Building and Maintaining an Intranet with the Macintosh

Tobin Anthony

Hayden Books

Hayden Books

Publisher
Lyn Blake

Publishing Manager
Laurie Petrycki

Managing Editor
Lisa Wilson

Marketing Manager
Nancy Price

Acquisitions Editor
Brian Gill

Development/Copy Editor
Beverly Scherf

Technical Editor
Tim Webster

Publishing Coordinator
Rosemary Lewis

Cover Designer
Karen Ruggles

Book Designer
Sandra Schroeder

Manufacturing Coordinator
Brook Farling

Production Team Supervisor
Laurie Casey

Production Team
Heather Butler,
Kim Cofer,
Terrie Deemer,
Tricia Flodder,
Aleata Howard,
Joe Millay,
Beth Rago,
Erich J. Richter,
Christine Tyner,
Karen Walsh

Indexer
Bront Davis

Building and Maintaining an Intranet with the Macintosh

Library of Congress Catalog Number: 96-75190
ISBN: 1-56830-279-7

Printed in the United States of America 1 2 3 4 5 6 7 8 9 0

Warning and Disclaimer

This book is sold as is, without warranty of any kind, either express or implied. While every precaution has been taken in the preparation of this book, the authors and Hayden Books assume no responsibility for errors or omissions. Neither is any liability assumed for damages resulting from the use of the information or instructions contained herein. It is further stated that the publisher and authors are not responsible for any damage or loss to your data or your equipment that results directly or indirectly from your use of this book.

About the Author

Tobin Anthony holds a Ph.D. in aerospace engineering but has been tinkering with Macintosh computers since the old Mac Plus days. A frothy Mac user, strict vegetarian, devout Roman Catholic, and lapsed private pilot, Tobin spends what little spare time he has with his wife Sharon and three children, Michelle, Austin, and Evan. Tobin works as a spacecraft control systems engineer at NASA's Goddard Space Flight Center in Greenbelt, MD. He has authored several technical articles and also has written extensively in the areas of the Web and CGI scripting. Email and Web stops are welcome at tobin@pobox.com and http://pobox.com~tobin.

Trademark Acknowledgments

All terms mentioned in this book that are known to be trademarks or services marks have been appropriately capitalized. Hayden Books cannot attest to the accuracy of this information. Use of a term in this book should not be regarded as affecting the validity of any trademark or service mark.

Dedication

To Sharon, the love of my life, thanks for minding the store, shredding my chapters, and just being plain superhuman.

Acknowledgments

To Jim Minatel, Doshia Stewart, Cheryl Willoughby and the gang at Que, thanks for making this happen. You guys are the greatest.

To Brian Gill and the crew at Hayden, thanks for picking up the book and giving me a fantastic team to work with. It was a crazy ride. Here's another priority FedEx coming at you.

To Beverly Scherf, this book would have been a lot less accurate, relevant, interesting, readable, and fun to write without you. Now please buy a newer version of Word!!

To Tim Webster, I'm indebted to your hard work, keen insight, and brutally honest technical editing (from which I'm still smarting).

To Mom and Dad, thanks for teaching me to love writing and to have a sense of humor about it.

To Zack Crues, thanks for getting me started with all this.

To my bosses at NASA, Frank, Marty, Alan, Dave M., and Dave W. (so much for streamlined management), thanks for the support and the time off for me to write this book.

To all the software authors who allowed me to discuss and include their precious work in this book, thanks for your cooperation and dedication to the Mac platform. You all write top-notch stuff.

To all the Mac Internet digerati, especially Chuck Shotton, Jon Wiederspan, Dave Winer, Peter Lewis, and many others, the quality of your work and contributions has made the Mac a major player in the Internet community. A lot of us would be running a different OS right now if it weren't for you guys.

Hayden Books

The staff of Hayden Books is committed to bringing you the best computer books. What our readers think of Hayden is important to our ability to serve our customers. If you have any comments, no matter how great or how small, we'd appreciate you taking the time to send us a note.

You can reach Hayden Books at the following:

Hayden Books

201 West 103rd Street

Indianapolis, IN 46290

Email addresses:

America Online: Hayden Bks

Internet: hayden@hayden.com

Visit the Hayden Books Web site at http://www.hayden.com

Contents at a Glance

Table of Contents

INTRODUCTION

Just when you thought you had the upper hand on the information revolution, you and your workplace are about to be blind-sided by what promises to be a momentous change in the way you do business. For years, you've lived with promise after promise of the paperless office. Well, guess what?! Intranets are going to help you establish a paperless office—for real!

Using technology that's getting heavy rotation on the Internet, you'll be able to develop services and applications that your coworkers can use to streamline their work routines. From now on, you won't have to shut down your Web browser when your boss walks by, as you'll be using it for your office work. The same thing with your FTP and email software. We'll even talk about how you can use your graphics applications to develop stunning and effective graphics for your Intranet Web pages. In short, you'll be using all of the tools that you've been brandishing on the Internet over these last few years to set up your Intranet—a private Internet. Well, not *all* of your Internet software...I haven't found a legitimate Intranet use yet for Marathon, but I'm working on it.

I like to think of an Intranet as a concept, rather than a physical mass of network hardware and chattering computers. Your Intranet users will utilize services that you'll develop and nurture. These services will grow in scope and sophistication along with your growing administrative expertise. No, I like to think of your Intranet as an amorphous information entity that encompasses and enhances the lives of your coworkers.

What I Already Know about You

You probably have some interest in setting up an Intranet in your organization. Either your boss has assigned you to set one up, or you've seen and heard enough about Intranets to have come up with the idea yourself. You've spent countless hours surfing the Web, have played around with Web servers, and have maybe cooked up some HTML. I'm expecting that you're familiar with some of the Internet buzzwords such as HTML, HTTP, CGI, and other hot button items.

You also probably have a couple of Macintosh computers lying around the office that are idly plugged into your building's local area network. You may not even have a local area network, so your Macs may be connected by some ancient LocalTalk cables to your seven-year old ImageWriter. That's okay too. In either case, we'll talk about how you can string your existing equipment and coordinate it with some new hardware to develop the basis for a fast and furious Intranet.

You've probably been forced to work with Windows and Unix servers for your work-related administration. You've always had that soft spot in your heart for the Macs, and you'd love to find a way to incorporate them into your complement of servers. Your bosses, however, scoff at the idea, deriding your Macs as toys, as they maintain a death watch on Apple Computer. In this book, I'll cover the many Mac-based solutions that exist for your Intranet needs. I'm hoping you'll gain an appreciation for the power and versatility of your Macintosh computers and will learn enough to be able to run several of your major Intranet services on your Mac.

Most importantly, if you're reading this book, or even just glancing through this section in the bookstore, I'm going to take a wild guess and say that you're the type of person who likes to think of yourself as slightly ahead of the pack. Maybe you were the first one in the office who understood the potential of Mosaic, back when the Web was an arcane playground for scientists, engineers, and grad students. You're the type of pioneer who's downloading Netscape beta versions and has a folder bulging with Netscape plug-ins. This type of pioneering spirit is what's drawing you to the Intranet.

What This Book Is

This book is a guide to building and maintaining an Intranet with your Mac. The information presented in this book comes from several years of my experience with both the Macintosh and the Internet in general. My experience has been supplemented by countless other users through email and Usenet postings. Like many Macintosh Internet enthusiasts, I started out running a crude Intranet in my office without really knowing it.

There are many facets to the creation and administration of an efficient Intranet. We will cover many of those topics in this book. My intention is to present as many topics as possible, so that the book will be sufficient enough to give you a head start on setting up a Macintosh-based Intranet.

What This Book Is Not

This book is not an introduction to the Internet. Many good books are out there to introduce you to the terminology used in this book. If you're not familiar with the Internet, it will be somewhat more difficult to come to grips with the concept of an Intranet. We'll discuss a lot of Internet terminology in detail here, so previous exposure to the medium will be helpful.

Furthermore, this book is not an introduction to the Macintosh. I'm assuming that you've used the MacOS enough to understand the vagaries of pointing, clicking, and dragging. There are not many strict DOS fanatics out there anymore, so chances are that you have some experience in window-oriented operating systems.

Getting the Most Out of This Book

This book is presented in a sequential manner that should mirror your development as an Intranet administrator. Chapter 1 explains the concept of Intranets in some detail. It discusses how people are using them, and it will try to spark some creative ideas in you as to what sorts of services you can provide. In Chapter 2, you'll learn about some of the wiring schemes you can use to establish the network part of your Intranet. You'll be exposed to some of the networking protocol and hardware buzzwords as well. Chapter 3 delves into your Mac server options. You'll learn about some of the features that you should look for in the Macintosh computers that you'll use to base your Intranet services.

Chapters 4 through 9 go into detail about the World Wide Web portion of your Intranet and how you can effectively customize this feature as your business link to the Internet. This is a good fraction of the entire book, but then again, your Intranet Web pages will play a hefty role in the services you'll provide to your users. Chapter 4 details the use of several popular shareware, freeware, and commercial Mac Web servers including WebSTAR, MacHTTP, and others. You'll learn enough in this chapter to get these applications up and running in no time. Chapters 5 and 6 deal with tips and information you can use to set up effective Intranet Web services. Chapter 5 talks about how you can set up a Web management philosophy, and Chapter 6 deals with some ways that you can present your HTML and graphics in a manner that makes your site easy to navigate and simple to use.

Chapters 7 and 8 are two of the most important chapters in this book. Chapter 7 deals with the Common Gateway Interface (CGI) and how you can write CGI scripts using several popular scripting environments under the MacOS. This chapter primarily covers AppleScript and Frontier; it also covers other environments such as CGI programming languages such as MacPerl, C/C++, and others. You'll also get a quick primer on imagemaps and how you can create them by using inexpensive shareware applications.

Chapter 8 discusses how you can incorporate databases as well as document search engines into your Intranet Web services. It covers a popular database, Butler SQL, and an associated CGI, Tango, that you can use to set up queries of your databases via the Web. You'll also look at some options you'll have to install document search engines on your Web pages. The importance of these tools to your Intranet users cannot be overstated. Finally, Chapter 9 details how you can go beyond HTML and graphics files to incorporate newer technologies into your Web pages. We'll talk about PDF files, VRML, and Java. Links are provided in these chapters to point you to other more comprehensive resources on these topics.

Chapters 10 through 14 deal with the non-Web elements of your Intranet. Chapter 10 talks about setting up FTP servers in your network. Chapter 11 covers setting up email and mailing list servers in your network. You'll eventually need to set up a domain name server, so we'll discuss how to do just that in Chapter 12. You may want to insulate your network from the Intranet as well as protect against accidental tampering from your users; for these reasons, we'll talk about how you can secure your Intranet in Chapter 13. The intent in Chapter 14 is to pull all these tools and topics together into a unified manner, detailing the types of Intranet services you can provide your users. I'll give you some rudimentary, but interdisciplinary, examples of possible services you can offer in your Intranet. The whole book is summarized in Chapter 15.

Appendix A introduces the software provided on the CD-ROM accompanying this book. Appendix B gives you several tips on how to convert or adapt your Intranet capabilities to establish a presence on the Internet. Appendix C discusses some of the high-end HTML editors, such as Adobe PageMill and the BBEdit HTML Tools, that you can use to create your Web pages; we'll also take a look at some of the Netscape HTML extensions that you can incorporate into some of your Web pages. Finally, there is a glossary of the more sophisticated terms used in this book.

Conventions

I've worked hard to make the presentation of this book as homogenous as possible. The material presented here is sophisticated, and the last thing you need is a steady onslaught of clip art and cartoons solely designed to break up the text (as well as your concentration). However, there are several conventions that I employ that should enhance the readability of this book.

From time to time, I set discussions and factoids apart from the flow of the book in special notes.

Software that's included on the CD-ROM is denoted with a CD icon.

This symbol ➥ has been used to represent program lines that have wrapped.

Very often, I'll include text from a script, or a snippet of HTML code in the middle of the chapter. When I do that, I'll set it aside in a monospaced font like this:

```
HTTP/1.0 200 OK
Date: Thursday, 01-Feb-96 19:15:32 GMT
Server: MacHTTP
MIME-version: 1.0
Last-modified: Friday, 21-May-96 14:11:08 GMT
```

At the end of each chapter, a list of URLs is presented that pertain to the material discussed in the chapter. Some of these links are included in the midst of the text, but the list at the end of the chapter is more comprehensive. Look for the bookmark file on this book's CD-ROM. For more information about this CD-ROM, see Appendix A.

Let's Keep in Touch

Intranets are a new and growing phenomenon. The Information Age has provided us with almost instant gratification in exchanging relevant information. I'd like this book to be no different. I'd be interested to see and hear how you implement the tools and technologies described in this book. Feel free to contact me with your observations, or flames, at tobin@pobox.com. Also, please drop by my Web site (http://www.pobox.com/~tobin) to see how I put the tools discussed in this book into action.

CHAPTER 1

Intranets—The Next Big Thing

Ready or not, Intranets are coming to a workplace near you. Intranets are going to profoundly change the way you and many other people work and do business. Kissing cousins of the Internet, Intranets are emerging in the workplace at a wild pace. It's a mad rush as businesses and organizations all over the globe are setting up private Intranets to allow employees to collaborate on tasks, exchange email, access databases, and other tasks—all using familiar networking technology customized to their particular needs. Much as the desktop computer transformed the workplace in the 1980s, Intranets will be transforming the office of the 1990s.

This book provides information on how you can configure an inexpensive yet highly flexible Intranet for your organization. While your Intranet will be based on the Macintosh operating system, you won't be limited to serving all-Mac networks. The beauty of the Intranet, as described in this book, lies within its cross-platform utility. A lot of the services upon which Intranets are based can serve Mac clients as well as Windows, Unix, and OS/2 clients. The services discussed in this book are applicable to nearly all the computers in your organization.

You're probably thinking, "This is great! I've got to set up an Intranet...but what is an Intranet?" Intranets are the hottest item in information technology today. While most of the world has invested large amounts of resources scrambling to get connected to the Internet, some organizations have set up private networks separate from the rest of the world. These private Intranets, as they are called, are focused entirely on the needs and affairs of the organization. Safely ensconced from the general Internet community behind secure barriers, these Intranets look very much like tiny little Internets serving hundreds or thousands of people instead of millions. Intranets do not have to be located in the same geographical location; you may have Intranet users in remote parts of the country that enjoy the same services and security as those users at your home site.

Your Intranet will be more than a self-contained network of routers, hubs, and other connection hardware. Your Intranet will be more of a concept than anything else. Users within your organization may already have network access to internal services or services out on the Internet. However, there may not be a coherent theme to the services available to members of your group. Sure, it's great to have email and maybe even access to a file server within your group, but what if you could enhance and streamline the work that people are already doing? What if you could provide services through your Intranet that are even above what is available to them currently? Your Intranet is less about wiring up computers to talk to one another and more about empowering your organization with new tools and capabilities beyond what's currently available.

The concept of Intranets is not new. People have been sharing data and exchanging email for several years now. In fact, many organizations conduct business using groupware applications. *Groupware* usually refers to a proprietary application that enables users to exchange data and email as well as collaborate on documents. The difference between commercial groupware applications and Intranets is that until this point, commercial groupware has tended to be built upon proprietary protocols and applications. The emphasis of Intranets has been the use of the open architecture embodied on the Internet, except they are adapted for the specific needs and purposes of the organization. TCP/IP-based Intranets are being constructed as low-cost alternatives to commercial groupware.

Intranets use the same tools and technologies as the Internet, but are adapted for private use. Many of the services provided by Intranets rely on the same networking protocols upon which the Internet was founded. Some services that major companies have provided on their Intranets include the following:

- ☐ Web forms to allow employees to update personnel information such as vacation balances, health plan preferences, or retirement account balances
- ☐ Databases linked with Web pages to manage internal paperwork as well as collaboration on corporate documents
- ☐ Videoconferences to allow users to communicate in real time with users throughout the company or throughout the world
- ☐ Corporate email service to allow users to exchange messages throughout the company or throughout the Internet
- ☐ Archives of meeting minutes, technical reports, or corporate memoranda

The rapid pace of Intranet construction and acceptance is aided by the familiarization of millions of people by the Internet and the World Wide Web (WWW) in particular. Within the past few years, millions of people have used the Web or similar facilities offered by the major online services such as America Online, CompuServe, and Prodigy. An Intranet, therefore, requires very little training for the average employee.

The Emergence of the Intranet

It's ironic that corporate America, which resisted the Internet as long as possible, is leading the charge to developing private Intranets. In retrospect, Intranets are a natural progression from the Internet for the following two reasons:

- ☐ **Floundering of online transactions.** Despite great advances in encryption technology, online commerce on the Internet has not yet taken hold. As a result, software companies needed a new market for which to develop products.
- ☐ **Proliferation of desktop computers.** Within the last 10 years, personal computers have become inexpensive enough to permit widespread usage throughout corporate America. Furthermore, with employees connected to local area networks for printing and email, these networks became fertile ground for conversion to Intranets.

As a result, it is projected that within a few years, sales of software and hardware devoted to Intranets will not only outstrip that associated with the Internet, but will outstrip it several times over. We have become used to thinking of the Internet as a large system linking millions of computers together. The indications are that if the Intranet concept takes hold, we'll think of the Internet as a medium that links together millions of Intranets.

Groupware versus Intranets

The idea of using a local area network to foster collaborative efforts in the workplace is not new. As mentioned earlier, groupware describes the class of software that allows users to exchange email, documents, and electronic forms. Most notable in this class is IBM's Lotus Notes application; other commercial groupware applications include Novell's GroupWise and Microsoft's Exchange. Lotus Notes serves millions of users around the world, allowing them to collaborate on projects.

Groupware, like Lotus Notes, is based on a proprietary format. Third-party software companies cannot easily extend the functionality of commercial groupware. Furthermore, groupware applications often are based on a networking protocol rather than the Transmission Control Protocol/Internet Protocol (TCP/IP) used by Intranets and on the Internet.

In contrast to commercial groupware, Intranets are based on open Internet protocols such as HTTP, FTP, and SMTP. While commercial groupware is moving toward TCP/IP, Intranets are built natively around the protocol. Intranets are being developed around the World Wide Web, with programmers customizing pages using HTML and CGI scripts. With people already using the Web on a daily basis, there is almost no learning curve with Web-based Intranets. Intranets are truly cross-platform, meaning that scientific, technical, and academic users running Unix workstations can participate as well. It costs much less to run an Intranet. Several types of Web browsers are on the market in addition to freeware and commercial Web servers. These browsers are no more than $40 per desktop and often can be obtained more inexpensively in bulk; Microsoft's Internet Explorer is even distributed free of charge. Intranets can be comprised of several different servers and can be accessed by any browser adhering to HTML standards. This is in direct contrast to commercial groupware applications, which do not easily work with other systems.

Intranets, however, are much less sophisticated than commercial groupware systems. Software suites like Lotus Notes and Microsoft Exchange are polished products that allow collaborative document processing, email, and electronic forms distribution. In contrast, Web-based Intranets are almost always homegrown without major third-party technical support. For example, if you want your marketing departments to be able to access a database containing sales data through your Intranet, a Web-based interface will need to be developed by your internal development staff. This interface will likely need to be developed or implemented by a local or outsourced programmer who will be your sole source of technical support.

Commercial groupware also excels in protecting your data. TCP/IP is a very well-understood protocol. This makes for great development opportunities, but is a disadvantage for security reasons. While there are proposals for secure TCP/IP layers, such as Netscape's Secure Sockets Layer (SSL), secure Web transactions do not enjoy the same level of confidence with users as does groupware.

Furthermore, applications such as Notes are better at allowing collaborative document processing. In this type of endeavor, users can work on the same document with each adding revisions to the final version. No widespread collaborative solution exists for Intranets at this time.

Table 1.1 compares the features of groupware and Intranets.

Table 1.1 *Commercial Groupware versus Intranets*

Feature	Commercial Groupware	Intranet
Protocol	non-TCP/IP	TCP/IP
Architecture	Proprietary	Open
Third-party support	Limited	Comprehensive
Cross-platform	Mac/Windows	Mac/Windows/Unix
Security	Advanced	Intermediate
User base	3 million	15–20 million (potential)
Collaborative tools	Advanced	Minimal
Cost/Desktop	$100–200	Free–$40

Intranets offer much of the functionality of commercial groupware at a lower cost. However, commercial groupware offers more in the way of security and capabilities at this time.

The Future of Groupware

The future struggle between commercial groupware and Intranets should prove to be interesting (and beneficial to the user) as the two sides gradually incorporate one another's capabilities. Commercial applications, such as Lotus Notes, with millions of users aren't going away overnight. Microsoft Exchange is being aggressively marketed by Microsoft as a groupware solution. In fact, IBM and Microsoft are developing Web-friendly versions of their groupware applications, allowing them to work better with Web servers and browsers. In contrast, Netscape Communications recently acquired Collabra, a maker of a groupware application that rivals Lotus Notes' capabilities. Netscape promises more groupware capabilities in its next version of its Web browser.

In all likelihood, users will benefit from the struggle between Netscape, Microsoft, IBM, Novell, and other vendors. Both groupware and Intranets are converging on the same goal albeit from different directions. The end result of this competition will be a series of inexpensive products that allow full cross-platform collaborative capabilities.

Uses for Your Intranet Server

Your organization spends a great deal of resources disseminating information throughout its workforce. An Intranet server can streamline the flow of information between personnel using a centralized information server. Your Intranet server can be harnessed for just this task.

In-House Documentation Archive

If your filing system is anything like mine, memoranda vanish without a trace once they hit your desk. The lucky ones make it to the recycling bin; at least they've got a chance to see the light of day as another memo. The Web makes an ideal platform for use as a document archive; in fact, that was the purpose for which it was originally designed.

Nowadays, internal documents are generated on a computer and are stored somewhere in electronic form. These documents can be stored in a database for access through an FTP or Web browser. In this manner, documents can be accessed through an interface between the document database and a specially configured Web page. If these reports and memoranda were consolidated within a group, personnel within that group would have access to the entire holdings within that database. Later in this book, we'll talk about how such an interface can be implemented.

NOTE 

> For an example of how such an archive was developed for the Unix platform, check out the WebLib home page at http://selsvr.stx.com/~weblib

Your Intranet also can be used to disseminate policy statements and administrative news. By establishing a home page on your server associated with administrative news, personnel would be able to consult this page for policy statements and directives from management. Company newsletters and HelpDesk information could also be posted on this server. In this manner, your organization would save a great deal of resources that would be required to print and distribute these directives among the workforce. Some alternative uses for an internal document server include the following:

- Management directives
- Organizational newsletter
- HelpDesk information
- Report and memorandum archive
- Searchable employee directories
- Organizational charts

In-House Software Archive

Large organizations usually standardize on some type of office automation software. Sometimes this software is purchased in large quantities for the use of employees throughout the organization. Rather than allocating valuable HelpDesk resources to install and configure the applications on personal computers throughout the company, the software could be stored on a centralized FTP server. The software would have to be covered under a site license or some arrangement that adheres to software licensing agreements. Instructions on how to load this software could be accessible through a HelpDesk Web page.

Electronic Mail

In addition to World Wide Web and FTP services, your Intranet can handle the administration of electronic mail throughout your organization. You have several commercial and shareware Macintosh options for serving email to your users. We'll discuss your email options in Chapter 11, "Email Services."

Bulletin Boards

Usenet was one of the earliest services offered on the Internet. It enables users from all over the world to post or request information on highly specific topics. Universities, government agencies, and large companies often set up local groups in conjunction with the public Usenet groups. These local newsgroups pertain to issues internal to the organization and exist as a means of information dissemination and collaboration to some degree. Setting up a Usenet feed to your Intranet is a daunting task. Usenet feeds require several gigabytes of storage since megabytes of new postings are generated each day.

You can still set up Web-based bulletin boards that fulfill the same function as Usenet groups. There are several shareware and commercial bulletin board applications at your disposal. Moreover, these applications will allow you to customize the output and operation of your bulletin boards more completely than a standard Usenet client. We'll talk about Web-based bulletin board software in Chapter 14, "Sample Intranet Applications."

Videoconferencing

You probably are familiar with QuickTime on the Macintosh and even Windows. QuickTime is an extension bundled with the MacOS that allows you to play movies using a variety of movie players. However, you can even use SimpleText to view some types of movies. Coupled with Intranet technology and the right equipment, you can record movies and play them over the Internet. With the right software, you can even videoconference between workstations.

Your Intranet can support videoconferencing if both parties have the correct (and often inexpensive) equipment such as Connectix's QuickCam or any other Mac-compatible video camera. Provided that remote users have the proper equipment and network configuration, you can even set up videoconferences inside your Intranet with employees who are in different parts of the country. You may not experience the full 32 frames per second that you see on television, but videoconferencing is the next best thing to being there. See Chapter 14, "Sample Intranet Applications," for more about videoconferencing.

Why the Macintosh?

I'll do my best to avoid a deep excursion into the operating system (OS) wars that have pitted PC and Macintosh users against one another. However, there's an interesting similarity between the Mac and the World Wide Web; as the Macintosh simplified personal computing with a revolutionary graphical interface, the Web offers the same friendly face for the Internet. The Mac and the World Wide Web have spurred explosive growth in personal computing and the Internet.

NOTE 

> I won't spend a lot of time telling you why the Macintosh is a better platform than a PC running Windows 95, but I'll let Apple tell you. Check out The Macintosh Advantage at http://www.apple.com/whymac/default.html.

Interestingly, Apple Computer has not benefited from the wild expansion of the personal computing market. Estimates of the Macintosh computer's share of the personal computing desktop market range from 7–12 percent as of this writing. While that is a larger share than that held by DOS or OS/2 machines these days, it's a distant second place to Microsoft's formidable troika of Windows 3.1, Windows 95, and Windows NT. There are several explanations for Microsoft's dominance of the desktop market, but for a desire to avoid another skirmish in the OS holy war, I don't intend to discuss them here.

Holding Its Own on the Net

The services that you will provide on your Intranet basically are the same services available on the Internet, but adapted for your own internal use. This book will tell you how to develop an Intranet using the Mac as a server platform. Even though the number of Macintosh computers is far outweighed by PCs running Windows, DOS, and OS/2, there are many Internet server applications written for the Mac. This section will discuss how you can adapt these applications to construct your Intranet. First, look at just how popular the Macintosh is as an Internet server platform.

According to a recent survey, Unix remains the most popular platform on which to institute an Internet server. This can be explained by the fact that TCP/IP is natively incorporated into the Unix OS. However, this survey showed some interesting statistics regarding the percentage of World Wide Web sites running under the MacOS. The results of this survey, tabulated in Table 1.2, show that of all Internet-capable operating systems, the MacOS operates the second-largest number of WWW servers.

NOTE

The full results of the survey performed by Mirai, a Chicago consulting firm, are available at http://www.mirai.com/survey/. Mirai expects to have results from an updated survey available in mid-1996.

Table 1.2 *Percentage of WWW Servers by OS (performed by Mirai, Oct. 1995)*

Servers	Percentage
SunOS	21.0%
MacOS	17.0%
Solaris	10.4%
Windows	9.7%
Other Unix	6.5%
Windows NT	4.5%
HP	4.1%
DEC-OSF	3.8%
BSD	3.4%
AIX	3.2%
SGI/IRIX	3.0%
Other OS	2.6%
OS/2 Warp	1.1%
NeXTSTEP	0.7%

Microsoft's Windows OS is found on 7 to 8 times as many desktop machines as the MacOS. Surprisingly, the MacOS runs nearly twice as many Web sites as MS Windows. Furthermore, the survey found that 40.9 percent of all respondents created World Wide Web site graphics using MacOS graphics applications. Windows and Unix accounted for 28.4 percent and 25.3 percent of all WWW graphics development, respectively.

Advantages of the MacOS as a WWW Server

Several explanations exist for the Macintosh's popularity as a World Wide Web server. The MacOS networking protocol, AppleTalk, is natively built in to the operating system. Although the Mac's native networking protocol, AppleTalk, is not routed along the Internet, it was a natural progression for Apple to develop EtherTalk in the late 1980s. EtherTalk allowed the Macintosh to use the AppleTalk protocol across a much faster Ethernet connection. Apple eventually developed MacTCP, which supports the movement of TCP/IP packets over the AppleTalk network.

Ease of Use

In 1993, the first World Wide Web servers were developed for various flavors of the Unix OS. By that time, Internet applications for the Macintosh had several years of heritage. The TCP/IP environment was well-defined for the Macintosh. The first Web server for the Macintosh, MacHTTP, was introduced shortly thereafter. With a double-click of the mouse, MacHTTP could be brought up and running. With the MacOS, there is no need to work with processes, daemons, and arcane configuration files. In contrast to Unix's arcane command-line interface, MacHTTP sports a menu-driven interface and a small, but simple-to-use configuration file. MacHTTP had brought simple-to-administer Web service to the masses.

The Frugal Mac

With the advent of the Power Macintosh in 1994, the performance gap between the MacOS platform and the Unix world narrowed.

The PowerPC chip running the MacOS is a descendent of the microprocessor architecture found in IBM's RS6000 workstation series. Moreover, it is much less expensive to operate a Power Mac World Wide Web server. A low-end Unix machine can be purchased for $10,000. Maintenance and configuration costs would be much higher than a similarly configured Power Mac. Furthermore, you can spend far less for a high-end Power Mac Web server. We will discuss the recommended configuration for a Macintosh World Wide Web server later in this book. My first Web site ran for several years on a Macintosh IIci powered by a Motorola 68030 processor. I only recently moved the server to a Power Mac.

NOTE

As of this writing, Apple's only models for the desktop are controlled by the PowerPC chip. This class of computers is referred to as Power Macintosh. For the sake of simplicity, I'll continue to refer to the computer platform as the Macintosh.

The Secure Mac

Another advantage of the MacOS over Unix is the inherent security built into the operating system. Unix was designed to allow users to access systems remotely. Hence, there are ways to compromise its security. The MacOS was built as a desktop operating system. The file-sharing capability of the Macintosh is crude when compared to the Internet's Telnet capability; however, this lack of sophistication is an advantage. There is no way to tunnel into the MacOS using another protocol. We'll talk more about securing your Intranet in Chapter 13, "Intranet Server Security."

Multitasking

Much is made of the fact that the MacOS is not a true multitasking operating system. It's true that you can run as many applications simultaneously as the resources on your Macintosh will allow, but the applications are not really running at the same time. Instead, the applications are competing for microprocessor time.

The MacOS is a cooperatively multitasking operating system. The main difference between Mac multitasking and true multitasking, as used in Unix, Windows NT, and OS/2, is that the MacOS, rather than the applications, is responsible for the bookkeeping required to run concurrently. Under the MacOS, applications relinquish control themselves and store their operating state themselves. Under true multitasking, the operating system takes care of these tasks, doing a much better job than the individual applications can. As a result, applications run much more smoothly under true multitasking than cooperatively multitasking operating systems.

Macintosh World Wide Web server administrators claim that a lack of preemptive multitasking doesn't prevent the Mac from remaining a viable platform for WWW service. They claim that network connections are the biggest obstacle to fast Web service. The most heavily accessed Web sites, such as Apple Computer's World Wide Web site, enjoy close to 100,000 accesses each day; that's only slightly more than one access per second. A high-speed network connection can transmit the HTTP instructions very quickly. The Mac conceivably would have enough time to answer the Web client request and send the network data on its merry way before receiving the next hit. A slower network connection means that the Mac frequently entertains simultaneous accesses. There is a definite disadvantage to the multithreading environment as opposed to the multitasking environment in these high-access cases. Conceivably, this problem could be solved through the use of a network of machines set up to handle different HTTP requests as Apple has done with its Web site.

When Not to Use a Mac as an Intranet Server

Because the emphasis of this book is the use of the Macintosh as an Intranet server, it's awkward to discuss situations where it may not be the optimal server solution. As mentioned previously, Unix is designed with inherent preemptive multitasking capability. This reduces the chance that a labor-intensive process will clog up the processor path. Therefore, systems with tens of thousands of hits each day will experience a heavy processing load. If the site is mainly serving small text or graphics files, a high-end Power Mac would have no trouble handling that load.

However, some Intranet sites are more sophisticated and serve more than just text and graphics. More sophisticated sites run external scripts that generate other Web pages or interact with databases. The MacOS does not have the same caliber of tools to run these scripts as does a Unix workstation. Hence a site that processes a lot of external scripts will incur a larger processing load than a system that just serves graphics and text.

There are several ways to run CGI scripts under the MacOS and we'll discuss those later in this book. These scripts cause the server to run much slower than if it were simply serving text and graphics. A server that expects several tens of thousands of hits per day and that is designed to repeatedly execute intricate CGI scripts may not be suited for implementation on a single Macintosh. A high-end Unix workstation or a network of multiple Mac servers may be more suitable for such a heavily accessed server.

Waiting for Copland

Transition of the Macintosh user base from the Motorola 680x0 chip architecture to a platform built around the PowerPC chip was painless for many reasons. Apple spent a great deal of time developing a PowerPC-based OS that could emulate the chip instructions of the 680x0 class of microprocessors. While ensuring backward-compatibility, Apple sacrificed performance; the 680x0 emulation requires more computational load than if the PowerPC were to execute an application written for its own chip instruction set. This is true of the MacOS as well; much of the operating system is borrowed from the 680x0 chip instruction class and is only being emulated on the PowerPC. This OS emulation has a negative impact on system performance.

Apple plans to release a new operating system in late 1996 that will utilize the native PowerPC instruction set. The new MacOS, code-named Copland (but also referred to by its probable name System 8), will also offer several desirable features including true preemptive multitasking, enhanced multithreading and protected memory partitioning (which will help prevent a program crash from bringing down the system). Many of the disadvantages that server administrators find using the MacOS in comparison with Windows NT and Unix should greatly diminish with the introduction of Copland.

Summary

My intent in this chapter was to introduce you to the concept of Intranets and to give you a feel for their relationship to the Internet. The concept of Intranets is not new; commercial groupware has provided much of communication and collaborative document processing offered by Intranets. However, TCP/IP-based Intranets are being constructed as low-cost alternatives to commercial groupware.

Furthermore, you saw that there are many advantages to basing your Intranet on Macintosh computers. Mac users have been working the Internet for years, so a large stable of tools and applications exists for the Macintosh. These same tools can be adapted for use in your Intranet. The inherent advantages of security, price, and ease of use have made the Mac a popular server platform on the Internet. This book will tell you how to make this popular Internet platform work for your Intranet.

Chapter 2, "Wiring Your Intranet," talks about how to construct the basic infrastructure of your Intranet. It discusses wiring and Internet connection options and how you can provide remote access to your Intranet. Feel free, however, to skip past this chapter and read one of the following chapters:

- ☐ Chapter 4, "Macintosh HTTP Servers," to learn about the different software you can use to set up World Wide Web services on your Mac.
- ☐ Chapter 7, "Writing CGI Scripts," to learn about writing scripts for your Web site. These scripts enable you to process data from HTML forms and return customized Web pages.
- ☐ Chapter 8, "Databases and Document Searches," to learn about how to allow your Intranet users a means of accessing your databases and searches document archives.
- ☐ Chapter 9, "Beyond HTML," to learn some techniques to spruce up your Web site beyond just using conventional HTML and graphics. We'll discuss Java, RealAudio, and other cool topics.

- Chapter 13, "Intranet Server Security," to learn how you can configure hardware to provide secure transactions within your Intranet and out to the Internet.
- Chapter 14, "Sample Intranet Applications," to learn about some services you can provide using the Web, FTP, and email technologies discussed in this book.
- Appendix B, "Establishing an Internet Presence," to learn more about adapting or expanding your Intranet to provide services to the Internet.

CHAPTER 2

Wiring Your Intranet

Before we talk about all the services that you'll provide on your Intranet, we need to talk about the hardware involved in your own internal network. To keep from putting the proverbial cart before the horse, we'll need to talk about your Intranet configuration as well as the computing hardware that you'll use to deliver the services we discussed in the previous chapter. The following chapter discusses the types of Macintosh computers that you'll be using to serve your Intranet. However, this chapter discusses the physical setup of your Intranet all the way down to the network connections on your users' desktop computers.

You may be working for a company or organization that already has an existing network. Your desktop computer may be already wired to the Internet, and you can even access a file server or email server from your site. This is fine, and it really gives you a leg up on using this book. You'll be able to march on to Chapter 3 and read about which Macintosh computers to use for your Intranet servers.

However, if you are with a smaller organization, or maybe you'd just like to learn more of the networking technology that network administrators throw around, this chapter is for you. This chapter covers the following topics:

- ☐ A brief primer on networking hardware and protocols
- ☐ Some possible wiring schemes for your network
- ☐ Ways to get connected to the Internet
- ☐ Providing access to your Intranet from remote sites

If you're like me, you're pretty comfortable with computers and you are undaunted by the concept of networking. However, you may not be up on a lot of the current terminology needed to fully understand your network. The next few sections cover the terms and buzzwords you'll need to understand and plan your Intranet's infrastructure.

Network Protocols

Information is transferred along networks such as an Intranet in packets that are strings of data no more than 500–1500 bytes in length. The manner in which they are transferred across a network is referred to as a *network protocol.* Packets are constructed differently using different network protocols, but usually they contain the desired information encapsulated by a header with data that details whether or not the packet arrived intact. Take a look at some of the network protocols you can use on your Mac-based Intranet.

TCP/IP

TCP/IP is a multilayered family of protocols upon which the Internet is built. Similarly, many of the services discussed in this book are based on TCP/IP. Many services such as FTP, Domain Name Service, and email are transmitted using TCP/IP. TCP/IP is comprised of two protocols: Transmission Control Protocol (TCP) and the Internet Protocol (IP). However, these two protocols are used together so often that you'll frequently see Intranets referred to as TCP/IP-based networks.

IP

Network protocols work to move packets across a network. Along the Internet, as well as your Intranet, IP defines the structure of the data packets that stream between clients and hosts. IP doesn't concern itself with the content of the data inside the packets, but is more concerned with providing a means of transporting that packet.

You're probably familiar with one aspect of IP, the IP address. Every computer on the Internet maintains an IP address, much like every working telephone maintains a phone number. If you're connected to the Internet, you're probably more familiar with your desktop computer's host name, which is something like spanky.dc.anyplace.com.

In reality, your host is known throughout the Internet using an IP address that's actually a unique numerical address. This address consists of four numerical fields: each field consists of a number from 0 to 255. Each IP address is associated with an easier-to-remember host name. You usually refer to the host names, but your computer works with the IP address. Your computer requires the use of a domain name server to associate a host name and an IP address; this is discussed in detail in Chapter 12, "Providing Domain Name Service."

IP packets, which can contain files or partial files sent by FTP, email messages, or Web browser requests, contain two destination IP addresses—the packet's final destination and that of your local router, which can further relay the packet to its source. From this router, the packets will bounce between other routers until they arrive at their destination. Routers are discussed in a later section in this chapter.

NOTE

> If you are sending an IP packet to another computer served on the same router as your computer, that router likely will have that destination computer's address stored in its table. In this case, the two IP addresses in the IP packet will be the same.

TCP

Your email message, file transfer, or Web browser request is made up of many IP packets. They may arrive at the destination computer in or out of sequence. They may take different paths between your computer and the final destination. Whereas IP doesn't care about the content or nature of the packets, TCP is the mechanism that breaks your request into packets, sends them across your Intranet or the Internet, and reassembles them in the correct order.

If these IP packets are not received in a proper order, TCP queries the sender for the original data until it receives the proper packet. Even if it's waiting for one tardy little packet, which it expected at the beginning of the transmission, TCP will allow your computer to reassemble the packets into the desired data format. This makes TCP/IP a very robust protocol upon which to base your Intranet transmissions. Furthermore, basing your Intranet on TCP/IP services allows you to interact more fully with the Internet.

MacTCP

Since the late 1980s, Apple has produced an adaptation of the TCP/IP layer for the Macintosh. Implemented as a control panel, MacTCP offers a means for Mac users to directly take advantage of TCP/IP services. MacTCP comes bundled with System 7.5; this integration of MacTCP and the MacOS allows a seamless interface for many TCP/IP applications. This is in contrast to PCs running Microsoft Windows, where there are many TCP/IP implementations for that operating system.

AppleTalk

Much like Unix, the MacOS has an advantage over most operating systems in that it utilizes a networking protocol that is native to the operating system. This protocol, AppleTalk, is built into the MacOS and allows easy printing and file sharing between computers. Since the early days of the Macintosh, users have been able to print documents simply by connecting cabling between their computers and a printer. AppleTalk would automatically configure the document for processing on the printer and send the requisite information to the device.

AppleTalk is not nearly as robust a network protocol as TCP/IP. AppleTalk does a lot of checking to make sure that the receiving computer is getting the correct information. The packets are of a different format but still are pushed through routers that are specially configured for AppleTalk.

Whereas TCP checks with the sending host to request wayward packets, AppleTalk engenders a great deal of communication between the sending and receiving hosts while packets are being transmitted. Network protocol specialists refer to AppleTalk as a *chatty* protocol for this reason. The rate at which a network can pass packets is known as the network's ***bandwidth***. Because of AppleTalk's propensity for chatty communications, you won't see the bandwidth out of AppleTalk networks that you see out of TCP/IP networks.

Apple does offer a version of AppleTalk for Windows. Running an Intranet solely based on AppleTalk would be possible, but not very easy. File sharing and printing would be possible, but much of the more powerful Intranet tools, such as Web browsers and FTP clients, require TCP/IP. You'll still use AppleTalk for your file sharing and printing, but AppleTalk alone will not serve all of your Intranet needs.

Open Transport

Open Transport (OT) is a new networking technology that greatly enhances Macintosh network services. Although OT 1.0 was originally released in late 1995, it wasn't until OT 1.1 came out a few months later that the bugs had worked out to a degree that ensured full use of the software for all Macintosh computers. OT will allow enhanced networking for Macintosh computers on TCP/IP and AppleTalk networks.

Open Transport supersedes both MacTCP and the AppleTalk software found in System 7.5.2 and earlier. Open Transport is fully PowerPC native, so Power Macs will see a networking performance boost. Furthermore, OT enables you to reconfigure your IP address on the fly; you can bring up another IP configuration simply by selecting an option on a popup menu without having to reboot your Mac. Chapter 4, "Macintosh HTTP Servers," talks more about IP streams and the 64-stream limit imposed by MacTCP; OT allows you maintain as many IP streams as your microprocessor and RAM will allow.

Network services found in future versions of the MacOS (Copland and beyond) will be based on Open Transport. By the time you read this, many Macintosh Intranet server applications will be reconfigured to take advantage of Open Transport advantages. Running OT will present your server with a great deal of advantages.

Wiring Protocols

As mentioned previously, you may already have existing wiring in your office. You may not be required to string up a series of cables to interconnect all your computers. In that case, you're one lucky administrator. However, this section will cover cabling terminology that is valuable to administrators with and without existing cable systems.

Ethernet

Although it's often, and incorrectly, referred to as a cabling system, Ethernet actually is a standardized cabling and signaling specification and refers to a slew of media and services. You can run many protocols over Ethernet including AppleTalk and TCP/IP. You also can run these protocols over a variety of wiring types including copper coaxial cable, fiber-optic cable, and unshielded twisted-pair cabling.

NOTE

Apple's implementation of AppleTalk that runs over Ethernet is known as EtherTalk.

Several types of Ethernet cabling systems are available for you to use to wire your Intranet. As of this writing, the most common scheme is twisted-pair cabling or 10BaseT. 10BaseT has ousted much of the old 10Base2 or coaxial thin-Ethernet cabling found in older local area networks (LAN); 10Base2 looks very much like the coaxial cable that leads into your cable TV set. 10BaseT connection hardware, such as routers and hubs, which we'll discuss below, is more expensive than 10Base2 but performs better under noisy or high-traffic environments. Furthermore, 10BaseT wiring is cheaper than thin-Ethernet and requires less skill to install. 10BaseT, to the untrained eye, appears very similar to common telephone wiring, even down the modular phone jack. Many computers have adapters that accept 10BaseT wiring. 10BaseT wiring is much lighter and easier to work with than thin-Ethernet cabling; network administrators find it easier to troubleshoot problems on 10BaseT networks than on thin-Ethernet systems.

NOTE

What's behind the name 10BaseT? The naming convention for 10BaseT, 100BaseT, and other cabling conventions is simple. For 10BaseT, the "10" stands for the transmission rate in megabits/sec (Mbps). The "Base" means that the cable admits baseband transmissions rather than broadband transmissions. The "T" stands for twisted-pair, meaning that 10BaseT Ethernet is running over unshielded twisted-pair cabling. Therefore, 100BaseT is similar to 10BaseT except that it transmits data at 100 Mbps.

With 10BaseT, you are limited to speeds of 10 Mbps. 100BaseT is a new Ethernet variant that supports network transmission speeds of up to 100 Mbps. Because of some confusion in the standards process, there are several competing 100 Mbps Ethernet implementations. 100VG-AnyLAN is a 100 Mbps Ethernet implementation that offers some enhancements over 100BaseT, but has little industry support.

NOTE

If you are working in an existing Intranet or LAN, chances are that it's based on 10BaseT. You may want to boost the productivity of your Intranet by providing 100BaseT. This is not a position to be taken lightly, as there's more that's involved than just replacing your hardware. All of your ancillary equipment, from your desktop computers' network interface cards (NIC) to the connection hardware behind the scenes, will have to be upgraded to accommodate 100BaseT. You may be able to use your existing wiring, but there still is a considerable amount of time and expense associated with such a move.

Your Ethernet-based Intranet wiring will require more than just cabling. We'll talk about ways to segment your sections of your Intranet in the section "Connection Hardware."

FDDI

Fiber Distributed Data Interface (FDDI) is a high-speed networking technology used as an alternative, in some instances, to 100BaseT. FDDI is almost always transmitted along a fiber-optic cable, which provides good signal-to-noise performance, but can be implemented along twisted-pair cabling as well. Like 100BaseT, you can get 100 Mbps along your FDDI connections; however, 100BaseT is limited to 250m-long segments, whereas FDDI connections can be several kilometers in length. Therefore, FDDI lends itself to use as a backbone transport mechanism. You can use FDDI segments to connect segments of your Intranet to one another.

On the flip side, FDDI is several times more expensive than 100BaseT or 100VG-AnyLAN. Furthermore, it is difficult to install. FDDI network cards are still more expensive than 100BaseT cards at this point, so running FDDI to the desktop is costly. FDDI may be supplanted by future technologies, such as ATM one day, but currently remains a popular backbone implementation.

ATM

Ask a network administrator about ATM and you won't hear about automatic teller machines. Instead, you'll hear about the Asynchronous Transfer Mode (ATM), which has been heralded as the next big advance in high-speed networking. In contrast to FDDI, ATM allows transmission speeds of over 600 Mbps. Furthermore, ATM is a scalable architecture, meaning that it can be implemented down to the desktop or as a backbone transport mechanism.

As a disadvantage, ATM is still an evolving architecture and is not yet in wide use. ATM connection hardware is more expensive than other options, making it more costly to implement as a full Intranet solution.

Connection Hardware

Your desktop computers will be connected to a network outlet by some network cable. The network outlet is connected to some type of connection hardware. This hardware funnels your network traffic in and out of your Intranet, and for large Intranets, your hardware intelligently routes your traffic to its destination and shields you from unwanted traffic. We'll talk about some of the hardware you'll use to bind your organization's computers into a full-fledged LAN.

Routers

If your Intranet is large, you'll want to have hardware in place that makes intelligent choices about directing your network traffic. For example, if you have a user trying to connect to a Web browser in one building, that traffic need not be broadcast to users on a network in another building. Routers, also called *gateways*, are used just for this very purpose. A router can be a regular computer running routing software or it could be a dedicated piece of hardware that is used only for routing data packets throughout your Intranet.

Routers maintain tables that they use to check whether they need to pass data to another section of your Intranet. Each packet contains the address of its destination, so routers inspect these addresses and send the packets off to the LAN that is closest to that final destination. This process is repeated as packets bounce from router to router until they arrive at their destination. This method of packet transfer occurs throughout the Internet and will work the same way through large Intranets.

Routers are improving with time and are posing less and less of a performance hindrance to your traffic. Usually network administrators shield large parts of a LAN behind different routers to insulate portions of the network from one another. Router software is improving in capacity and functionality and can more efficiently direct your network traffic to its proper destination. Routers can work with different protocols, such as AppleTalk and TCP/IP, providing the router software is configured with the appropriate software.

Bridges

A bridge will connect to distinct segments of your network cabling and transmit traffic between them. Routers are in effect bridges, but standard bridges apply no intelligence to the traffic passing through them. You use bridges to extend the length of your networking cable. 100BaseT has a maximum segment length of 250 meters; you can connect several of these segments together with bridges to extend the network over long distances.

Learning bridges are a special form of bridges. Learning bridges actually take notice of the hardware address attached to the packets transferring between segments. Each device on your Intranet, whether it's a printer, a computer, or a router, maintains a unique address, known as a Medium Access Control (MAC) address, associated with the network interface. Network cards have unique MAC addresses, as do computers such as Quadras and Power Macs, that contain built-in networking hardware. Learning bridges take notice of the MAC addresses on either side of the connection and record that information for further use. Some packets that are directed to computers within the bridged segment need not travel outside the bridge. A standard bridge would blindly pass the packet on and eventually a router would bounce the packet back inside the bridge to the destination. A learning bridge would know that the source and destination computers are on the segment and would not transfer the packet out to the other segment. This prevents undue network traffic outside the affected segments.

NOTE

Routers and bridges perform essentially the same function but are concerned with different elements of the Ethernet packet. Routers are concerned with the destination IP address, whereas bridges are concerned with the actual MAC address. Routers slow traffic somewhat, as calculations are made as to where the packets need to be directed. Bridges place fewer restrictions on the packets but cannot segregate traffic to remote LANs as routers can. Usually, several Ethernet segments are bridged together behind a single router.

Hubs

A hub is an amorphous term used to describe a variety of network connection hardware. Hubs, also known as concentrators, connect several network entities together in a star-like fashion. You can hook up routers, bridges, and even cable segments to a hub. The hub acts to coordinate the traffic from all of its connections and move it out to another portion of the LAN. Conversely, hubs also receive traffic and divert it to the proper input port.

Getting Wired on the Inside

You've read about wiring and hardware that can connect your segments together. Now it's time to put this knowledge together to develop a coherent and scalable Intranet architecture. My intent is to give you a general feel for how you can deploy your network components so as to create a robust and scalable Intranet. I'll refrain from making any specific recommendations for any make and model of any of your networking hardware.

Wiring Schemes

In developing a comprehensive wiring scheme, start big and work your way down. First, look at your Intranet's connection to the Internet and work your way down to the desktop. The implementations discussed in this section are by no means the only way that you can institute your Intranet but are more of an illustration at how the connection hardware and your cabling can be combined to form a usable network.

Deploying Your Routers

Depending on the size of your Intranet, you may want to install more than one router. If you plan on instituting a firewall or any of the security measures mentioned in Chapter 13, "Intranet Server Security," you'll need at least one router to regulate traffic in and out of your Intranet. This router will filter out traffic that does not belong in your Intranet. Similarly, it will direct traffic coming out of your Intranet to the proper destination.

If your Intranet is small, say 100–200 nodes, you may well be served by using only one router. This would suit a small network where traffic flows throughout the entire Intranet. However, your organization may be large enough that your network could exist over several buildings. Some types of traffic, such as email, printing, and file sharing, often occurs within a building. You don't necessarily want to blast these packets throughout your Intranet, so routing according to buildings is a good idea.

The Backbone's Connected to the...

The function of your Intranet's backbone is to coordinate and expedite your network traffic. This backbone will connect the major parts of your Intranet by using a high-speed Ethernet medium. If your Intranet lies between several remote sites, such as buildings, your backbone will link your building routers into a high-speed network. If your small Intranet is served by a single router, you can use a high-speed network medium to connect several network segments.

For connections between routers that lie geographically distant, FDDI is a good choice for a backbone transport medium. FDDI brings fault tolerance and proven technology to your Intranet backbone. You can string FDDI segments that are several kilometers in length. Furthermore, stringing fiber optic cable over long distances will allow you to avoid many of the performance and reliability issues that come with stringing long lengths of copper wiring. You can deploy this FDDI backbone as a ring structure. In this way, routers have a continuous path to one another and there are fewer chances that some anomaly or obstacle will impede your network performance.

If your Intranet is small and only consists of a single router, you can still construct a backbone between your hubs. You can connect the hubs via a high-speed backbone. Installing FDDI in such a geographically contained environment may be cost-prohibitive. Therefore, one of the 100 Mbps Ethernet options, such as 100BaseT, makes an excellent backbone for a small Intranet.

NOTE

Your backbone will most likely provide the fastest transmission speed within your Intranet. Therefore, it's a good idea to connect those machines, which may see a lot of internal Intranet access, such as Web and FTP servers, directly to your backbone. If that's not possible, these servers should have their own connection to a local hub. If high-traffic servers are placed on a segment with other nominally-used nodes (such as printers or normal desktop computers), these other nodes, as well as your server, will notice a huge performance hit. Providing these servers with an isolated high-speed network access will improve their performance.

Building Bridges

No matter what the size of your Intranet may be, you will likely need to segment your client desktop computers. A segment is just a segregation of geographically contained network hosts. You may have 10–20 computers on a segment, which is often referred to as a rib. You can wire these segments using 100BaseT cabling. In fact, you can even string 100BaseT cabling down to the desktop. There are many 100BaseT NICs for Macintosh computers and PCs, and 100BaseT interfaces come standard with many high-end Unix workstations.

Bridging these segments allows you to overcome the 250 meter limit imposed on 10BaseT segments. Advanced bridges, as we discussed in the above section, will actually filter out packets that do not need to traverse outside of the segment. These bridges will connect to various hubs deployed throughout your Intranet.

Deploying Your Hubs

Like bridges, hubs will play a large part in your Intranet architecture regardless of the size of your network. For large Intranets, you'll deploy hubs inside your principal routers. If you choose to deploy a router for each building, for example, on your network, you can install a hub on each floor in your building. These hubs receive and disburse traffic from several connected bridges.

Smaller Intranets can use hubs to access the 100BaseT backbone. You can still use the hubs to distribute traffic throughout your backbone. You can even bridge a couple of segments and concentrate those bridges in your hubs. This smaller Intranet model is simply a scaled-down version of what we've proposed for a larger Intranet model.

Tapping into the Desktop

To connect your users to the network, you'll have to provide them with NICs. These cards will need to work with the medium that you've defined on your segment. 100BaseT NICs for PCs and Macintosh computers are becoming more prevalent. You'll need to construct segments that are not crowded with users, but also adhere to the 100BaseT 250 meter limit. These two constraints are mutually exclusive and require a great deal of consideration when planning your segments.

NOTE

Many newer Macintosh computers come with onboard network interfaces; you simply purchase a transceiver that works with the segment Ethernet medium. You could also circumvent the onboard network interface and purchase direct 100BaseT cards that plug into NuBus slots on your Mac. 100BaseT NICs that have been developed for the new PCI-based Power Macs offer a huge increase in performance over the standard onboard network interface.

Connecting to the Internet

Although your Intranet is primarily concerned with the needs of your business, you'll still need to exchange information with the outside world. For this reason, you'll have to have some sort of connection to the Internet. This opens a Pandora's box of concerns. Security is a major concern, as giving your Intranet access to the Internet conversely gives the Internet access to your Intranet. Your Intranet security options are discussed in Chapter 13, "Intranet Server Security." You'll also have to provide a roadmap for your users to get out onto the Internet; likewise, you'll have to direct

Internet users to those hosts that you decide to provide access. Domain name service is discussed in detail in Chapter 12, "Providing Domain Name Service." As far as what you plan on publishing to the Internet, you can skip to Appendix B, "Establishing an Internet Presence."

First and foremost, you need to acquire a physical connection to the Internet. The popularity of the World Wide Web, online services, and the Internet in general has given rise to a wealth of options for you to connect to the Internet. Over the past year or two, many companies have started to offer Internet access over phone links, much like the online services have done for their proprietary systems for years. These companies, known as Internet Server Providers (ISP), provide you with access to the Internet for a monthly fee. Let's look at your options.

Getting Your Own Connection

The Internet is comprised of a large number of smaller networks combined together over a high-speed backbone. If you need high-speed access to the Internet, you may want to tap into this backbone. The Internet was initially developed out of the U.S. government's desire to link federal labs with academic institutions. Until recently, the U.S. government oversaw the operation of the Internet backbone. This responsibility is now divided between several Network Access Providers (NAP). These NAPs tend to be large telecommunication companies such as Sprint, MCI, and some of the regional Baby Bells.

T1 or T3 Lines

You can purchase a T1 or T3 line directly from the NAP that administers the Internet backbone in your area. This is what ISPs do. You can circumvent the ISP and purchase an internet connection from a NAP. A T1 line is rated at 1.5 Mbps, whereas a T3 line is much faster, rated at 45 Mbps. You'll need to purchase an IP router as well as a T1 adapter. This T1 adapter converts the packets obtained from the T1 line into a format usable on your Intranet. The advantage of a T1 line is that you pay a fixed fee regardless of the traffic volume. However, this cost is in the neighborhood of several thousand dollars per year.

Fractional T1 Lines

You can actually purchase a fractional T1 line from a NAP. The bandwidth of such a line is rated at roughly 256 Kbps. One advantage to the fractional T1 approach is that you'll have the necessary equipment in place if you decide to take the plunge and purchase full T1 access in the future. The other advantage is that fractional T1 is obviously cheaper than normal T1 access.

Using an Internet Service Provider

Your other option is to go through an ISP for your Internet access. You'll pay access fees and maybe even usage fees according to the traffic volume flowing in and out of your Intranet. You won't have to worry about maintenance and upkeep of Internet connection, but you'll pay dearly for the convenience.

Conventional Modems

Many ISPs are configured like the commercial online services. You dial the ISP's phone number over conventional phone lines using a 14.4 or 28.8 modem. This is an extremely slow way to access the network but is definitely your least expensive option. It may be incongruous for your Intranet to be based on 100BaseT wiring while relying on modems for Internet access; however, this is your least complicated option as you need no other hardware, outside of your users' modems, to make the connection. You can even set up modems that your users can use over the Intranet as shared devices much as printers and file servers are used; keep in mind that these shared modems would be serving several people simultaneously, thereby fracturing the already slow modem bandwidth.

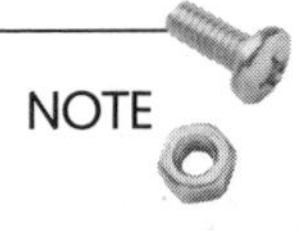

NOTE

The terms 14.4 and 28.8 are used as shorthand for 14,400 and 28,000 Kbps modems throughout the book. Most 28.8 modems also use compression algorithms, which can effectively boost your connection speed under ideal conditions to 56 Kbps. In reality, line losses and limitations of the phone line will cause you to average out to about 75 percent of your modem's top-speed capacity.

One disadvantage of using modems for Internet access is that many analysts feel that copper phone wiring is nearing the theoretical speed limit of data conversion. You probably won't see faster modems than 28.8 modems in the future. Communication technology will likely banish modems to the dustbin of history as new and more efficient communications protocols are implemented.

ISDN

One technology that shows more promise is the Integrated Services Digital Network or ISDN. ISDN goes one step better than modem technology. Whereas modems encode and decode data into a format suitable for transmission over phone lines, ISDN encodes the data into a digital form and transfers it over the conventional phone lines.

ISDN provides a maximum of 128 Kbps, so it far outstrips the capabilities of conventional 28.8 modems. ISDN modems exist and are being produced in rapid numbers as more ISPs are providing the service. However, you'll pay both an access fee and a usage fee for ISDN from most ISPs. Your ISP will charge for the privilege of receiving the service and will also charge you by the amount of time the connection is active. The telephone companies are beginning to provide ISDN access at competitive rates, but flat-fee ISDN service is rare (where a flat fee is charged regardless of the connection time or traffic volume).

ISDN is a very new service, and like ISPs a few years ago, is the scene of intense and aggressive price competition. This is good for you, the consumer, as it may not be long before flat-fee ISDN access costs what ISPs charge for 28.8 Kbps access today.

Colocation

Yet another option is for your organization to sign on with an ISP and locate your server with the ISP. In this way, your server will have immediate access to a T1 line or greater. You'll have to connect to the servers via FTP (with your Web server to test the HTML upload) to update your servers. It also would be a little sticky to arrange for your users to have access to the server if you set up some type of firewall. With colocated services, you'll avoid any kind of linkage fees that you incur with the other ISP services; however, you'll get charged per megabyte of storage.

You have a variety of Internet access methods that vary from slow and cheap to fast and expensive (see Table 2.1).

Table 2.1 *Comparison of Internet Connection Schemes*

Service	Speed	Advantage	Disadvantage
Modem	28 Kbps	Inexpensive hardware	Slow access speeds
ISDN	256 Kbps	Less expensive hardware	Access and usage fees still high
Fractional T1	256 Kbps	Allows upgrade to T1	Expensive to install and maintain
T1/T3	1.5 Mbps/ 45 Mbps	Access is directly from Internet	Expensive
Collocation	Same as ISP	Cheaper than owning T1 line	Servers must be administered remotely

Registering Your Nodes

After you've set up your Internet connection, you'll need to start registering your node names with the InterNIC organization. Before you even set up your users' host names, you have to submit your proposed domain name. (Domain names are discussed further in Chapter 12, "Providing Domain Name Service.") This chapter gives details on how you can register your domain name, as well as how the Internet domain hierarchy is organized. For this reason, the discussion of node registration is deferred to Chapter 12.

You can divide your Intranet into subnets. A subnet is a group of machines that are grouped together by function (not necessarily geography). You can assign two or three of the four fields in the standard IP address. For example, IP addresses on all the computers defined in the 128.183.250.xxx domain start with the same first three fields. You may want to set up different subnets throughout different locations in your Intranet. By setting up subnets, you can improve network hardware performance as well be able to restrict Web access to certain subnets (look in Chapter 4, "Macintosh HTTP Servers").

Providing Remote Access to Your Intranet

One service that your users will find most beneficial is the ability to access your Intranet from a remote site. As a result, you'll need to provide the same services away from the office that your Intranet users receive in the office. They'll need to be able to check their email, Web-based administrative forms, schedule meetings, and download files via FTP.

SLIP and PPP

I purchased a 12 Kbps modem in 1990 along with my Macintosh IIsi (which with a 20 MHz 68030 chip seemed pretty fast to me at the time). In just over five years, the average baud rate of a Mac or PC modem has increased over 20 times! While 28.8 Kbps is still a far cry from the bandwidth provided by ISDN or T1 lines, it is tantalizingly close to giving you the impression that you're on the Internet for real.

Two protocols allow you to emulate TCP/IP over a conventional phone line: Serial Line Internet Protocol (SLIP) and Point-to-Point Protocol (PPP). A computer running SLIP or PPP over a modem connection needs to be connected to a computer that serves those protocols. When connected, the client computer appears to the Internet as just another node, although a very slow one. You'll be able to take advantage of any TCP/IP application such as email, Web browsing, FTP, and other services from any location with a phone.

PPP is generally perceived as more reliable than SLIP, although I've never seen a study that validated this commonly held belief. However, PPP is used more heavily than SLIP, by both Windows and MacOS users. To serve PPP, you'll need to procure a specific PPP server, such as offered by the Xylogics Remote Annex (http://www.xylogics.com). The Remote Annex machine is specifically configured to route protocols such as AppleTalk and TCP/IP over phone lines.

NOTE

What about Apple Remote Access? Apple Remote Access (ARA) is used similarly to PPP, in that ARA users appear as nodes on AppleTalk networks while connected through a phone line. Performing tasks on an AppleTalk network is much slower through ARA than it is under normal AppleTalk. Earlier in this chapter, we discussed the fact that AppleTalk is a much chattier and less efficient protocol than TCP/IP; this becomes painfully obvious when running ARA, even over a 28.8 modem.

Using ARA, you can perform any function that you can over a real AppleTalk network. You can mount a remote volume and even print a file on a remote printer. However, file sharing is prohibitively slow over ARA, and a transfer of an equivalently sized file takes much less time using FTP than when using ARA. Running a remote application such as a word processor or spreadsheet is not practical over ARA.

Using Xylogics Remote Annex server, you can provide ARA service, but you need to weigh the burden of administering an additional service like ARA over the benefits it would bring to your Intranet. With the exception of remote printing, there appears to be few advantages of ARA over PPP.

Summary

A great deal of material was covered in this chapter, but you'll need to examine many of the resources listed in the links at the end of this chapter for more information on setting up and maintaining your network hardware. The intent of this chapter was to expose you to the issues you'll face in building your Intranet from the ground up. If you already participate in an existing local area network, my hope was to educate you about much of the current networking terminology. In either case, networking hardware is a rapidly evolving market, and through careful planning, you can plan your resources so as to build a robust infrastructure with which to develop your Intranet.

From here, we're going to spend the next several chapters discussing your Intranet Web services. You can of course jump to the following related chapters in the book:

- ☐ Chapter 12, "Providing Domain Name Service," to learn about how Domain Name Service and how you can implement a domain name server on a Mac.
- ☐ Chapter 13, "Intranet Server Security," to learn how you can configure hardware to provide secure transactions within your Intranet and out to the Internet.
- ☐ Appendix B, "Establishing an Internet Presence," to learn more about adapting or expanding your Intranet to provide services to the Internet.

Links Related to This Chapter

Apple Open Transport Home Page	http://www.macos.apple.com:80/macos/safe/network/transportover.html
Mark Sproul's Open Transport Page	http://msproul.rutgers.edu/macintosh/OpenTpt.html
Xylogics Remote Annex	http://www.xylogics.com

Usenet	comp.dcom.modems comp.dcom.cabling comp.dcom.lans.ethernet comp.protocols.ppp comp.sys.mac.hardware

CHAPTER 3

Choosing Your Server Hardware

With the introduction out of the way, it's time to talk about the hardware upon which you'll build your Intranet service. The popularity of the Macintosh as an Internet server platform makes it an ideal choice as the foundation of your Intranet.

One of the criticisms leveled at Apple regards the large number of different Macintosh models sold and then discontinued by the company. This means, however, that there are a significant number of models that you can use as Intranet servers. The newer machines coming out of Apple, on the other hand, sport new technology that poses a distinct advantage over the earlier models.

The following are some of the questions you will face when selecting your killer workstation:

- ☐ Do you go for an older Mac or a new workstation?
- ☐ What's all this business about PCI and Open Transport?
- ☐ What type of specialized Web servers is Apple offering these days?
- ☐ Should you run Unix on your Mac?

These topics will be addressed in depth in this chapter. Keep in mind that Apple has plans for new computer models in the near future (what else is new?). Specific Macintosh models will be discussed here, but the intent of this chapter is to introduce you to your current and future hardware options and give you enough information to make an informed decision about your server.

Out-of-the-Box or Off-the-Shelf?

Any budding Mac WebMaster will talk about how he started using MacHTTP on an old SE/30 that he found abandoned on a shelf in an old broom closet. My story started some years ago on a lovable Macintosh IIci computer that I used for my word processing and general engineering work. It hummed away on my desk serving HTML while I did work. I eventually upgraded its RAM and disk space and tossed an accelerator card inside.

My souped-up Macintosh IIci did a fine job at serving my Web page and a 5-second audio greeting from my daughter. I started experimenting with imagemaps, CGI scripting, and even some rudimentary database work. It wasn't long before I moved my server to a Power Mac running WebSTAR (MacHTTP's commercial descendant), which was far more capable of handling the extra workload.

NOTE 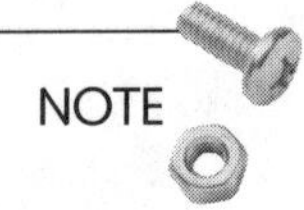

> More about MacHTTP, WebSTAR, and other HTTP servers is discussed in Chapter 4, "Macintosh HTTP Servers."

Another yarn I spin is about the email system we used in our office. Some time ago, we decided to move from a proprietary mail application to a more open system. We moved our new post office to a Macintosh IIci, which ended up serving about 100 users. Keep in mind that this is a recent story. This mail server is still humming on a six-year-old computer! Granted, that Macintosh IIci does little else but serve email, but imagine running a similar system using an old 386-based machine.

You probably have a similar story to tell. The fact is that even your older Macintosh can play a part in your Intranet as low-level WWW, FTP, domain name, or mail servers. Having said that, the newer Macintosh computers sport many new features that allow them to excel as network servers.

As an Intranet administrator, you'll want to build a service that is robust and, most importantly, inexpensive. If your office has a strong Mac presence, chances are that you can incorporate a lot of seemingly obsolete models into your service. Your organization may be large enough and your ambitions grand enough that you will require the latest and greatest Macintosh computers to run your Intranet applications. Your Intranet actually is a combination of several different services such as FTP, Web, email, domain name service, and others. You may want to emphasize different Intranet services in your organization; serving these particular elements will require more robust hardware.

Your decision between using new or used Mac hardware really depends on the sophistication of your Intranet. There's a place for your older Macintosh II series machines and Quadras, as well as for some of the new gee-whiz Power Mac computers. You will most likely deploy older machines for some purposes and newer machines for more arduous tasks. These issues are discussed in the following section.

Using Older Macintosh Computers

Newer Macintosh computers, like any other desktop computer, simply work and move data faster than older models. However, there are instances where you can use your older machines as servers within your Intranet. Some of the less computationally intensive services offered by your Intranet will be email and domain name service. Any of the late-model Macintosh II series would work well as an email or domain name server. These services require transfers of small amounts of data from a hard drive back out to your Intranet.

When you start talking about large-scale data transfer, such as with FTP and Web servers, you may be better off procuring a newer Power Mac. In addition to a more optimized architecture, the peripherals associated with the new machines, such as hard drives and the onboard Ethernet connection, are simply of a more advanced design. Hard drive access time, defined as the amount of time it takes for a drive to locate a desired sector on a disk, has decreased steadily in recent years as advances in hard drive technology have occurred. The 16-bit network cards in older machines are going to transfer data more slowly than modern onboard Ethernet connections. In addition to working faster than your older models, it's also likely that your newer computers will come equipped with more hard drive space and RAM than your older models, making them more useful for storing and serving large amounts of data.

Even the slower machines will work well as low-level FTP and Web servers if you have relegated them to low-level tasks. The MacOS is a robust operating system, and the older machines have retained a great deal of their utility. The slower processing speed of the older Macintosh computers is not an absolutely limiting factor for use as Intranet servers. In the following section, the real data transport limitations of your computers will be discussed.

Your Server's Bottleneck

It's hard to believe that only a few years ago, Intel and Motorola microprocessors ran at 4 to 8 MHz. This is in comparison to the 150 MHz Pentium and PowerPC processors used by high-end computers today. The history of desktop computing to date has been dominated by a relentless drive to increase the speeds of these chips. If the 1980s were the decade of the CPU, however, the 1990s promise to be the decade of the network connection.

All of a sudden, the issue is no longer how fast your processor is, but rather how fast your network connection is. Think about it, what would you rather be doing? Running Netscape Navigator on a Macintosh IIci with a high-speed fiber connection or a Power Mac with a 28.8 modem?

NOTE

Personally, I'll take the IIci. Nowadays, network bandwidth is king. The 1980s saw an exponential growth in CPU speed. I feel that the 1990s will see a similar growth in network access. At home, I've already gone from using a 1200 baud modem that I purchased in 1990 to using a 28.8 modem. I have a powerful new Power Mac at home running on a 28.8 modem, but it's a lot less useful for Net applications than my older and slower Power Mac at the office with a fast Ethernet connection. The higher speed access by the typical end-use has changed the overall content of the Web. I'm never going to knock a computer with a high-speed microprocessor, but for Internet and Intranet applications, I'll take a slower computer with a faster connection any day.

Regardless of whether you're serving email, Web pages, or any other TCP/IP traffic, your true bottleneck is going to be your ability to get data in and out of your computer. The processing speed is important, but a slow network connection will be the most significant factor affecting your Intranet performance.

There are two elements to this network connection: your bus speed and your network connection. Your microprocessor uses a *data bus* to transfer information to other peripherals such as hard drives, network cards, or video cards. To communicate with an Ethernet network, the Mac passes data to an Ethernet card in an expansion slot. Newer Macintosh computers actually have the Ethernet connection built into the motherboard. Until recently, Apple used the NuBus standard to communicate to cards in expansion slots. Recently, Macintosh computers have been developed to use the Peripheral Component Interconnect (PCI) standard to transfer data to peripheral cards in expansion slots. The PCI standard supports data transfer at faster rates than does NuBus and is an accepted standard in the Windows/Intel computer platform. PCI is discussed further in the section "The PCI Architecture" later in this chapter.

Your network connection is what allows your Mac to communicate with a larger collection of computers. In the old days, Macintosh computers used to be grouped together in AppleTalk networks using LocalTalk connections. AppleTalk is the MacOS-native networking protocol; you use it to print documents or share files with other computers. LocalTalk connections are extremely slow in comparison to Ethernet connections; Ethernet traffic can move up to 40 times faster than traffic on a LocalTalk network. Therefore, many Mac networks have discarded LocalTalk and now use Ethernet as a basis for their local area networks, as we discussed in Chapter 2. You probably could have figured out the naming convention, but AppleTalk is referred to as EtherTalk when run over an Ethernet network.

Therefore, both your data bus speeds and your network connection are bottlenecks in your Intranet. A fast processor will not help you get data in and out of your computer any faster. For Intranet applications that require fast data transfer, maximizing your data bus and network connection speeds will result in greater server performance.

This is not to say that processor speed is irrelevant. You may want to relegate certain tasks to ancillary computers. You may, for example, want to offload the tasks of executing CGI scripts or database queries to a separate computer, leaving a primary computer to serve HTML. These ancillary computers will be executing intensive tasks, and faster Power Macintosh computers will naturally execute them more rapidly.

Deploying Your Hardware

Depending on the scope of your Intranet services, your server complement may be comprised of several different Macintosh computers. Another factor in this deployment is the size of your Intranet. For a small 10-person office, you may be able to fit all the services discussed in this book onto one computer. For a large organization, consisting of several hundred to a thousand users, you may divide your server functions between several computers of varying capabilities.

The first thing you'll need to decide is which services you want to provide. These services will likely include the following:

- ☐ Web-based administrative information, such as database queries, document collaboration, and bulletin boards
- ☐ Electronic mail distribution
- ☐ Document archival through FTP
- ☐ Domain name service provision to allow your Intranet users to talk to the Internet

You'll have to decide which Mac models you want to use for these services. You'll also need to decide, based on your resources, how many computers you can spare for this effort. My advice is to think big. Plan for twice the computer you think you will need and expect to generate twice as much network traffic than you anticipate.

Your Web services will likely be the centerpiece of your Intranet. If at all possible, you'll want to procure a newer Mac, or Mac clone, with the most memory and hard drive space you can afford. If a new Mac is out of the question, you need to find the most potent Mac in your arsenal for recycling as your main WWW server. The types of models you should consider are discussed in the sections "The Macintosh Family Tree," and "Apple Internet Server Solutions," later in this chapter.

Figure 3.1 shows a suggested tree of evolution for your Intranet hardware configuration. The progression of server evolution marches from left to right as you acquire more resources. If you're just starting out with a small Intranet and not much in the way of spare change, for example, you can easily set up WWW and email servers on two older Macintosh computers. As your Intranet becomes more popular, managers will probably flood you with cash, so you can replace the WWW server workstation with a new Power Mac or Workgroup Server. Your Intranet may become even more popular within the company, so you may get a promotion as well as a staff. You may decide to add FTP services and a new Mac on which to host them. This can become an even bigger hit; so you may become a huge hero in the company. As your budget and staff grow, you may decide to provide domain name service allowing users to access the Internet; this will enable you to share the HTTP load between several Macintosh computers like the big kids do. Soon your whole organization may be buzzing about how you've turned things around with your Intranet, and you'll chuckle thinking about how you started with just a pair of old Macintosh computers.

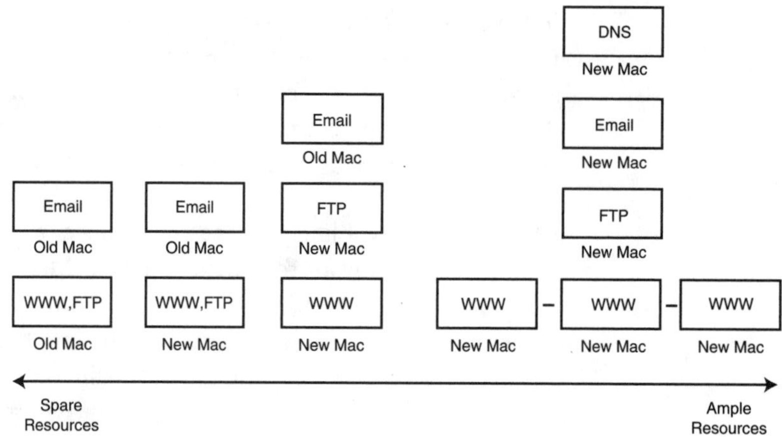

Figure 3.1 *You can add services and model upgrades as your Intranet grows and you acquire more resources.*

Macintosh Models Available to You

This section discusses some of the different types of Macintosh computers offered by Apple. Some of the new technology offered by Apple is exciting and poses some great benefits for your Intranet services. This section discusses some of this new technology while also revisiting some of the older types of Macintosh computers that you can recycle as Intranet servers.

The Macintosh Family Tree

Since its introduction in 1984, the Macintosh has grown and matured in performance and reliability. Even though the MacOS looks different nowadays, the system works pretty similarly to what was on the original Mac. Apple has produced several families of the Macintosh in this time span. The models that should interest you are outlined as follows:

- **68030/68040 machines.** Any Macintosh II-class or Quadra-class machine, except for the Macintosh II itself.
- **Power Macintosh computers.** Any Mac powered by the PowerPC chip series.

- ☐ **Workgroup Server.** A special class of Macintosh designed especially to serve documents via AppleTalk or EtherTalk.

Note that the Performa class of Macintosh computers, which is provided primarily through consumer channels and geared to the home user market, is not mentioned. As a result, it comes bundled with a great deal of software appealing to a home user, but nothing especially useful for your Intranet.

68030/68040 Machines

The Macintosh IIx was the first Mac based on the Motorola 68030 chip that was comparable to the Intel 80386 chip. Other 68030-based Macintosh computers include the Macintosh IIcx, IIci, IIsi, IIfx, and IIvx computers as well as the LC class of Macintosh. The faster 68040 chip powers the Quadra and Centris classes of Macintosh computers. Apple no longer manufactures computers of this class; only Power Macs and other PowerPC-based computers (PowerBooks, Workgroup Servers, and so on) are produced at this time. However, these older machines can be upgraded with extra RAM to be extremely reliable servers. While their performance will be markedly below that of newer Power Mac computers, these systems can easily run the latest MacOS versions.

NOTE

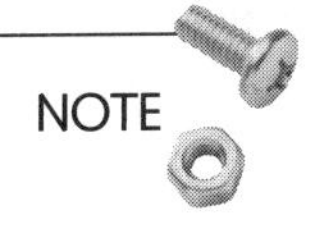

The term *680x0* refers to the chip architecture used on the pre-Power Mac models. Along with the models discussed above, some 680x0-based Macintosh computers included the original Mac, the Macintosh Classic, the SE, SE/30, and the Macintosh II.

Power Macintosh

In early 1994, Apple began the transition of the Mac architecture from the Motorola 680x0 architecture to an advanced chip known as the PowerPC. To ensure backward compatibility with earlier Macintosh computers, Apple built a 680x0 emulator into the MacOS. When Power Mac computers run software originally designed for an older Mac, the software is run in a slightly slower emulated mode. Therefore, those commercial and shareware applications written specifically for the PowerPC Macs will run much faster and seamlessly than their 680x0 equivalents.

The Power Mac computers will run future versions of the MacOS. With several Web and FTP server applications optimized to run on the PowerPC chip, the Power Mac is an ideal platform upon which to base your Intranet services.

Apple Internet Server Solutions

Apple has developed Power Mac computers that are specifically designed to operate as high-performance network servers. Known as the Apple Internet Server Solutions (AISS), these computers are differentiated from Power Macs in their expandability, robustness, and bundled software. These extra features cause the AISS machines to be more expensive than normal desktop Power Mac computers. AISS configurations are used to serve many high-traffic Web sites.

Apple Workgroup Servers

As of this writing, Apple produces three different Apple Workgroup Server (AWG) models: the 6150, 8150, and 9150. The models continually are updated with faster versions of the PowerPC microprocessor. These servers differ from the conventional desktop Macintosh computers in the following ways:

- AWGs come with larger disk drives than those found in conventional Power Macs and also contain room for multiple disk drives.
- AWGs come with digital audio tape (DAT) drives and backup software to use to safeguard information on your disks.
- AWGs come with various network management applications that help troubleshoot server problems.
- AWGs support data safety, using a system of Redundant Array of Independent Disks (RAID). RAID is a means of grouping relatively inexpensive drives as a single logical unit to achieve a faster and more reliable disk storage system.

Like Apple's newer Power Macs, the AWG PowerPC processors reside on upgradeable daughtercards. This means that you can pop the microprocessor out of the logic board and replace it with a much faster version, thereby protecting your investment in the machine.

AWGs currently are used as high-performance Web sites in many locations. At this time, Apple Computer maintains a QuickTime VR Web site comprised of a system of three AWG 8150s in tandem. This system of servers, combined as a "redundant array of inexpensive computers," or RAIC, publishes 3 GBs of data each day.

AISS Software

Bundled with the AWG servers, Apple offers a CD-ROM that contains a great deal of software that you can use to set up your Intranet Web services. This software includes a variety of applications including a WWW server, an HTML editor, a domain name server, CGI scripting tools, Tango and Butler SQL database applications, and other software. The CD-ROM is only available by purchasing one of the AWG server models and is not sold separately. Many of the applications listed on the AISS CD-ROM are provided as demo versions on this book's CD-ROM.

Macintosh Clones

It was not until 1995 that the first Mac clones began to appear. For the first time, Apple Computer was no longer the sole source for Mac. The most robust and competitive offerings come from Power Computing Corp. The reliability and compatibility of these computers have received high marks from analysts and users. These computers cut few corners and furthermore appear to offer a lot of Mac for the buck.

Currently, the high-end of Power Computing Mac clones come in 132 and 150 MHz PowerPC versions. Besides exceptionally quick processors, these computers offer several amenities that lend to their use as Intranet servers; these amenities include large amounts of RAM and hard drive space. The PowerWave series, as the high-end computers are known, do not come with the networking tools that accompany the AWGs; instead, these computers are comparable to the high-end desktop Mac models. However, Power Computing offers a great deal of flexibility in constructing and selecting the various options for your computers.

Other Hardware Concerns

The Mac models you choose for your server options will depend on your resources. There are some additional considerations you'll need to keep in mind when selecting and configuring your computer hardware.

Buying RAM

The more applications you run on your machine, the more RAM you'll need to add to your Mac. Most Power Macs come with 8 MB or 16 MB of RAM. If you expect your servers to see a lot of traffic, or if you expect to run multiple servers on the same computer, load the computer with as much RAM you can afford. RAM is rarely a bad investment, as RAM requirements for Mac applications have increased with time. It's a safe bet that as your server applications grow in sophistication over the next few years, their RAM requirements will grow as well.

NOTE

> You can install RAM on many Macintosh computer models yourself. When doing so, pay close attention to the instructions for your computer. Some models require you to install RAM chips (also known as Single- and Dual-Inline-Memory-Modules—SIMMS and DIMMs) in pairs in certain slots on your Mac's motherboard. Power Macs use DIMMs, while older Macintosh computers use SIMMs.

One useful utility used by many Mac owners is Connectix Corp's RAM Doubler. RAM Doubler is a memory management tool that allows applications on your Mac to use more RAM than what's physically installed on the computer.

When you look at the About this Macintosh option (found under the Apple icon at the upper left of your desktop), you see a display similar to that shown in figure 3.2. You see a listing of the active applications currently running; you can also tell how much RAM is allocated to each application and how much RAM is available to the application. RAM Doubler effectively doubles the RAM installed using SIMMs or DIMMs.

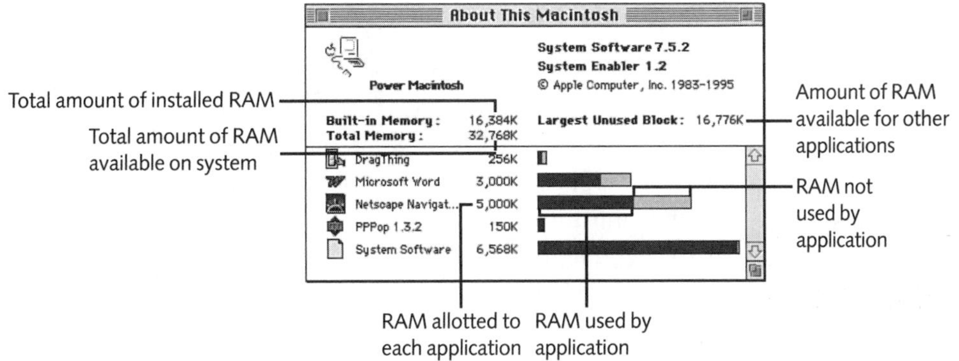

Figure 3.2 *A lot of the RAM reserved for your applications is not available for other applications. Among other memory-saving features, RAM Doubler distributes unused RAM to other applications.*

RAM Doubler does this in the following three ways:

- RAM Doubler distributes the RAM unused by the applications to other applications that need it. By selecting an application icon and opening the Get Info box (done by pressing Command-I), you can reserve a certain amount of RAM for the application. Normally, the application doesn't use all the RAM you've reserved for it (as seen in figure 3.2). RAM Doubler redistributes this RAM to other applications.

- Many applications reserve some of their allocated RAM for certain tasks such as launching or quitting. RAM Doubler compresses and redistributes this RAM to other applications as needed.

- As a last resort, RAM Doubler will reserve space on your hard drive for virtual memory. You'll notice a performance hit when this happens, as your hard drive will be accessed frequently in these instances.

RAM Doubler is compatible with many older Macintosh computers as well as the newer models. Check with your individual server applications to see if they're compatible with RAM Doubler.

Buying Big Enough Hard Drive Space

Along with RAM, you'll always need more disk space than you think. In addition to RAM requirements, hard drive space required for server applications has grown in recent years. Many high-end Internet and Intranet administrators combine several hard drives into a single unit using RAID technology (which is discussed in the section "RAID" later in this chapter).

Buying Scaleable Machines

One advantage of the Workgroup Servers discussed earlier is their scalability. These machines give you enough space to add peripherals such as hard drives, CD-ROM drives, backup tape drives, and other such devices. Using old hardware is nice and inexpensive, but be sure that your solutions are scaleable in that you can add modern peripherals as needed. The old Macintosh II with the 8-bit Ethernet card may not be the best networking solution for you.

New Macintosh Technology

The Mac has undergone a radical makeover in the last two years. Because of heavy competition from Windows/Intel-based PCs, the Mac has become less costly, more powerful, and more laden with features than ever before. Some of these new advances will be discussed in the following sections.

The PCI Architecture

The expansion slots in the back of your Mac accept cards that provide a variety of functions. You can insert a video card, a graphics accelerator card, a CPU accelerator card, an internal modem, an Ethernet card, or a variety of other cards. Until recently, the slots in the back of your Mac accepted cards using the NuBus standard. In late 1995, Apple began to build the Macintosh with a different type of expansion bus. This standard, the Peripheral Component Interconnect or PCI, is new to the Mac but is actually popular with Pentium-based PCs.

Cards and boards adhering to the PCI standard will deliver higher performance at a lower price than those based on the NuBus standard. This move to PCI has many graphics and video professionals drooling at the thought of using high-end PCI video cards. Furthermore, as PCI cards are very popular with the larger Intel-based PC market, it is hoped that many of these cards will now become available, with minor modifications, to the Power Mac. The crossover between these markets remains to be seen, but many of your peripherals will take advantage of this new bus standard.

RAID

RAID is a means of combining a series of disks into a single conglomerate that acts as a single drive. This enables you to store data with more reliability than if you stored your data on a similarly sized single hard drive. For example, if you have five 1 GB disks, you have a better chance at recovering your data if one of those drives crashes than if you were operating a single 5 GB disk. Therefore, for systems where you are storing or publishing large amounts of data, RAID is a desirable storage option. Apple RAID software is included with the AISS CD-ROM.

Open Transport

Open Transport (OT) is Apple's new PowerPC-native networking and communications system for the MacOS. Open Transport 1.0 was released with the first PCI-based Power Macintosh computers in late 1995; this release gave many users of these Macintosh computers a lot of trouble, so it wasn't until OT 1.1 was released a few months later that the system came into widespread use.

Open Transport actually replaces the conventional AppleTalk and TCP/IP implementations under the MacOS. Much of this is transparent from a user's perspective. As an Intranet administrator, the most obvious benefit you will see is the ability to employ more than the 64 TCP/IP streams allowed by MacTCP. Think of an IP stream as a toll booth. A packet of information has to get in and out of your server using an IP stream. The more toll booths you have, the shorter your wait to get through. Similarly, the more IP streams you have, the more data you can get in and out of your server. Under OT, the number of streams you can maintain are constrained by your RAM and processor power.

By the time you read this, most MacOS Internet applications will have OT-compliant versions available. These applications should see an improvement over the MacTCP versions.

Unix on the Macintosh

There seems to be some strange and mysterious alliance between Unix and the MacOS. Despite the arcane command-line driven interface behind Unix, many Mac users seem to be conversant with the operating system. Unix ruled the Internet long before Mac and PC users discovered it. Many of the Internet protocols are natively supported within Unix. Furthermore, NCSA's original httpd Web server originated under Unix. Many Web and Internet/Intranet tools exist under Unix. Now Unix exists on the Mac.

Running Unix on the Mac has several advantages. For one thing, Unix is natively multitasking, meaning that processes can be run simultaneously; this allows operations, such as Web services, to be greatly enhanced. Until Copland, the next major MacOS release, Mac users will have to make do with multithreaded processing. Similarly, the MacOS file system has difficulties with large file systems; Unix has no such problems. Several flavors of Unix have been ported to the Mac, and several Mac Internet servers are actually running Unix.

Apple Unix

Apple Unix (A/UX) is the original Unix port to the Mac, courtesy of Apple. Apple Unix had a cult following within the Mac community. A result of the PowerPC consortium was that Apple threw its weight behind IBM's Unix implementation, AIX. Apple Unix is no longer supported by Apple but is still used as a server platform. Apache, the popular freeware alternative to NCSA's httpd Web server, for example, is developed and available under A/UX.

Apple recently released two new servers, Network Servers 700 and 900, which actually run a version of AIX with a slight MacOS tinge. These servers are geared toward publishing production markets, but it will be interesting to see if these machines will be used for high-powered WWW servers.

MachTen

MachTen from Tenon Intersystems is a commercial port of Unix to the Mac. MachTen 4.0 is developed for the PowerPC platform. MachTen runs on top of the MacOS so that you can easily alternate between the two operating systems. MachTen comes bundled with NCSA httpd and other IP tools that support advanced networking protocols not yet supported by OT.

Linux

Linux has taken the PC world by storm. Linux is a freely distributed port of Unix to the Intel PC market. Originally developed by a European college student, Linux source code is freely accessible; successive versions of the OS have been developed through a group effort of the Internet community. As an open system, no one really owns Linux, but Apple recently threw its weight behind a Linux port to the Power Mac. This port should be available by the end of 1996 and will give many Mac users an inexpensive but powerful Unix presence.

Why Unix?

Many Mac users have a special attachment to the Mac because of the MacOS's ease-of-use and expanded functionality. This begs the question of why Mac users would be interested in running another OS on their computers? Until Copland, Unix will be the only way that Mac Intranet administrators can beat the MacOS file system limitations and lack of multitasking. Furthermore, more WWW servers are running on top of Unix than any other operating system (the MacOS rates second—see the latest survey results at http://www.mirai.com/survey). Hence, there are many freely accessible Unix tools that you can use on your Intranet.

Summary

The Macintosh platform has undergone huge changes in recent years. The next few years promise to be even more transitional, as the wild ride of the Internet/Intranet will continue to drive software and hardware development. You will need to keep abreast of the different developments in the Mac hardware field in order to keep your Intranet services as flexible as possible.

For the next few chapters, we are going to discuss some of the software that you'll use to construct your Intranet services. Chapter 4 discusses "Macintosh HTTP Servers," but feel free to jump to any of the following related chapters:

- ☐ Chapter 13, "Intranet Server Security," to learn how you can configure hardware to provide secure transactions within your Intranet and out to the Internet.
- ☐ Chapter 14, "Sample Intranet Applications," to learn about some services you can provide using the Web, FTP, and email technologies discussed in this book.
- ☐ Appendix B, "Establishing an Internet Presence," to learn more about adapting or expanding your Intranet to provide services to the Internet.

Links Related to This Chapter

Connectix Corp	http://www.connectix.com
Apple Internet Server Solution FAQ	http://www.solutions.com /AISS-FAQ/AISS_FAQ.html
QuickTime VR	http://qtvr.quicktime.apple.com
Power Computing	http://www.powercc.com
Tenon Intersystems	http://www.tenon.com
Linux for Power Macintosh	http://www.mklinux.apple.com/
WWW Server Survey	http://www.mirai.com/survey

CHAPTER 4

Macintosh HTTP Servers

It was shortly after the introduction of Mosaic in late 1993 that Chuck Shotton developed and released MacHTTP. At that time, MacHTTP was a freeware port of the commonly used Unix HTTP server from the NCSA. It enabled a Macintosh with a reasonably fast network connection to serve HTML files and graphics. Like most Macintosh applications, MacHTTP was simple to launch, configure, and maintain. A few clicks of the mouse, and you were off serving Web pages.

There is a good chance that your Web service will be the most visible part of your Intranet presence. If your organization is connected to the Internet, most of your users not only have access to Web browsers, but also have experience with them as well. You'll include FTP and email services within your Intranet suite of capabilities, but your Web services will most likely be the cornerstone of your service. Great care must be taken in the configuration and operation of your Web server software. The servers discussed in this chapter go way beyond the power and performance of the original MacHTTP application. We will discuss some of the options you have for the Intranet Web service including the following:

- ☐ An overview of the HyperText Transport Protocol
- ☐ Installation and configuration of MacHTTP
- ☐ Installation and configuration of WebSTAR
- ☐ Installation and configuration of InterServer Publisher

- ☐ Use of some shareware and freeware HTTP servers
- ☐ A contrast and comparison of the available server options

Introducing Terms and Technology

Before discussing implementation and use of the various HTTP servers for the Mac, let's cover some of the terms and technology that are used in this book. Although the servers mentioned here offer plug-and-play operation, to fully configure and utilize your server to its full potential, you'll need to understand some of the basic nomenclature.

This is where the book gets a little dry. Page after page of software description can get a little...well, boring. However, these descriptions are necessary to understand the workings of the program. My intent is to make the documentation task-driven rather than feature-driven. When you read software documentation, notice that the literature steps you right across the menu bar, spitting out a paragraph on each menu. That's good for reference material, but the approach in this chapter, as well as the rest of the book, is to teach you how to work the various tasks, like adding users or setting privileges. It's my sincere hope that this chapter, as well as the following chapters, will be more informative than if you were just to plow through your software documentation.

HyperText Transport Protocol

HyperText Transport Protocol (HTTP) is the most common method of transporting data between Web browsers and clients. The protocol was developed in 1989 for the purpose of transporting documents along the Internet via a hypertext interface. In contrast to FTP, an HTTP connection between computers requires few resources. The protocol was designed to nimbly recover text and other data from HTTP servers with very little overhead required from the browser or server computers.

The HTTP specifications undergo periodic review by a committee of Internet specialists. As with most committees, these specialists take a great deal of time and care before approving new sets of standards. The current standard is HTTP/1.0, which supersedes the original HTTP/0.9. Further versions of HTTP are under review; they will provide greater capabilities to Web browsers in the areas of performance and security.

An HTTP connection between a Web client and server can be separated into four separate actions:

- **Connection launch.** The HTTP server constantly listens on a certain IP port for a request from a Web browser. This port usually is specified as port 80, but nonstandard ports can be included in the URL.
- **Client request.** After a connection is established, the browser sends a request to the server. In addition to querying the server regarding a CGI script, or a certain image, sound, or HTML file, the browser sends a little information about itself (mainly the type of file formats it can understand).
- **Server response.** The server, having digested the request from the browser, sends an HTTP message to the browser. The server communicates to the browser the following information: the level of HTTP being supported, the format used to convey the response, and the response itself.
- **Connection close.** Having sent the message, the connection is terminated by either the client or server.

NOTE

An Internet Protocol (IP) port is a channel through which information enters and exits your computer. Think of IP ports as channels on a CB radio; your radio can send and receive conversations on multiple channels on the same radio. Your computer contains many IP ports that are implemented in software rather than hardware. Different types of IP traffic (HTTP, Usenet, email, and so on) are directed to different ports on your computer.

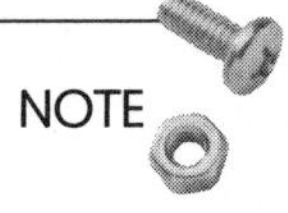
NOTE

Depending on your security arrangement, which we'll discuss in Chapter 13, "Intranet Server Security," you may want to direct your Intranet Web services to a nonstandard IP port, that is, a port other than 80. You may want to assign your Web server to a port that is higher than that used by normal IP traffic such as 8080. In this way, if Internet users have access to your server, they will not immediately be able to access your Web site.

As opposed to FTP or Telnet connections, the HTTP connection does not stay open. As a result, a server can maintain many more HTTP connections for a given length of time than it can support remote logins.

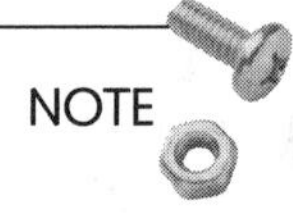
NOTE

For more specific information on HTTP, visit the World Wide Web Consortium HTTP draft specification at http://www.w3.org/hypertext/WWW/Protocols/HTTP/HTTP2.html.

MIME

The Multimedia Internet Mail Exchange (MIME) message representation protocol is a means of conveying information about a file that is being sent through the Internet. This protocol conveys information about the message through MIME headers but leaves the message content or body in the form of plain ASCII text. For this reason, MIME is an excellent means of transferring files between different platforms. For example, you can use the email program Eudora to send a graphics file from your Mac to a PC user. If the PC user also is running Eudora, or any other MIME-capable mail reader, the program will read the MIME header and attach the relevant tag to the file to make it readable by the correct application.

Much like HTTP, MIME content headers are under a standards process. The key information in the header is the MIME type and subtype that identify the type of message content. The MIME type usually will consist of one of the types listed in Table 4.1.

Table 4.1 *Common MIME Types*

Type	Column
Application	Defines client applications
Audio	Defines audio formats
Image	Defines image formats
Message	Used for electronic mail messages
Multipart	Used for transmission with multiple parts
Text	Defines text formats
Video	Defines video formats
X-string	Denotes an experimental MIME type not recognized as a standard

The content header is comprised of a type and subtype. The subtype specifically defines the message content within the context of the MIME type. An HTTP server, for example, will send the following MIME type/subtype in response to a Web client query:

```
text/html
```

This header information tells the browser to expect some text, and specifically, some HTML text. Web browsers, as opposed to other applications, understand that MIME types need to be interpreted as HTML and displayed accordingly. Similarly, a MIME header containing the information

```
image/gif
```

would tell the browser the following ASCII text actually is a GIF image. The browser then displays the GIF within the window or launches a GIF-viewing application.

A variety of MIME subtypes are defined for each type. The HTTP server needs to correlate the type of information it's serving to a certain MIME type. If it's serving a JPEG file as part of a Web page, for example, it needs to know that

- The file is a JPEG formatted-file
- Image/JPEG is the standard MIME classification for that file

The Web server needs to have some means of identifying files and the relevant MIME types in order to tell the browsers what to expect. How to do this for the various server applications is covered later in this chapter.

What You'll Need

You're going to be investing a lot of time in developing a server that other people will depend on you to maintain. For that reason, you'll need to stay abreast of the latest MacOS system software developments. The software in this chapter requires at least System 7.0. There are strong advantages, however, to maintaining the most recent system software version. We discussed your options for configuring your Mac hardware in Chapter 3, "Choosing Your Server Hardware," but it is assumed that you have at least 8 MB of RAM (16 MB is preferable) and sufficient hard drive space to contain the various applications as well as the files that you want to serve.

NOTE

Some of the software on this CD-ROM is either shareware or a demonstration version of a commercial application. Purchase of this book does not fulfill your shareware obligations.

NOTE

The latest Apple System Software updates are available at the Apple WWW site at http://www.support.apple.com/wwwdocs/apple_sw_updates.html.

Just as important, you'll need to have remote access to your organization LAN as discussed in Chapter 2; it is assumed that you at least have access to MacTCP 2.0.6. Open Transport is a follow-on application to MacTCP, which, at the time of this writing, has just been released for most Mac models. Although some of the software in this chapter will run under Open Transport, it is not yet a required element for running your Web server application.

NOTE

Drag-and-drop refers to the feature enabling you to open files by dragging them onto application icons or aliases. I sometimes launch a local session of Netscape Navigator by dragging a copy of an HTML file on top of it. Navigator displays the file upon launching.

Several of the applications in this chapter work with AppleScript, which is Apple's own MacOS scripting language. Using AppleScript, you can create and run small applications using the AppleScript language. This language is easy to understand and implement into AppleScript executable files.

NOTE

A friend of mine was convinced that System 7 is a nefarious plot by Apple to make users purchase more RAM and faster Macintosh computers. Similarly, you may be asking why you should upgrade to 7.5 because the earlier System 7 versions are free. With System 7.5 you get AppleScript and MacTCP bundled free. You also get drag-and-drop and a scriptable Finder all for less than $99. The scriptable Finder is useful as it enables you to build scripts by having the Script Editor record your work. Your PC friends will likely have to accumulate similar applications from various sources, whereas you have a slew of relevant tools just bundled with your operating system.

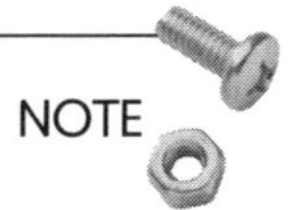
NOTE

Apple maintains several mailing lists related to authoring and providing Internet services. Check out http://www.solutions.apple.com/apple-internet/ for the mailing list home page.

Using MacHTTP

MacHTTP is the granddaddy of all Mac Web servers. It's one big reason why the Mac has such a large presence among Web servers on the Internet. Its simple installation, configuration, and maintenance have won the praise of many Internet enthusiasts inside and outside the Macintosh community.

NOTE

MacHTTP is not found on this server but is available at the URL listed at the end of the chapter. It also is distributed at the major FTP archives.

Requirements

MacHTTP 2.2 requires System 7 and MacTCP. You'll need AppleScript to allow MacHTTP to support such advanced features as searchable documents and imagemaps. AppleScript comes with System 7.5 and later. Don't worry if you're not running System 7.5 because MacHTTP comes bundled with AppleScript. The application requires only 600 KB of RAM and under 2 MB of disk space. MacHTTP 2.2 comes as a fat binary. MacHTTP is a shareware application; consult the MacHTTP documentation for instructions on how to pay your shareware fee.

NOTE

When an application is described as a *fat binary* it means that it will run on either a Power Mac or a normal 680x0-based Mac (also nicknamed 68K-based Mac). All Macintosh models before the Power Mac were based on a Motorola 68000-based microprocessor. The original Macintosh used a 68000 comparable to Intel's 8086. The Macintosh II came out in 1987 based on the 68020 chip. Later Macintosh IIs were based on the 68030 chip, and the Quadra and Centris models were based on the 68040, roughly equivalent to the Intel 486 chip. The PowerPC chip, which runs the Power Mac platform, uses a markedly different chip instruction set. However, it can run applications written for older Macintosh computers under a slower emulation mode. A fat binary file contains code that will run on the older Mac as well as a Power Mac. As a result, the file is slightly larger than either a straight 68K-based or Power Mac-based version.

Installing MacHTTP

CD-ROM

MacHTTP is included on the CD-ROM that comes with this book. Locate the folder entitled MacHTTP Software & Docs and drag it to your hard drive. Double-click the MacHTTP 2.2 application and you've just started publishing on the Web. As long as the software is running, you will be able to serve documents.

Test the server by determining at what address your MacHTTP server is publishing. If your server IP address is www.anyplace.com, then the server's default URL is http://www.anyplace.com. A browser seeking that URL will key in on the directory where MacHTTP is located and running. For example, if a browser requests the following URL:

```
http://www.anyplace.com/images/logo.gif
```

your MacHTTP server will look in its own folder for a folder entitled Images. In this Images folder, it will look to publish a file called logo.gif. Note that you do not reference anything relative to the Mac's root folder. You will want to avoid spaces and other Mac-unique characters in your file folder names whenever possible.

NOTE

> One useful feature of Mac Web servers is that they do not provide access to areas on your server outside the served folder. If you keep MacHTTP in a certain folder, for example, users cannot access any information or files outside that folder.

You can test the server by entering the server's default URL into your browser. To fully test your system, run the browser on a remote computer; in this way, you can test MacHTTP as well as your network connection. If you have your network configured correctly, the MacHTTP default page will appear in your browser.

NOTE

> Like other applications used to provide your Intranet services, you may want to add an alias of the MacHTTP application into the Startup Items folder of your System folder. Whenever your computer is restarted, this application will be one of the first to launch.

If you are running System 7 earlier than System 7.5, or do not have AppleScript installed, you will need to install it to do some of the CGI exercises discussed in Chapter 7, "Writing CGI Scripts." Like installation of any other System extensions, you drag the contents of Apple's Scripting System to the location specified by the folder names. If you are running a Power Mac, copy the contents of both folders to the Extensions folder inside your System folder. The Scripting Additions folder needs to be copied to the Extensions folder. Similarly, the MacTCP folder contains the MacTCP control panel that should be installed in the Control Panels folder in your System Folder, if you have not done so already.

NOTE

To reduce clutter in your MacHTTP folder, move some of the extraneous folders out to another location. First, go into the Tutorials folder and remove the Extending MacHTTP Scripts and bring it into the same folder as MacHTTP. Rename this folder Scripts. Move the Documentation folder and the remainder of the Tutorials folder to a location where they can be referred to later. Your MacHTTP folder now contains the application, associated files, an Images folder, and a Scripts folder. When you start adding images and CGI scripts, you can neatly store them in the appropriate folders.

Configuring MacHTTP

MacHTTP configuration is managed by editing the MacHTTP.config file in the MacHTTP Software & Docs folder. Some of the configurations listed here are duplicated by menu options within MacHTTP, but those are covered later. You can edit this file in SimpleText or any text editor. Several keywords are in this file that you can modify to configure MacHTTP service. These keywords are described in Table 4.2.

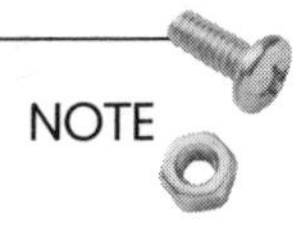
NOTE

If you edit MacHTTP.config using SimpleText, the MacHTTP keywords appear in boldface type.

Table 4.2 *MacHTTP Configuration Keywords*

Keyword	Description (Default value in parentheses)
VERSION	MacHTTP version number (2.2)
DEFAULT	Default MIME type (text/html)
INDEX	Default home page location (Default.html)
ERROR	Default error page location (Error.html)
NOACCESS	Default location of security error page (Noaccess.html)
LOG	Name of MacHTTP log file (MacHTTP.log)
TIMEOUT	Length of time until inactive connections time out (60)
MAXUSERS	Limit on maximum number of concurrent users (10)
MAXLISTENS	Limit on maximum number of preconnection Listens (10)
PORT	HTTP communication port (80)
PIG_DELAY	Number of ticks (1/60 sec) that MacHTTP gives top priority to MacHTTP request response (30)
DUMP_BUF_SIZE	Maximum number of bytes into which file transfers are divided (4096)
NO_DNS	Toggles DNS lookups (Commented out)
Suffix Mappings	Used to link MIME headers with MacOS file types
REALM	Means of localizing server access
DENY/ALLOW	Restrict or enable server access by IP address

Default File Locations

When a browser successfully contacts a MacHTTP server, similar to any other server, it gets one of the following four pages in response:

- The desired page
- The default page for that directory
- An error page when the URL is incorrect
- A message denoting a lack of access privileges

You can set up these pages several ways by entering their locations within MacHTTP.config. The keywords for these pages are listed in Table 4.2. The files can exist anyplace inside the MacHTTP folder providing you enter the folder path correctly. The INDEX keyword is used to enable someone to enter a URL such as

```
http://www.anyplace.com
```

and have it access

```
http://www.anyplace.com/Default.html
```

depending on which default HTML file is specified.

NOTE

The message files in MacHTTP.config do not have to be HTML files. You can display images, or even CGI scripts, or any other type of file as long as you've entered the correct suffix mapping in the configuration file.

NOTE

The DEFAULT keyword must describe a file name, not a path name like the other file keywords. MacHTTP does not index directories as other HTTP servers do. Directory indexing occurs when you supply a URL of a directory with no file name appended; with the CERN and NCSA servers, you then have access to the entire folder and enclosed folders. You may or may not want this to happen. Chuck Shotton, MacHTTP's author, felt that this was a huge security risk, and therefore it is not supported by MacHTTP.

NOTE

> The MacOS does not natively support case sensitivity. Requesting the file Image.gif is the same as requesting the file IMAGE.GIF. The same is true of MacHTTP service as well.

Configuring Connection Limitations

You can specify certain parameters that customize MacHTTP's connection characteristics. In Table 4.2, we see the TIMEOUT keyword is used to specify the amount of time that an HTTP connection stays open. At the beginning of this chapter, we talked about how HTTP is designed to be a nimble protocol that maintains short connections. If for some reason, a client request connection stays open, you can terminate it after a set amount of time; the default value is one minute.

The maximum number of users and listens on your server is set by the MAXUSERS and MAXLISTENS keywords. A *user* is defined as a client with an open connection to your server. In contrast, the server listens for requests from other browsers. With MacTCP, you are limited to 64 connections of which MacHTTP can claim as many as 48. These 48 IP connections are divided into actual requests and listens that are Requests for Requests. By setting the MAXUSERS keyword to a high value, you are doing two things. First, because MacHTTP can process only one request at a time, a large number of users results in frustrating delays for the other users. Secondly, you theoretically restrict MacHTTP's capability to listen for other connections. MAXUSERS and MAXLISTENS are restricted between 3 and 48, but default to 8 users and 5 listens respectively.

NOTE

> In March 1996, Apple released System 7.5.3, which contains a new networking transport mechanism known as Open Transport (OT). OT is the modern networking and communications subsystem for the MacOS and replaces earlier versions of AppleTalk and MacTCP. Useful features that OT gives TCP/IP users include a removal of the limit on consecutive IP streams. The number of
>
> *continues*

streams available to your Macintosh will be limited by the microprocessor speed and available RAM. Furthermore, you will be able to change your IP configuration (such as IP address) on-the-fly without having to reboot your computer.

You can configure the IP port on which MacHTTP listens for connections using the PORT keyword. By Internet convention, HTTP is allotted to port 80, which is the MacHTTP default. However, you can run multiple MacHTTP servers on your Macintosh by having the different applications run on different IP ports. By convention, common IP services utilize ports under 1024, so it's recommended that you configure the PORT keyword to something greater than 1024.

Configuring for Performance

You can modify several parameters to configure MacHTTP's performance. PIG_DELAY is a means of determining how much time MacHTTP will spend processing requests at the expense of other processes on your Macintosh. This parameter is required, because the MacOS is a cooperative multitasking, rather than a preemptively multitasking, operating system. PIG_DELAY defaults to 30 ticks (where a tick is equivalent to 1/60 of a second). You can set this as high as 120 at the expense of your other applications.

By breaking up the response into smaller file partitions, MacHTTP can swap slow connections with fast connections, freeing up the faster connections. By setting the parameter DUMP_BUF_SIZE accordingly, you can tell MacTCP the maximum size into which you want to divide a response. The default is 4096 bytes, but you can set the block size as low as 256 or as high as 10240 bytes.

When we talk about how MacHTTP logs connections, you'll see that MacHTTP lists the mnemonic IP address, as opposed to the numerical address, when it can get them. If you're really committed to getting the actual mnemonic IP address, you can tell MacHTTP to look up numerical IP addresses. If so, leave the NO_DNS commented out. There is a performance penalty in having MacHTTP look up the host names, and you can always look up the host name later. We'll talk more about domain name service in Chapter 12, "Providing Domain Name Service."

Suffix Mapping

To construct a MIME header to inform the Web browser what sort of files are included in the response, MacHTTP needs some means of mapping the Mac file type to a certain MIME type and subtype. This is done using the suffix mapping within MacHTTP.config.

The suffix mapping syntax is

```
<transfer type><suffix><Mac file type><MacOS Creator
Code><MIME Type/Subtype>
```

The transfer type tells MacHTTP what type of file is being mapped. The options include TEXT, BINARY, SCRIPT, CGI, and ACGI. ACGI stands for Asynchronous CGI, which is discussed in Chapter 7, "Writing CGI Scripts." The next field contains the suffix at the end of the file name. If the Mac file type is known, that is included next. If the file's creator code is known, this information is included in the mapping entry. Finally, the appropriate MIME type and subtype are listed as well.

NOTE

Each Mac file contains a four-character creator code. This code tells the operating system which application created the file. Each application has a unique case-sensitive creator code. Although it seems counter-intuitive to assign a suffix to a Mac file, it prevents Webmasters from having to use a resource editor like ResEdit to determine the creator code of a file created by GraphicConverter versus a code for a Photoshop file. Also, there are many different types of HTML editors, each with a different creator code. It's a lot simpler to leave the creator code off the mapping and just include an HTML suffix; otherwise, you'll need to update your config file every time you install new software.

If a file is included in the HTTP response that does not conform to any of the criteria, MacHTTP sends the default mapping, telling the browser it's sending down an HTML file. This default mapping is

```
TEXT .html TEXT * text/html
```

The asterisk denotes that the creator code for the default HTML setting is unknown or left out. Examples for various MIME suffix mapping entries are in the MacHTTP.config file.

MacHTTP sets up MIME headers that tell the requesting Web browser what sort of files are included in the response. It is essential that the browser have the same MIME type information in order to process the file. If you want to serve BinHex files, for example, you would use the following suffix mapping

```
TEXT .hqx TEXT BNHQ application/mac-binhex40
```

The browser knows nothing about the file name, its suffix, its creator code, or even if it's a Mac file. It just knows that the MacHTTP is telling it that its MIME type is application/mac-binhex40. To decode the file, the application that decodes BinHex files needs to be resident on the browsing computer, and the browser needs to have that application identified with the MIME header application/mac-binhex40.

Configuring for Security

MacHTTP secures HTTP connections two ways. Both of these methods require modifications to the MacHTTP.config file. The first method involves using the DENY and ALLOW parameters. As described in Table 4.2, these keywords restrict or allow access to the server by host name or IP address. When MacHTTP detects at least one entry of either keyword, it automatically implements a DENY * setting restricting access to all connections. You have to add appropriate ALLOW keywords to allow entry by desired users.

You can restrict access by partial domain listings. For example, if you insert the listing

```
ALLOW anyplace.com
```

no one except those users in the anyplace.com domain can access the site. Similarly, look at the following entry

```
ALLOW 128.183.4
```

This restricts everyone except those whose address begins with 128.183.4. Note that this entry will allow users with an address 128.183.40.* or any other address that begins with the number following the ALLOW keyword. To only allow users from the 128.183.4.* subnet, you would have to add a trailing period after the subnet address.

Another useful means of restricting access is to restrict it according to file name. In this way, you can allow users unrestricted access to certain files. However, certain other files can be restricted according to a phrase in the URL. This is accomplished with the REALM keyword. For example, you can create a secure group entitled BeanCounter; only members of this group are allowed to access any file containing the string financial.

```
REALM financial BeanCounter
```

Now go into the MacHTTP application. Under the Edit menu, choose the Passwords option. You'll see a menu similar to what is displayed in Figure 4.1. Reading the MacHTTP.config file, MacHTTP will determine that the REALM BeanCounter exists and will allow you to add users and passwords to that realm. Now members of this realm will be the only users able to access any file containing the phrase financial.

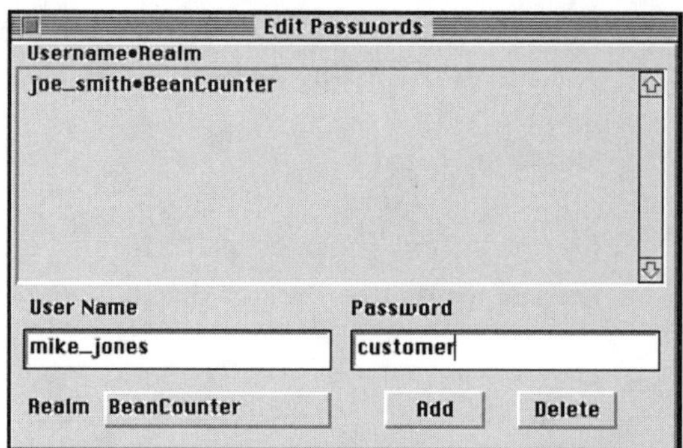

Figure 4.1 *MacHTTP allows you to define users and passwords to restrict access to certain files.*

Running MacHTTP

Now that you've configured MacHTTP the way that you want, it's time to start using the application. Several capabilities within the program enable you to further customize its usage.

Logging Accesses

After you've started publishing your Web server, expect a flood of the unwashed masses to show up at your doorstep. Soon enough, you'll see the MacHTTP log filling up with users. This information will be displayed in the status window (see Figure 4.2). Note that you will receive information about the date and time of the access, the user's IP address, what file was accessed, and how many bytes were transferred. When you restart MacHTTP, the status window will be empty, but the MacHTTP.log file will still maintain the previous accesses.

The top two lines of the status window give more information. The statistics are displayed to enable you to tune the MacHTTP.config parameters for better performance. The display can be summarized as follows in Table 4.3.

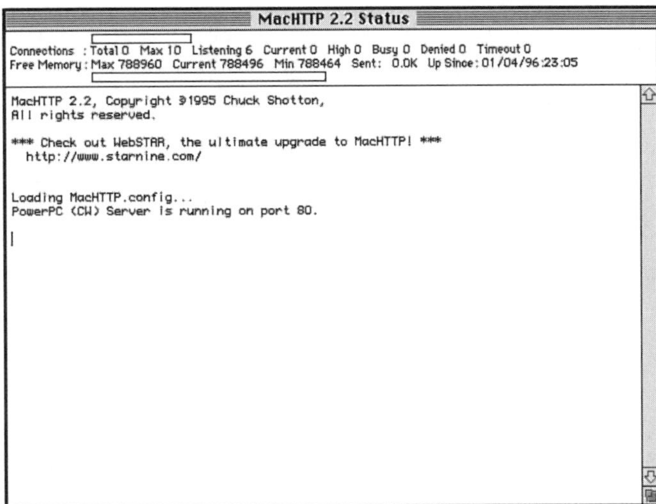

Figure 4.2 *The MacHTTP status window provides information about accesses to your server.*

Table 4.3 *MacHTTP Statistics Display*

Statistic	Description
Total	Represents total number of connections recorded while MacHTTP has been active.
Max	Displays MAXUSERS parameter.
Listening	Displays MAXLISTENS parameter.
Current	Represents number of current connections to the server.
High	Displays historically highest number of users.
Busy	Shows how many clients have been refused service because number of users has exceeded MAXUSERS. Use this statistic to tune MAXUSERS.
Denied	Shows how many requests were denied access for security reasons.

continues

Table 4.3 *Continued*

Statistic	Description
Timeout	Shows the number of connections that have timed out. A large number of timeouts may mean that your server is not keeping connections open long enough and that the TIMEOUT option needs to be increased.
Free memory Max	Represents the historically highest amount of memory available to MacHTTP.
Current	Represents the current amount of free memory available to MacHTTP. Unless you are using a memory-management tool like Connectix Corp.'s RAM Doubler, this memory may not all be available to the application. It should be monitored as to how close it is to the minimum memory statistic below.
Min	Represents historical low of RAM available to MacHTTP. MacHTTP must have at least 150 KB to run certain CGI scripts. Use this statistic to determine how much memory should be allocated to MacHTTP.
Sent	Details the total amount of data transferred in kilobytes.
Up Since	Displays time that server was launched.

NOTE

WebStat and ServerStat are programs that use the MacHTTP log file to summarize and compile reports about accesses. They will be discussed in Chapter 5, "Managing Your Intranet Web Services."

Verbose Logging Messages

Under the Option menu, you can drag down to Verbose Messages to cause MacHTTP to provide more status information with each access than what is described above. This information will be more comprehensive than you might need, because it pertains to high-level MacTCP information, but it may aid in identifying connection problems.

Suspending Logging and Refusing New Connections

If you need to edit your log file or edit some of the HTML pages you're serving, you can suspend the access logging or even refuse new connections. Both of these options are available under the Option menu. When suspending logging, your users will still be able to access the server, but their actions will not be recorded. When refusing new connections, users will be notified that connections are being refused temporarily.

Hiding the Status Window

You can hide the status window by toggling Hide Window in Background. Then when you leave MacHTTP, the status window will disappear. The window reappears when you return to the application. This is useful especially if you use the Macintosh for other applications and need to conserve your screen real estate. You can always hide the window using the standard MacOS tricks of choosing Hide MacHTTP from the application menu or Option-clicking on the desktop.

Serving Nonstandard Mac Files

You may want to serve other types of files from the standard JPEG, GIF, HTML, audio formats. For example, you may want to serve Microsoft Word documents or Microsoft Excel spreadsheets to both Macintosh or Windows users. To do this, you must configure your suffix mappings with the information that informs the browser as to the type of file you are sending. If you wanted to publish a Microsoft Word file, for example, you would install the following entry in your MacHTTP.config file

```
BINARY .msw WDBN MSWD application/msword
```

Because the Microsoft Word files actually are binary files, you need the BINARY keyword. The suffix you assign to Microsoft Word files is arbitrary as long you're consistent; I have chosen .msw. The file type and case-sensitive creator codes are given as well as WDBN and MSWD. The standard MIME type for Microsoft Word files is application/msword. The browser will have to have this MIME type defined and will have to define Microsoft Word as a helper application for files of this type. Clicking on a link that serves a *.msw file will cause the server to send the file down to the browser; the browser will then launch the file inside Microsoft Word. This can be done for any file for which the browser has a defined MIME type/subtype.

NOTE

You can define other nonstandard MIME types to serve Mac files. The convention is to append an x to the front of the MIME subtype. For example, a sample MIME header for a Canvas document would be application/x-canvas.

WebSTAR

CD-ROM

WebSTAR is the commercial follow-up to MacHTTP. Chuck Shotton, MacHTTP's author, was hired in 1994 by StarNine Technologies Inc. (which has since been acquired by QuarterDeck). Shotton and StarNine still support MacHTTP; however, it is clear, as with most shareware/commercial pairings, that the development emphasis will be on WebSTAR and its ancillary programs.

StarNine claims that WebSTAR offers more functionality than MacHTTP. These are summarized here:

- **Multithreaded operation.** Multiple threading is the closest you'll come to preemptive multitasking with the current MacOS. WebSTAR enables you to use multiple threads, which StarNine claims make WebSTAR 3 to 4 times faster than MacHTTP. The multiple thread processing is enabled by the Thread Manager extension bundled with WebSTAR as well as the MacOS from System 7.5 and later.
- **WebSTAR Admin.** Whereas MacHTTP required you to edit an ASCII text file to configure MacHTTP, WebSTAR is customized through a separate application, WebSTAR Admin. Furthermore, WebSTAR Admin can be operated over a local area network to administer a remote WebSTAR server.

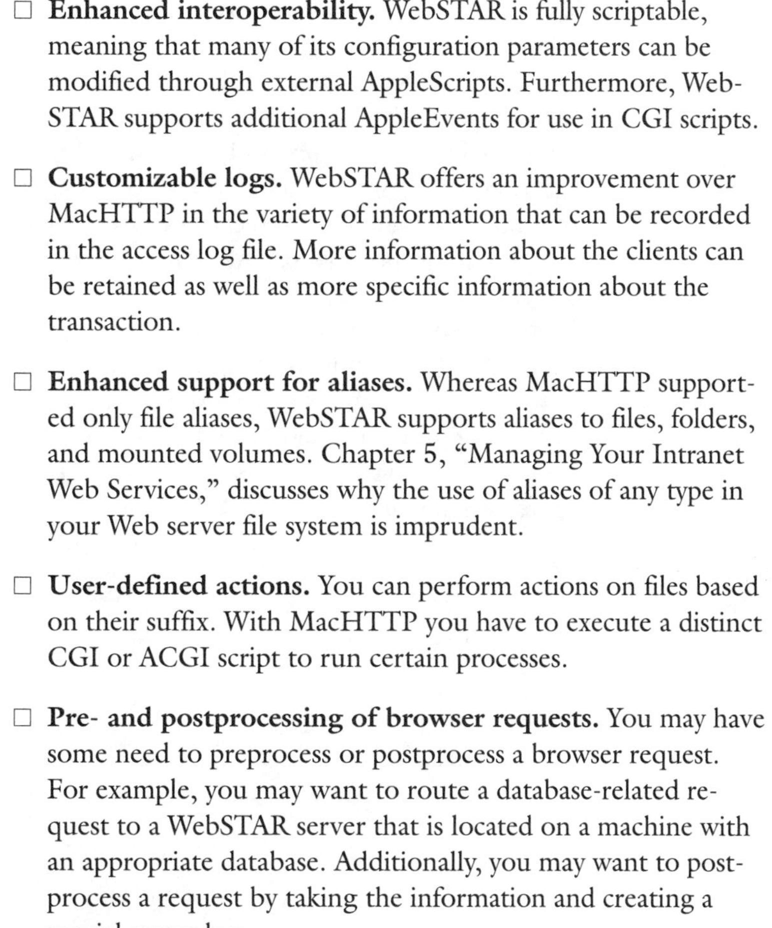

- **Enhanced interoperability.** WebSTAR is fully scriptable, meaning that many of its configuration parameters can be modified through external AppleScripts. Furthermore, WebSTAR supports additional AppleEvents for use in CGI scripts.

- **Customizable logs.** WebSTAR offers an improvement over MacHTTP in the variety of information that can be recorded in the access log file. More information about the clients can be retained as well as more specific information about the transaction.

- **Enhanced support for aliases.** Whereas MacHTTP supported only file aliases, WebSTAR supports aliases to files, folders, and mounted volumes. Chapter 5, "Managing Your Intranet Web Services," discusses why the use of aliases of any type in your Web server file system is imprudent.

- **User-defined actions.** You can perform actions on files based on their suffix. With MacHTTP you have to execute a distinct CGI or ACGI script to run certain processes.

- **Pre- and postprocessing of browser requests.** You may have some need to preprocess or postprocess a browser request. For example, you may want to route a database-related request to a WebSTAR server that is located on a machine with an appropriate database. Additionally, you may want to postprocess a request by taking the information and creating a special access log.

Installing WebSTAR

One disadvantage of WebSTAR is that it requires more memory than MacHTTP. StarNine recommends that you assign at least 1 MB RAM to WebSTAR for the default 12 connections; 3 MB RAM should be allotted for 25 connections. The correct amount of RAM for your usage should be allocated by reviewing the memory statistics discussed later in this section.

To install WebSTAR, drag the WebSTAR folder onto your hard drive. Double-click on the Installer icon inside the folder. The Installer will load MacTCP, AppleScript, some scripting extensions, and the Thread Manager extension into the System folder.

The Installer will load WebSTAR Admin into the WebSTAR folder. WebSTAR Admin is the administrative utility used to customize WebSTAR. Whereas the MacHTTP.config file was required to configure MacHTTP, WebSTAR Admin provides the same functionality. Moreover, you can install WebSTAR Admin on a separate Macintosh to remotely administer WebSTAR. You can even administer multiple WebSTAR servers with one copy of WebSTAR Admin. For now, move WebSTAR Admin to its own directory.

More discussion about organizing your Web server folders is in Chapter 5, "Managing Your Intranet Web Services." You should, however, partition your WebSTAR folder into separate folders that contain script, image, and HTML files. A sample WebSTAR folder hierarchy is shown in Figure 4.3. The WebSTAR Settings file will appear when you first launch WebSTAR.

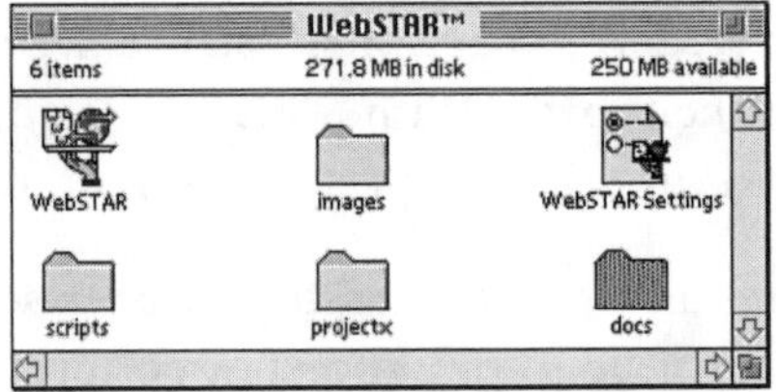

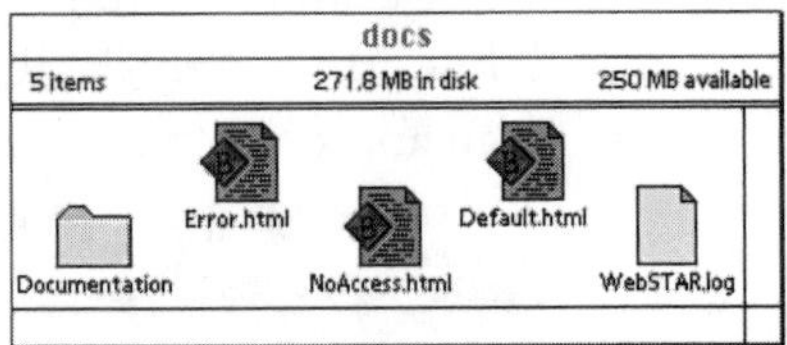

Figure 4.3 *A WebSTAR folder can be partitioned with scripts, images, default files, and HTML in separate folders.*

Setting Up WebSTAR Admin

WebSTAR Admin does not support remote administration through IP connections. Therefore, you are limited to administering only those servers that reside on a local AppleTalk network. This unfortunately limits your capability of remotely administering a site from your home. Many Internet service providers (ISPs) support SLIP and PPP. If you work in a large organization, chances are that they maintain a private PPP service. Almost all ISPs, as of this writing, offer some form of PPP service.

Few providers, however, offer remote AppleTalk access. This usually is provided through a protocol known as Apple Remote Access (ARA). As much as PPP enables you to act as a node on the Internet, ARA enables you to participate in an AppleTalk network through your modem. While connected to ARA, you can print and access other computers as if you were connected through your AppleTalk port, albeit much more slowly. If you want to administer your server from home or another remote location, you must have access to an ARA server, or you will have to invest in hardware that allows such access.

You have the option of running WebSTAR Admin either on the same computer that WebSTAR resides or on a different computer. The first case is trivial, so we'll cover what is required to run WebSTAR from a remote computer. To access a WebSTAR server through a remote server, you will need to make the application and its host computer accessible to you through the local AppleTalk network. This is easily done through System 7's file sharing capability. There are three steps to this process:

- ☐ Enabling WebSTAR's host Macintosh to support file sharing and linking
- ☐ Creating access privileges on the host Macintosh
- ☐ Enabling WebSTAR to support links to other applications

If you participate in a local AppleTalk network, chances are you have file sharing turned on already. Even so, let's review how it is done.

NOTE

File sharing was introduced as a feature of System 7 back in 1991. It allows peer-to-peer sharing of data and applications. Essentially, every properly configured Mac on a AppleTalk network with file sharing turned on is an AppleTalk server. Users can log on to your computer and exchange files. You can even run applications resident on other Macs over the network. Program linking is a lot like running an application over the network, except that you are allowing applications to communicate with one another.

All these actions must take place on the WebSTAR host computer; let's assume that you have WebSTAR residing on a remote machine. Choose the Sharing Setup control panel. A dialog box like that shown in Figure 4.4 will appear. It's advisable to enable file sharing if you like as well; be advised that you open your server up to huge performance hits if someone launches a huge application on it. Enter the appropriate user information and click the bottom button to enable program linking.

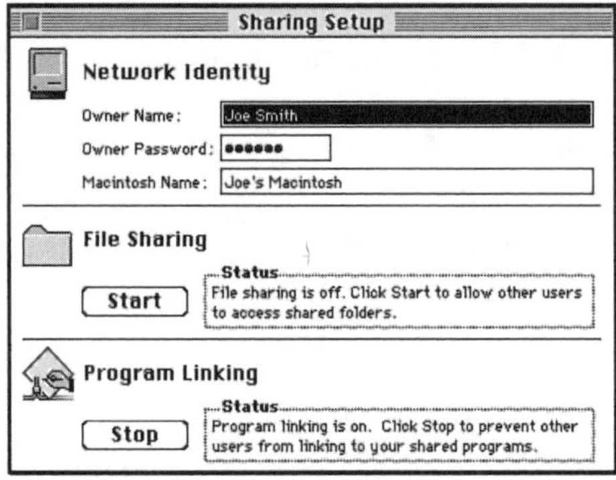

Figure 4.4 *Program linking can be enabled in the Sharing Setup control panel.*

Now you'll want to allow access to the Macintosh so that you can link WebSTAR Admin to WebSTAR on this machine. To do this, select the Users & Groups control panel. Double-click on the user to whom you want to give administrative privileges. You'll see a display similar to that in Figure 4.5. Click on the bottom checkbox in the user's profile box to allow the user to link programs to this Macintosh.

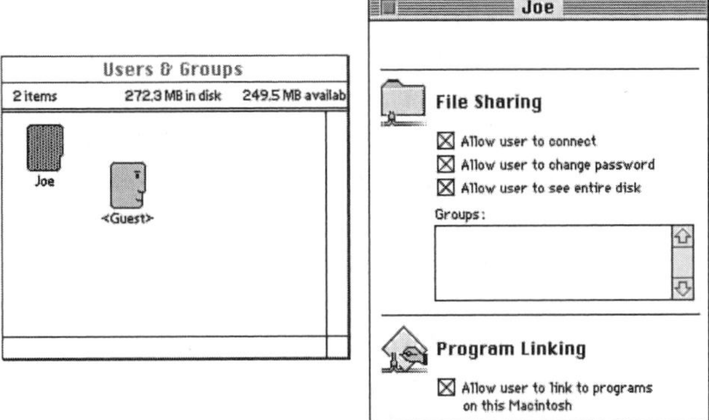

Figure 4.5 *You can enable program linking for users through the Users & Groups control panel.*

Finally, you'll want to enable WebSTAR to link to other programs, in this case, WebSTAR Admin. To do this, click on the WebSTAR application and choose Sharing from the File menu. If it is not already checked, click on the checkbox to enable WebSTAR to link with WebSTAR Admin as shown in Figure 4.6.

Figure 4.6 *You need to enable program linking on WebSTAR to allow it to communicate with WebSTAR Admin.*

Configuring WebSTAR with WebSTAR Admin

Now go back to the computer where you have WebSTAR Admin. To do this, use WebSTAR Admin to configure the parameters that you previously entered in the MacHTTP.config file when you worked with MacHTTP. As a result, you need to have an active WebSTAR session before you can run WebSTAR Admin. Do this by double-clicking on the WebSTAR application. The status window appears, but we'll talk about that later.

The first time you start the application, you'll be asked for an evaluation key or serial number. You can validate the software by contacting StarNine (800-525-2580 or keys@starnine.com) for an evaluation serial number. The eval key will enable you to run the program (as a trial) for several weeks after which time the key will expire. You'll be expected to purchase the software if you have further interest in using it.

After WebSTAR is active, launch WebSTAR Admin. If you are running WebSTAR Admin from a remote computer, you'll be asked to find the AppleTalk zone and computer on which WebSTAR is running. If you're running the two applications on the same computer, you will see a dialog box similar to that shown in Figure 4.7. Choose the WebSTAR application and click OK; if you are running multiple WebSTAR servers on the same computer, you will have a choice of several different servers.

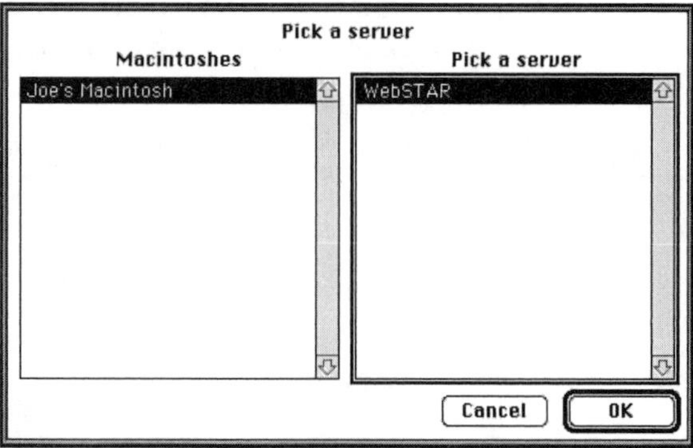

Figure 4.7 *WebSTAR Admin lets you choose which server to administer.*

After you pick a server, a monitor window for that WebSTAR process will appear (see Figure 4.8). The IP address and port number appear in the title bar. This is useful when you are running WebSTAR on multiple servers and want to display multiple monitor windows.

The upper-left of the window presents a running histogram detailing the number of current connections along with the maximum number of users. The thermometer graph below it details the amount of free memory used by WebSTAR versus how much is allotted to it. Monitoring both of these graphs will enable you to tune the performance of the server.

In the right-hand section of the monitor window, you see displays of several configuration parameters. All of these parameters were covered in the MacHTTP configuration discussion. However, it can be seen that the WebSTAR version number is included in this window as well.

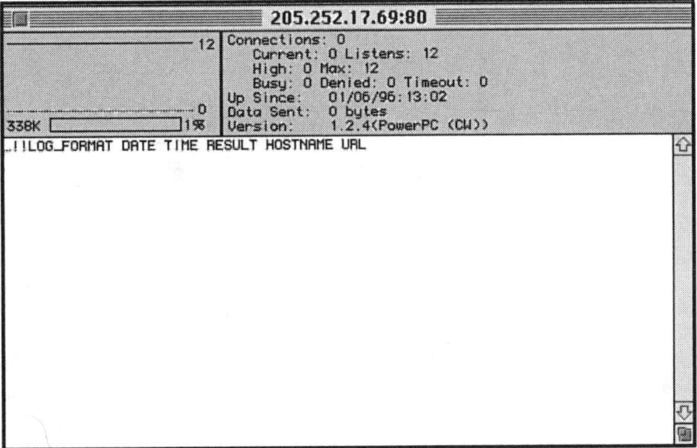

Figure 4.8 *The WebSTAR Admin monitor window enables you to monitor and configure a WebSTAR server process.*

Several configuration options are available under the Configure menu. Although they offer much the same functionality as the MacHTTP configuration file, the interface is more intuitive in WebSTAR.

Suffix Mapping

WebSTAR offers a simple means of modifying the suffix mapping used to encode MIME messages. In the Configure menu, choose Suffix Mapping and a dialog box will appear similar to that shown in Figure 4.9. A list of default suffix mappings is found in the dialog box. The data for each mapping is arranged using the same fields we encountered in the MacHTTP.config file.

NOTE

> If you are just reading the WebSTAR section of this chapter, a full discussion of how WebSTAR and MacHTTP use suffix mappings to create MIME message headers is provided earlier in this chapter.

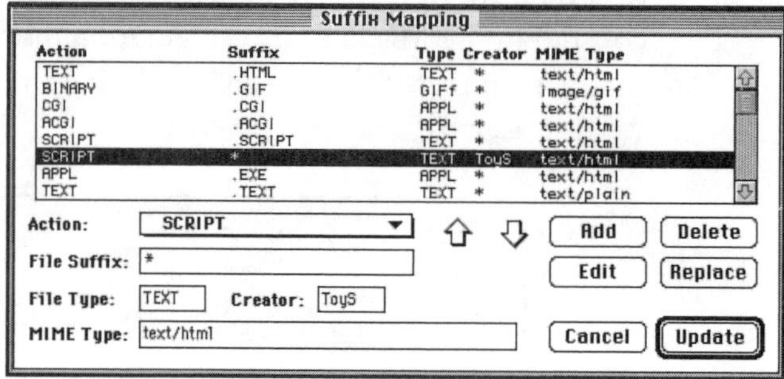

Figure 4.9 *Suffix mappings can be added with WebSTAR Admin's suffix mapping editor.*

You can add, delete, or edit these mappings. Several action keywords already are defined in the dialog box; the options include TEXT, BINARY, SCRIPT, CGI, and ACGI depending on which describes the file. The arrow keys move the entries up and down.

Actions

A useful feature of WebSTAR is the addition of user-defined actions. For example, if you had a special form that you wanted handled by a special CGI script, you could add the suffix *.form to that file and define that it would be handled by a particular script. This is useful if you customized one particular script that can be used by a variety of forms located all over your server. In this manner, the URL included in the form would be overridden by the user-defined CGI.

To do this, you can click on the Configure menu and choose the Actions item. This brings up the actions editor as shown in Figure 4.10. With this editor, you can add, delete, and edit user-defined actions. In the application field, you enter the name of the application or script that you want to process this type of file. You need to use the colon separator to denote the file location including the necessary folders; the locations are referenced from the folder containing the WebSTAR application. Enter the action name in the Action Name field. After pressing the Update button, you should be able to access these new actions in the Suffix Mapping dialog box.

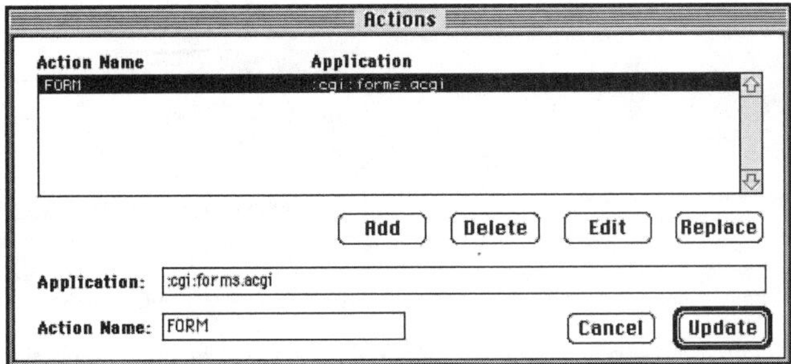

Figure 4.10 *User-defined actions can be created with WebSTAR Admin's Actions editor.*

Restricting Access to Your Server

The concept of security realms in WebSTAR is equivalent to that used in MacHTTP. A *realm* is a means of adding security to a series of files and folders; only those users belonging to certain realms are allowed to connect to URLs that contain certain strings. You can add and edit realms by clicking on the Configure menu under the Realms item; see Figure 4.11 that shows the Realms dialog box. You add the realm name and matching string in the appropriate fields.

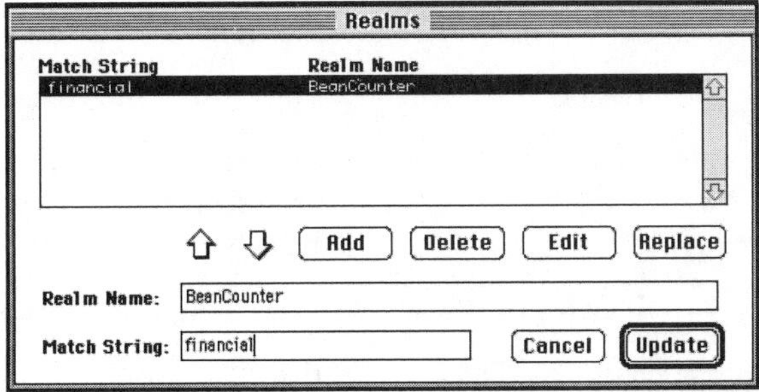

Figure 4.11 *You can restrict access to certain documents and folders using the WebSTAR Admin Realms editor.*

You add passwords to the realms using the Password editor. Open the editor by clicking on the Add Passwords editor under the Configure menu item. This allows you to assign user names and passwords to various realms. The available realms are listed in the popup menu at the bottom of the editor as shown in Figure 4.12.

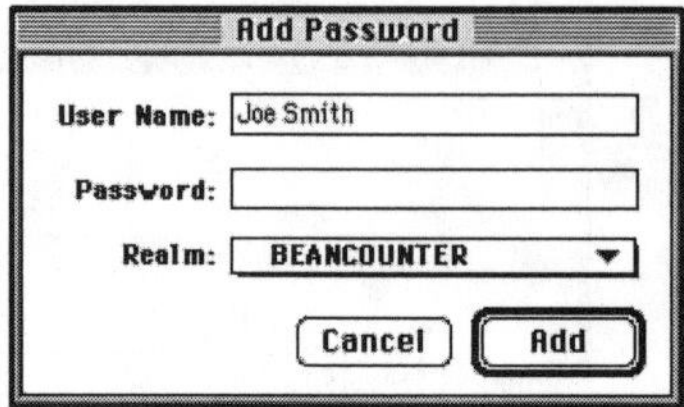

Figure 4.12 *Web Admin offers a simple means of adding password protection to your files and folders.*

Specifying the WebSTAR Log Format

WebSTAR Admin offers a flexible means of customizing your server access log. Click on the Log Format item underneath the Configure menu to open up the editor as shown in Figure 4.13. In this editor, you have 13 options that can be added to your server log file. These options detail information about the requester and the transaction.

Log Format Option	Description
AGENT	The identity of the WWW browser client.
BYTES_SENT	The number of bytes that were transferred in the transaction.
DATE	The date of the transaction.
FROM	Contents of the HTTP From: field. Some browsers include the user's email address if available.
HOSTNAME	The client's IP address.
METHOD	If a form was involved, this string details the method: GET or POST.
PATH_ARGS	The path arguments if the command is a request for a CGI script.

Log Format Option	Description
REFERER[sic]	The URL from which your server was referred.
SEARCH_ARGS	The search arguments if the command is a request for a CGI script.
TIME	The time of the transaction.
TRANSFER TIME	The amount of time (in 1/60ths of a second) needed to complete the transaction.
URL	The URL requested by the browser.
USER	The user's name if the request was authenticated.

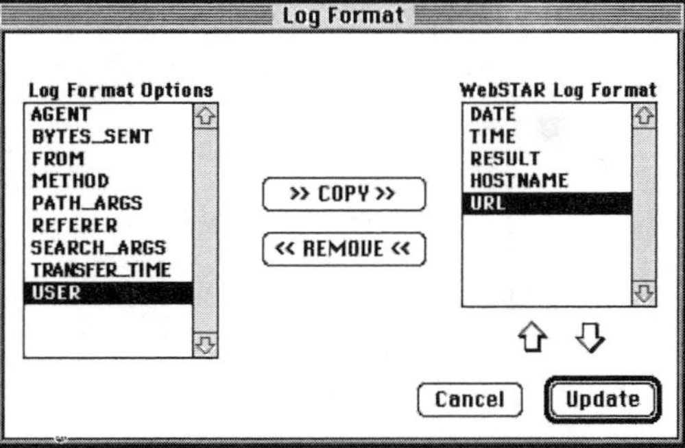

Figure 4.13 *You can specify options for formatting your server access log with WebSTAR Admin's Log Format editor.*

Using the Log Format editor, you can add or remove any of these options customize your WebSTAR access log. These options are added and removed through the Cancel and Update buttons. Furthermore, the options can be positioned relative to one another via the up and down arrow buttons.

Keep in mind that as you add more logging options your server will slow as your log file grows in size that much faster. For sites with thousands of accesses per day, an additional option can add thousands of bytes to the file each day. It can become time consuming to develop statistics for large log files, so only include the options you absolutely need.

NOTE

Other applications such as WebStat and ServerStat can maintain sophisticated logs for MacHTTP and WebSTAR. You can even use these applications to display the logs as HTML. See Chapter 5, "Managing Your Intranet Web Services," for more details.

Configuring Server Access Parameters

You can configure the miscellaneous parameters using the Misc. Settings option under the Configure menu. In this dialog box, shown in Figure 4.14, you see many of your old friends from the MacHTTP.config file. There is a checkbox for DNS lookups and two new fields. As mentioned earlier, you can assign certain CGIs to preprocess or postprocess various URLs. These CGIs would be listed in the appropriate fields here.

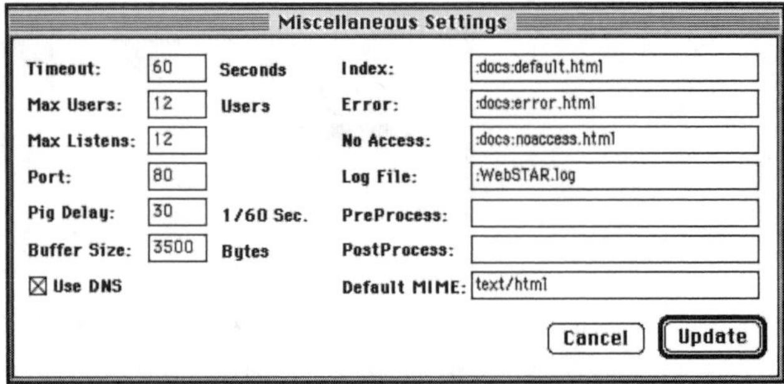

Figure 4.14 *WebSTAR Admin offers a compact means of modifying access parameters.*

Using WebSTAR

The WebSTAR Status Window should look familiar to you, as it's almost the same display that we saw during our MacHTTP discussion. This is obvious from a comparison of Figure 4.15 to Figure 4.2. The same is true with the menu items under Option: you can suspend logging, refuse connections, change to verbose logging, and hide the window in the background, similar to how we learned how with MacHTTP. One new feature that is extremely useful is the Serial Number tool. This tool enables you to display your serial number and technical support ID. You can store several serial numbers depending on how many WebSTAR ancillary applications you have running. This tool is available under the Serial Numbers item in the Menu dialog box.

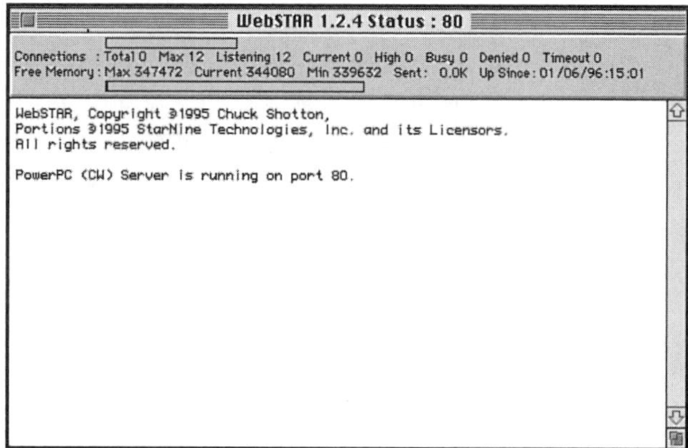

Figure 4.15 *Look familiar? The WebSTAR status window is similar to the MacHTTP status window.*

You can run multiple WebSTAR servers on the same Macintosh, although you will need a distinct serial number for each application. With a fast Mac and network connection, you could be able to serve different directories with simultaneous WebSTAR processes. Keep in mind that you'll still be working against MacTCP's 64-connection limit. WebSTAR will allow you to utilize up to 50 of those connections, compared to MacHTTP's 48, which gives you slightly more margin to install multiple servers. This is providing you don't intend to run a lot of other servers on the machine.

WebSTAR's greatest strength lies in the way it utilizes specialized CGI scripts. Preprocessing and postprocessing URLs offer a lot of promise, as do user-defined additions. Keep in mind that these modifications are not supported on other platforms at this time. Adding some of these features to your code limits its portability to servers running under other operating systems. How to work with CGI scripts is discussed in more detail in Chapter 7, "Writing CGI Scripts."

Other WebSTAR Applications

WebSTAR BG is a relative newcomer to the StarNine stable of products. It's essentially a background-only version of WebSTAR. There's no direct interface to the application, but it uses the same settings file as normal WebSTAR. The advantages of using it, according to StarNine, is that it's slightly faster than even running a Power Mac-native version of normal WebSTAR. Because it runs in the background, it will be harder for careless users to accidentally shut the system down.

StarNine also took over Microsoft Mail back in 1994. StarNine Mail, as it's now called, enables you to exchange SMTP mail with other users. The extended AppleEvents supported by WebSTAR enabless sophisticated integration between StarNine Mail and WebSTAR. ListSTAR is a mailing list application from StarNine that we will discuss later in this book.

WebSTAR/SSL is a WebSTAR add-on application that employs the Secure Sockets Layer (SSL) protocol developed by Netscape Communications. This application enabless secure transactions between a WebSTAR/SSL server and a secure browser such as Netscape. Secure transactions enable financial and confidential Web traffic to occur.

InterServer Publisher

InterServer Publisher is a fully featured Intranet server developed by InterCon Systems. In contrast to MacHTTP and WebSTAR, which only serve Web pages, InterServer Publisher serves files through the Web, FTP, and Gopher with one application. This section discusses the Web server aspects of InterServer Publisher. For more information about FTP, see Chapter 10, "FTP Services."

Installing InterServer Publisher

In the InterServer Publisher on the CD-ROM, double-click on the InterServer Installer icon. You'll be presented with the standard installer dialog box. Furthermore, you'll be queried as to whether you want an Easy Install or a Custom Install. The Easy Install option will add a lot of ancillary software such as the following:

- ☐ Clip art
- ☐ HTML Pro editor
- ☐ GraphicConverter
- ☐ InterCon's own Web browser, NetShark

MacTCP is installed during an Easy Install if you do not already have a copy; if you have one but it's not as recent as version 2.0.6, the installer will replace your version. Like other MacOS installation procedures, you can always pick and choose which features you would like to see added. Select where you want the application installed and proceed with the installation.

Let's assume that you performed the full installation of InterServer Publisher. The installer then inserts the InterServer Publisher extension into the Extensions folder of your System folder. Unlike other installations you may have run, you are not required to restart your Mac after the installation.

The InterServer Publisher extension does all of your Web, FTP, and Gopher service. There are four applications used in conjunction with the extension. These applications are described here.

Application	Description
InterServer Publisher Setup	Initializes Publisher and configures WWW, FTP, and Gopher service
StartServer	Starts Publisher service
StopServer	Stops Publisher service
InterServer Log Viewer	Views access log window without using InterServer Publisher Setup

These four applications are all that you need to run your Web server. Just double-click on the StartServer icon and you are ready to start publishing on the Web.

Using InterServer Publisher Setup

The InterServer Publisher Setup application is the most involved of all the ancillary applications you'll need to run to set up Web services using InterServer Publisher. Double-click on the InterServer Publisher Setup icon to launch the application. If you have not launched the StartServer application, launching Setup will initiate this process.

The InterServer Publisher Configuration editor will appear on your desktop. It looks quite similar to the old pre-System 7 control panel arrangement as shown in Figure 4.16; as in the figure, the Minimal configuration panel should be active. In the field marked General, you need to specify your server's node name. To enable your Web service, simply click the box entitled Enable World Wide Web server. Presto! You're back on the Web!

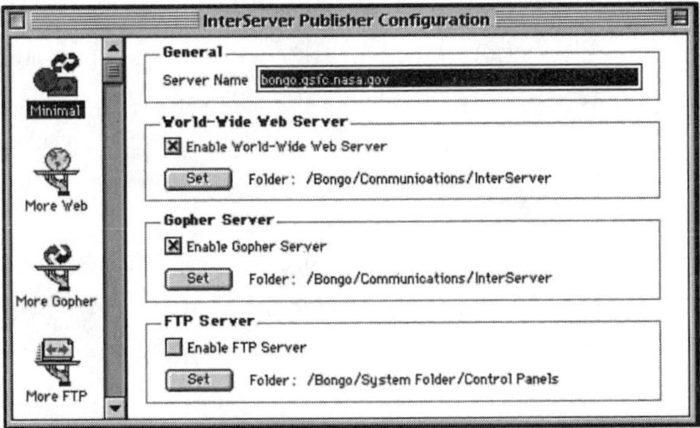

Figure 4.16 *The InterServer Publisher minimal configuration allows you to customize important features of your Web services.*

To further configure your Web server, you then need to click on the More Web configuration panel. In this panel, shown in Figure 4.17, you have additional parameters with which to customize your server. You can enter the maximum number of simultaneous Web connections. Sizing this number higher allows you to enable more users to connect to your server, but can slow down your HTTP processing. This number will likely need to be adjusted after viewing the server statistics.

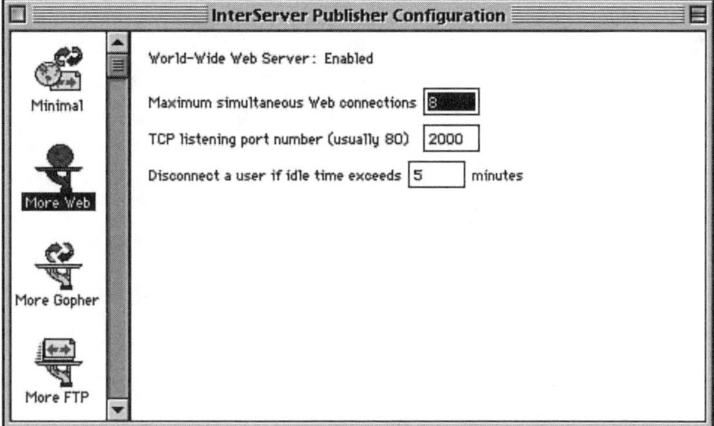

Figure 4.17 *Additional configuration of InterServer Publisher Web services can be effected with the More Web configuration panel.*

You can then set your TCP port. By convention, Web servers are assigned port 80, but you can set this to a different port if you desire. Remember to set your port to a number higher than 1024 to avoid conflicting with other IP services.

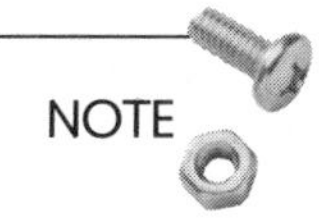

NOTE

As mentioned previously, your Intranet services will likely be located behind a firewall of some type, as described in Chapter 13, "Intranet Server Security." If not, then you may want to set your Intranet Web pages to a nonstandard IP port to help keep out prying eyes.

You also can specify the time that you want to hold open idle connections. Remember that the more connections you hold open, the fewer chances you have to handle other HTTP requests. As HTTP is such a nimble protocol, it requires little time to transfer data. If a connection is held idle for a long period of time, there is probably a network fault impeding the connection. You should therefore set this number to no more than one minute.

NOTE

Because of the limitation of MacTCP connections, InterServer Publisher limits you to a total of 50 connections shared between your FTP, Gopher, and WWW servers.

Securing Your Server

You can use the InterServer Publisher Setup application to secure your server in the following ways:

- ☐ Specify domains and addresses to be allowed and denied access to the server
- ☐ Set up user accounts and passwords
- ☐ Utilize security realms to restrict access to certain files and folders

Keep in mind that further discussion about securing your server is in Chapter 13, "Intranet Server Security."

Restricting Host Access

In the InterServer Publisher Setup application, click on the Host Access configuration panel. The display should look like Figure 4.18. You can enter the domain or IP address in the Web Allow or Web Deny. For example, to allow access only to members of the domain anyplace.com, you would enter @anyplace.com in the Web Allow field. Conversely, you could deny access to the entire domain by entering @anyplace.com into the Web Deny field.

You also can specify subnets that you want to restrict or enable access to your server. For example, you may have information that you want to restrict to your organization's marketing subnet; similarly, you may want to restrict access to certain data only by your organization's R&D labs. If your organization is large enough, you will end up instituting subnets for your larger groups.

As an example, entering the string 128.184.22 in the Web Deny field restricts any address in the 128.184.22.xxx subnet. Entering any domain in the Web Allow field, leaving the Web Deny field empty, enables only that domain to access the server. Conversely, entering any domain in the Web Deny field, leaving the Web Allow field empty, restricts only that domain from accessing files on that server.

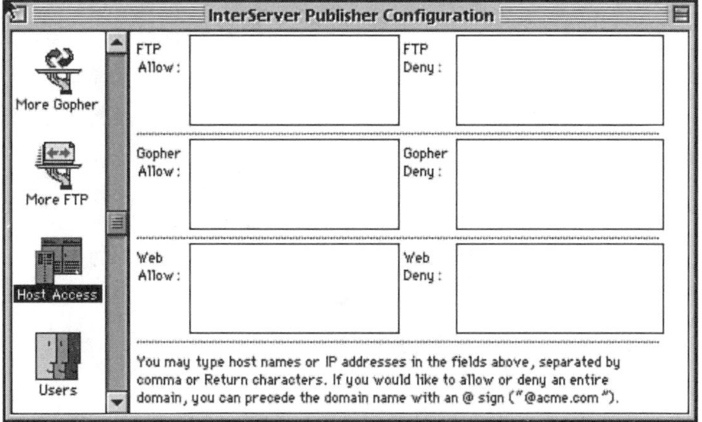

Figure 4.18 *The Host Access configuration panel enables the InterServer Publisher Setup application to restrict or enable access based on the user's Internet address.*

Adding Users to Your Server

You cannot only restrict or enable access by domain, but you also can customize the privileges of individual users. Users with similar privileges are grouped into realms; members of realms have access to certain files and folders. Before we talk about realms, we need to learn how to add users to the system so that we can create realms.

Scroll down the left side of the Setup application and click on the Users configuration panel. A dialog box similar to that shown in Figure 4.19 will appear. In the top right of the window, there are three buttons: New, Rename, and Delete. Click New to create a new account. A new dialog box will appear, and you can enter the user name. Click OK to close the New dialog box. Back in the Setup application, you can enter a password for this new user. Note from Figure 4.19 that the password field is blocked, but unfortunately there is no password verification scheme. You then enter a case-sensitive password for the user. After you have accumulated enough user accounts, you will be able to change the user names or even delete accounts using the Rename and Delete buttons. For now, ignore the checkboxes in the bottom half of the box; they are more relevant for the FTP services.

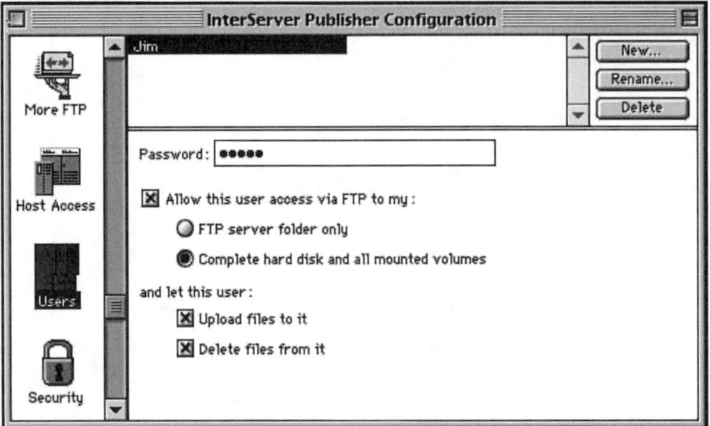

Figure 4.19 *Security realm user accounts can be created using the Users configuration panel.*

Creating Security Realms

After you have accumulated a stable of potential users, you can arrange them into secure realms. Attributes of these realms can be configured to permit all the relevant users to access certain parts of the file system. After privileges have been assigned to a realm, members of that realm can access files that contain certain key-words. These realms are constructed using the Security configura-tion panel.

Upon clicking on the Security configuration panel, as shown in Figure 4.20, you will see a list of user accounts that you have creat-ed. Once again, there are three buttons in the upper right of the dialog box. To create a new realm, click the New button. You'll be prompted for the name of the new realm. Enter the name and click on OK.

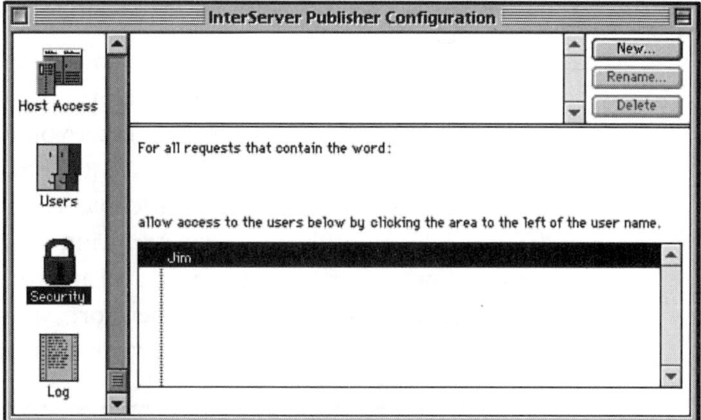

Figure 4.20 *Using the Security configuration panel, you can create realms that enable access to restrict folders or files.*

Members of a particular realm can access files that contain a certain string. For example, you may want to restrict access to a certain set of Web pages to members of your financial management time. If the access keyword for a realm is financial, members of that realm will be able to access any file or folder with a name containing the string financial. By selecting a realm in the Security configuration panel, a field opens up in the middle of the dialog box into which you can enter a realm keyword. In the user list field at the bottom of the page, you can add users to the realm by clicking on the column to the left of the user names. You can create several realms in this manner. As expected, you can rename and delete realms using the appropriate buttons in the upper right of the dialog box.

Maintaining an Access Log

InterServer Publisher allows you to record a log of Web, FTP, and Gopher accesses. The access history is written in a tab-delimited text file, the contents of which can be pasted into a spreadsheet such as Microsoft Excel, or a database such as FileMaker Pro. As users access your server, pertinent information is written to the log file. You can manually archive versions of the log file or have archives created automatically. Furthermore, InterServer Publisher allows you to view the log remotely.

Configuring Your Log Characteristics

Click on the Log configuration panel in the InterServer Publisher Setup application. A dialog box similar to that shown in Figure 4.21 will appear. You can specify whether you want to archive the log file manually, automatically archive it, or have the file archived when it gets to a specific size. Your choices of periodic archiving are daily, weekly, monthly, or yearly. Archiving your log file keeps the file size down and allows the individual archives to be small enough to be perused at a later date. Furthermore, you can click the appropriate checkbox if you desire to view your log archives remotely.

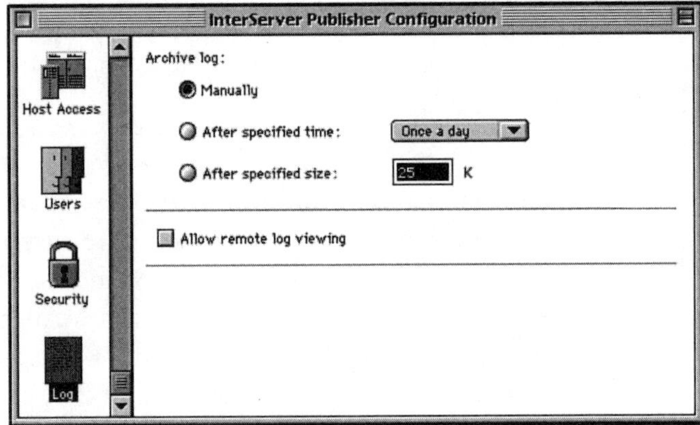

Figure 4.21 *You can specify certain access log characteristics using the Log configuration panel.*

The InterServer Publisher log file can be viewed by clicking on the Setup menu and dragging down to Show Log File. The following access data will be displayed under each entry of the log.

Log Field	Description
Date	Date of access
Time	Time of access
Server Type	Type of access (Web, FTP, Gopher)
Status	Indication of successful transfer
Client IP Address	IP address of client
Client Node Name	Client host name (if available)

Transfer Size	Number of bytes transmitted during request
Connection Duration	Duration of HTTP connection
Authenticated User Name	User's name if transaction was authenticated
Requested File	File requested by client
Additional Notes	Various information provided by the server

These fields are not configurable.

Archiving Your Log File

As mentioned previously, you will want to trim the size of your log file periodically to prevent it from becoming too large. This is done by periodically saving your log to a separate file and clearing the log contents. You can maintain a series of archives to peruse your access statistics.

One way to archive your log file is to do it manually. First, double-click on the StopServer application, which causes InterServer Publisher to refuse new connections. Find the log file, named Current Log and give it some other name. The log files are stored in the InterServer Publisher Logs folder in the Preferences folder in the System folder. Then activate the StartServer application to restart your server. A new log file will be created.

If you enabled remote viewing of your access log, you can access the current log and any archives you may have created. You can bring up the log page in a Web browser using the following URL:

```
http://your_server_address/.log
```

Your current log and any archive logs are available through hypertext links on the resulting Web page.

The InterServer Log Viewer is an application that you can use to view the current log if you are running Publisher on the same Macintosh. It's a means of viewing the log file without having to open up the InterServer Publisher Setup application.

Administering InterServer Publisher

Now that you've learned how to configure InterServer Publisher, you need to learn how to administer the ongoing Web service. There are several tools and tips at your disposal.

Using the Status Window

The Status window is available under the Setup menu item under Show Status window. This window allows you to monitor current connections on your server. Each entry in this window details the following information: connection type; Web, FTP, or Gopher; client address; server activity; and completed percentage of the request. At the bottom of the Status window, the number of available free connections for each protocol is displayed. You can close a connection by selecting a transaction and clicking the Close Transaction button at the top of the window.

Setting Up Your Web Sharing Folder

Okay, you're almost there! It's time to start populating your Web Sharing folder. In the InterServer Publisher Setup application, you specified which folder would contain your HTML documents. This folder now becomes the root folder for your Web server file system. Folders in this folder can contain Web documents provided they are indexed correctly in the Web browser. By default, Publisher enables you to specify a default file, index.html, for a Web folder. In this way, if a browser requests a URL that contains no file name, Publisher assumes a default file name of index.html.

NOTE 

You do not need to store BinHexed and MacBinary versions of files in your InterServer Publisher file system. Publisher will send BinHex or MacBinary versions of the files if the file listed in the URL is appended with a .hqx or .bin suffix. This is important, as Publisher's lack of suffix mapping would make serving Mac files otherwise difficult.

A Look at InterXTML

InterXTML is an extension of HTML that is unique to InterServer Publisher. These tags add functionality to your Web pages that are normally only available with CGI scripts. The tags are processed by InterServer, which sends out standard HTML, so there is no incompatibility with certain types of browsers. On the other hand, moving these pages to another server may be problematic.

InterXTML tags can enable you to do the following:

- Create a directory listing of the files in your Web page
- Create counters displaying the number of Web page accesses
- Display the date and time of the most recent Web page modifications

Use of the InterXTML tags adds functionality; but it also poses an added load to your server as compared to normal HTML. Furthermore, use of the InterXTML tags prevents you from porting your code to other servers, even those running under the MacOS. We will discuss the InterXTML tags more fully in Chapter 7, "Writing CGI Scripts."

NetPresenz

NetPresenz is an FTP server for the Macintosh that runs Web and Gopher services as well. It's written by Peter Lewis, the author of several Internet applications for the Macintosh, such as Anarchie and Internet Config in addition to other important programs. NetPresenz is primarily an FTP server, but it will serve text and graphics files as well as CGI applications through HTTP connections. I will defer discussion of NetPresenz until we talk about FTP servers in Chapter 10, "FTP Services." In that chapter, we'll discuss how to set up NetPresenz and will also briefly cover how to configure the application to serve Web files as well.

httpd4Mac

The httpd4Mac server is the only free Web server discussed in this chapter. This server is in beta format (version 1.3b) and runs only on 68K Macs, but it's useful enough to be discussed in this chapter. It's designed as a no-frills server that just serves text and graphics; needless to say, CGI script support is not included in this version. It has a minimal interface, but it requires only several hundred kilobytes of RAM.

Installing httpd4Mac

Open the httpd4Mac folder and double-click on the httpd4Mac icon. The first time that you launch the application, it will look for a Preferences file. This file can be either in the Preferences folder inside the System folder or it can be in with the application itself. If it does not find a Preferences file in either case, it will create one in the Preferences folder and quit. You are then free to edit the well-commented Preferences file called httpd_prefs; you also have the option of moving it to the httpd4Mac folder. Instructions for editing the httpd4Mac Preferences file are given here.

NOTE

Background-only applications cannot be easily turned off once you've launched them. You usually end up having to restart the computer, as recommended by the author of httpd4Mac.

Configuring httpd4Mac

Configuring httpd4Mac consists of editing the file httpd_prefs created when you first launch the application. This file can be edited with a simple text editor like BBEdit or SimpleText. There are several keywords that can be modified to configure httpd4Mac's performance.

httpd4Mac Configuration Parameters

Parameter	Description
check_syntax	httpd4mac checks your HTML syntax and reports errors through notification window.
notify	On/off toggle, which tells httpd4Mac to notify user of various status messages.
create_access_log	On/off toggle, which tells httpd4Mac to create a new access log upon each restart.
log_access	On/off toggle, which controls whether accesses are logged.
create_error_log	On/off toggle, which tells httpd4Mac to create a new error log upon each restart.
log_errors	On/off toggle, which controls whether accesses are logged.
access_log_name	Specifies access log file name.
error_log_name	Specifies error log file name.
log_creator	Defines creator code for log file name. This is important as it enables you to specify which application will open upon double-clicking the log file.
dnr	On/off toggle, which controls whether host names of accessing browsers need to be determined.

continues

Continued

Parameter	Description
log_q	Tells httpd4Mac how deep to make the access log queue. If you have a great deal of accesses, this queue stores the access information in a queue before logging them. This parameter specifies how long that queue will be.
translate_iso	On/off toggle specifying whether to translate 8-bit ISO characters.
http_port	Specifies HTTP port number.
streams	Dictates how many MacTCP streams to assign to httpd4Mac.
send_timeout	httpd4Mac sends data back to the client in fixed 20K buffers. The application will time-out when the buffer has taken longer than the amount of time specified by this parameter.
debug	On/off toggle telling httpd4Mac to write debugging information to a file entitled http_debug_log.
verbose	On/off toggle affecting verbose log messaging.
debug_buff	If debugging is turned on, this parameter specifies how many buffers are assigned for debugging messages.
cache_life	Specifies after how many seconds should objects be deleted from the cache buffer.
cache_check_on	On/off toggle, which tells httpd4Mac to check file creation dates versus cache creation dates. If file is newer than cached version, it is sent to the browser.
mime_def	Provides MIME type translation.
time_zone	Time zone offset from Greenwich Mean Time for time stamping your logs. You can also enter your time zone (EST, CDT, and so on).

The httpd4Mac MIME definition parameter, mime_def, is configured as follows:

```
mime_def 'creator_code' & 'suffix' = MIME type/subtype
➥7¦8
```

Like the other Web servers, the creator_code is used if no suffix is appended to a file. The 7 or 8 at the end of the line denotes either 7-bit or 8-bit encoding; a 7-bit encoded file denotes a text format, whereas an 8-bit file denotes a binary format. Like the other servers, you can leave an '*' as a wildcard. An example MIME definition for an HTML file would be

```
mime_def '*' & html = text/html 7
```

The mime_def parameters need to be lowercase. The httpd4Mac default MIME type is text/plain.

NOTE

httpd4Mac only serves the data fork of a file. Therefore, you cannot send binary files, such as MS Word or Excel documents, directly down to the browser. httpd4Mac's author, Bill Melotti, recommends a work-around by transforming the file into a 7-bit format using the BinHex compression scheme; in this manner, the encrypted information is stored in the data fork. You can then assign a MIME type of application/mac-binhex40; the browser will know to launch a helper application, which can decrypt the file back into its binary format.

Other Web Servers

Other commerical Web servers are available but were not reviewed for this chapter. With time, there may be more servers hitting the market as well. Both of the servers offer Internet services beyond HTTP.

NetWings Internet Server

NetWings Internet Server is available from Netwings Inc. The application offers Web services, including CGI scripting through AppleEvents, but also offers Gopher, email, and other administrative tools. The software is built upon the 4D database system.

OneSite/Web

Delphic Software has announced the OneSite/Web HTTP Server for the Macintosh. Delphic offers OneSite/Web as a freeware Web server with OneSite/Web+ offered as a fully functional Web server. OneSite/Web+ will also offer Gopher and FTP services. Delphic plans for a suite of Internet tools for the Macintosh, including NNTP, DNS, UDP, BootP services in addition to email and listserv functionality as well.

Determining Your Server

Of the Intranet server options mentioned in this chapter, it's hard to beat MacHTTP in terms of bang for the buck. If you plan on running a small Web server with a few hundred accesses a day and some nominal CGI scripting, it's hard to beat MacHTTP's price and power. NetPresenz and httpd4Mac offer bare-bones service for straight text and graphics service and may be your choice if your resources are limited.

If your Intranet is going to be servicing a large organization, your choices at this point are between WebSTAR and InterServer Publisher. Both systems sport highly configurable interfaces and offer high performance. WebSTAR has a huge market share, and you will be able to get assistance from many people through Usenet. On the other hand, InterCon Systems has a long heritage with Macintosh Internet applications and InterServer Publisher offers FTP and Gopher services in addition to HTTP.

Summary

The Macintosh maintains a sizable presence on the Internet mostly because of the ease of use and relative power of the servers mentioned in this chapter. These servers range from bare bones to highly sophisticated. The Mac server market has come a long way from the original MacHTTP release. Servers like WebSTAR, InterServer Publisher, and NetPresenz provide much the same functionality as more established Unix HTTP servers but without the complexity.

The sophistication of the servers mentioned here does not detract from their simplicity and ease of use. These servers can be used to provide simple text and graphics for the simplest of Intranets or can provide powerful applications, secure transactions, and high-speed service for large and demanding intranets.

In Chapter 5, "Managing Your Intranet Web Services," we'll move beyond the dry mechanics behind operating Web servers and we'll talk about managing them. You'll be introduced to some of the administrative tools and techniques available for aiding in your Intranet Web service management. Or if you like, you can jump to the following chapters:

- Chapter 7, "Writing CGI Scripts," to learn about writing scripts for your Web site. These scriptsenable you to process data from HTML forms and return customized Web pages.
- Chapter 8, "Databases and Document Searches," to learn about how to enable your Intranet users a means of accessing your databases and searches document archives.
- Chapter 9, "Beyond HTML," to learn about some techniques to spruce up your Web site beyond just using conventional HTML and graphics. We'll discuss Java, RealAudio, and other cool topics.
- Chapter 13, "Intranet Server Security," to learn how you can configure hardware to provide secure transactions within your Intranet and out to the Internet.

- Appendix C, "Perfecting HTML," to learn about HTML editors as well as some new and advanced HTML techniques, such as frames and server-push/client-pull techniques.

Links Related to This Chapter

Apple System Software Updates	http://www.support.apple.com/wwwdocs/apple_sw_updates.html
Apple Mailing Lists	http://www.solutions.apple.com/apple-internet/
StarNine Technologies	http://www.starnine.com
InterCon Systems	http://www.intercon.com
Peter Lewis	http://www.share.com/peter-lewis/
httpd4mac	http://sodium.ch.man.ac.uk/pages/httpd4Mac/home.html
NetWings	http://www.netwings.com
Delphic Software	http://www.delphic.com
Usenet	comp.sys.mac.comm comp.infosystems.www.servers.mac

CHAPTER 5

Managing Your Intranet Web Services

Publishing a full-fledged Intranet Web server is a multidisciplinary effort. We've talked about the rigors of choosing your server hardware and software, not to mention the effort of HTML programming, CGI scripting, and graphics design. As administrator of your Intranet, you will need to not only marshal your technical talents, but also your organizational skills as well. If Web services play a large role in your Intranet, you will need to very carefully organize the content and structure of your Web site. In this chapter, we'll cover the following topics:

- Management of the server's content
- Tips for organizing your documents and graphics files
- Tools to aid your server administration

NOTE

As mentioned previously, I'll assume that you have worked extensively with HTML and graphics to be aware of the nomenclature used here. If not, consult *Teach Yourself HTML in a Week*, published by Sams.net Publishing.

Managing Web Server Content

Managing the content of your server's documents is important because the Web server may be the most visible portion of your Intranet. If you are the only person within your organization with access to your server, then the problem is a lot less complicated than if several people are contributing to the server's development. The latter arrangement is more of a management challenge, so in this section, we'll talk about how to manage your server with multiple contributors.

Server Management Models

The easiest management model for your server is one where the server is just sitting at your desk. For example, I have managed a Web and FTP server at work for several years. The server applications reside on the same Mac that I use for most of my daily work. It's a low-access server, as I get only 100–200 hits/day. I manage the server content, updating it whenever I get around to it. I maintain a personal home page, and some bookmarks and files that I serve to others in my line of work. It's a tiny little server but hey, it's mine.

You may have more grandiose aspirations. Running a workgroup server or a more organized server representing your organization will take a lot of your time. It might take more time than you have, so you may be considering getting some help developing and organizing your server. This gets a little sticky because now you have to develop an efficient management scheme to provide consistent server content. There are several models that you can employ in developing and maintaining your server:

- **Managed access.** Colleagues and developers have restricted access to the system.
- **Centralized access.** The administrator is the only person with access to the system. This person approves and installs all contributed content on the system.
- **Distributed access.** A team of administrators is managed by a central administrator. Members of the team manage different areas of the server and work with users to publish files on the server.

Let's talk about how these management models can be implemented.

Managed Access

In a managed-access server model, users have access to certain areas of the server. For example, a project team has access to the file server structure assigned to that project team. Users within the organization are able to post their personal home pages in folders assigned to them, but they are restricted from accessing other parts of the server. The server would continue to be managed by a centralized administrator, but virtually unrestricted content would be placed on the server. A systems administrator maintains the machine and creates accounts but exerts no managerial control over the content. A schematic of this model is shown in Figure 5.1.

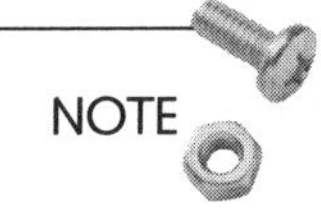

NOTE

We'll talk more about security issues in Chapter 13, "Intranet Server Security," but you should be aware of the risks involved with allowing other users upload privileges to your server. Unscrupulous users within your Intranet could put potentially invasive and harmful programs on your server, which could compromise the server contents. These privileges should be doled out with caution.

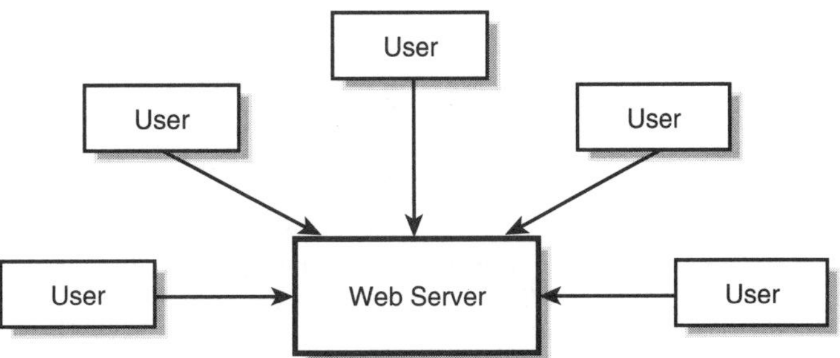

Figure 5.1 *The managed-access server model enables users to upload documents to certain areas of the server.*

This model is adequate for small organizations, but could lead to chaos for large groups. This type of model is ideal for a server that just publishes personal Web pages. For more professional intentions, a different organizational structure would be required.

Centralized Access

In a centralized-access server structure, a central administrator is the sole contact to the server. Users can submit upload requests to the administrator, but are restricted from performing the upload themselves. The administrator has the full authority of the Web site including content, privileges, and organization.

The centralized-access strategy is adequate for organizations without a lot of technically literate employees who don't frequently update Web pages. This strategy could work well in a group where people know enough to work a word-processing application but want to stay away from FTP, TCP/IP, HTML, or any other scary acronym. Users within the group would need to forward the content to the administrator; the administrator would convert it to HTML and upload it to the server. This again may work well for small groups with period server updates, but it still may be unsuitable for larger groups. A diagram of this strategy is given in Figure 5.2.

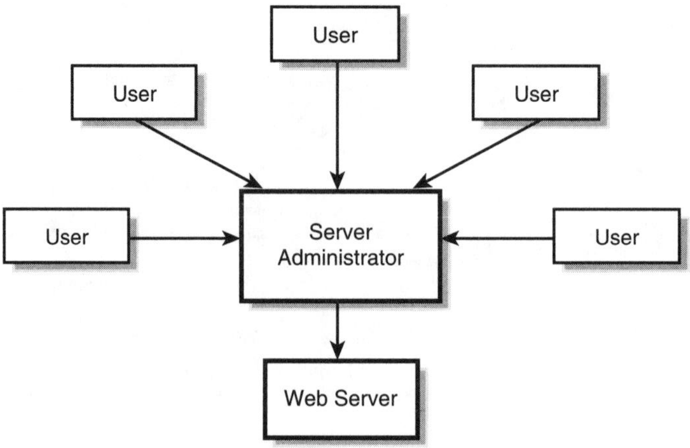

Figure 5.2 *There is only one point of contact to the server in the managed-access server topology.*

Distributed Access

In a distributed-access strategy, a centralized team of developers creates content for the server. The team is headed by a central administrator who serves as an editor-in-chief of the Web-site content. The development team edits, converts, and archives documents contributed by the users; the team also creates a lot of the specialized CGI scripting necessary to perform workgroup or other functions.

This model is used by large organizations and corporations to maintain their Web presence as well as manage content from their employees. Larger sites may receive hundreds of thousands of hits each day; the technical issues involved with serving that volume of traffic would be shared by a team of individuals. A diagram of this model is shown in Figure 5.3.

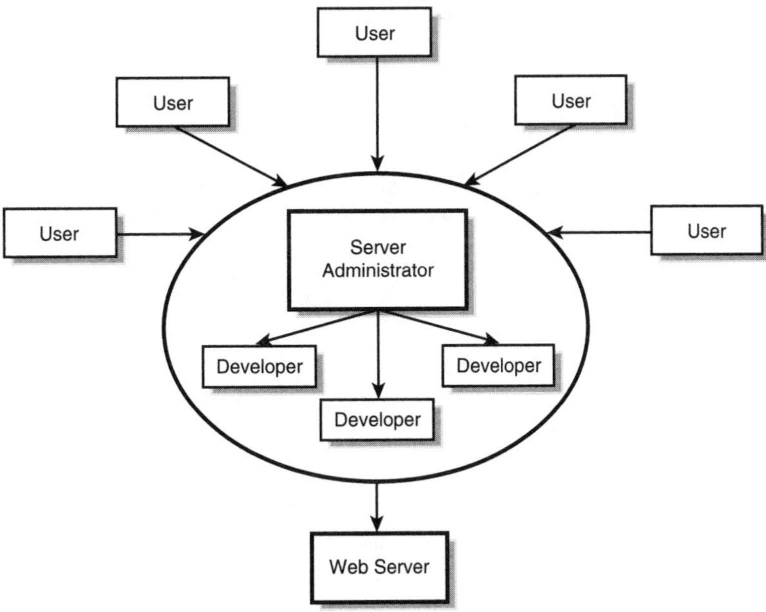

Figure 5.3 *The distributed-access server model is designed to work well for groups with large or popular Web sites.*

Choose the Strategy for You

Your organization likely fits one of the descriptions mentioned earlier. It's also likely that your server will evolve as your organization finds uses for it. There are plenty of large Web sites that started out as a little old Mac server somewhere. It's important that your server organization affords you the flexibility to efficiently publish your presence on the Web.

Controlling Access

The models described above are predicated on the idea that you can secure parts of your server and restrict access to certain parties. The MacOS is not a multiuser operating system in the same sense as Unix; however, there are provisions for enabling users FTP access. The topics of securing your server as well as managing FTP access to your Macintosh server will be covered in Chapter 13, "Intranet Server Security."

Efficient Directory Structure

Going back to my example server, I started some time ago keeping all my document files in my MacHTTP folder. Like I said earlier, it's a small server. When I started adding more files to the server, things became chaotic. I had image files in the same folder as my AppleScript CGIs and they were all mixed in with my HTML files. You can imagine what my bedroom looked like as a kid.

As your server grows, you'll be faced with the daunting task of organizing your offerings in a coherent manner. Keep in mind that as your server needs increase, so will the capability of available Macintosh hardware. Furthermore, at some point, you may be forced to duplicate or move your server files to another platform, such as a Windows NT or a Unix machine. Here are some tips to keep your server file system flexible and portable.

Using Relative URLs

A popular HTML command is the <BASE> tag. This command lends itself to use of relative URLs, which are used to address documents that reside on the same server. The argument of the <BASE> tag contains the root URL from which your files are served.

Relative URLs versus Absolute URLs

Do this

```
<BASE HREF="http://www.anywhere.com">
...
<A HREF="sample1.html>Item</A>
<A HREF="sample2.html>Item</A>
<A HREF="/test/sample3.html>Item</A>
```

Instead of this

```
<A HREF="http://www.anywhere.com/sample1.html>Item</A>
<A HREF="http://www.anywhere.com/sample2.html>Item</A>
<A HREF="http://www.anywhere.com/test/
➥sample3.html>Item</A>
```

Use of relative URLs enables your files to be transported en masse to, or mirrored on, another server without a large edit of your code. Undoubtedly, you'll upgrade your server hardware at some point. You'll probably have to change your server IP address and maybe even the directory in which your server application is located. Using relative URLs enables you to transport the server files easily via FTP or some other media such as tape backup.

Organizing Your Directory Structure

If you've used the MacOS for some time, you're probably comfortable with the folders and files on the system. You've seen how long it takes to open a folder with 1,000 files in it. Like other operating systems, folders really exist so that you can find files reasonably quickly. The same is true of your Web server file structure. The key is to keep similar files in similar directories.

Figure 5.4 shows a sample server file system. Note that images and scripts are kept in separate folders. The HTML files are kept free in the server folder. Project-specific HTML folders can be included as well to facilitate development and service of project-specific work.

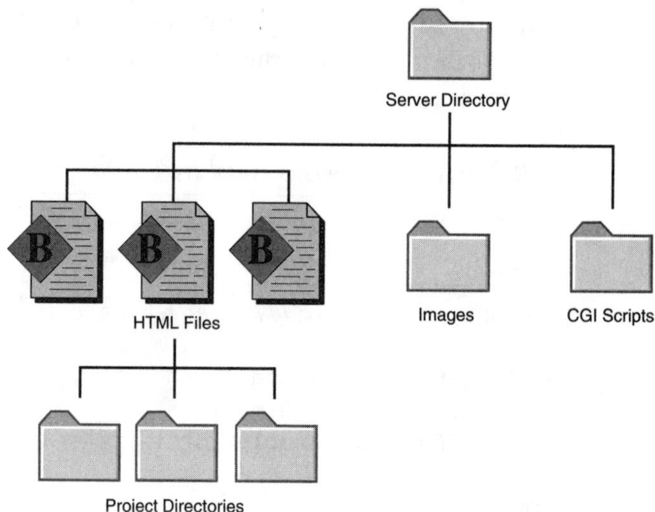

Figure 5.4 *An organized file system is one where HTML files, images, and scripts are maintained in separate folders.*

By keeping images in the same folder, you facilitate their access through the server file system. If you need to access a company logo, for example, you can reference it using the <BASE> tag and a relative URL with the same address from anywhere in the file system. The same is true of CGI scripts.

Using Aliases

Aliases are an easy way of making copies of files that act as pointers to the original copy. To take advantage of the Mac's Drag and Drop feature, I keep aliases of my favorite applications on my desktop; I can then open files by dragging them onto aliases as if I had dragged them onto the real applications. Furthermore, they only take up a couple of kilobytes of disk space.

Keeping aliases in your server directories can be problematic for several reasons—the first of which is that they are not transportable. If you have to port, or duplicate, your server files to a computer using another operating system, the aliases will have no relevance outside the MacOS. Also, aliases do not disappear when you delete the original. Granted, there are shareware applications you can use to manage your aliases efficiently, but I recommend that you avoid using them in your server directories entirely. There's really no need to copy files throughout your server directory if you use relative URLs. For example, use of relative URLs allows you to refer to the same GIF file, in many different HTML documents, without having duplicate versions of that file.

Making aliases to directories outside your file server directory structure is not a good idea for the reason that it spreads your server files out all over your Macintosh. You are looking to establish a compact file system for your server. Aliasing directories that are outside this system means that when you move your server directory, you'll have to remember to move the aliased directory as well. Aliased directories destroy this compactness that you should be striving to achieve.

Administrative Tools

There are some tools worth having that will aid in maintenance of your Web pages. The applications listed here are by no means the only tools in their respective classes. For discussion on some useful HTML editors, see Appendix C, "Perfecting HTML."

Spreadsheet-to-HTML Table Conversion

Microsoft Excel has become the de facto spreadsheet standard on the Mac. It's used for many purposes including tabular display of data. It may be advantageous for you to publish some of your data on the Web. This can be done in two ways: 1) publish the Excel documents in an encoded format to be read by an Excel application on the user's computer, or 2) convert the table to HTML 3.0 table definitions. With the second option in mind, there are several tools available to perform the conversion. Some of these are mentioned here:

NOTE

When you convert your spreadsheet to HTML 3.0 format, you will lose any formulae, macros, and other Excel-specific features. You can add these features by coding them with JavaScript. See Hayden's *JavaScript for the Macintosh* for more information on programming with JavaScript.

MS Excel to HTML Converters

xl2html.xls	http://www710.gsfc.nasa.gov/704/dgd/xl2html.html
Excel to HTML	http://rhodes.edu/software/readme.html
Internet Assistant for Microsoft Excel	http://www.microsoft.com/macoffice

The first two applications are actually macros written in Microsoft's Visual Basic (VB) programming language. As a result, both applications require use of Microsoft Excel 5.0. These utilities have become very popular, like any other VB macros, they can run just as easily under Windows as they can under the MacOS. Microsoft's Internet Assistant for Microsoft Excel is a freeware utility that walks users through the process of converting spreadsheets to HTML tables.

HTML Grinder

HTML Grinder is a powerful text-processing application designed to aid in making simultaneous changes to multiple text files. The Grinder is not a text editor but a batch text processor. You drag a collection of HTML files onto the Grinder; the files then appear in a dialog box similar to Figure 5.5. Some of the possible tasks you can perform include the following:

- **Find and Replace text.** You can find and replace text throughout a series of files. This is useful in changing the <BASE> tag if you move to another server or to another directory on your server.
- **Date stamp.** You can automatically date stamp your Web pages.
- **Netscape Color editor.** You can select Netscape color codes and insert them in your document. Like some HTML editors, HTML Grinder uses the Apple Color Editors to help determine the Netscape color codes.
- **Creator code changing.** This tool is useful for changing the creator code on a batch of files. File creator codes tell the

MacOS which application created that file. Double-clicking on the files opens the application designed in the file's creator code. This can be tedious if you do not own the application that was used to create the file. This HTML Grinder tool enables you to change the creator code of a file to that of an application that you own.

- **Linking your pages.** Using the HTML Grinder, you can insert hypertext in your pages that links the pages together. This will allow users to navigate through a list of sequential pages using Next and Previous links. With another tool, you can construct an index linking to various spots in your pages.

- **Creating Stretch lists.** Stretch lists operate much like the way the MacOS lets you view folders and files when viewing the files by Name or Date. You can nest text inside your pages; by clicking on the stretch icons, you can make the text visible within the Web browser. This has the appearance of stretching the page.

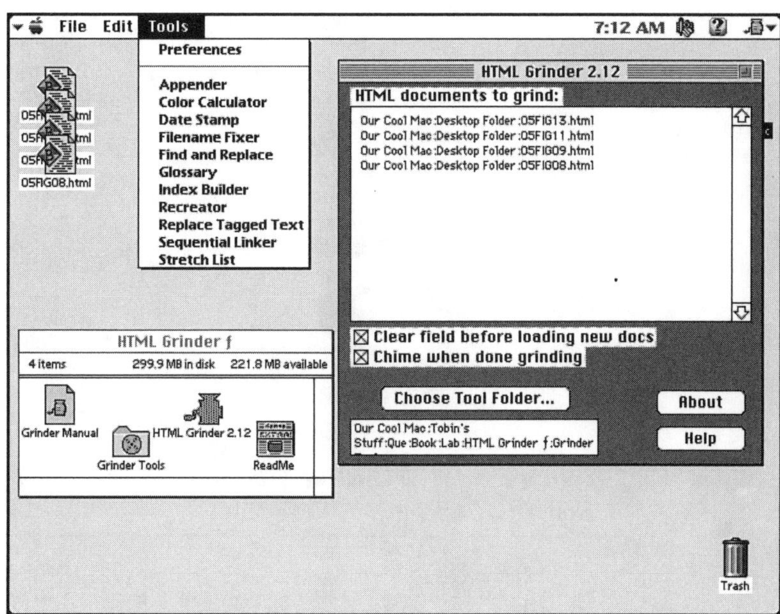

Figure 5.5 *HTML Grinder performs a variety of tasks on files dragged and dropped onto it.*

Clay Basket

Clay Basket is yet another tool that purports to be more than just a text editor. In fact, Clay Basket isn't really a text editor at all. Clay Basket is designed to aid in, as the author Dave Winer calls it, Web-site building. The freeware application enables you to develop Web sites from a top-down approach—you develop the outline of the site first before developing the content of the individual pages.

Clay Basket works in conjunction with text editors, such as BBEdit and PageMill, and browsers like Netscape to allow you to construct and manage Web pages. Clay Basket is a full-featured outliner as shown in Figure 5.6. In this figure, an example included with the Clay Basket distribution, you can see that the hypothetical Web site is displayed in outline form. Using the software, you can click on one of the files to edit it or you can preview it with Netscape.

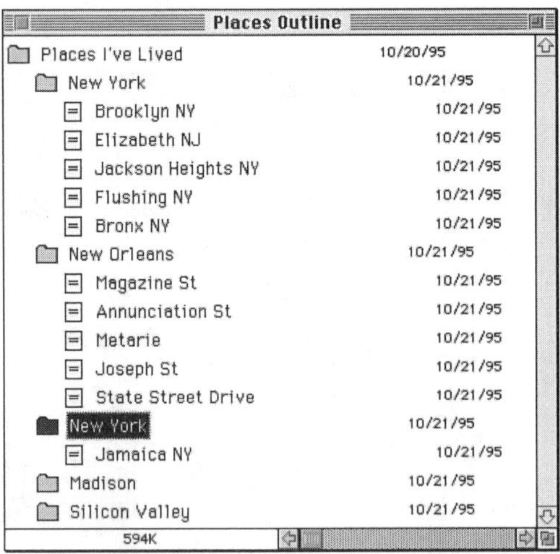

Figure 5.6 *The Outline View in Clay Basket aids in managing entire Web sites.*

By constructing the outline, you are constructing a hierarchy of Web pages. You can automatically link these pages together with a simple click of the mouse. While in outline view, you can launch any text editor to modify the file. Clay Basket supports a wide variety of templates to use in file creation.

Most important, Clay Basket works with the Frontier scripting environment. Originally a commercial product, Frontier is now a freely accessible scripting environment that was actually introduced before AppleScript; the scripting language used by Frontier is known as UserTalk. Apple bundled AppleScript with System 7.5; this eventually pushed Frontier to freeware status. Frontier will execute AppleScript files, but it offers more functionality than its Apple-supported scripting rival. Clay Basket uses Frontier scripts for many purposes; using Frontier scripts, Clay Basket enables you to assemble a glossary of links. When you are typing your HTML file, you can describe a link by including it in double quotes. Clay Basket uses a Frontier script to search your collection of URLs to look for an association between the link you've double-quoted and any link in your glossary. If it finds such a link, it automatically replaces the text with the HTML linking code. Other such Web-site management features can be employed using Clay Basket and the Frontier scripting environment.

Maintaining Server Statistics

You will no doubt be interested in seeing who has visited your site and what they've been downloading. For this reason, you'll want to employ some sort of statistics calculation application. Two Macintosh applications for this purpose are WebStat and ServerStat.

WebStat

WebStat is a simple application that reads the MacHTTP log file. The application will also work with the WebSTAR log file as well. MacHTTP can be configured to write certain pieces of information into its log file. For the most part, this information consists of the user's login time, IP address, and download information. WebStat takes this log file, and processes and tabulates the information in an HTML report suitable for publishing on your site.

You configure the WebStat application by editing the WebStat.config file in the distribution folder. Using the configuration file, you can customize the statistics generation in the following ways:

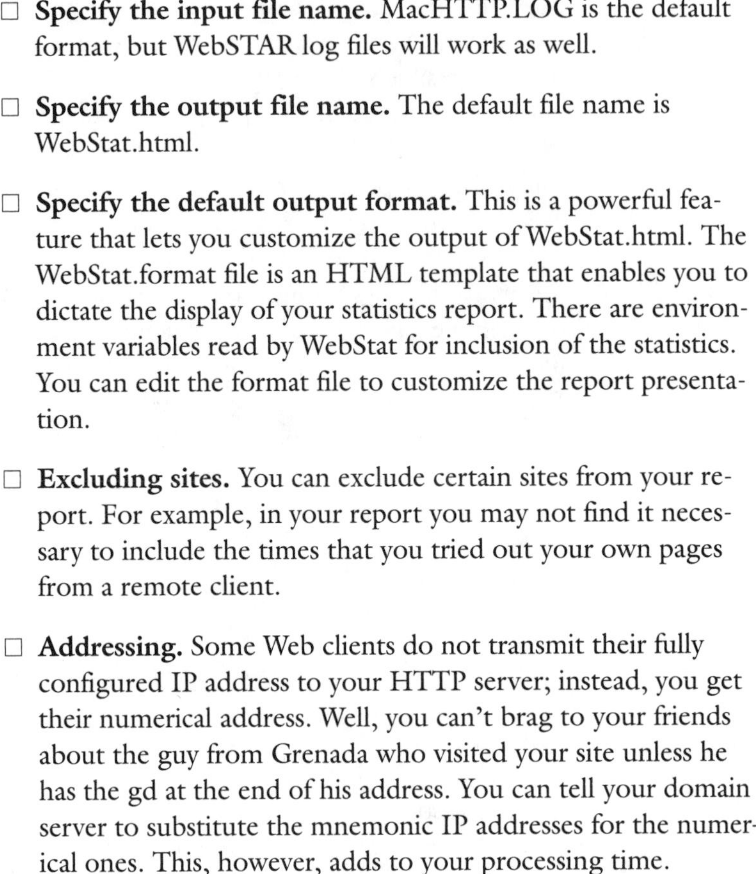

- **Specify the input file name.** MacHTTP.LOG is the default format, but WebSTAR log files will work as well.
- **Specify the output file name.** The default file name is WebStat.html.
- **Specify the default output format.** This is a powerful feature that lets you customize the output of WebStat.html. The WebStat.format file is an HTML template that enables you to dictate the display of your statistics report. There are environment variables read by WebStat for inclusion of the statistics. You can edit the format file to customize the report presentation.
- **Excluding sites.** You can exclude certain sites from your report. For example, in your report you may not find it necessary to include the times that you tried out your own pages from a remote client.
- **Addressing.** Some Web clients do not transmit their fully configured IP address to your HTTP server; instead, you get their numerical address. Well, you can't brag to your friends about the guy from Grenada who visited your site unless he has the gd at the end of his address. You can tell your domain server to substitute the mnemonic IP addresses for the numerical ones. This, however, adds to your processing time.

WebStat will then sort your access statistics by summary (number of files and bytes downloaded), day, hour, weekday, IP domain, IP subdomain, and files that were downloaded. As your MacHTTP file grows larger, WebStat takes more and more time to process it. This requires periodic culling of your log file for accesses that are too old to be of interest. Every month, I manually remove listings that are more than two months old on my server. Depending on the number of accesses you get, you may have to edit your file more frequently.

To run this program on a periodic basis, you need some sort of Cron utility. Cron is a Unix system utility that runs scripts at predetermined times. There are several Cron utilities for the Macintosh. The WebStat author recommends the use of Cron for the

Macintosh, by Mark Malson; the URL for the application is given in the WebStat README file. Although it worked fine for many months on my Mac IIci, I have not been able to get Mark's Cron utility to work without crashing my new Power Macintosh server. Instead, I recommend using Chris Johnson's Cron utility; it's a little harder to use but works quite well.

ServerStat Lite

ServerStat Lite, derived from its commercial cousin ServerStat, is a freeware statistics generation package. ServerStat Lite functions much like WebStat, although it produces statistics for WebSTAR and GopherSurfer, as well as MacHTTP. Rather than rely on text-based configuration files, ServerStat Lite offers a graphical user interface to customize statistics generation and reports. Reports can be written in HTML or plain text for editing purposes. Furthermore, ServerStat Lite is scriptable, using AppleScript and UserTalk scripts for complete customization.

ServerStat offers more functionality than ServerStat Lite. ServerStat is Power Macintosh native and also supports Open Transport. ServerStat is also more scriptable, and enables you to customize its operation to a greater degree than ServerStat Lite. Furthermore, ServerStat reports can contain links to different areas on your site.

Summary

As you can see, there's more to publishing a Web site than just hanging graphics HTML off your server. As an Intranet administrator, you'll have to administer your server keeping your links fresh and your content interesting. Luckily, there are several tools at your disposal to help you with Web server administration.

In the next chapter, we'll talk about some of the tips for using graphics and HTML efficiently to construct a Web site that's easy to browse. Of if you like, you can jump to the following chapters:

- ☐ Chapter 7, "Writing CGI Scripts," to learn about writing scripts for your Web site. These scripts enable you to process data from HTML forms and return customized Web pages.
- ☐ Chapter 8, "Databases and Document Searches," to learn about how to enable your Intranet users a means of accessing your databases and searches document archives.
- ☐ Chapter 9, "Beyond HTML," to learn about ways some techniques to spruce up your Web site beyond just using conventional HTML and graphics. We'll discuss Java, RealAudio, and other cool topics.
- ☐ Appendix C, "Perfecting HTML," to learn about HTML editors as well as some new and advanced HTML techniques, such as frames and server-push/client-pull techniques.

Links Related to This Chapter

xl2html.xls	http://www710.gsfc.nasa.gov/704/dgd/xl2html.html
Excel to HTML	http://rhodes.edu/software/readme.html
Internet Assistant for Microsoft Excel	http://www.microsoft.com/macoffice
Matterform Media	http://www.matterform.com
HTML Grinder	http://www.matterform.com/mf/grinder/htmlgrinder.html
Clay Basket	http://www.hotwired.com/staff/userland/yabbadabba/
WebStat	http://snodaq.phy.queensu.ca/Phil/phil.html
Mark Malson's Cron	http://snodaq.phy.queensu.ca/Cron.sit.Hqx

Chris Johnson's Cron	http://gargravarr.cc.utexas.edu/cron/cron.html
Kitchen Sink Software	http://www.kitchen-sink.com/
ServerStat Lite	http://www.kitchen-sink.com/ss.html

CHAPTER 6

Creating an Efficient Web Site

In your travels throughout the Web, you've probably come across sites that you felt were very well designed. They had good information, were graphically pleasing, and were easy to navigate. In short, these sites were very browsable.

Nothing is more frustrating than accessing a site that has good information content, but is difficult to browse. These kind of sites contain pages that are all in plain text with an abundance of network-busting graphics, and you have to hit the Back button on your browser because there are no links to the home page. The usability of your site within your organization is heavily dependent on its browsability and ease of use.

As an Intranet administrator, you can think of your users as captive users. They have to access your site to work with administrative or technical data within your organization. However, putting up clunky Web pages that are difficult to browse will only make your users reluctant to access them.

Some of the topics that we'll discuss relevant to your site's browsability include:

- ☐ Effective use of browsing navigation tools
- ☐ Tips for effective HTML design
- ☐ Effective use of lists
- ☐ Creative uses of graphics in your pages
- ☐ Creative design of tables

An Efficient Web Site

So what are the qualities of an efficient Web site? First, there should be a compelling reason to visit the site. Users within your Intranet will be looking for relevant information on your Web site. Second, effective sites use some navigational and layout design techniques that we'll discuss in this chapter. They are easy to navigate, and when you get lost, there's always a link back to the previous page or back to the home page. Let's discuss some of these techniques.

Maxing Out on HTML

As a text processing language, HTML 2.0 is fairly limited in features. With HTML 3.0 still in the proposal stage as of this writing, it seems that the Web community will need to find ways to creatively use HTML 2.0 to display effective Web pages.

Netscape HTML Extensions

In Appendix C, "Perfecting HTML," we will talk about the different flavors of HTML and how the Netscape extensions differ from standard HTML. With a huge market share and millions of dollars worth of stock behind it, chances are that Netscape Communications will have a large say in the direction that HTML will take over the next few years. However, many people are nervous about what they see as a Netscape hegemony over HTML, similar to what Microsoft has with operating system and office automation software. With Microsoft's introduction of its Internet Explorer Web browser in early 1996, a whole new set of specific HTML extensions were introduced as well. With several different flavors of HTML being supported by major browsers, you will have to decide which set of extensions you will support within your Intranet. This will more or less dictate the type of browser upon which your users will have to standardize.

NOTE

Although Internet Explorer accepts many of Netscape's HTML extensions, Microsoft has included support for extensions beyond those used by Netscape Navigator. Specifically, Internet Explorer enables you to play background sounds and display floating marquees on pages. For more information, see the URL at the end of this chapter.

Having said that, the Netscape extensions can be pretty useful. Background GIFs and text colors add a new dimension to your page layout. Netscape Navigator was one of the first browsers to support HTML 3.0 tables. Despite the reviled <BLINK> environment, Netscape has introduced some novel extensions, such as frames, which have been adopted throughout the Web. The current convention is that if you plan on using the Netscape extensions, notify your users in some way that non-Netscape browsers can interpret. The most common way is to include a GIF or announcement that you are using Netscape-enhanced HTML. The graphics in Figure 6.1 are often used in this manner.

Figure 6.1 *These images are often used to warn users of Netscape-enhanced pages. They can be found on Netscape's home pages starting at http://www.netscape.com.*

NOTE

The images in Figure 6.1 are often used to link to the Netscape Communications home page (http://www.netscape.com) so that the user can download a copy of the browser. Sometimes the icons are linked to an archived copy of the browser itself. The Netscape 2.0 icon is used to denote that the page uses Navigator 2.0 features such as frames and Java applets.

NOTE

When developing HTML pages, one good practice is to maintain a stable of browsers, such as Mosaic and MacWeb, to determine how compatible your Netscape-enhanced pages are with other Web clients.

Realize that when you use the Netscape extensions, you are potentially using nonstandard HTML. If you have standardized upon Navigator as your Intranet's standard Web browser, then your users should have no trouble with your pages. Many functions of the current Netscape extensions will be incorporated into the eventual HTML 3.0 standard.

Using Lists Effectively

Lists are one of the original and most heavily-used HTML environments. The list environment is used to represent distinct items of information in an ordered format. HTML 2.0 offers little flexibility in setting up lists; the Netscape extensions offer few added features. We'll discuss the three major list types: ordered lists, unordered lists, and definition lists. There are several guidelines that you should observe when developing HTML lists.

NOTE

I like to use the word *tag* to describe HTML commands such as `<P>`, `<NOBR>`, and `<HR>` that stand by themselves and need no complementing tag. I use the term *environment* to describe HTML commands that require beginning and closing tags. Headers (`<H1>...</H1>`) and bold type (`<B>...</B>`) are examples of what I refer to as HTML environments. Note that environments are denoted with starting and closing tags.

Using Ordered and Unordered Lists

Ordered and bulleted lists are popular list environments. With standard HTML 2.0, there are not a lot of options at your disposal. As a review, the Netscape HTML extensions allow you the following flexibility:

- Unordered list bullets can be made into hollow circles and squares instead of just the usual discs.
- Ordered list headings can be preceded with uppercase and lowercase alphabetic, uppercase and lowercase Roman numeral, and numeric characters.
- Ordered list numerical prefixes can be set to start at any particular number.

Directory and menu lists are similar to unordered lists and do not provide much more functionality.

Using Definition Lists

Definition lists are useful for providing definitions of various list items. My favorite use for a definition list is to provide a description of a hotlist or list of links. An example of this is shown below in Figure 6.2 along with the associated HTML code.

```
<H2>Example of a definition list of links</H2>
<DL>
<DT><A
HREF="http://docs.kb.bib.dk/Interviews/WWW/Links/
➥Links.html">Net.Personalities</A><BR>
    <DD>Interviews with various WWW and Internet
➥Personalities
<DT><A HREF="http://www.webcrawler.com/">WebCrawler</A>
    <DD>A Popular WWW Searching Tool
<DT><A HREF="http://www.apple.com">Apple Computer</
➥A><BR>
    <DD>Apple Computer's Home Page
</DL>
```

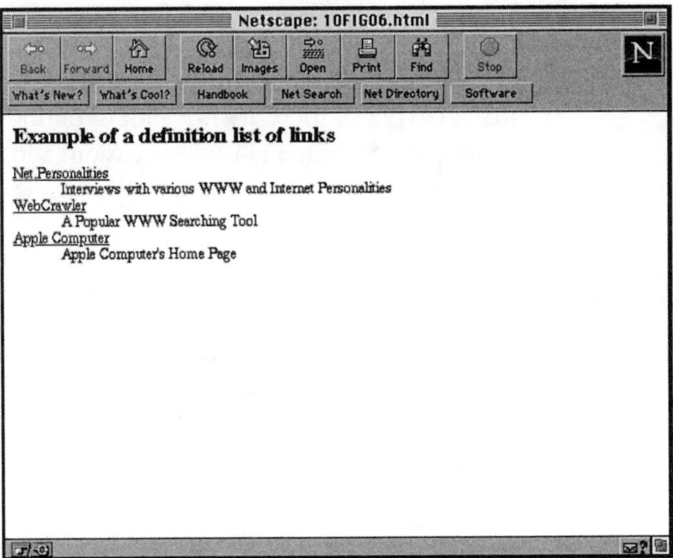

Figure 6.2 *The definition list can be used to present a descriptive list of hotlinks.*

Managing List Length

One of the most annoying things I see on the Web is lists that go on and on forever. Long lists can be distracting and difficult to navigate. For the sake of readability, you should break up exceedingly long lists into separate pages. However, if you need to keep the list as a single entity, there are two ways to make it more readable.

The first way is to use anchors to index various portions of your text. In this way, you can sport a table of contents at the top of the page with links to the various list elements. An example of this is shown below in Figure 6.3 along with the associated code.

```
<HTML>
<HEAD>
<TITLE>Indexed List Example</TITLE>
</HEAD>
<BODY>
```

```
<!--header-->
This is an index to the list below.
<DL>
    <DT>Click <A HREF="#1st">here</A> for first element
    <DT>Click <A HREF="#2nd">here</A> for second
➥element
    <DT>Click <A HREF="#3rd">here</A> for third element
    <DT>Click <A HREF="#4th">here</A> for fourth
➥element
</DL>
<!--end of header-->
<DL>
    <DT><H4><A NAME="1st">First List Element</A></H4>
        <DD>This item contains a lot of material about
➥the first element of this list. While you may think
➥stretch lists are a little complicated, they are
➥actually quite simple when used with HTML Grinder.
➥They save space on your browser window.
    <DT><H4><A NAME="2nd">Second List Element</A></H4>
        <DD>This contains some information about the
➥2nd list element
    <DT><H4><A NAME="3rd">Third List Element</A></H4>
        <DD>This contains some information about the
➥2nd list element
    <DT><H4><A NAME="4th">Fourth List Element</A></H4>
        <DD>This contains some information about the
➥2nd list element
</DL>

</BODY>
</HTML>
```

In the index at the top of the page, you see a small definition list; each item has anchor tags that refer down to the items in the definition list at the bottom of the page. By clicking on one of the links in the index, the browser window scrolls to the point where the referenced list item is at the top of the window. If you absolutely need to keep a list on one single page, this is a useful technique.

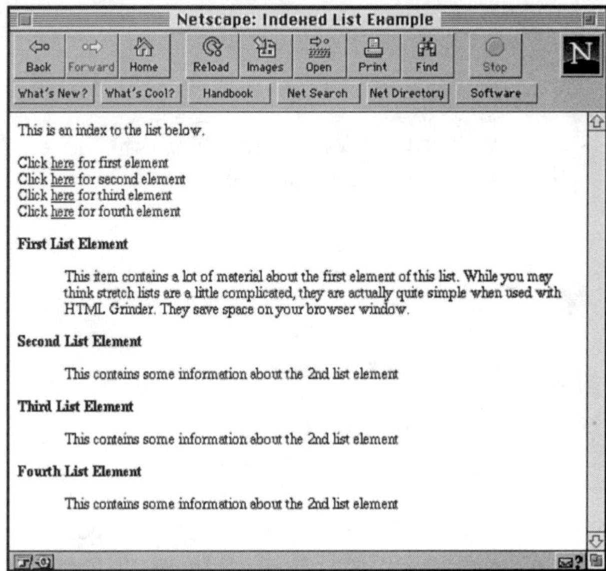

Figure 6.3 *You can index HTML anchor tags to reference items in a list environment.*

The other technique is to use stretch lists as implemented by HTML Grinder. Stretch lists do not use the HTML list environment, but are a means of making HTML mimic the behavior exhibited by the MacOS when you view folders by name. Stretch lists enable you to display the primary headings in a list format as shown in Figure 6.4. By clicking on a link, you can expand that list item as shown in Figure 6.5.

The stretch list is actually a clever means of redistributing HTML text in a document. The HTML Grinder application has a Stretch List tool, or wheel, which allows you to build stretch lists. It's an easy task to do. You first need to format your original document in a way that HTML Grinder can interpret.

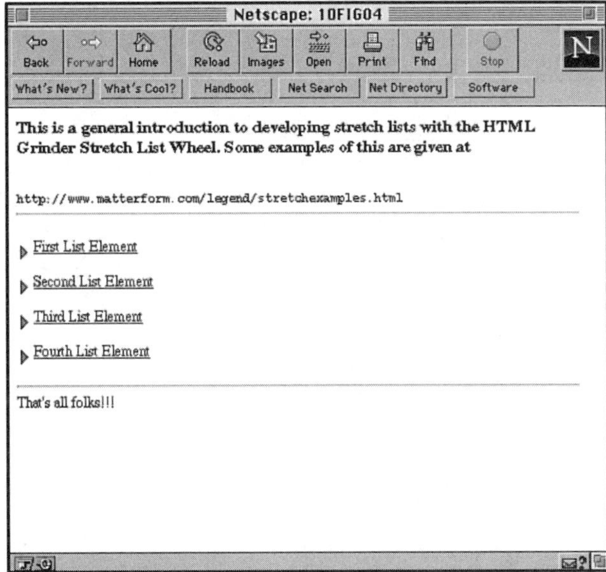

Figure 6.4 *A stretch list mimics the MacOS View by Name paradigm.*

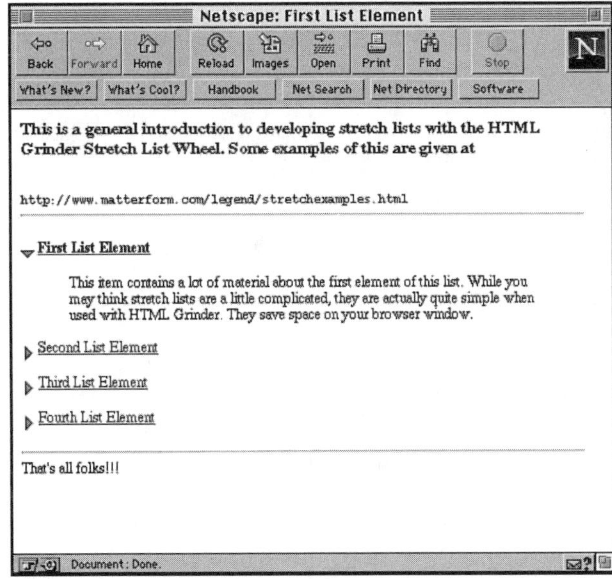

Figure 6.5 *By clicking on a link, you can expand that list item on a stretch list.*

The following code contains a simple list that we are going to crank through the HTML Grinder.

```
<!--header-->
<H3>This is a general introduction to developing
➥stretch lists with the HTML Grinder Stretch List
➥Wheel. Some examples of this are given at</H3>
➥<BR><TT>http://www.matterform.com/legend/
stretchexamples.html</TT>
<HR>
<!--end of header-->

<H4>First List Element</H4>
This item contains a lot of material about the first
➥element of this list. While you may think stretch
➥lists are a little complicated, they are actually
➥quite simple when used with HTML Grinder. They save
➥space on your browser window.
<H4>Second List Element</H4>
This contains some information about the 2nd list
➥element
<H4>Third List Element</H4>
This contains some information about the 2nd list
➥element
<H4>Fourth List Elemen</H4>
This contains some information about the 2nd list
➥element

<!--footer-->
<HR>
That's all folks!!!
<!--end of footer-->
```

NOTE 

> Before you use the HTML Grinder to make a stretch list, make a backup of your HTML code, because the stretch list creation is not undoable.

You need to define the *stretched* and *nonstretched* versions of the document using header and footer comments. You also need to denote your primary list headers in some sort of environment; this environment can be a heading, a physical or logical markup, or any other closed set of tags. The environment needs to be unique to the desired list headers in the document. In the preceding example, <H4> tags were used.

Take your file and drag it onto the HTML Grinder application. From the Tools menu, select the Stretch List option. A dialog box appears, similar to that shown in Figure 6.6. You need to specify which environment you used to designate your primary list headings. You also need to specify the comment strings you used to denote the beginning and end of your headers and footers. Lastly, you can specify your expanded and condensed item icons. The HTML Grinder has two default icons, similar to the MacOS list icons, in the Grinder Tools folder. Move or copy these icon files (they're only 9K) over to your HTML code folder. Press Create Stretch List to create your stretch list.

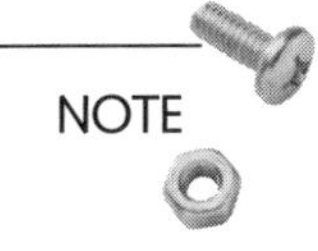

NOTE

> The HTML Grinder will ask you for a serial number if you have not registered the software. It will allow you to create a stretch list while in demo mode, but this grace period will expire within a few weeks. As with all shareware on the CD-ROM, purchase of this book does not fulfill your shareware obligation.

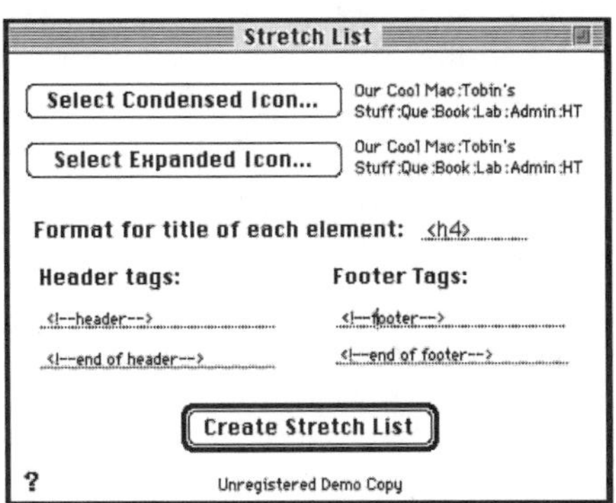

Figure 6.6 *The HTML Grinder Stretch List dialog box allows you to create stretch lists.*

Your HTML file will be converted to represent an unexpanded stretch list as shown in Figure 6.5 with your primary item headers transformed into hypertext. The Grinded code in the new HTML file is given here:

```
<title>10FIG04</title>

<!--header-->
<H3>This is a general introduction to developing
➥stretch lists with the HTML Grinder Stretch List
➥Wheel. Some examples of this are given at</H3>
<BR><TT>http://www.matterform.com/legend/
stretchexamples.html</TT>
<HR>
<!--end of header-->
<p>
<img align=center src="condensed.gif"> <a
➥href="10FIG041.html">First List Element</a><p>
<img align=center src="condensed.gif"> <a
➥href="10FIG042.html">Second List Element</a><p>
<img align=center src="condensed.gif"> <a
➥href="10FIG043.html">Third List Element</a><p>
<img align=center src="condensed.gif"> <a
➥href="10FIG044.html">Fourth List Element</a><p>

<!--footer-->
<HR>
That's all folks!!!
<!--end of footer-->
```

Clicking on any of the item headers will give the appearance of expanding that list item as a new page appears with an *expanded* icon replacing the *condensed* icon and the list item text appearing as well. What has actually happened is that the HTML Grinder has created an additional page for each expanded link. These additional pages contain the original list with one item expanded. In the unexpanded list, these list headers point to associated additional pages. The Stretch List is a clever and very useful means of maintaining large lists.

NOTE 

> Because of the mechanism that HTML Grinder uses to expand list items, you can expand only one item in a stretch list at a time. This may prove useful for large lists, because it means your page will never grow to undue lengths.

Using Tables Effectively

Even under HTML 2.0, tables can be a highly flexible means of displaying information. Once again, the Netscape extensions allow greater flexibility in table definition.

Setting Table Borders

HTML 2.0 enables you to set up tables with borders; Netscape enables you to display these tables with various border widths. Thick borders can be especially eye-catching. Some examples of thick table borders are shown in Figure 6.7. Borders are also an interesting way to frame certain graphics. The picture in Figure 6.8 is framed with a 5-pixel border.

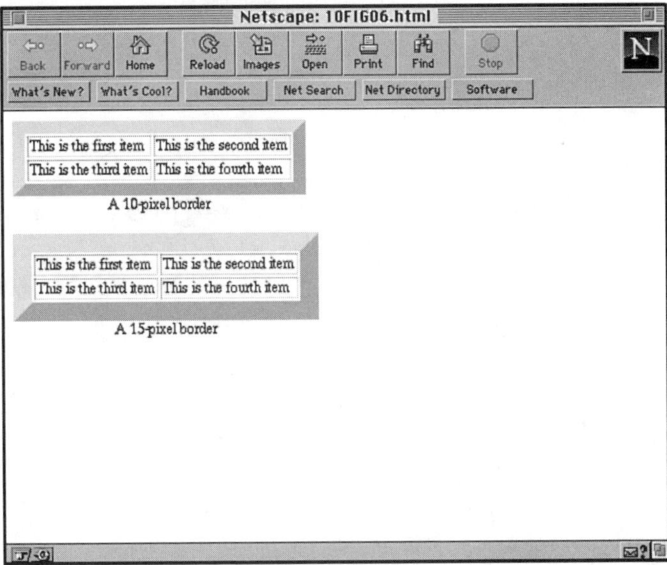

Figure 6.7 *Table borders can be constructed with various widths using Netscape HTML extensions.*

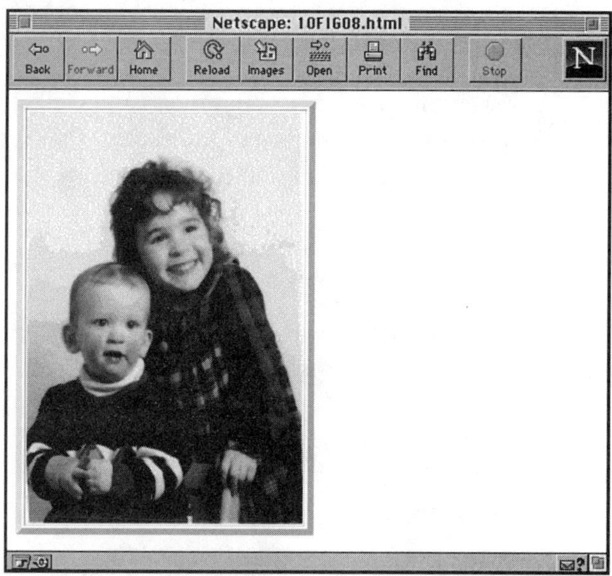

Figure 6.8 *You also can use the Netscape table border capability to frame images.*

NOTE

Tables also can be used to align images. You can create a table without borders and include an image or icon in each cell. They will appear to be aligned with one another. This is most noticeable by including images of equal size.

NOTE

Similarly, you can use tables to align columns of text to pictures. Check out examples of this in the Salon e-zine at http://www.salon1999.com.

Using Graphics Effectively

The Internet has been serving text documents for a long time; the appeal of the Web, however, is that you can integrate text and graphics on the same page. This new flexibility enables you to customize the look of your pages. The tips we'll cover in this section will enable you to supply graphics that add style to your documents, while ensuring their browsability.

Using Imagemaps

We've talked about the utility of imagemaps. Not only can they provide a compact means of setting up links to different pages, but they can provide an attractive addition to your page's layout. Imagemaps, such as the one shown in Figure 6.9, can be decorative and useful at the same time.

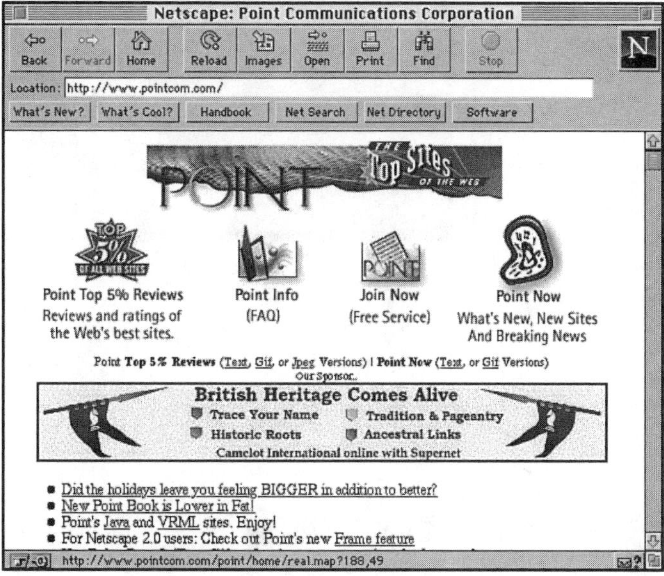

Figure 6.9 *The Point Communications home page sports an attractive imagemap as a means of accessing other pages on the site.*

In addition to making your page a whole lot prettier, imagemaps can add insight into your page more effectively than simply stringing up links using HTML. An example of this is shown in Figure 6.10. In this example, you can click on various geographic locations on a map of the United States to obtain more information on the various NASA centers. For example, you would click on an area of the map near Houston, Texas, to obtain more information on the Johnson Space Center located in Houston. In this way, the user gains insight into the location of the different NASA centers more than if the NASA center links were posted in a table or an unordered list.

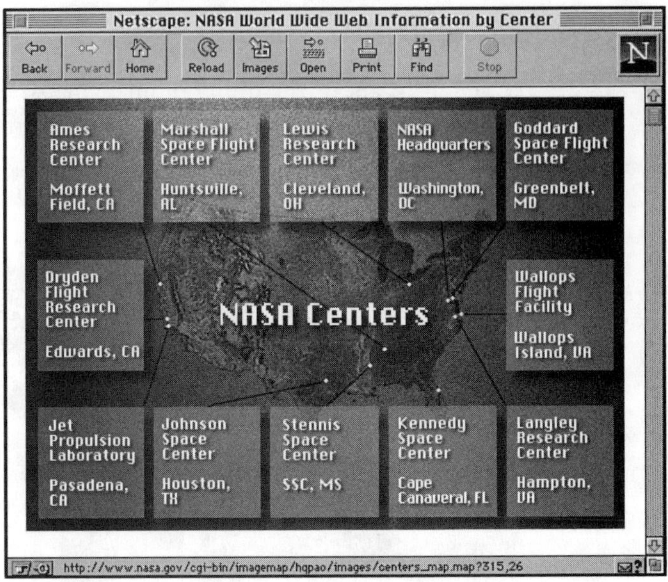

Figure 6.10 *This imagemap from the NASA Web site lets you click on geographic locations on the U.S. map to obtain more information on the various NASA centers.*

The HTML 3.0 proposals also provide use for *client-side* imagemaps. With conventional, or *server-side*, imagemaps, the user clicks on an area of the map. The browser sends the location of the click to the Web server which in turn relays this information to a special application known as a CGI script. This script translates the coordinates of the map click to a URL and passes the URL back to the server. The server processes the URL and returns the corresponding HTML back to the browser. With client-side imagemaps, the server is left out of the picture. Association between areas of the map and associated URLs is made within the HTML code. Many experts feel that client-side imagemaps present more utility in that they are faster because the server is not called into action. Similarly, you can test client-side imagemaps offline when you don't have access to a server.

NOTE

See Chapter 7, "Writing CGI Scripts," for more information about imagemaps and CGI scripts.

Alternatives to <HR>

We'll talk about the importance of modularity in your documents. One way to break up the flow of text in your pages is to use the horizontal rule as discussed in Chapter 5. However, there are graphical alternatives to the horizontal rule. These graphics are usually transparent and because they are small in size, take very little time to load. An example of some of these horizontal-rule alternatives is given in Figure 6.11.

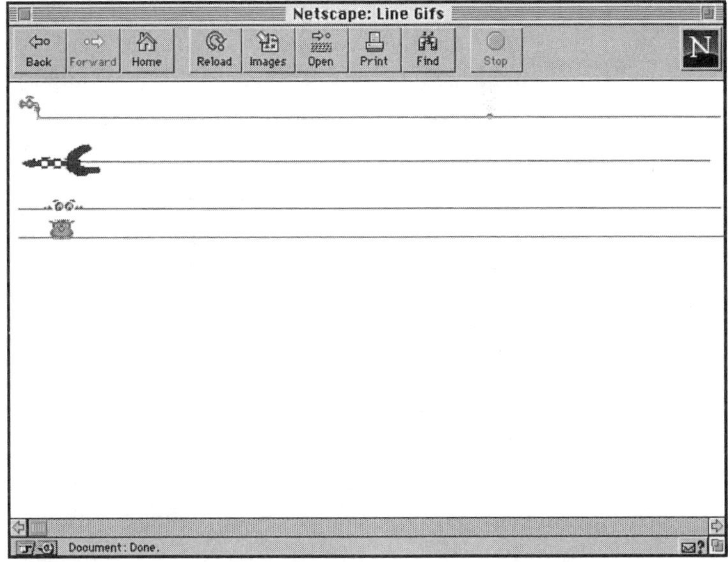

Figure 6.11 *These transparent GIFs can be used as alternatives to HTML's horizontal rule.*

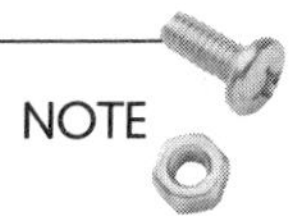

NOTE

You can check out Yahoo's list of icon archives at http://www.yahoo.com/Computers/World_Wide_Web/Programming/Icons/.

Using Background and Text Colors

Netscape 1.1 introduced the capability of modifying colors of the browser text and background window; you can even set up an image to serve as a background to your browser window. These features were initially supported only by Netscape, but the latest version of Mosaic now accommodates these HTML extensions as does Microsoft's Internet Explorer. Soon after Netscape 1.1 was released, the Web exploded in a collage of bizarre colors and graphics. These graphics reduced the legibility of these documents below the level of comprehensibility. It didn't take long for people to find the right RGB codes to produce green text on a bright orange background.

NOTE 

> If you find the different graphical backgrounds annoying, there's hope. Many browsers, such as Navigator and Internet Explorer, enable you to override the background colors and graphics with a preset color scheme.

In the early Macintosh development, studies showed that the text and background color combination that was easiest for people to read was the conventional black on white. Recent studies by graphics designers have confirmed these results. You can use color combinations different from this optimal configuration with only a minimal loss of readability. First, let's talk a little bit about the way these colors are formed.

One way to establish a particular color is to describe its relative amounts of pure red, green, and blue components. This scheme, known as the RGB (Red, Green, Blue) color scheme, enables you to precisely define a particular color. The MacOS enables you to specify the relative amount of each component using a relative scale of 0 to 65535. For example, the Apple Color Table defines pure white to consist of a relative scaling of 65535 for all three components; in contrast, black has a 0 relative scaling for all three components.

As mentioned previously, Navigator uses the same RGB convention to specify text and background colors. However, the relative scaling of the red, green, and blue components is specified using hexadecimal (or base 16) codes instead of decimal (conventional base 10) representations. As a result, there are far fewer possible color combinations using the Navigator system than there are using the Apple Color Table.

NOTE

> Hexadecimal numbers are often used in computing applications because they describe a base 16 number system. Our standard number system is base 10. The hexadecimal system uses the familiar base 10 numbers and then uses a combination of alphabetic characters to describe numbers equivalent to 11 through 16.

I have found that light pastels are best for background colors because they offer the best contrast with text. You can determine a pastel by noting that two of the indices will contain quite similar values, while the third contains less similar values. For example, a light cyan contains 50 percent red, but full green and blue. This translates to a background color code of 7FFFFF (the number FF is a hexadecimal number representation). In contrast, a harsh green that contains neither red nor blue corresponds to a code of 00FF00. I find the stronger colors to be useful for text and the lighter shades acceptable for background colors. The important thing to remember is to provide enough contrast between your text and background to ensure legibility.

NOTE

> ColorMeister is an application that you can use to determine the Navigator color codes. You can use either the standard MacOS color wheel or RGB guide to express a color in its hexadecimal equivalent.

With these HTML extensions, you also can change the colors of active, visited, and unexplored links. Since Mosaic's introduction several years ago, the convention has been to assign unexplored links a royal blue with visited links displayed in a magenta color. Surprisingly, this convention is maintained on a lot of pages even when the body text is a different color. This possibly results from the fact that the link colors tell you something about the status of the link, whereas normal text color is simply decorative. The only rule of thumb I would suggest is to not reverse the link color convention. I have seen some pages where visited links are blue and unexplored links are red. This can be very confusing even to veteran Web surfers. There are aesthetic reasons for changing the link color convention, but the contrast between explored and unexplored link colors should be large enough to dispel any ambiguity.

Background images are used in lieu of background colors. Desktop texture utilities have been around for several years; these utilities enable you to replace the standard desktop with images or customized patterns. System 7.5 even comes with a desktop pattern control panel. Again, the point is to provide enough contrast between text and background to make the document legible. The most legible documents use backgrounds that are semitransparent or use muted hues. Figure 6.12 shows two examples of text and background images. The first example shows a muted gray background that is easy to read; but the second window is more difficult to read, because there is little contrast between the text and the image. To make the document readable, a white, or similarly contrasting, text color should be used.

NOTE

A link is active when you click on it or activate it. Note that the color changes from its original color when you click on a link. The link describing the Netscape HTML extensions is given at the end of this chapter.

GIF versus JPEG

Two major graphics formats are published on the Web at this time: the Graphics Interchange Format (GIF) and the Joint Photographic Experts Group (JPEG). Originally, Mosaic did not support the JPEG format, and such images had to be viewed offline; the only images you could view in a browser window were GIF images. The original version of Netscape supported inline JPEG displays; because other browsers now do this, there's a legitimate question as to which format you should be using.

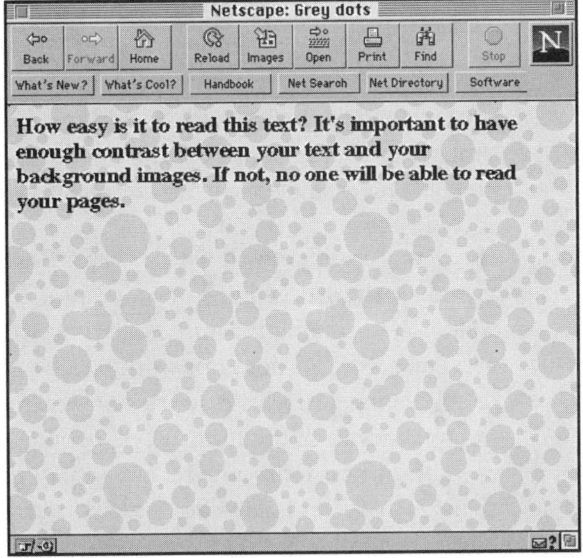

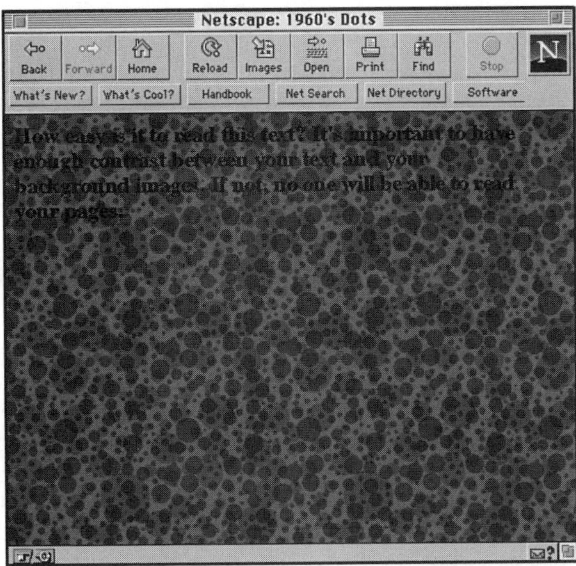

Figure 6.12 *The page on the top is readable because of the contrast between the text and background image; for the same reason the page on the bottom is not easily readable.*

The JPEG format was developed for displaying photographs; you can support 24-bit color with a JPEG image. This is useful only if your monitor supports 24-bit color. This gives almost photographic quality to inline images viewed within a browser. GIF files, on the other hand, support 8-bit color yielding 256 possible colors in an image. This is fine for clip art, but insufficient for photographs.

JPEG was also designed with a very efficient compression scheme to reduce the size of large photographic files. This scheme works well with photographic images, natural scenery, or any other complex image. JPEG does not work so well for some line art, lettering, or simple images. This compression scheme is designed to exploit the weaknesses of the human eye; people can perceive small changes in brightness far more accurately than they can detect small changes in color. Therefore, artwork with sharp contrasts can look blurry and indistinct. However, image quality also depends on the level of compression and whether the art has been anti-aliased.

NOTE 

GIF files can better display inline alphanumeric characters at small sizes, meaning GIF is the preferred format for imagemaps.

On the other hand, the GIF encoding scheme is very efficient at compressing images that have large patterns of similar color, such as icons or cartoons. JPEG cannot compress such imagery as efficiently. GIF compression can be lossless when working with small files; JPEG tends to lose image quality with each image compression. A JPEG image is expanded and compressed each time it is edited with a graphics application such as GraphicConverter or Adobe Photoshop. This degree of loss can be traded off with the final image size using one of the applications previously mentioned; even so, the degree of quality loss is generally less than human perception.

So the question still is: which image format should I use? The rule of thumb is to use GIF files to store images of simple icons, line art, imagemaps, and especially any form of black-and-white artwork; use JPEG to store complicated imagery such as photographs and artwork. For complicated images, you receive better quality and smaller files with JPEG than with GIF.

NOTE

The quality of color inherent in an image is related to the size of the computational word used to describe the number of colors available to express each pixel. For example, say that you want to display a piece of clip art in black and white. You would assign one bit for each pixel—if the bit is on, the pixel is white and if it's off, the pixel is black. With more bits per pixel, you can describe various shades of gray or colors. With 24-bit color supported by JPEG, you can theoretically describe 2^{24}, or 16,777,216 colors in a JPEG image. Naturally, the more color you describe in an image, the larger your file will need to be. Eight-bit color files are much smaller than files containing images described with 24-bit color.

Photographs versus Clip Art

Ever wonder why it takes so long to download certain graphics files? The short answer is that some files are larger than others. Fundamentally, downloading text and graphics through the Web is a file transfer using HTTP. The larger the amount of text and graphics you download, the longer the transfer will take. The question is, why are some graphics files larger than others? Much of it has to do with the size of the graphic and the format, GIF or JPEG, in which it is saved. A navigation arrow may be a couple of kilobytes, but a photograph, which can take up more space in your browser window, may be stored in a larger file.

Much of the difference results in the way that the graphic files are stored. A GIF file supports limited numbers of colors and therefore requires 8 bits per image pixel to describe the image colors. Furthermore, the GIF encoding algorithm works much better with color patterns; space can be saved by using an algorithm to describe color patterns. In contrast, a photograph can have no discernible pattern of color, making it difficult to condense using an encoding scheme.

As a result, clip art and drawings that use few colors require less file space than photographs. When there's a choice, rig up your own clip art for mundane uses as navigation buttons and banners; store these images using GIF files as previously mentioned. Use photographs only when they contribute to the content of the page.

NOTE

Your page will load more quickly if you minimize the number of images on the page. The browser sets up a separate HTTP connection for each image, so there's extra overhead involved with starting up each connection in addition to the actual image transfer.

Overall Page Design

To create a truly browsable Web site, you'll need more than snazzy graphics and HTML tricks. You'll need to organize your pages into a format that is accessible by the reader. The tips in this section detail some of the ways you can organize your pages into an accessible format.

Modularizing Your Pages

Maybe I'm stuck in the remote-control generation, but I have trouble with pages that are more than three browser screens long. For one thing, it's hard to keep track of excessively long material and the page, with associated graphics, takes too long to load. Just as you limit the length of your paragraphs, you will want to limit your individual Web documents to no more than three screens.

NOTE

To design your pages in a modular fashion, you can use Clay Basket. The application contains an outline tool that aids you to develop interconnecting pages. HTML Grinder also has a Sequential Linker tool that enables you to set up navigational hypertext to connect existing HTML pages.

You also can use horizontal rules, tables, and figures to break up the flow of your document. The idea of publishing Web pages is to utilize the media to the fullest extent possible. If your document is too long and text-based, you might as well publish it on a Gopher or FTP archive.

Publishing Online Documentation

One of the main uses of your Intranet Web server will be to publish a document of some type, such as a software manual, a technical paper, or a list of frequently asked questions (FAQs) for the benefit of your readers. With these types of documents, you'll want to break it up into sections or modules as described previously. However, you may want to allow users to download copies of the documentation in a single file rather than require them to repeatedly browse the same pages on your site. For this reason, you may want to store the document in a single file written in a cross-platform format, such as PostScript or Portable Document Format (PDF). Providing this documentation in a single file enables users to make hard copies of the material if they desire; in addition, it can lighten your server load a bit.

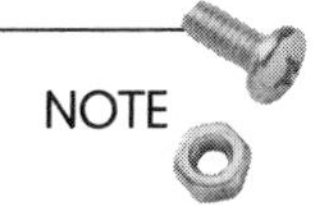

NOTE

> Adobe Systems, Inc. has introduced the Portable Document Format for use as a cross-platform document format. You can view PDF files with the freeware Adobe Acrobat Reader utility. PDF files are created by high-end applications such as FrameMaker or Adobe Acrobat Pro. You can convert PostScript files to PDF using Adobe Acrobat Distiller. You can even use the Acrobat Netscape Navigator plug-in module, which enables you to read PDF files within Navigator pages. See Adobe's home page for more information (http://www.adobe.com).

Navigation Tips

Another feature of browsable Web pages is the ease of navigation. If your Intranet Web pages are going to contain diverse types of information, chances are you'll have several sets of pages relating to different topics. You may have them set up in a complicated hierarchy that seems logical to you, but unfamiliar to your Intranet users. You also have to provide for the fact that many of your users will not be hitting your home page and may be barreling into some obscure location within your site. If your pages are disjointed and difficult to traverse, users will get frustrated. In this section, we'll discuss ways that you can make your site more navigable.

Your users will probably hop from page to page within your site. Well, that's great, but ideally, you want them to know where they're hopping. This can be done with some sort of navigation buttons. For example, the pages in the Web site shown in Figure 6.13 have a series of navigational buttons for the user to move through documentation. Note that the buttons enable you to move forward and backward by page or by section.

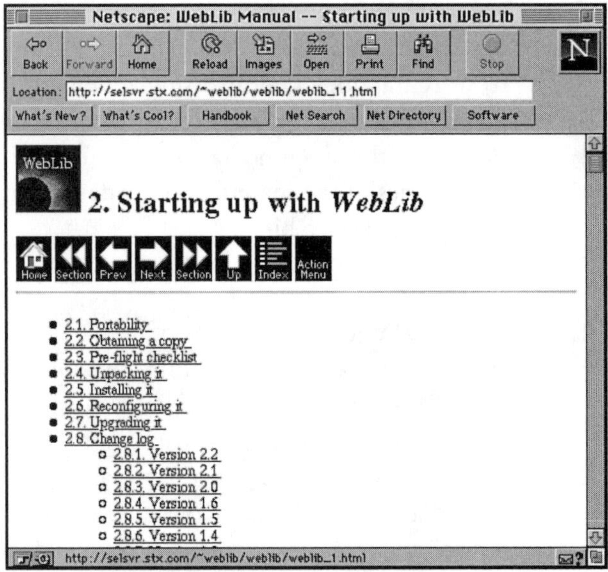

Figure 6.13 *The WebLib project (http://selsvr.stx.com/~weblib/) Web pages use a series of navigational buttons to enable users to step through the online documentation.*

The page in Figure 6.13 utilized different images for different commands. You can place the same functionality within an imagemap. Figure 6.14 shows an example of a navigational image used in the Apple Computer home page. The image is broken up into several areas that are linked, by an imagemap script, to various pages.

An important feature to note from both examples is that you should always include a link to the home page in your navigational display. If users become lost in the bowels of your Web pages, they can always come back to the top level by hitting a link to the home page. Having a home page link on all your pages enables users to start at the top, where you might have additional information available.

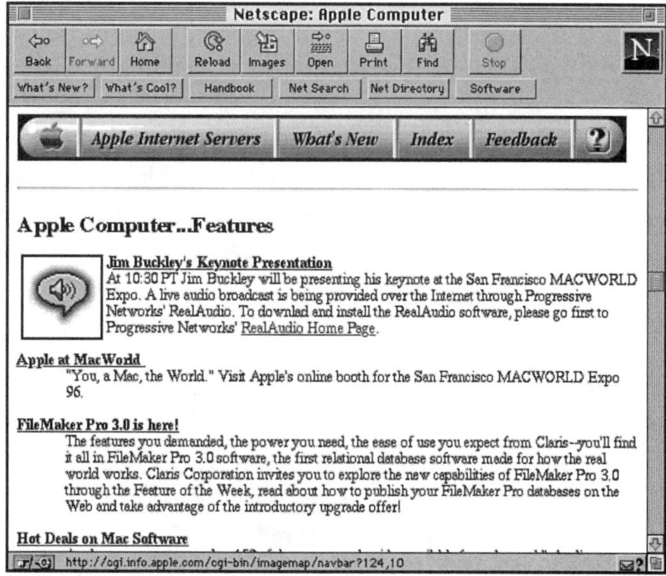

Figure 6.14 *The Apple Computer home pages use a navigational imagemap to enable users to move to different portions of the site.*

NOTE

Some of your users will have image loading turned off; also, transmission problems may prevent graphics from loading accurately at times. For either reason, you will want to have a hypertext version of your navigation buttons available somewhere on the page.

Similarly, you should include a text description of your images using the ALT keyword. An example is given below:

<IMG SRC="me.gif" ALT="Picture of me in bathing suit">

If me.gif does not load for some reason, the Web browser will display the text in the ALT tag instead.

Providing Credit Where Credit Is Due

If your users have questions on your content or your Web-site organization, you should provide a means for them to contact you. Your organization may be large enough that not all of the users might know you by name or email. You should identify yourself by name and email address in the footer of each of your pages. Setting up an email hypertext link is simple through use of a mailto HTML tag. If your organization allows you the privilege of a personal home page, include a link to your page; you can provide more detailed locator information on the home page.

NOTE

> If you are reluctant to publish your name or email address on your Web pages, set up an email account so that you can receive mail at webmaster@host.your_domain_name. Identify this address on the page as a means of providing feedback to you. We'll talk more about setting up these types of accounts in Chapter 11, "Email Services."

Maintain Fresh Links

Using administration tools such as Clay Basket, it will be difficult for you to publish stale links within your own document. Some of the HTML validation services mentioned in Appendix C, "Perfecting HTML," will check your internal links for you. If you are going to maintain links to pages located outside your Web site, you need to prepare against publishing stale links. You should constantly check to see that your links go to the correct places.

Adobe is distributing SiteMill, a site management tool for Web administrators. SiteMill provides a means of testing the connections between your links and is specifically geared to managing large sites. Like Clay Basket, SiteMill presents you with an outline view of your Web site. However, SiteMill enables you to check for the accuracy of your links. When you change the name of a file, SiteMill will warn you of the number of documents that will need to be updated as a result of that change.

NOTE

A *stale link* is a hypertext link of some sort that points to a nonexistent page. Most Web servers produce a default error page when requests for erroneous or stale links are made.

Tips for Keeping Your Users' Interest

Okay, now you know your Intranet users are going to be using your Web pages because they're told to do so. Still, you want to do things to increase acceptance of your pages within your organization. In a sense, you are marketing your pages to your organization. If they are hard to use, uninteresting, or unusable, you may see your Intranet waste away from disuse.

Much of the information you post on your Intranet Web pages will be administrative; you'll have to think hard about how to make that material presentable. The tips discussed in this chapter should help. Beyond that, there are some things you can do that will personalize your pages to gain acceptance within your company.

Spotlight People and Organizations

You can prepare little reports on people or groups within your organization. These are similar to "up-close-and-personal" interviews that you find published in many company newsletters. You can include photographs and even recorded greetings from these individuals. If you want to highlight a certain group, you can discuss members of the group or even publish a group photograph. Change the link periodically and watch your users vie for the spotlight!

Social Calendars

Your organization might sponsor social events. Publish a listing of these events whether they involve Christmas parties, summer barbecues, or trips to local sports events. You also can think about posting links regarding events that are of local interest to employees within your company.

Publishing Cool Links

Keep a list of hotlinks handy that are relevant to your users' interests. You may want to keep links to Yahoo, Infoseek, Alta Vista, or some of the other popular search engines. You also can publish links to companies or organizations that have similar interests to your own.

Summary

There are two keys to keeping your site on the cutting edge: know your audience and keep browsing the Web. By knowing your audience, you know what to publish and how to publish it. For example, you may be developing Intranet forms and Web pages for use by your nontechnical administrative staff. You will need to design these pages differently than if you develop pages targeted for scientists and engineers. There will be varying levels of computer expertise in your organization, and you will need to customize your content to reflect the understanding of your specific Intranet users.

Second, by surfing the Web, you can get information about what's hot and what's not. Many times, I will see pages that will make me ask, "How did they do that?" Downloading the HTML source code usually answers that question. You can learn more about proper HTML style and design by looking at links to related pages than you can from using almost any other source.

Your Intranet users are more or less captive users. They'll have to use your site if you post administrative applications that they'll need to use. However, your site will gain more acceptance within your organization if you structure the content in a way that makes your pages easy to browse.

We're ready to talk about CGI scripting in the next chapter. We'll discuss some of the scripting environments available to you on the Macintosh including AppleScript, Frontier, and MacPerl. I've even included some simple examples. If you want to skip the next chapter, you can jump to the following chapters; however, CGI scripts will greatly enhance the services that you can offer your users, so I recommend that you read that chapter at some point.

- Chapter 8, "Databases and Document Searches," to learn about how to allow your Intranet users a means of accessing your databases and searches document archives.
- Chapter 9, "Beyond HTML," to learn about ways some techniques spruce up your Web site beyond just using conventional HTML and graphics. We'll discuss Java, RealAudio, and other cool topics.
- Appendix C, "Perfecting HTML," to learn about HTML editors as well as some new and advanced HTML techniques such as frames and server-push/client-pull techniques.

Links Related to This Chapter

World Wide Web Consortium	http://www.w3c.org
HTML Proposals, Specs, and Other Info	http://www.w3.org/hypertext/WWW/Mark-Up
Tips on Writing HTML Beginner's Guide to HTML	http://www.ncsa.uiuc.edu/demoweb/html-primer.html
Composing Good HTML	http://www.cs.cmu.edu/~tilt/cgh/
Guides to Writing HTML Documents	http://union.ncsa.uiuc.edu:80/HyperNews/get/www/html/guides.html
Netscape HTML 2.0 Extensions	http://home.netscape.com/assist/net_sites/html_extensions_3.html
Netscape HTML 3.0 Extensions	http://home.netscape.com/assist/net_sites/html_extensions_3.html
Microsoft HTML Extensions	http://www.microsoft.com/ie/author/html-spec/html_toc.htm

JPEG FAQ	http://www.cis.ohio-state.edu/hypertext/faq/usenet/jpeg-faq/top.html
Adobe Systems, Inc.	http://www.adobe.com
Usenet	comp.infosystems.www.authoring.html comp.infosystems.www.authoring.images

CHAPTER 7

Writing CGI Scripts

By now, you know enough to get your server up and running. You can create and publish HTML documents and display images. This is important, but your Intranet will require more advanced capabilities. Your pages need to do something. You know, search databases, compile HTML form data input, and even keep track of page accesses. As an Intranet administrator, your Web services need to be more specialized and more feature-oriented than what is seen out on the Internet.

It's time to talk about creating dynamic documents on your Intranet. One of the earliest means of creating documents on-the-fly is through the use of the Common Gateway Interface (CGI). Using CGI scripts, your server can interact with third-party applications that can execute document searches, query databases, or return a dynamically created HTML page. These types of services give a professional bearing to your Intranet.

This chapter discusses how CGI scripts can be implemented on your Macintosh Intranet Web server. Specifically, it covers the following topics:

- ☐ A brief introduction to the Common Gateway Interface
- ☐ A discussion of how you can implement CGI scripts using MacPerl, AppleScript, and Frontier
- ☐ A look at some Server Side Includes that are used to extend functionality to your pages without using CGI scripts.

The emphasis of this chapter will be on developing the kind of knowledge that you can use to customize your Intranet Web service.

The Common Gateway Interface

Typically, Web servers respond to requests from Web browsers in the form of HTML documents and images. The browser sends a URL to the server, and the server sends the file—whether it's an HTML document, GIF or JPEG graphic, audio file, or movie—to the browser via an HTTP connection. Sometimes, the browser sends a URL that does not point to a document, but instead points to an application. The server activates this application which then responds to the browser with the requisite information. This application is referred to as a CGI script. This section covers how this script interacts with the Web server and browser.

Basic Scripting Concepts

The process through which the Common Gateway Interface works is quite simple. The following steps detail the process through which output is returned to a form request.

1. The browser accumulates data from an HTML form and prepares it for transmission to the Web server.

2. The Web server extracts the CGI application name from the URL and activates the application.

3. The Web server transfers the information from the HTML form to the CGI application. The data is transferred into a format that is readable by the CGI script.

4. The CGI script processes the form data and prepares a response. This processing can include a database query, a numerical calculation, or an imagemap request. The response is usually in the form of an HTML document. However, the response is cleverly phrased by the CGI application to convince the Web browser that it originated from the server. In addition to just sending an HTML document in response,

CGI scripts can send mail, update a guestbook, or almost any task that you can accomplish through clever programming.

5. The CGI application passes the response to the server, which immediately redirects it to the Web client. The server does not process the response in any way.

This process is outlined in Figure 7.1. Note that the server merely passes information to the script. The script receives the data from the Web server through some mechanism unique to the language in which the script was developed. As long as this mechanism is in place, any programming language can be used to implement a CGI script.

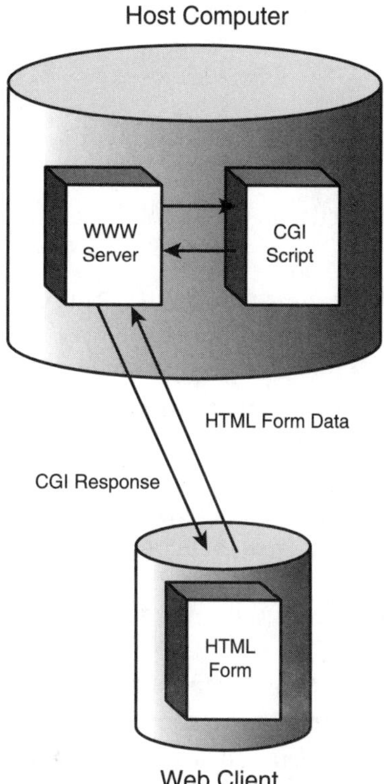

Figure. 7.1 *The Web browser transfers HTML form data to CGI scripts. These scripts process the data and return some form of result, usually another HTML page.*

How to Trick a Web Browser

Web browsers communicate with Web servers via the HTTP protocol. Not only does this protocol specify the physical packet structure of the protocol, but it also defines the manner in which the server and browser exchange information. For example, a Netscape Navigator client might send the following text to a Web server for a simple file request:

```
GET /test23.html HTTP/1.0
Accept: text/html
Accept: www/source
Accept: image/gif
Accept: image/jpeg
User-Agent: Mozilla/2.0 (Macintosh; I; PPC)

 ...a blank line...
```

NOTE

> See Chapter 4, "Macintosh HTTP Servers," for a more in-depth discussion on the MIME encoding protocol.

```
GET /test23.html HTTP/1.0
```

This message header informs the server that the browser is looking for the file text23.html and intends to use version 1.0 of the HTTP specification.

```
Accept: text/html
Accept: www/source
Accept: image/gif
Accept: image/jpeg
```

The browser then informs the server as to which file formats it can interpret. In the above message, this list is truncated from what browsers usually express, but the server is informed that the client can interpret several text and graphics MIME types.

```
User-Agent: Mozilla/2.0 (Macintosh; I; PPC)
```

The browser then informs the server as to its brand of client; in this example, the browser is defined as Netscape Navigator.

Finally, the browser passes a blank line to complete the request.

The server will respond with a message generally like the following:

```
HTTP/1.0 200 OK
Date: Thursday, 01-Feb-96 19:15:32 GMT
Server: MacHTTP
MIME-version: 1.0
Last-modified: Friday, 21-May-96 14:11:08 GMT
Content-type: text/html
Content-length: 7562
 ...a blank line...
<HTML><HEAD><TITLE>Article....
```

In this response, the server provides enough information to allow the browser to process the requested data. This response can be analyzed line by line.

```
HTTP/1.0 200 OK
```

The server denotes that it too is providing data using the HTTP v.1.0 protocol. Furthermore, it returns an HTTP code of 200 OK which tells the browser to relax and that the requested file was not only found, but is being returned in this message.

```
Date: Thursday, 01-Feb-96 19:15:32 GMT
Server: MacHTTP
```

The date and server type are described in the header. The server type is included because the browser may interpret certain features not described in other servers.

```
MIME-version: 1.0
```

The server tells the Web client which version of MIME encoding is being used, so that the browser can reprocess the data.

```
Last-modified: Friday, 21-May-96 14:11:08 GMT
Content-type: text/html
Content-length: 7562
```

The browser is also informed as to the MIME type of the data and the size of the file; this last datum is important because as it allows the browser to inform the user as to the progress of the data transfer. After inserting a blank line, the server returns the file data.

The server needs to be flexible enough to provide the file in a format that is accessible to the client. For example, the server would need to provide a GIF file if a browser, which could only process GIF files, requests a file that is offered in JPEG.

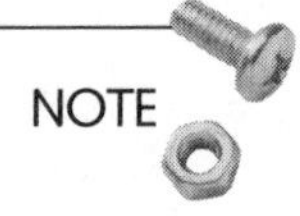

NOTE

The client and server header formats are defined in RFC 822. The Internet Engineering Task Force (IETF) maintains an archive of all active Request for Comment (RFC) documents at http://ds.internic.net/ds/dspg2intdoc.html.

As mentioned previously, the HTTP server doesn't process output from a CGI application; the response is merely funneled through the server back at the browser. The message, however, must be configured so as to conform to the HTTP message header specifications.

Using Forms to Talk to the CGI Script

By using an HTML form page, you can allow users to enter data that is processed by a CGI script. As discussed earlier in this book, users can enter text and specify options using forms developed with HTML. The types of data input options are as follows:

- Checkboxes
- Multiline text entry fields
- Popup selection menus
- Radio buttons

Figure 7.2 shows an example of an HTML form that you can use to transfer data to a CGI application. Note that this sample page contains text, checkboxes, and radio buttons. The HTML code for this page is shown following:

```
<HTML>
<HEAD>
<TITLE>
Forms Test
</TITLE>
</HEAD>
<BODY>
<FORM ACTION="http://hoohoo.ncsa.uiuc.edu/cgi-bin/
➥post-query" METHOD=POST>
A normal text field:
<TEXTAREA NAME="comments1"></TEXTAREA><p>
<HR>
<DL>Please indicate your favorite holiday:
<DD>
<INPUT TYPE="radio" NAME="holiday"
➥VALUE="Christmas">Christmas
<DD>
<INPUT TYPE="radio" NAME="holiday"
➥VALUE="Thanksgiving">Thanksgiving
<DD>
<INPUT TYPE="radio" NAME="holiday"
➥VALUE="Easter">Easter
<DD>
<INPUT TYPE="radio" NAME="holiday" VALUE="NYDay">New
➥Year's Day
</DL>
<DL>Please put a check next to the applications you
➥own:
<DD>
<INPUT TYPE="checkbox" NAME="msword" VALUE="No"
➥CHECKED>Microsoft Word
<DD>
<INPUT TYPE="checkbox" NAME="photoshop"
➥VALUE="No">Adobe Photoshop
<DD>
<INPUT TYPE="checkbox" NAME="netscape"
➥VALUE="No">Netscape
<DD>
<INPUT TYPE="checkbox" NAME="excel"
➥VALUE="No">Microsoft Excel
</DL>
<INPUT TYPE="submit" VALUE="Submit This Form">
</FORM>
</BODY>
</HTML>
```

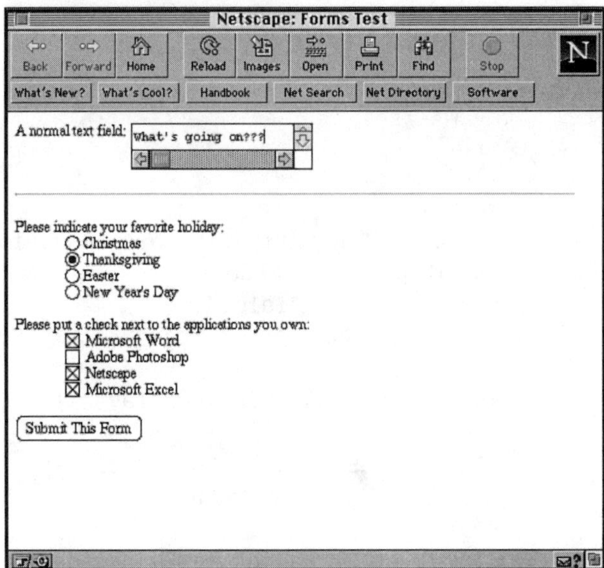

Figure 7.2 *There are several types of HTML form fields available to retrieve information from Web users.*

Note that all of the form elements in the preceding code use the NAME attribute. The idea is that the user enters text in a field or checks a radio button; this data is assigned a variable corresponding to the value of the NAME attribute. The CGI script uses these data by referencing the corresponding variable name. For example, the response from a post-query script to the preceding example is shown in Figure 7.3.

Links to HTML Forms Tutorials

Intro to CGI Scripts and HTML Forms	http://kuhttp.cc.ukans.edu/info/forms/forms-intro.html
NCSA Forms Tutorial	http://kuhttp.cc.ukans.edu/info/forms/forms-intro.html
Carlos' Form Tutorial	http://robot0.ge.uiuc.edu/~carlosp/cs317/cft.html

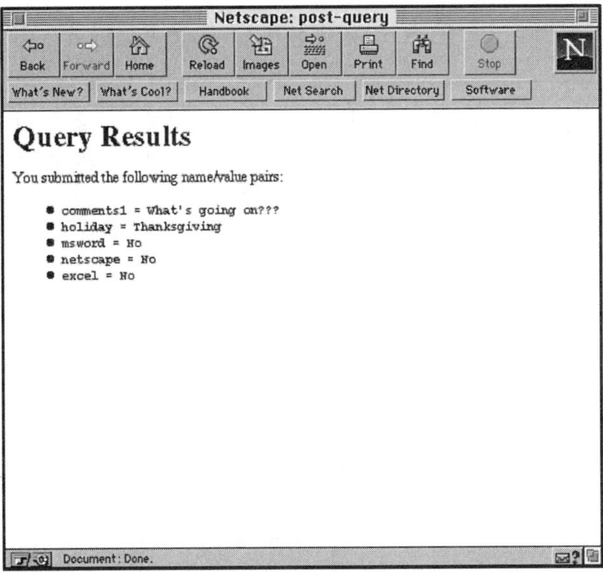

Figure 7.3 *A post-query script is useful for displaying the values of an HTML form.*

NOTE

A post-query script is a generic term for any script that merely echoes back the results of an HTML form submission. It is useful to have such a script on your server to aid in CGI script debugging. The NCSA httpd distribution for Unix systems contains a post-query CGI that you can use. Check out http://hoohoo.ncsa.uiuc.edu/cgi-bin/post-query.

Two alternative methods of transferring form data to a CGI script are POST and GET. These are the possible values of the METHOD attribute in the opening <FORM> tag. The GET method of transferring data is somewhat antiquated and dates back to the old Gopher days. You are limited to passing no more than 4 KB of data back to the server using GET. POST, however, allows transfer of up to 24 KB of data. This results from the fact that a request made through the GET method concatenates all the HTML form variables into a single string; this string is appended to the URL in the HTTP message that identifies the CGI script. Requests made through the POST method combine all the form parameters into an internal variable that is passed to the script.

The Macintosh CGI Environment

CGI scripts on your Macintosh Web server will interact with the servers we talked about in Chapter 4. In the section, "Macintosh CGI Scripting Languages," we'll talk about the various options you have for developing CGI applications to work with your HTTP server. Before discussing your scripting options, let's talk about how CGI works on the Mac.

Apple Events

CGI scripts work differently on various operating systems. For example, on the Unix operating system, servers transfer data using standard input and Unix environment variables, depending on whether or not the transfer method is POST or GET. Similarly, a Windows HTTP server uses content files to transfer information to the CGI script. Under the MacOS, HTTP servers and CGI scripts transfer data using Apple events.

Apple events are a feature of the MacOS that allows communication of data between applications. Unseen by the user, Apple events flit back and forth carrying various pieces of information between applications. For example, Web browsers use Apple events to launch helper applications to view particular files; through Apple events, a browser starts the viewing application and transmits the newly downloaded file for interpretation.

At first, Apple events received very little attention among the Macintosh development community. The Finder supported only the most fundamental Apple events; even so, System 7.0 used these operations to open and close applications and print documents. With later versions of the MacOS, more Apple events were defined, thereby allowing a wider variety of information to pass between applications.

Macintosh HTTP servers utilize Apple events to communicate HTML form data to the CGI scripts. The scripts need to be written in languages that can accept Apple events. The output of these scripts usually consists of HTML which is sent back down to the browser.

Script Processing

In the early days of MacHTTP, CGI scripts could only be executed synchronously; in these instances, all server activities are suspended until the CGI application is completed. An asynchronous CGI script is executed asynchronously, meaning that the script shares server resources with other processes. The script is alternatively suspended and executed depending on the needs of other processes. Synchronous CGI scripts are denoted by the .cgi suffix; asynchronous CGI scripts are labeled with the .acgi suffix. Macintosh Web servers, as well as other servers, process CGI applications differently based on these suffixes.

A script needs to be developed using a multithreaded or finite-state machine architecture in order to take full advantage of asynchronous script handling. For the Mac, this means the script is developed using the Thread Manager libraries. The Thread Manager is a system extension that comes with the MacOS as of System 7.5. Multithreaded computing is the next step below true multitasking on the computer processing hierarchy. With true multitasking, processes are computed simultaneously with the operating system performing the bookkeeping regarding process status. In the multithreaded MacOS, the applications have to keep track of which process reliquishes and assumes control. The latter arrangment is not as efficient as true multitasking.

CGI Variables

Macintosh HTTP servers rely on an Apple event to not only start up the CGI application, but to pass the HTML form data as well. This Apple event is composed of two parts: the class WWW and the actual event sdoc. These parts must be separated with the capital omega character, Ω.

The WWWΩsdoc Apple event is sent by the HTTP server. Included in this event is the information obtained from the HTML form. Your CGI needs to do the following:

- ☐ Respond to launch call from server.
- ☐ Wait until server sends an Apple event containing data from Web browser.

- ☐ Retrieve data from Apple event and parse the data accordingly.
- ☐ Process the data and formulate an appropriate response such as a properly formatted HTML document or graphic image.
- ☐ Quit once all processing has been completed.

We discussed earlier how the sdoc Apple event is used by the Macintosh WWW server to transmit information from the Web browser to the CGI script. This Apple event contains information that is useful for CGI script processing. A summary of the CGI variables sent to the server is shown in Table 7.1.

Table 7.1 *CGI Variable Description*

Variable	Description
path_args	The data after the $ and before a ? in a URL
http_search _args	Search arguments, which follow the ? in a URL such as in an <ISINDEX> tag or imagemap request
post_args	The data typed into the form
method	The method used to convey the information to the server, typically GET or POST
user_agent	The type and version of Web browser initiating the request
client_address	The IP address used by the Web browser
server_name	The IP address of the Web server
server_port	The IP listening port used by the server (usually 80)
username	The validated user of the Web browser
password	The validated user's password
script_name	The full path name of the CGI script
referrer	The URL of the page containing the script
content_type	The MIME content type of post_args
full_request	The full WWW client request as seen by the CGI script

In addition to the standard variables listed here, the CGI script works with variables obtained from HTML form fields and imagemap requests.

Macintosh CGI Scripting Languages

Several scripting language options are at your disposal, some of which are free or included with your operating system. These languages perform the same function: they retrieve form variables from the HTTP server, process the data, and return a response to the requesting browser. The ease of this process varies between languages. There exists, for each of these scripting languages, a wealth of CGI script archives that perform a variety of common tasks. These languages include:

- AppleScript
- UserLand's UserTalk
- MacPerl
- InterCon's InterXMTL
- HyperCard
- C/C++

In the following sections, we'll discuss the merits and disadvantages of these various scripting languages. None of the sections below are intended to be a comprehensive guide to the respective languages. For a more in-depth treatment of these languages, you should check out the computer section of your local bookstore.

You'll need the following applications available to write and test your CGI scripts:

- An HTTP server application such as MacHTTP, WebSTAR, or InterServer Publisher.

- An editor to use to formulate your CGI script. Most scripting languages come with a native editor. For example, AppleScript comes with the Script Editor. Think C++ comes with a native editor as well. Use of these editors expedites script compilation and debugging; however, you can use a common editor such as BBEdit to develop scripts in any of these languages.
- An HTML editor. I recommend either Adobe PageMill or BBEdit 3.5 (or later) with the BBEdit HTML Extensions.
- A Web browser such as Microsoft Internet Explorer or Netscape Navigator.

It's advisable to edit your scripts and HTML on a local Mac, run your Web server on a remote Mac, and use an FTP application such as Anarchie or Fetch to transfer your scripts to a CGI folder. In this way, you'll be testing your scripts as many others will be using them.

I also recommend that you organize your Web server folder into separate folders for HTML documents and CGI scripts. I keep a folder called Test in my MacHTTP folder, in which I install my test scripts. Similarly, I store CGI scripts in a folder entitled CGI.

AppleScript

AppleScript is the MacOS system-level scripting language; it binds the operating system with AppleScript-aware applications to automate and customize operations within the MacOS. For example, you can create an AppleScript that can do some of the following example tasks:

- Perform a complicated Finder function, such as change the folder view to View by Name
- Open a Web or FTP client to a particular URL
- Copy cells from a table from a Microsoft Excel spreadsheet and paste them into a Microsoft Word document, all without having to open the applications directly

With the advent of System 7.5, AppleScript became more accessible to Mac users for two reasons. First, and perhaps most importantly, AppleScript and the associated Script Editor were bundled freely with the operating system. The Script Editor is used to edit and construct AppleScript applications. Secondly, the Finder became scriptable and recordable under AppleScript. This latest feature enables you to construct AppleScript applications simply by telling the Script Editor to record your actions. This does not have great value with regards to CGI scripting, but it's a potent means of creating organizational tools for your desktop environment.

Using the Script Editor

Along with the AppleScript extension, which resides in the Extensions folder, the AppleScript package comes with a utility known as the Script Editor. This utility is a rudimentary text editor that allows you to create and compile AppleScript applications. Although you could create scripts using a conventional editor such as SimpleText or BBEdit, you'll need the Script Editor to check your syntax and actually create AppleScript applications.

NOTE

Commercial alternatives to Apple's Script Editor are available. Full Moon Software's ScriptWizard (http://www.fullmoon.com/fmsdl/products/fms_scriptwiz.html), Main Event's Scripter (http://www.yy.net/bis/mainevent/scripter.html), and Late Night Software's Script Debugger (http://dev.info.apple.com/solguide/script.html) are some examples of commercial AppleScript editors that provide more functionality than Apple's Script Editor.

Let's get started with AppleScript. Double-click on the Script Editor application and you should see a window similar to that in Figure 7.4. Note that there are two windows within the Editor. The top window is the Description window which is used as you might imagine. You can enter comments about the script, your name, your email, and your excuses why it may not work. The lower window is the Scripting window to enter your AppleScript commands.

NOTE

Don't worry, it's not just you. The default Screen Editor window is much too small to do any real work. You need to resize the window to a normal size to write your scripts. When you open a script with the Script Editor, the window will size to fit the script. You can set the default window size by clicking on the Script Editor File menu and dragging down to Set Default Window Size.

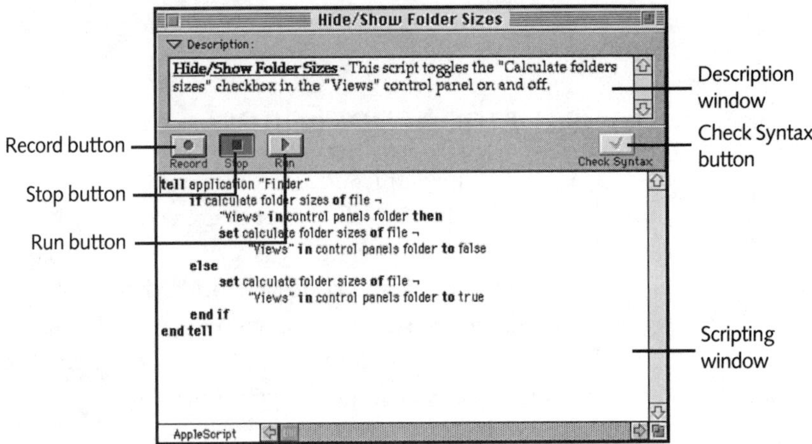

Figure 7.4 *Within the AppleScript Editor window, you can record, run, and check the syntax of your scripts.*

Creating Scripts

Four buttons are located between the two windows: Record, Stop, Run, and Check Syntax. These buttons are designed to aid you in composing and executing scripts. Using the Record button, you can create scripts, much as you can create macros with QuicKeys or other macro packages. Simply clicking the Record button and then running scriptable applications and Finder operations, you can create a rudimentary script. You can watch the Script Editor fill up with commands as you perform operations. Clicking on the Stop button ends the script generation.

Clicking on the Run button executes the script you have just recorded. You'll see your actions mimicked by the script with application windows opening and closing. You probably won't encounter any errors if you run a recently recorded script; if you do encounter errors, the Script Editor will return an appropriate message.

You also can compose a script from scratch using AppleScript syntax, much as you would with any programming language. The Script Editor offers some rudimentary editing functions. You can use the Check Syntax button to validate your script. Furthermore, the script formatting will change from a roman font to a display similar to that shown in Figure 7.4, where various AppleScript reserve words appear in bold type and the looping constructs are indented accordingly.

Saving Scripts for Reuse

To reuse the script over a long period of time, you'll eventually have to save the script to disk. You have several options with which you can save your files. They include straight text files, compiled scripts, and applications. Each brand of script is identified by an icon (see Table 7.2).

Table 7.2 *Script Editor Saving Options*

Type	Description
Script Text	Script can be edited with any text editor. Useful for constructing script.
Compiled Script	Script is executable through the Script Editor. Can still be edited.
Application	Script can be run without the Script Editor. Cannot be opened with text editor.

Text-Only Scripts

The text-only script is usually the first stage of script construction. In this step, you will most likely be constructing and modifying your script, so you'll want to save it in an accessible format. You cannot run the script at this point without checking the script syntax. Text-only scripts can be opened with other text editors.

NOTE

When you save a script, the Script Editor will want to compile it for you. For large uncomplicated scripts, you may not want to, or not be able to, compile when you save it. Holding the Shift key down when you're saving the document suppresses compilation.

Compiled Scripts

If your AppleScript syntax is correct, you can save your script as a compiled script. This enables you to edit and run the script within the Script Editor.

Applications

If you want to run your script without the inconvenience of opening the Script Editor, you can save it as an application. Your script then acts like any other Macintosh application; double-clicking on it executes your AppleScript commands; furthermore, you can create aliases of AppleScript applications and install them in your Apple Menu Items folder. Many of the tasks performed in System 7.5's Speakable Items folder are compiled AppleScript applications. AppleScript applications require less space than normal scripts, because much of the work is performed by the system software.

NOTE

One useful feature of the Script Editor enables you to save your application so that it will display the contents of the Description window in a dialog box. The user then has the option of quitting or running the application after reading the script description.

Other Script Saving Options

You may have reason to store your script in a format that will prevent other users from editing your script. For this reason, you may want to save your script using the Save As Run-Only option under the File menu. A copy of your script will be saved as a run-only compiled script or application.

If you want to save your script as a Run-Only application, you'll need to have compiled it correctly. You'll be presented with two additional saving options. Clicking on the Stay Open checkbox causes the application to stay open until it is closed by the user (if a splash screen was presented) or until it is closed by an Apple event. Clicking on the Never Show Startup Screen checkbox prevents the splash page from appearing.

NOTE 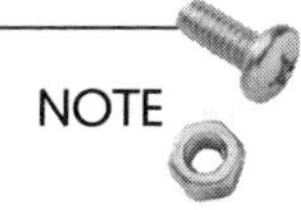

When you save the file as a run-only application or compiled script, you will no longer be able to edit the script, so be sure to save a backup copy.

Developing CGI Scripts with AppleScript

As with all languages discussed in this chapter, I'm going to skimp on describing AppleScript language and syntax. You will be better served by referring to several of the AppleScript books out on the market. Try to look at the examples in this section and understand the structure of the script. As you'll soon find out, CGI scripts have the same basic structure, even if they're constructed in different languages. When constructing your own AppleScript CGI scripts, refer to the examples shown here and extend them with Apple-Script knowledge gleaned from other sources.

You will need to save your CGI scripts using the Run-Only option. Furthermore, you will need to activate both of the checkboxes. AppleScript CGI scripts need to stay open for a period of time after activation; allowing the splash screen to activate would interfere with communication between the Web server and the script.

Extending AppleScript through OSAXen

AppleScript maintains a very limited vocabulary. This is by design; the language itself maintains a simple structure with many of the sophisticated tasks performed by the scripting additions. Scripting additions are very special types of system extensions. They can be found in the Scripting Additions folder in your Extensions folder. These tools in effect are external software libraries that extend the AppleScript vocabulary. Such a library is often referred to as an OSAX (Open Scripting Architecture Extensions), or in the plural form OSAXen.

NOTE

> Apple set up a system to allow future scripting of the operating system using Apple events. This system is known as the Open Scripting Architecture (OSA). The Open part of OSA refers to the fact that internal mechanisms are in place to be used by any third-party scripting environment, such as UserLand's Frontier.

OSAXen are often compiled in a language such as C or Pascal, rather than AppleScript itself. As a result, AppleScript performance is enhanced by using OSAX. The scripts described in this section will use OSAXen designed to aid in CGI processing. AppleScript itself would be able to handle these tasks, but the use of OSAX commands greatly speeds up the processing; this is desirable for all applications, but especially CGI processing.

NOTE

> OSAXen exist in scripting environments other than AppleScript. HyperTalk, for example, uses external commands (XCMDs), and external functions (XFCNs) which are technically defined as OSAXen. You can tell whether a file is an OSAX by peeking at its file type with a resource editor like ResEdit or File Buddy. If it's an OSAX, its file type will be `osax`.

CD-ROM

You will need a variety of scripting additions to enhance the performance of your CGI processing. Some of these tools are useful for general scripting purposes. The most useful OSAX available for AppleScript CGI usage is the Parse CGI OSAX from Clearway Technologies; this software is available on this book's CD-ROM. This library allows you to decode, parse, and access the HTML form information passed to the CGI application from the Web server. It replaces some of the older OSAXen. The ScriptWeb (http://www.scriptweb.com) archive maintains many OSAXen for use in CGI scripting as well as general AppleScript use.

NOTE

Keep in mind that you can avoid using OSAX if you want. OSAX functions can almost always be duplicated using AppleScript. However, OSAXen are usually constructed using compiled C or Pascal code, and therefore offer subroutines that run many times faster than AppleScript equivalents.

Sample AppleScript CGI Script

In this section, we'll look at a simple, but comprehensive AppleScript CGI script. We'll dissect the script and look at how the script interacts with the browser and processes the data.

Let's take a look at a sample HTML forms page that queries and accepts data from the user.

```
<FORM METHOD=POST ACTION="http://cgi-test/cgi/
➥test_as.cgi">

Enter your first name here:
<INPUT NAME="first_name" SIZE=35>
</TEXTAREA><P>

Select the movie you like best
<SELECT NAME="movie" SIZE=5>
<OPTION> Apollo 13
<OPTION> Star Wars
<OPTION> Howard's End
<OPTION> Taxi Driver
<OPTION> Pulp Fiction
</SELECT><P>

<DL>
<DT>How old are you?
<DD><INPUT TYPE="radio" NAME="age"
➥VALUE="young">Younger than 24
<DD><INPUT TYPE="radio" NAME="age" VALUE="middle">24-35
```

```
<DD><INPUT TYPE="radio" NAME="age" VALUE="old">Older
➥than 35
</DL>

Press here to submit form
<INPUT TYPE="submit" VALUE="Submit Form">
</FORM>
```

This simple example is shown in a Netscape Navigator browser window (see Figure 7.5). In this figure, we see that the HTML page uses a variety of form types to convey data to the CGI script. As with AppleScript and the other languages discussed here, instruction on programming with HTML forms is best left to the many other books devoted to this topic.

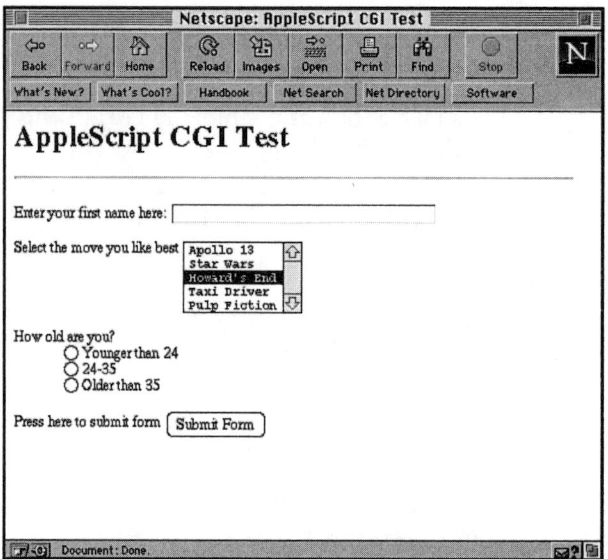

Figure 7.5 *The data from this HTML form example will be passed to the AppleScript CGI example.*

Now, let's develop a CGI script to process the data you may enter from the CGI page. The example script is shown here:

```
-- Set up global variables
global crlf
global http_10_header
global datestamp
```

```
-- define a variable equal to a carriage return and a
➥line feed
set crlf to (ASCII character 13) & (ASCII character 10)

-- set the current date to a variable
set datestamp to current date

-- set up number of seconds that script will remain
➥idle before terminating
set idletime to 15

-- define a standard HTTP 1.0 header
set http_10_header to "HTTP/1.0 200 OK" & crlf & ¬
    "Server: MacHTTP" & crlf & ¬
    "MIME-Version: 1.0" & crlf & ¬
    "Content-type: text/html" & crlf & crlf

-- This is the handler that processes Apple events sent
➥from MacHTTP.
-- WWWΩsdoc is the event sent with GET or POST methods.
-- process Apple event sent by the WWW server
on «event WWWΩsdoc» path_args given «class
➥post»:post_args,«class addr»:client_address
    set formdata to parse CGI arguments post_args
    set full_name to CGI field "first_name" from
➥formdata
    set rock to CGI field "movie" from formdata
    set age to CGI field "age" from formdata
    set return_page to http_10_header & ¬
          "<HTML><HEAD><TITLE>AppleScript CGI Test
➥Results</TITLE></HEAD>" & ¬
          "<BODY><H1>AppleScript CGI Test Results</
➥H1>" & return & ¬
          "<H2>Parse CGI Test</H2>" & return & ¬
          "<HR>" & return
    -- list form variables
    set return_page to return_page & ¬
          "You are coming from the IP address: " &
➥client_address & "<P>" & return & ¬
          "Your first name is " & return & first_name
➥& "<P>" & return & ¬
```

```
            "Your favorite movie is " & movie & "<P>" &
➥return & ¬
            "You consider yourself to be of the " & age
➥& " age group" & "<P>" & return & ¬
            "</BODY></HTML>"

    return return_page
end «event WWW¬sdoc»
-- Following handlers quit applications if idle after
➥"idletime" seconds
on idle
    if (current date) > (datestamp + idletime) then
            quit
    end if
    return 5
end idle

on quit
    continue quit
end quit
```

Let's go over the example section by section.

Variable Initialization

```
-- Set up global variables
global crlf
global http_10_header
global datestamp

-- define a variable equal to a carriage return and a
➥line feed
set crlf to (ASCII character 13) & (ASCII character 10)

-- set the current date to a variable
set datestamp to current date
-- set up number of seconds that script will remain
➥idle before terminating
set idletime to 15
```

At the start of the script, we need to define the variables used in the script. The global statements are used to define the script global variables. The variables function much as global variables do in more sophisticated programming languages; global variables are available inside subroutines that might exist within the AppleScript.

The variable crlf is set to the ASCII equivalent of a combined character return and line feed. This variable is useful in constructing the HTTP 1.0 header. The variable datestamp is also set to the current date, as determined by the server. The script is designed to quit after a certain amount of time; this predetermined time is set in the idletime variable.

Setting Up the HTTP 1.0 Header

```
-- define a standard HTTP 1.0 header
set http_10_header to "HTTP/1.0 200 OK" & crlf & ¬
        "Server: MacHTTP" & crlf & ¬
        "MIME-Version: 1.0" & crlf & ¬
        "Content-type: text/html" & crlf & crlf
```

In this part of the script, we're beginning to formulate a response to server to convey back to the browser. To do this, we need to construct an HTTP 1.0 header. This header tells the Web browser several things about the content of the message.

We begin by constructing the HTTP 1.0 header variable entitled http_10_header. This variable is constructed using a concatenation of text strings, carriage return/line feeds, and AppleScript continuation symbols. The line continuation symbol, obtained by pressing Option-L, allows you to construct a variable over several lines. In this variable, we are tricking the browser into thinking it's receiving a message from the Web server. Therefore, we need to construct the message header as a server would.

This is accomplished by returning the HTTP code of 200, which tells the browser that its request was received and a completed response is on its way back. The next line tells the browser that the server is MacHTTP; you'll have to substitute the name of whichever browser you end up using. After telling the browser that content is being sent using version 1.0 of the MIME encoding protocol, we tell the browser that the content is of MIME type text, subtype html. The browser then knows to process the response as an HTML file.

Defining the Apple Event Handler

One of the more complicated AppleScript constructs is the handler. At the risk of over-simplifying the description of handlers, they can be described as subroutines that get executed when a certain event takes place. We'll use a handler to receive and interpret the WWW-Ωsdoc event.

```
on «event WWWΩsdoc» path_args given «class
➥post»:post_args,¬
«class addr»:client_address
...
end «event WWW¬sdoc»
```

The « and » characters are obtained by using the Option-\ and Option-Shift-\ combinations. In this handler, the post_args and client_address variables are obtained from the WWWΩsdoc Apple event. The variables from the HTML form are contained in the post_args variable and need to be extracted later in the script.

Processing the Form Data

```
set formdata to parse CGI arguments post_args
set full_name to CGI field "first_name" from
➥formdata
set rock to CGI field "movie" from formdata
set age to CGI field "age" from formdata
```

The statements above extract data from the post_args variable using the parse CGI arguments command from the Parse CGI OSAX previously described. This command is intrinsic to the OSAX and is used to read the content from post_args and assign the content to AppleScript variables.

NOTE

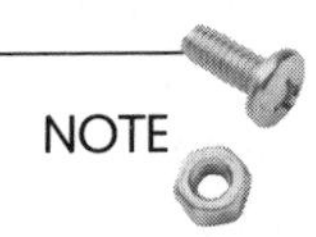

> The Parse CGI OSAX is described in the previous section, "Extending AppleScript through OSAXen." The Parse CGI OSAX home page is given in the list of links at the end of this chapter.

```
set return_page to http_10_header & ¬
        "<HTML><HEAD><TITLE>Test 4</TITLE></HEAD>" & ¬
        "<BODY><H1>Test 4</H1>" & return & ¬
        "<H2>Parse CGI Test</H2>" & return & ¬
        "<HR>" & return
```

In the statements preceding, we are continuing to construct the CGI response. The entire response will be contained in the variable return_page; return_page consists of the text string http_10_header and a series of additional strings concatenated to one another. These strings are added to one another using the ampersand symbol. Note that the return_page string contains HTML commands along with the return variable we defined at the beginning of the script. These HTML commands are processed by the browser and displayed on the screen as if they came from HTML files.

```
set return_page to return_page & ¬
        "You are coming from the IP address: " &
➥client_address & "<P>" & return & ¬
        "Your first name is " & return & first_name &
➥"<P>" & return & ¬
        "Your favorite movie is " & movie & "<P>" &
➥return & ¬
        "You consider yourself to be of the " & age & "
➥age group" & "<P>" & return & ¬
        "</BODY></HTML>"
```

In the statements above, we include the form data and the Web Browser's IP address in the CGI response. Remember that the client_address CGI variable is sent by most browsers to the server. This variable is included in the Web server's Apple event transmission to the CGI script.

Overriding the Stay Open Option

By checking the Stay Open box, your AppleScript CGI application will stay open indefinitely. As mentioned earlier, your script needs to be active for a period of time to allow your Web server enough time to transfer the browser request. However, you may not want to have the application open indefinitely. If you are running many CGI scripts simultaneously, you can easily consume your server resources. For this reason, you may want to close down these scripts soon after they are accessed. The following statements of the sample script perform this very function.

```
-- Following handlers quit applications if idle after
➥"idletime" seconds
on idle
      if (current date) > (datestamp + idletime) then
          quit
      end if
      return 5
end idle

on quit
      continue quit
end quit
```

The variable datestamp is set at the beginning of the program's execution. The variable idletime was also set at that time; this variable is defined to be the amount of time (in seconds) that the program will stay active after launch. When the script is idle for idletime seconds, the handlers in the above code cause the script to self-terminate. If the application is not idle and is instead processing an Apple event, the idle handler returns a value of 5, meaning that the server quit handler will be queried in 5 seconds.

This quit handler enables you to insert some extra AppleScript commands before shutting down the script. You could perform such tasks as logging the CGI script access or writing some other type of data to a file.

You'll want to set idletime high enough to keep the application open for Apple event requests. Keep in mind that any CGI request received while the application is quitting is lost. When this happens, the user will have to resubmit the browser request with an annoying loss of a few seconds. You don't want the application to be opening and closing every few seconds if it's a popular script, such as a search script. For this reason, you'll have to adjust idletime accordingly.

The Results

Given the form setup in Figure 7.5, this very simple CGI script returns the result shown in Figure 7.6.

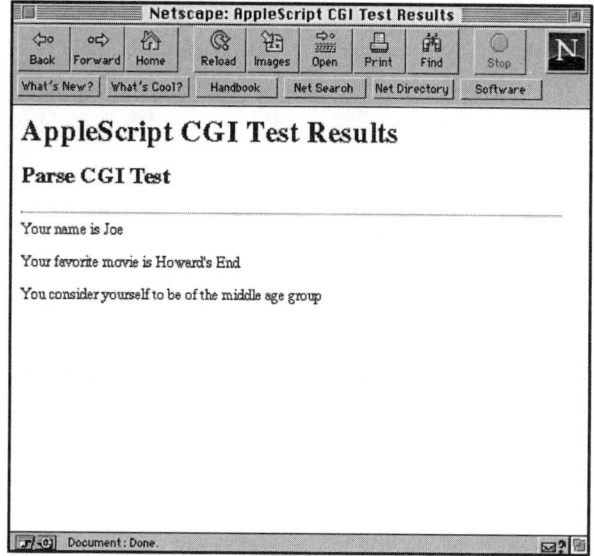

Figure 7.6 *Is it or isn't it? This Web page is not really a file containing HTML, but is actually HTML returned from a CGI script.*

Ideas for AppleScript CGI Scripts

The advantage of using AppleScript is that you have access to inter-application communications. The Apple event handler in AppleScript works cleanly with other Macintosh applications. Therefore, you can include information processed by these other applications within your CGI scripts.

Interfacing with FileMaker Pro

Regardless of the operating system, one chief application of Web servers on all platforms is the interaction with external databases via the World Wide Web. One of the prominent database applications on the make is Claris' FileMaker Pro. The ROFM CGI (formerly FMPro CGI (http://rowen.astro.washington.edu/) was developed for the purpose of allowing you to edit, add, and delete records in a FileMaker Pro database.

More information on database searches via the Web is available in Chapter 8, "Databases and Document Searches."

Other Applications

Again, the opportunities for interactions with your AppleScript CGI scripts is limited by your imagination. In addition to general CGI processing, you can program your scripts to extract actual words out of Microsoft Word documents and enter them in Microsoft Excel spreadsheets. AppleScript's native handling of Apple events enables you to interact with MacOS applications nearly seamlessly.

Frontier

UserLand Frontier is the first comprehensive scripting system developed for the Macintosh. Frontier is actually the environment in which you develop scripts. The scripting language itself is known as UserTalk. Frontier was originally offered as a commercial product; soon after Apple's decision to bundle AppleScript and the Script Editor with System 7.5, Frontier became freeware.

Frontier has several advantages over AppleScript. Frontier is PowerPC-native, meaning that Frontier applications run much faster on Power Macs. AppleScript applications run in emulation mode on the Power Mac and therefore cannot take full advantage of the PowerPC architecture. Furthermore, Frontier is multithreaded; this means you need the Thread Manager extension installed in your Extensions folder. Both of these features have direct relevance to CGI scripting.

NOTE

Pre-system 7.5 users can get a copy of the Thread Manager at ftp://ftp.support.apple.com.

In this section, we'll take a brief look at the Frontier scripting environment. After this, we will discuss Frontier's utility as a CGI scripting environment.

Introduction to Frontier

UserLand's Frontier is actually a scripting environment of which UserTalk is the scripting language. However, it is difficult to disassociate the two. Whereas you could develop AppleScript without the Script Editor, UserTalk is designed specifically to work within Frontier's hierarchical structure. We will discuss the structure of Frontier, but we'll give only a brief tutorial on the UserTalk language. You are referred to the DocServer database distributed with the Frontier application.

CD-ROM

Installing and Opening Frontier

Frontier is available on this book's CD-ROM. There is a PowerPC-native and PowerPC non-native version. Select the version compatible with your Mac and move the folder to a suitable location on your computer.

Double-click on the Frontier application. You should see a small menu bar appear, as shown in Figure 7.7. This menu bar is the starting point for developing scripts in Frontier. Click on the flag to toggle the visibility of four buttons used to aid in your script writing. Clicking on the Menu Bar button enables you to adjust the items in Frontier's menus. Clicking on the Object DB button opens up the Frontier object database. This database is an integral part of the Frontier application and will be discussed later in this section. The Quick Script button enables you to generate a short script for debugging or diagnostic purposes. Clicking on the Tech Support returns a menu detailing your technical support options.

Figure 7.7 *Frontier's Main window is the starting place for your script development.*

Quick Scripts

To get a feel for the syntax, let's try running a very quick script. Click on the Quick Script button. The Quick Script window will appear. In this window, type the following:

```
msg("Intranets are big!!")
```

and then click the Run button. Now look in the area of the Main window above the buttons. As shown in Figure 7.8, you will see the phrase "Intranets are big!!" In contrast, type the phrase:

```
dialog("Intranets are big!!")
```

and click the Run button. You will see a dialog box pop up with the phrase "Intranets are big!!" in the main part of the window. Click OK, and the window disappears.

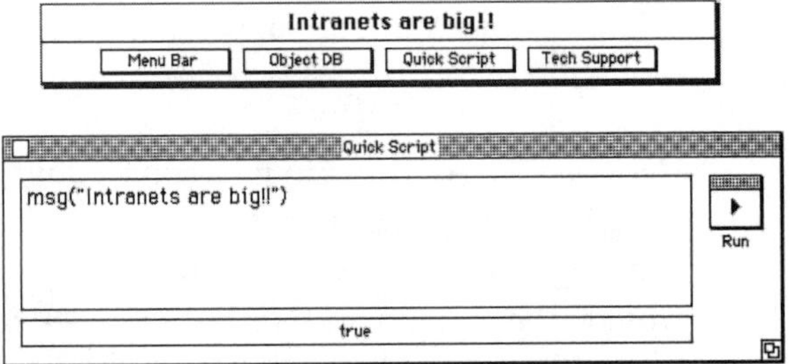

Figure 7.8 *The Quick Script window enables you to write short scripts with outputs appearing in the Main window. These scripts are useful for printing diagnostic messages.*

The Object Database

In order to write more complicated scripts, we need to discuss the Frontier Object Database that is the foundation of the Frontier scripting environment. Double-click on the Object DB button on the Frontier Main window. A table similar to that shown in Figure 7.9 will appear. This table is Frontier's Object Database; the actual file in which the database is stored is known as Frontier.root and is usually located in the same folder as the Frontier application. This file, along with the application itself, contains everything you need to run Frontier. All your scripts and variable definitions will be stored in this file.

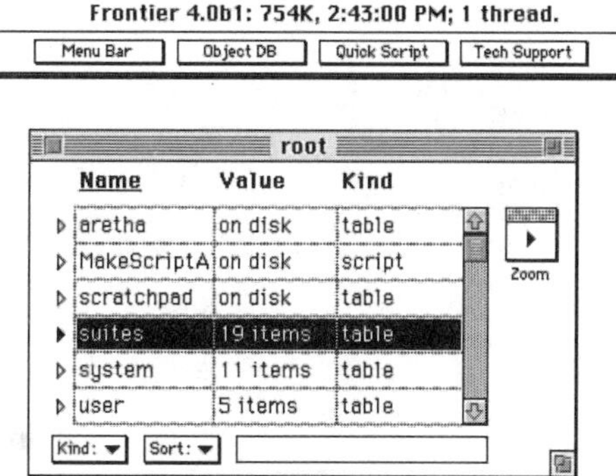

Figure 7.9 *Many types of Frontier objects are stored in the Object Database.*

The Object Database is a hierarchical table of variables. These variables can consist of a variety of objects; the major Frontier object types are shown in Table 7.3. A variables object type is listed in the column under the Kind heading. Table contains scripts, variables, outlines, menubars, and other objects associated with a certain function. Note that tables can even contain other tables. You can have up to 25 levels of objects, but for the sake of good organization it's better not to go use more than 8–10 levels.

Table 7.3 *Description of Frontier Objects*

Object	Description
table	Table containing other objects
boolean	Boolean value (True, False, 1, 0)
character	ASCII character
number	Integer
floating-point number	Double-precision number
date	String containing date and time
direction	Set of directions useful for navigational applications
string	String of text
word processing text	Document in word processing window
picture	PICT file
outline	Frontier outline
script	UserTalk script
menu bar	Menu
binary	Binary data representation

The Object Database enables you to group objects according to their function. For example, the table system.extensions.trigCmd can be found by going to the Object Database and double-clicking on the system table. This brings up a table of objects inside the system table. Double-click on the extensions table and then double-click on the trigCmd table. The trigCmd table contains a series of UserTalk scripts, as shown in Figure 7.10. Double-clicking on one of the scripts in this table brings up the actual UserTalk code to perform a sine, cosine, or some other trigonometric calculation. If the various trig scripts had required certain variables, integer or floating-point numbers could have been stored in tables inside the system.extensions.trigCmd table and accessed by the scripts.

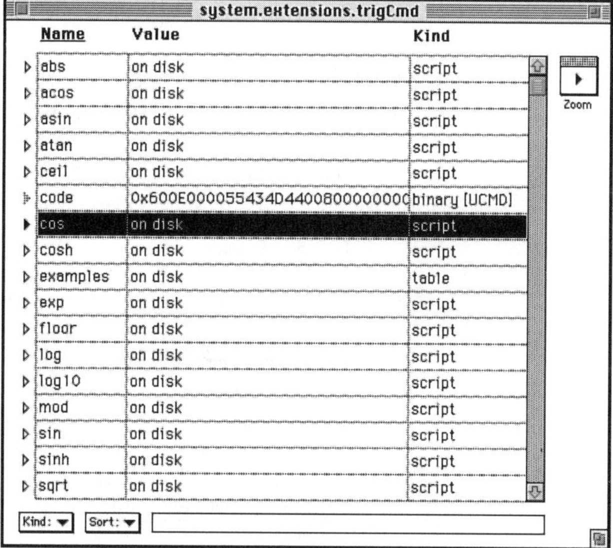

Figure 7.10 *The system.extensions.trigCmd table contains a series of scripts, which can be used by other UserTalk scripts or even external applications.*

Running a Simple Script

Before we discuss CGI scripting with Frontier, we need to look at some simple script examples. You can use Frontier's hierarchical structure to develop scripting applications.

1. Open the Object Database.
2. If there is not already a table entitled scratchpad, create one. You can do this by clicking on the Table menu and selecting Create Sub-Table.
3. You will be queried for the name of the new table, so enter scratchpad.
4. Once inside scratchpad, go back up to the Table menu and create another table called color_test.
5. The names of the variable in this example are arbitrary but must match the names used in the script.

6. Once inside the new table, create a table called colors.

7. Using the New Special command under Table, create a series of strings. Label them, as shown in Figure 7.11.

8. Go back to the color_test table and create a new script. This is done by clicking on New Script under the Table menu and naming the script.

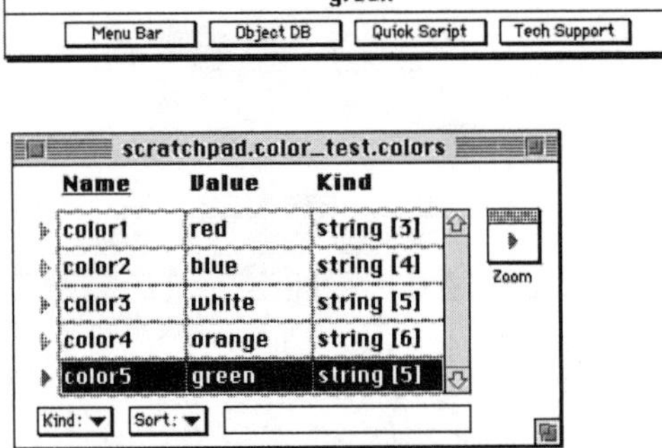

Figure 7.11 *This table contains a series of text strings.*

9. The script window should be empty. If it is not empty, delete whatever lines are there by clicking on the heading marks and pressing the Delete key. Insert the following lines into the script window.

```
local (i)
for i = 1 to 5
    msg(scratchpad.color_test.colors[i])
```

Your script should look similar to the script window in Figure 7.12. The table color_test now contains two elements: a script and a table of five strings.

Make sure that you press the tab key to indent the msg statement. The local(i) statement defines a local variable i which is used in a for loop. Note that the for loop has no end statement, unlike Pascal and C. Frontier depends heavily on the outline view in this window to indent parts of your code; these indentations define the looping constructs and obviate the use of begin and end statements prevalent in other languages.

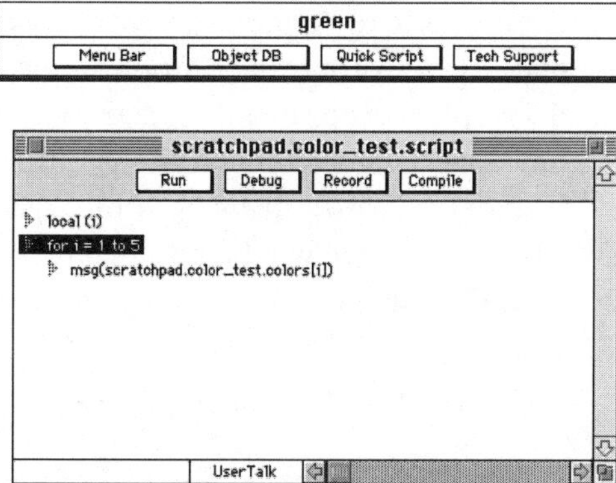

Figure 7.12 *The Frontier scripting environment allows you several options in running and debugging your UserTalk scripts.*

The msg command returns the value of its parameter to the status window in the Frontier Main window. In this case, we are cycling through the strings in the table scratchpad.color_test.colors; note that the individual colors are identified by an array-like index appended to the table name. Pressing the Run button causes all the strings in the table to be rapidly displayed in the Main window.

This very simple example demonstrates the hierarchical nature of the Object Database in addition to some rudimentary UserTalk syntax. There's a great deal more to UserTalk and Frontier than what is described here. The intent of this section was to give you enough exposure to the environment to be able to program some rudimentary scripts. You are referred to the DocServer application for detailed information about UserTalk and to the Frontier user manual included in the software distribution.

Developing CGI Scripts with Frontier

Now that we've covered some rudimentary Frontier scripting principles, let's talk about how to develop CGI scripts for your Web server using Frontier. Frontier works much the same way that AppleScript does; Frontier receives Apple events from the HTTP server and processes them through UserTalk scripts.

Comparable to AppleScript, you can develop external Frontier applications. In contrast to AppleScript, these applications, known as desktop scripts or droplets, activate Frontier and do not run autonomously. This actually saves a great deal of overhead because Frontier will most likely be running continuously on your server. Therefore, there will be minimal delays resulting from initializing your CGI scripts.

The Frontier CGI Framework

Another interesting feature of Frontier CGI scripts is that the scripts reside within the Object Database. With Frontier running continuously on your server, there is very little overhead in running your scripts. However, Frontier needs to be able to trap the WWWΩsdoc Apple event to gather the HTML form and CGI variables. An entire new framework needs to be introduced to Frontier to allow this communication.

The Frontier CGI Framework (http://www.webedge.com/frontier/cgiframework.html) is a sophisticated series of Frontier scripts and objects to provide this very function. The CGI Framework is included on this book's CD-ROM. In order to install the scripts into the Object Database, open the CGI Framework folder and double-click on the Frontier script Installer. This file is a special type of Frontier application, called an import/export file, that transfers its own collection of hierarchical scripts and objects into the Object Database in Frontier.root. By clicking on the installer file, you transfer the Framework scripts to your Frontier.root database. Specifically, the Framework will install new tables, entitled webServer and webServerScripts in the root table.

In addition to giving your CGI scripts a home, the Frontier CGI Framework adds several types of macros that aid your CGI script development. For example, in AppleScript we had to construct an HTTP response header from scratch. The Framework provides this functionality with the webserver.httpHeader script, which can be called from within a UserTalk CGI script.

After double-clicking on the Installer script, you will be queried for your Web server address. Enter your server address and press OK.

Note that the script is asking for an address and not a URL; do not include the http:// prefix. The script will then query you for the location of your existing CGI scripts. You may have MacPerl or AppleScript CGI scripts in a certain folder; select this folder in the dialog box. Finally, the script will ask if you want to read the webServer.readme file. This file describes the UserTalk commands introduced by the Framework and is well worth reading.

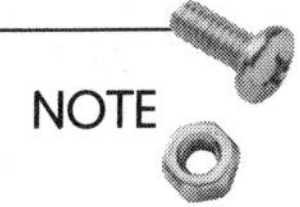

The webServer.readme file is of the object type wp text. This object represents a sophisticated word-processing capability within Frontier. You customize the fonts and style of the document. When in an object of this type, scripts provided by the Frontier CGI Framework even enable you to create HTML code.

Customizing Your Server

Now that you have told Frontier how to handle and create your CGI scripts, you need to configure your Web servers so that they know to contact Frontier to process the CGI requests. The process is different between MacHTTP and WebStar. InterServer Publisher does not yet support suffix mapping, so this type of interface is not possible.

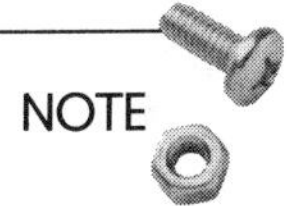

For more discussion on suffix mapping, refer to Chapter 4, "Macintosh HTTP Servers."

With MacHTTP, open the MacHTTP.config file and add the following line:

```
ACGI .FCGI APPL * text/html
```

Open the MacHTTP Support 1.0 folder on this book's CD-ROM. There are two Frontier scripts that you will need to run to allow MacHTTP to work with Frontier. First, you need to create aliases to your Frontier CGI scripts. Double-click on the Make Script Aliases script. This rifles through the CGI scripts you have constructed in your suites.WebServerScripts table and creates aliases in your HTML folder. After doing this, double-click on the traps.WWWΩ for MacHTTP script. This installs the proper scripts into Frontier.root, enabling Frontier to pick up the required Apple events from MacHTTP.

NOTE

> The aliases you create with Make Script Aliases script are not really aliases to the individual Frontier scripts. These are actually aliases to the Frontier application itself. The alias names alert Frontier as to which scripts need to be executed.

Sample Frontier CGI script

Let's develop our own script. Open the suites.WebServerScripts table and create a script entitled survey. Our intent is to duplicate the simple example shown earlier in this chapter, in the section "Sample AppleScript CGI Script."

```
on survey (Params)
        local (htmltext = webServer.httpHeader ())
        on add (s)
             htmltext = htmltext + s + cr

        add("<HTML><HEAD><TITLE>Frontier CGI Test
➥Results</TITLE></HEAD>");
        add("<BODY><H1>Frontier CGI Test Results</H1>");
        add("<HR>");
        with Params^,argTable
             add("You are coming from the IP address: " +
➥clientAddress + "<P>");
             add("Your first name is " + first_name +
➥"<P>");
             add("Your favorite movie is " + movie +
➥"<P>");
             add("You consider yourself to be of the " +
➥age + " age group" + "<P>");
             add("</BODY></HTML>")
        return(htmltext)
```

Keep in mind that the indenting shown here is derived from Frontier's outline view; there's no need to add the tabs and spaces manually. Let's analyze this script section by section.

Preamble

```
on survey (Params)
        local (htmltext = webServer.httpHeader ())
        on add (s)
             htmltext = htmltext + s + cr
```

In this part of the script, is declared the subroutine survey with the parameter Params. Scripts from the Frontier CGI Framework package all the CGI data variables passed from the Web server into the array Params. We then declare the variable htmltext as a local variable, assigning it the default value of webServer.httpHeader. This variable is equivalent to a standard HTTP 1.0 header of code 200; this code signifies a successful response to the browser request. Finally, we define a small subroutine where s is a text string; this subroutine concatenates the variable htmltext, the subroutine input string, and a carriage return into one text string.

NOTE 

Information on HTTP header codes can be found at http://www.w3.org/pub/WWW/Protocols/.

NOTE 

Form data obtained by the POST method is automatically parsed into the Params array. Form data obtained by the GET method needs to be parsed using the CGI framework verb webServer.parseArgs.

HTML Headers

```
    add("<HTML><HEAD><TITLE>Frontier CGI Test Results</
➥TITLE></HEAD>");
    add("<BODY><H1>Frontier CGI Test Results</H1>");
    add("<HR>");
```

In these statements, we use the add routine to create HTML header code.

Processing the Form Data

```
with Params^,argTable
      add("You are coming from the IP address: " +
➥clientAddress + "<P>");
      add("Your first name is " + first_name + "<P>");
      add("Your favorite movie is " + movie + "<P>");
      add("You consider yourself to be of the " + age
➥+ " age group" + "<P>");
      add("</BODY></HTML>")
return(htmltext)
```

Most of these statements are enclosed in a `with` statement. This enables us to refer to a variable without prepending the subtable names every time they're used thereafter in the code; this is a programming shortcut and not an essential part of the program's logic. The caret (^) following the Params database makes all the elements of the array available to the following statements. Form data is written to a subtable known as argTable. The variable names of the form fields, as defined in the original HTML code, are carried over into the Frontier script. Therefore, the text field first_name is available as argTable.first_name. Finally, the variable htmltext is returned; this variable contains the entire CGI response. Remember to compile the script before executing it.

Now process the HTML code, as shown in Figure 7.13. Make sure that you have an alias to the survey script in your CGI folder and that it's referenced in your form statement. A typical response to the query is shown in Figure 7.14.

Frontier versus AppleScript

In terms of usefulness as a CGI script environment, Frontier has several advantages over AppleScript. As mentioned previously, Frontier takes advantage of the PowerPC architecture; Frontier scripts and applications will run much faster on Power Macs than on older 680x0-based Macintosh computers. AppleScript scripts and applications will run under 680x0-emulation mode, which is much slower.

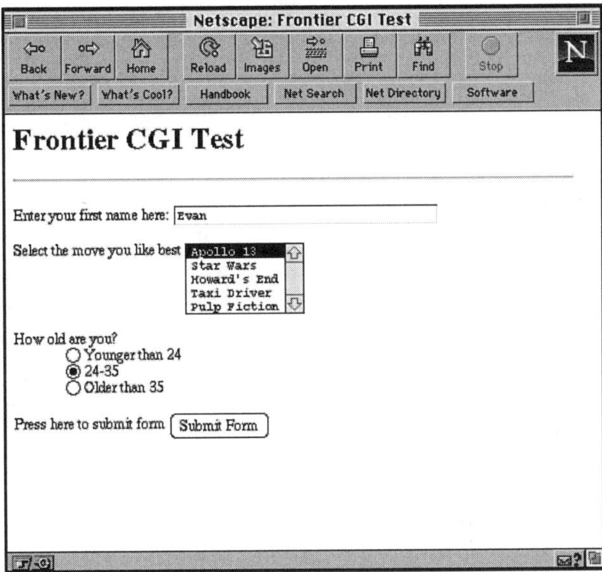

Figure 7.13 *This simple HTML form is used to query the Frontier CGI script.*

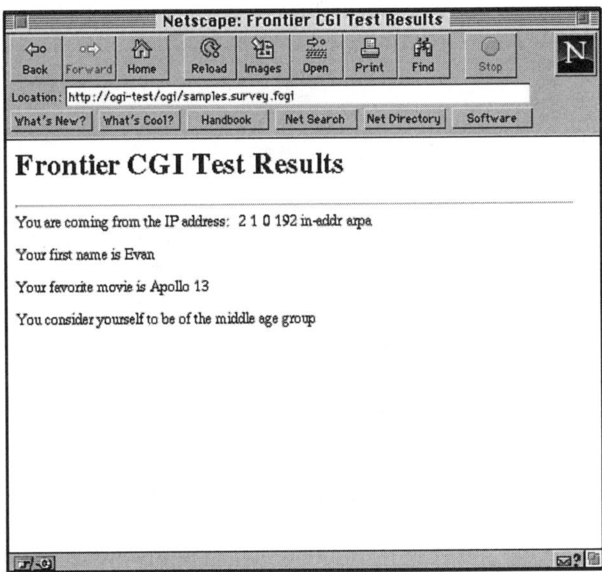

Figure 7.14 *This HTML page was generated by a Frontier CGI script.*

Multithreaded processing is very important for CGI scripting. An application—such as an AppleScript application—that is not multithreaded processes events on a last-in, first-out queue. When your server receives multiple requests for a CGI script, the older requests are forced to wait for newer requests to be answered. This may result in many CGI timeouts. Multithreaded applications, such as those constructed with Frontier, are more efficient, in that events are handled simultaneously and do not preclude one another.

Furthermore, Frontier's Object Database contains all the functions that Frontier CGI scripts might require. AppleScript applications frequently make use of external libraries residing in various OSAXen. Adding a new separate application for each CGI script creates more overhead for your server; this has the effect of slowing all of the processes.

One advantage of AppleScript is its more comprehensible syntax. UserTalk retains many C-like constructs, which are difficult for many novice programmers to master. AppleScript syntax is easy to understand and is closer to conversational English than it is to another programming language. Furthermore, several AppleScript books are available on the market.

Servers that receive a lot of CGI script requests will enjoy better performance with Frontier applications. More and more Web administrators are moving their scripts to the more flexible environment exhibited by Frontier. If your Intranet Web server is going to see a lot of CGI action, you may well be advised to use the Frontier CGI environment for your scripts.

Other Frontier Intranet Applications

Frontier can be set up as a URL handler for Navigator. By running Frontier in conjunction with Navigator, you can embed scripts within a browser window. Setting up a link with the following address:

```
<a
➥href="usrtlk:dialog.alert%20(%22Hello%20World!%22)">here< a>
```

will execute the UserTalk command

```
dialog.alert ("Hello World!")
```

Embedded scripts present almost limitless possibilities for you to customize services on your Intranet. For example, you could easily develop embedded scripts on your Intranet Web pages that can work with Mac clients to do the following:

- Mount remote AppleShare volumes
- Perform software installations
- Launch Macintosh applications
- Update FileMaker Pro or Tango databases

And the list goes on and on. As you become more comfortable with Frontier, you'll be able to add more sophisticated capabilities to your Mac Intranet clients.

NOTE

> You can embed AppleScript in your Web pages just like you can with Frontier. However, you'll need a copy of Flypaper or Web Runner (http://www.pass.wayne.edu/~eric/applescript.html).

Additional CGI Scripting Languages

AppleScript and Frontier are two of the most popular CGI scripting languages for the MacOS. However, you can employ any language that can interpret Apple events directed from the HTTP server. Some of these alternative scripting environments are discussed in this section.

MacPerl

The Practical Extraction and Report Language (PERL or most commonly, Perl) is a popular text-processing language with its origins in the Unix operating system. Perl offers much of the utility of C and C++, but with easier syntax rules. As a result, Perl is wildly popular as a CGI platform in the Unix environment and has been ported to the major OS platforms, such as OS/2, MacOS, DOS, and Windows NT.

Perl is a compiled language and sports one of the fastest compilers of any high-level language. However, Perl scripts are compiled at run-time; so using Perl scripts as CGI applications will give them that interpreted "feel." The ubiquity of Perl throughout the major operating systems ensures that you will find a vast resource of CGI scripts available for your perusal. With minor modifications, you can incorporate these Perl scripts into your server.

MacPerl is a port of the Perl language to the MacOS. Scripts developed in MacPerl are compatible with the popular Unix Perl distribution. This proves to be a huge incentive for using MacPerl as your CGI scripting environment. Scripts that you develop for your Mac WWW server will work on other server platforms as well. The converse is even more important; there are huge libraries of Perl CGI scripts available. These scripts will port to your Mac server with minimal modifications.

> To develop MacPerl CGI scripts that work with the MacHTTP or WebStar server applications, you will need the MacHTTP Script Extension included with the MacPerl distribution on this book's CD-ROM.

C/C++

Many CGI applications written for the MacOS are developed using C or even C++. These languages exist for the Mac but require external compilers and libraries to handle Apple events. Symantec's Think C/C++ and Metrowerks' CodeWarrior are good examples of

C and C++ compilers for the Mac. Even so, these environments required extensive libraries to process HTML form data. This difficulty is a trade-off, because scripts compiled using these languages will tend to run faster than interpreted scripts written in other languages. Your scripts, in addition, will also be portable to Unix or Windows servers (although not as portable as Perl); this enables you to share CGI scripts with users of other systems.

HyperCard

HyperCard sports a user-interface language, HyperTalk, of which AppleScript is highly derivative. The two languages share much in the way of structure and even grammar. HyperCard is a multimedia authoring tool with roots deep in the Mac family tree. It is one of the oldest Mac applications for the Mac, dating back to the days of the venerable Macintosh II.

HyperTalk is able to handle Apple events and can therefore manage inter-process communication. However, HyperTalk has always been criticized for its slow performance. Even though you can now compile external applications with HyperCard, these applications are not optimized for performance and tend to run much slower than applications compiled with higher-level programming languages. Similarly, CGI processing with HyperCard yields even slower performance than AppleScript CGI scripts do. For this reason, HyperCard is not a popular CGI scripting platform for the Mac.

Application Programming Interfaces

Yet another alternative to conventional CGI scripting lies with development of Application Progamming Interfaces (APIs). An API can be thought of as a series of subroutines that a third-party developer can use to extend an application. For example, Netscape offers information about the Server APIs. In this way, you could write applications using these Netscape APIs that enable the Netscape server to perform functions that you would normally accomplish through CGI scripts. However, your code would actually be integrated with the server in a manner more cohesive than what can be accomplished through CGI scripting.

NOTE

WebSTAR 3.0 will allow you to utilize a WebSTAR API so that fast server extensions can be developed. This capability should be available in mid-1996.

Server Side Includes

Server Side Includes (SSIs) are an alternative to CGI scripts. Using SSIs configured with your Web server, you can develop customized pages on-the-fly without the overhead of running an external application. SSIs are a standard complement to the NCSA HTTPd server, from which MacHTTP and WebStar are derived. However, there are several types of SSIs available for Mac Web browsers. You must keep in mind that using SSIs will enable you to accomplish useful things on your Web server while restricting the portability of your code to other servers and systems. In this section, we'll look at several kinds of SSI-type features available to you. Once again, you'll need to consult the documentation accompanying these packages for a full discussion of the syntax and usage of these HTML extensions.

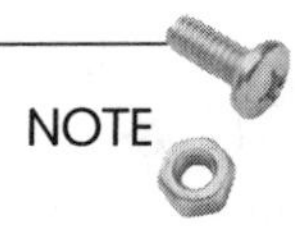

NOTE

Quarterdeck has said that a future release of WebSTAR will include support for SSIs. This capability should be available in mid-1996.

InterServer Publisher InterXTML

InterXTML is a set of extensions available to Web pages served by Intercon's InterServer Publisher. Like other SSIs, you insert InterXTML tags into your HTML code. The tags are processed by Publisher and converted into HTML. For this reason, you are able to serve files that use XTML to ordinary Web browsers.

You notify Publisher that your HTML document contains InterXTML tags by inserting the following statement at the beginning and end of the file:

```
<InterXTML>
...
</InterXTML>
```

The main capabilities of InterXTML can be divided into three areas:

- You can display access counters telling users how many times your pages have been accessed.
- You can display the modification dates of your Web pages. This is useful for allowing your users to see how current the information is on your pages.
- You can provide listings of your directories in the form of HTML documents. Special InterXTML tags enable you to import the file properties, such as file names and icons for use in your HTML pages.

Access counters and modification dates are cute add-ons to your pages that inform your users how many times certain pages have been accessed or how recently your page was modified. Access counters are neat, but are more prevalent out on the Internet and would not have a great deal of utility within your Intranet. InterXTML tags that display your files' modification dates have greater utility, in that they will convey just how recent certain documents are on your server.

InterXTML lets you publish directory listings on your pages. As mentioned in Chapter 4, Unix Web servers enable you to list the contents of directories simply by specifying the directory in the URL. For security reasons, this feature wasn't implemented in MacHTTP, WebSTAR, or InterServer Publisher. However, InterXTML enables you to not only display the folder contents in a Web page, but also enables you to display the file icons, names, comments, size, and other information as well. This InterXTML feature has great potential by enabling you to automatically develop file descriptions that your Mac, Window, and Unix Intranet users can peruse and use to download files in your archives.

NetCloak

NetCloak, from Maxum Corp, is a set of server extensions similar to InterXTML. Unlike InterXTML, NetCloak works with any Web server that understands certain Apple events. NetCloak extensions allow you the following capabilities:

- You can secure documents or even sections of documents from certain users based on user name or domain name.
- You can exhibit different parts of your document at different times of the day or year.
- You have full access to many CGI variables, such as user client, user IP address, browser type, and other types of data.
- NetCloak enables you to develop simple macros that contain frequently used HTML code.

NetCloak enables you to implement several features that may have a lot of appeal within your Intranet. With NetCloak's security features, you can cloak sections of a document that you want to restrict viewership to the members of management in your organization. Groups within your organization can post work schedules viewable only to relevant members. Using NetCloak macros, you can customize your pages by adding standardized headers and footers.

For customizing your HTML forms, check out Maxum's NetForms HTML extensions package.

Tips for Writing CGI Scripts

Now that we've covered some of the environments that you can employ to develop CGI scripts, we can discuss some tips that you can keep in mind while developing these new applications.

Portability

In developing your Intranet, chances are that you are starting small. You may even be running your Web server on a 680x0-based Mac. As your own Net grows, you may have a desire to expand your server to a different Mac model, different server software, or even (gulp!) a Unix or Windows NT platform. If you do plan to migrate your software to a different environment, you'll need to ensure that your CGI scripts are portable. For example, you get several benefits by using SSIs; however, SSIs are usually specific to the server software. Using proprietary adjustments such as SSIs enable you to do sophisticated HTML processing, but at a cost of portablity.

Optimize for Your System's Needs

Perl is a wonderful CGI language and is perfectly capable of handling many types of scripting objectives. However, Perl is an interpreted language, as opposed to C++ which is a compiled language. Perl scripts are therefore going to run more slowly than C scripts that perform the same functionality. Compiled applications will run much more quickly than their interpreted peers.

Using the Script Libraries

Make sure that you can develop scripts that are complicated, but available on the Net. Surfing the various CGI archives still will enable you to pull down popular scripts. At the very least, scripts found on the archives present a good starting point for your scripting development.

Building Imagemaps

Anyone who's surfed the Web for a long period of time has run across imagemaps. Imagemaps are graphical images that contain designated "hot" areas that act like buttons. Clicking on one of the "hot" areas brings up another page or performs some type of action. Imagemaps make use of CGI scripts, so this is an appropriate time to discuss how imagemaps work.

How Imagemaps Work

Very often, you will want to present a user with a list of options—go to next page, go to previous page, go to home page, send mail to Web administrator, and others. You may want to display these options on various pages. You could do this using a bulleted list or some other variation of standard HTML. However, imagemaps enable you to present options to your user in a graphical format. Imagemaps are really just a list of URLs that present navigation options to the Web user.

The imagemap process works something like this:

1. The user is presented with an imagemap that has several links to other documents buried within it.

2. The user clicks somewhere on the image.

3. The Web browser records the location of the click in the imagemap's frame of reference and passes that information on to the Web server.

4. The Web server passes the click location to a CGI script (which was designated in the imagemap URL), which then correlates the click location with a predetermined hotspot on the map.

5. If there's a URL associated with that hotspot, the CGI script returns that URL to the server. If no hotspot was activated, then a default URL is returned.

6. A page corresponding to the URL returned by the CGI script is loaded into the user's Web browser. Life is good.

What You'll Need to Build Imagemaps

The only trick to imagemaps is defining the hotspots on the graphics image. There are three things that you'll need to develop imagemaps. You'll need the following:

- ☐ A graphics image
- ☐ A software application that lets you define the hotspots and associate them with URLs
- ☐ A CGI script that translates the click locations to URLs

Let's look at these elements one at a time.

Getting a Graphics Image

You need to produce a graphics image on which you want to build an imagemap. You can use any graphics application you like, providing that the end result gives you a graphics format that you can display on your Web pages. Deneba Canvas (http://www.deneba.com) and Adobe Photoshop (http://www.adobe.com) are two popular applications for building these types of images on the Mac.

> The latest versions of both Canvas and Photoshop produce JPEG and GIF graphics. Other Mac graphics applications may not produce files in these formats. However, most applications will produce PICT files which can then be translated to GIF or JPEG, using applications such as GIFConverter, GraphicConverter, or JPEGView (http://www.med.cornell.edu/jpegview.html).

Because you'll likely include text in your image, GIF is a good format to use for imagemaps. As we talked about in Chapter 6, "Creating an Efficient Web Site," GIF files store and display text more efficiently than JPEG files. If your image is comprised of a photograph or some complicated graphic that does not contain text, then you may be better off using the JPEG format.

Creating the Hotspots

In order to create hotspots on a graphic image, you'll need a special imagemap creation application. There are several specific Mac applications for this purpose. We'll talk about WebMap in this section. However, several high-end HTML editors have imagemap creation capability built into the software.

Adobe PageMill has an easy-to-use imagemap creation tool built into the editor. For more information about PageMill, see Appendix C, "Perfecting HTML."

Using an Imagemap CGI Script

You'll also need to create or a CGI script that will map the user mouse clicks to your predetermined hotspots. We'll be discussing the application MapServe for that purpose in this section.

Creating Imagemaps with WebMap

WebMap 1.0.1 is a shareware application designed to build imagemaps from existing PICT, GIF, or JPEG files. WebMap 2.0 is in beta testing as of this writing and should be available by the time you read this. However, this version of the software will be strictly commercial as opposed to shareware. Look on this book's CD-ROM for a link where you can download a copy of WebMap 1.0.1.

Creating Imagemap Hotspots

Developing an imagemap in WebMap is extremely simple. Double-click on the WebMap icon to launch the application. Load the test.gif graphics file into WebMap using the Open command. You should see a series of shapes. The toolbar lets you define a series of shapes superimposed on the image. You have the choice of using a rectangle, circle/oval, or polygon.

Two types of imagemap standards are in use at this time. The imagemap files are formatted differently, depending on whether they adhere to the CERN or NCSA standard. The NCSA standard allows the use of ovals in addition to circles and is more widely used than the CERN standard. WebMap defaults to the NCSA standard, but you can alter this under the Preferences command.

Note that you can use the shapes on the toolbar to draw the hotspots you'll need to define in the imagemap. Simply click on the desired shape around the desired area and the phrase [Undefined] will appear in the URL column. Double-click on the [Undefined] phrase and enter the URL you'd like to associate with that hotspot.

NOTE

> You use the WebMap polygon tool like you do with a polygon tool in any drawing program. You close the polygon by double-clicking the starting point of the shape.

You cannot expect the user to be able to click right in the desired shapes; they might accidentally click a region of the imagemap where you have not defined a link. Therefore, you'll want to define a default URL that will be called by the CGI script when the user clicks a portion of the image not defined by a hotspot. Under Edit, choose Set Default URL to define the URL returned in these instances.

Creating the Imagemap File

Once you've defined all your shapes within WebMap, you'll need to write the information to a file that can be read by a CGI script to process the map. This is done by clicking on File and choosing Export as Text. WebMap will prompt you for the map file location; create a folder accessible by your Web server in which you'll store your imagemaps and the imagemap CGI application. Before saving the document, you'll be able to check whether or not you want the file in CERN or NCSA format. For the example shown in Figure 7.15, WebMap will create the following output:

```
default http://www.anywhere.com/oops.html
circ http://www.anyplace.com/page2.html 76,2 231,67
rect http://www.anyplace.com/page3.html 147,75 292,145
poly http://www.anyplace.com/page1.html 0,87 3,154
➥83,158 123,118 74,69 0,87
```

Note that this file contains a default URL and three shapes. The shapes are listed in terms of imagemap coordinates in x,y pairs. While working in WebMap, the coordinates of your mouse location are given in the lower left portion of the screen as designated in Figure 7.15. Save this file with the .map suffix in your predetermined imagemap folder.

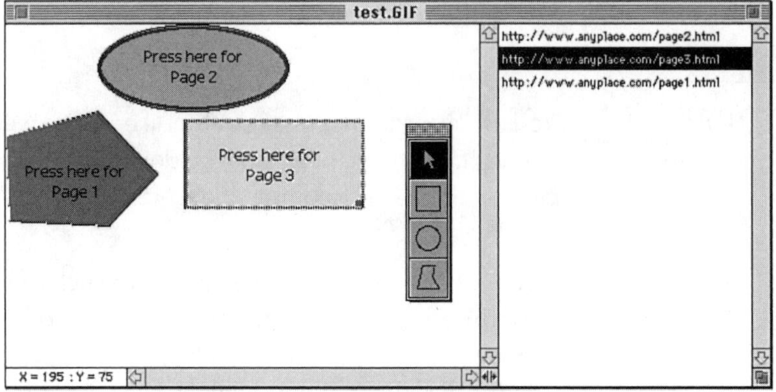

Figure 7.15 *WebMap provides a graphical interface for you to develop imagemap files.*

Using an Imagemap CGI Script

Now that you've got your imagemap file configured, it's time to introduce it to your server. You'll need a CGI application that is specially configured to serve imagemaps. One application that works well with WebSTAR, MacHTTP, or any other CGI-enabled Mac HTTP server is the shareware application MapServe. MapServe consists of an asynchronous CGI that is launched when referred in a URL. Look on this book's CD-ROM for the link to MapServe's home page where you can download a copy.

Place the MapServe.acgi file in a folder accessible by your Web server. You may want to store your imagemap files in the same location. In your Web pages, you can access your imagemap using a URL constructed as such:

```
<A HREF="/<imagemap path>/mapserve.acgi$test.map">
<IMG SRC="test.gif" ISMAP></A>
```

In the above statement, you've included information about the location of the CGI script as well as the imagemap file name.

You've bracketed the test.gif image discussed above with the imagemap anchor. Note that the ISMAP attribute was used in the <IMG> tag telling the browser that this image is actually a clickable imagemap. A user clicking on this image will bring up one of the URLs you specified using WebMap.

NOTE

The MapServe documentation includes information on how you can set up MapServer as a user-defined action in WebSTAR. In this way, you can tell WebSTAR to run MapServer when a file containing a .map suffix is included in a URL.

Client-Side Imagemaps

Imagemaps are often used for navigation aids. Many Web authors direct users to different parts of their site using elaborate graphics. However, this may seem like a waste of time and processing. With imagemaps, you are calling up a CGI which does nothing but redirect you to another Web page. This is somewhat underwhelming compared to the power and flexibility you can express using the CGI scripts we've discussed above. Furthermore, you need to have access to a Web server to use your imagemaps. Many Web authors test their pages on a local machine before moving them to the permanent server site. On a local machine separated from your HTTP server, your imagemaps will be useless, but awfully pretty graphics files.

Netscape has instituted support for HTML 3.0 client-side imagemaps in the Navigator browser. The idea behind client-side imagemaps is that you no longer require the use of a CGI script to direct users to other Web pages. Client-side imagemaps are set up much like conventional imagemaps, except that the shape definitions and URLs are included in the HTML code. As a result, client-side imagemaps execute much more quickly than conventional imagemaps. See Appendix C, "Perfecting HTML," for a more specific discussion of client-side imagemaps.

Summary

CGI scripting should be an integral part of your Intranet Web services. With these scripts, you'll be able to offer useful services to your Intranet users. There are several programming languages to use for your scripting environment. Frontier and AppleScript are perhaps the two most popular although MacPerl has a large following as well. The future should bring server side includes, robust Java implementation, and APIs to the MacOS; so CGI scripting may have a totally different look before too long.

In Chapter 8, "Databases and Document Searches," we'll see how sophisticated CGI scripts can be used in searching documents and accessing databases. You may be interested in jumping to one of the following chapters:

- ☐ Chapter 4, "Macintosh HTTP Servers," to learn about the different software you can use to set up World Wide Web services on your Mac.
- ☐ Appendix C, "Perfecting HTML," to learn about some advanced HTML programming features, as well as how to use some popular HTML editors including Adobe PageMill and BBEdit.

Links Related to This Chapter

StarNine Technologies	http://www.starnine.com
InterCon Systems, Inc.	http://www.intercon.com
AppleScript Home Page	http://dev.info.apple.com/solguide/AppleScript.html
ScriptWeb	http://www.scriptweb.com/scriptweb
Late Night's Script Debugger	http://dev.info.apple.com/solguide/script.html

Main Event's Scripter	http://www.yy.net/bis/mainevent/scripter.html
Full Moon's Script Wizard	http://www.fullmoon.com/fmsdl/products/fms_scriptwiz.html
Parse CGI Home Page	http://marquis.tiac.net/software/parse-cgi-osax-12.hqx
ROFM CGI	http://rowen.astro.washington.edu/
MacPerl Q&A	http://err.ethz.ch/members/neeri/macintosh/perl-qa.html
MacPerl FTP archive	ftp://ftp.share.com/pub/macperl
MacHTTP CGI Script extension	ftp://err.ethz.ch/pub/neeri/MacPerlBeta/
Frontier Home Page	http://www.hotwired.com/ staff/userland/aretha
Frontier CGI Scripting	http://www.webedge.com/frontier
Low Tech Object DB	http://www.scripting.com/root.html
Maxum Corp	http://www.maxum.com
Usenet	comp.infosystems.www.servers.mac
	comp.infosystems.www.authoring.cgi
Apple Mailing Lists	http://www.solutions.apple.com/apple-internet/

CHAPTER 8

Databases and Document Searches

This book has covered elementary CGI scripting, but you've really just scratched the surface on what you can do on the Web. Don't get me wrong—access counters, post-queries, and server-side includes allow you to put lots of cool features on your home page. Still, you might wonder if there's more to CGI scripting than the little parlor tricks we discussed in Chapter 7. Now we'll talk about adding raw power to your Web site by allowing your Intranet users to search documents and databases.

This is where a lot of the utility of your Intranet comes into play. With a simple and inexpensive Web browser, your users can gain access to the vast amounts of information your organization has stored in piles of forgotten documents and databases. With a minimal amount of setup, you can configure your existing databases and documents for access via the Web.

When you think about it, most of the work performed by members of your organization exists somewhere on someone's computer. File after file are safely stored on different desktop computers, unreachable by anyone but their author. With modern CGI technology, you can allow your users to search these documents, regardless of their format and location within your Intranet.

The work involved in programming databases is way too involved for this chapter. Modern databases are written using sophisticated programming languages; constructing them requires a great deal of study, experience, and sweat; you won't be learning how to develop databases in this chapter. However, you will be exposed to the following:

- A brief introduction to databases and their uses on the Macintosh
- An introduction to Tango—an application that lets you customize a Web front-end to your databases
- Different methods you can use to search documents on your Intranet Web sites

Database Primer

Let's first discuss databases and how they're used in the modern workplace. There are several different flavors of databases in the computing world. Databases have grown in sophistication over the years. Whereas older databases stored information in static formats, much like library card catalogs, modern databases are dynamic applications with which sophisticated modeling and analyses can be developed.

Introduction to Databases

Databases are applications that store sets of data in an easily retrievable format. In that sense, an Excel spreadsheet is a rudimentary database. In a spreadsheet, you can store data in a tabular format that is easy to read and retrieve.

Modern databases allow administrators and analysts to work with the data in a far more sophisticated fashion than afforded by an Excel spreadsheet. Nowadays, you can set up sophisticated rules using advanced programming languages to manipulate and organize your database contents. Furthermore, you can develop sophisticated graphical user interfaces to interact with your database. These interfaces can access your database from remote computers, even those running different operating systems. For example, you can run a compiled database front-end on a Mac that interacts with a database that resides on a Unix machine. This type of operation, between a front-end interface and a database, is known as a client-server relationship.

Databases are comprised of tables; these tables are comprised of columns and rows. When you add data to a database, you add it in terms of rows. This is very much like the familiar spreadsheet data format you see in Microsoft Excel. However, databases differ from spreadsheets, in that you display spreadsheet information in rows and columns; with Microsoft Excel 5.0, you can even have multiple spreadsheet tables in the same document. In contrast, database information is stored in rows, columns, and tables; this organization is often unseen by the user. Database contents are often displayed in formats developed by the user. For example, you could display information from a financial database in a spreadsheet format or include it in any report or table format.

Sophisticated databases do more than just store data or give you graphical means of accessing the data. Advanced programming using the Sequential Query Language (SQL—pronounced "sequel") is possible. SQL is a standardized database manipulation language that allows you to develop sophisticated programming constructs. You can develop if-then clauses or looping constructs that operate on the contents of your databases. Rather than just store the data, you can create new data based on SQL operation of your database contents. Furthermore, SQL allows you to develop sophisticated control and procedural structures as well, much like C/C++ and Pascal.

Many of the larger Web sites allow access to internal databases. Some of the larger Web search tools, such as WebCrawler, Lycos, Alta Vista, and others, actually send automated programs out on the Internet to access Web pages. The search engines then download those pages to a large internal database on the search service's site. When you search for a keyword to be found on a Web page, you are actually searching an internal database. Similarly, lots of companies post online catalogs where you can peruse their product offerings; often you are cruising through a gateway into that company's internal database. We'll spend some time talking about how you can use an application, known as Tango, on your Web server to provide access for your Intranet users to your internal databases.

Databases on the Macintosh

There are many types of database applications for the Mac. Recently, the viability of the MacOS as a database platform was given a boost by ports of the Oracle and PowerBuilder front-ends. Oracle Power Objects and Powersoft's PowerBuilder are recent additions that enable you to develop graphically oriented applications on the Mac that interact, via the Internet, with databases that exist on Windows NT or Unix workstations. However, there are standalone databases that reside under the MacOS.

FileMaker Pro

Claris FileMaker Pro (http://www.claris.com) is a popular database application for the MacOS. The product recently underwent an upgrade, transforming the database architecture to a relational foundation. This is relevant, as a relational database allows you to store data based on common threads or concepts that you define.

There are several CGI scripts that have been developed, which allow you to link your Web server to FileMaker Pro. These CGI scripts allow you to query the database via an HTML forms interface. Users can set up database queries that until recently had only been possible using compiled database front-ends.

4th Dimension

ACI-US 4th Dimension (http://www.acius.com) is a sophisticated cross-platform client-server application. 4D, as the application is often referred to, sports an object-oriented layout editor, a powerful programming language, and an optional language compiler that can be used develop faster client applications. 4D also comes bundled with tools that allow you to develop Web and CGI interfaces.

Butler SQL

Butler SQL, from EveryWare Development Corp. (http://www.everyware.com), is a high-end relational database for the Mac. Like 4D, it is a client-server cross-platform application. Butler SQL is built on a powerful programming language, Data Access Language (DAL); it comes with several tools, such as ButlerTools, which allow you to easily develop database applications. Butler SQL also supports the Open Database Connectivity (ODBC) standard that allows it to connect, via TCP/IP and other protocols, to databases on different platforms and from many different manufacturers, such as Oracle, Sybase, and Informix.

Using Butler SQL

In Chapter 7, you learned a great deal about CGI scripting on the Mac. The sophisticated features of your Intranet will require some advanced CGI scripts. Your databases, however, are sophisticated data storage facilities. It's one thing to program a simple access counter script or an HTML form query. However, writing CGI scripts, in languages like AppleScript, UserTalk, or Perl, to search and retrieve data from your database requires a considerable amount of effort and skill.

EveryWare Development Corp.'s Tango is a means of streamlining CGI development. Tango offers a graphical interface for linking between your Web server to a variety of databases. Most notably, Tango comes bundled with EveryWare's Butler SQL database. Specifically, Tango was originally designed to work with Butler SQL; however, Tango now adheres to the Open Database Connectivity (ODBC) standard so that Tango can work with several types of databases including Oracle, Sybase, and Informix.

Using Tango's graphical interface tools, you can develop interfaces between your Web server and your database. Specifically designed to work with StarNine's WebSTAR Web server, Tango prevents you from having to develop code using complicated database syntax or even HTML. By not having to do with the vagaries of these languages, you develop custom CGIs in a drastically reduced amount of time.

NOTE 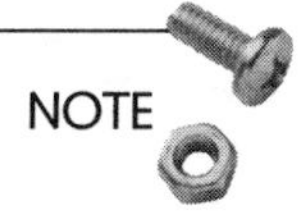

See Chapter 4, "Macintosh HTTP Servers," for more information on WebSTAR.

Introduction to Butler SQL

Before we talk about Tango and the various tools allowing you to construct Web pages, let's discuss the underlying database structure through which Tango is derived. EveryWare's Butler SQL is a popular client-server database for the Macintosh. However, you are not limited to just serving Macintosh computers; with proper network configuration, clients under both Windows and Macintosh platforms can access Butler SQL databases.

Once again, the intent of this discussion on Butler is not to educate you on the use of the database. EveryWare provides hundreds of pages of documentation on Butler, and I can't hope to give you a more specific introduction than that. My intent is to introduce you to the Butler SQL application, talk a little about how it works, and give you examples of how it works with Tango to display database contents on the Web.

Installing Butler SQL and Tango

My intention in this section is to introduce you to the capabilities of Tango and some of the tools that you can use to expose your databases to your Intranet. You'll need at least 12 MB of RAM on your Mac to comfortably run the operating system, Butler SQL, and WebSTAR.

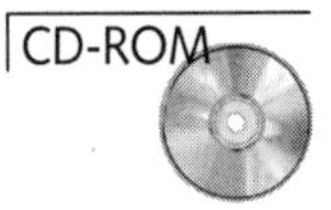

Go to the Butler SQL/Tango folder on this book's CD-ROM. Double-click on the Butler SQL Test Drive Installer icon to install the software on your startup disk. Take the Tango folder and move it inside of your WebSTAR folder. This Tango folder contains the Tango CGI and various databases that you'll need to run the demos in this chapter.

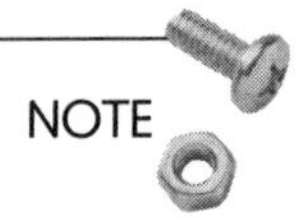

> You can run Tango on a different computer than your WebSTAR server. You can even install Tango and Butler on Macintosh computers other than your WebSTAR server. All computers need to be accessible on the same local or wide area network. However, for the purposes of simplicity, I'll assume that you'll be running Butler

SQL, Tango, and WebSTAR on the same computer. The Tango documentation details how to install the applications on different computers.

The Butler SQL/Tango Installer will insert several folders in your computer's Preferences folders. Specifically, the Public Databases folder inside the Butler Preferences folder needs to house the Butler databases that you wish to query through the Web. For each example in this section, you will need to move the relevant Butler database to this folder.

A Brief Butler SQL Primer

The version of Butler SQL that comes on this book's CD-ROM is actually a limited demo version that restricts you to creating databases of no more than 100 records per database table. Let's look at the tools and applications that work with Butler SQL.

In your Butler SQL Test Drive folder, you'll see the Butler SQL Test Drive application. Like the full-featured Butler SQL application, Butler SQL Test Drive, Butler as we'll refer to it in this chapter, is a relational SQL database. The version of Butler is distributed on the CD-ROM as a fat binary, meaning that it will work with 680x0-based Macintosh computers as well as Power Macs.

Similar to an HTTP server, Butler serves data based on requests. These requests are phrased in SQL and are answered by Butler using desired contents of the server specified in the SQL request. Butler actually employs a SQL dialect known as Data Access Language (DAL) but will understand requests using any language that adheres to the SQL standard.

The Butler application really does nothing more than accept requests and send data to clients. Most of the database configuration is done by the ancillary applications such as ButlerTools, described in the next section. You can set up Butler connections with the Butler applications through communication links that EveryWare calls ports (not to be confused with IP ports). You can set up Butler ports that allow users to link to the Butler server through System 7 file sharing, network, modem, or serial connections.

Creating Databases with ButlerTools

ButlerTools is the application that you use to create and maintain Butler databases. With ButlerTools you also can import existing data from ASCII files, spreadsheets, or other databases into your Butler databases. You also use ButlerTools to create users and groups, thereby defining their database access privileges.

Let's take a look at a database using the ButlerTools application. Double-click on the ButlerTools application icon. Once the application has launched, click on File and select Open Database. Locate the Seminars_db database and open it; on the CD-ROM, this file will be located in the Tango folder. You will see a window containing the names of the tables contained in the Seminar_db database, as shown in Figure 8.1.

Figure 8.1 *ButlerTools allows you to examine the number of tables contained in a Butler database.*

In this window, you see the three tables that comprise the database: Customers, Registrations, and Seminars. You can tell how many rows of data are contained in each table. Double-click on the Customers table; you should see a window much like that shown in Figure 8.2. Each of the columns in the table is listed along with its variable type, length, column title, and initial value. You can modify any of these parameters by either clicking on the Schema menu and selecting Edit Column, or by simply double-clicking on the column. For example, clicking on the Student column gives you a window as displayed in Figure 8.3. Using this editor window, you can change any of the column parameters.

Butler data types are varied in scope. You can store data as Boolean, integer, or floating point representations. You also can store dates, time, text strings, documents, sounds, small graphics, and even movies. Some of these data types can describe data as large as 2 GB that is useful for indexing large documents and files in a Butler database.

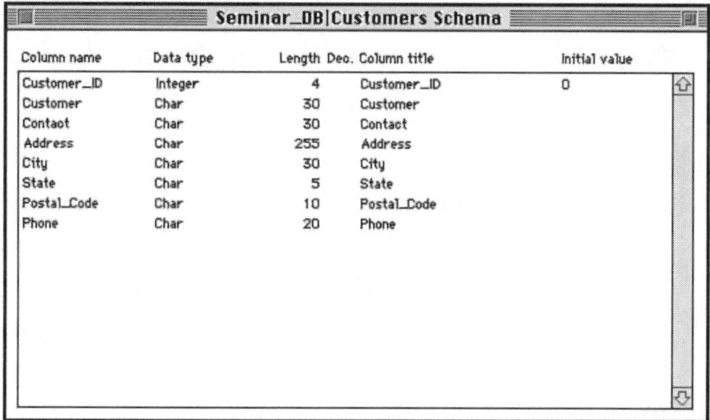

Column name	Data type	Length	Dec.	Column title	Initial value
Customer_ID	Integer	4		Customer_ID	0
Customer	Char	30		Customer	
Contact	Char	30		Contact	
Address	Char	255		Address	
City	Char	30		City	
State	Char	5		State	
Postal_Code	Char	10		Postal_Code	
Phone	Char	20		Phone	

Figure 8.2 *The tables of a Butler database are comprised of different columns.*

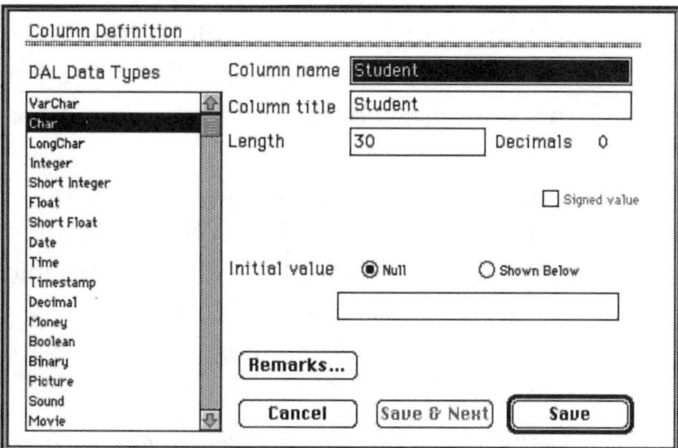

Figure 8.3 *You can define the data types of the individual columns in each table.*

ButlerTools also allows you to import data into a specific Butler table. This data can come from any program that will export data into a tab-, space-, or comma-delimited text file. Virtually any spreadsheet or data analysis package can export files in this format.

Another useful feature of ButlerTools is the development of database access privileges. You can assign user and group access privileges for each database and database table available on your Butler server. Butler allows different users to connect through communication ports. ButlerTools allows you to protect or restrict access to Butler databases or tables within the databases.

ButlerClient

ButlerClient is a basic DAL client application you can use to troubleshoot and test your DAL code. Using ButlerClient, you can send sections of DAL code to your server, have them executed, and observe the results. In this way, you can test how your server would respond to an actual database query.

Other Butler Front-Ends

Included with this Butler demo are several toolkits that you can use to develop interfaces to Butler using AppleScript, FirstClass, and HyperCard. With ButlerLink/AppleScript, you can develop scripts that will query and return information from Butler databases. For example, you can develop a script that is executed each morning that pulls down data from a financial database.

ButlerLink/FirstClass database extensions are FirstClass database add-ons for accessing Butler SQL databases from SoftArc's FirstClass (http://www.softarc.com) communications system. With FirstClass, you could set up a bulletin board system that could serve the contents of a Butler database.

ButlerLink/XCMD is a means of setting up a HyperCard interface to your database. HyperCard can be configured to display textual, numerical, and graphical data from your Butler database.

Introduction to Tango

Now that you have had a brief glimpse of Butler, it's time to figure out how to implement a Web-based front-end to your Butler databases. Tango adheres to the ODBC standard that allows you to interact with any ODBC-compliant database applications including Butler (of course), Oracle, Sybase, Informix, FoxPro, as well as Excel and several others. Tango allows you to interface with these databases without having to deal with SQL, CGI scripting languages such as C/C++ and Perl, or even HTML.

Examples Using Tango

We're going to run some of the examples that are included in the Tango demo. Later in this section, we'll look at some of the tools involved in setting up these examples. To run these examples, or any other Tango query, you'll need to have the following conditions in place:

- The Butler SQL Test Drive application must be running. Double-click on the Butler SQL Test Drive application in the Butler SQL folder.
- The WebSTAR server must be running.
- The Tango folder must be located inside of the WebSTAR folder.

Open the following URL:

```
http://<your server name>/Tango/default.html
```

You'll need to substitute the address of your Butler/SQL server for <your server name>. Figure 8.4 shows the Tango default page. You have several examples listed in the page. Clicking on any of the links in the list shown here will activate some of the Tango demos.

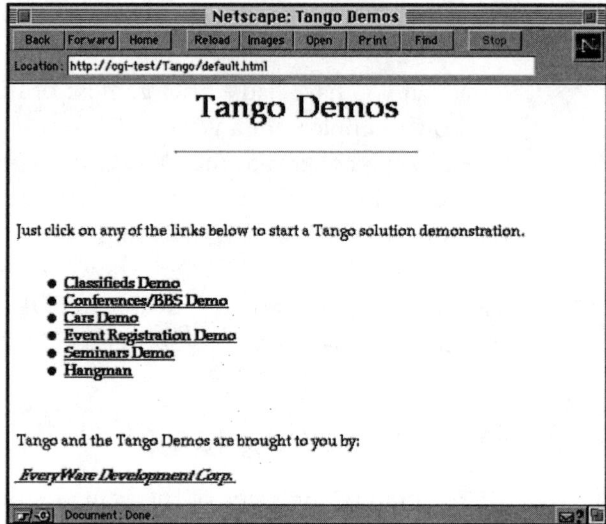

Figure 8.4 *This default Tango page is a jumping point for several of the demos discussed in this section.*

Automobile Classifieds Example

Before running the demo, you'll need to move the relevant Butler database to the Public Databases folder buried deep in your Preferences folder. In the Tango folder, that you've just moved to your WebSTAR folder, open the Car_demo folder. Each demo folder has a nested folder entitled Utilities. You'll find the Tango databases located in these Utilities folders; in this case, either move, alias, or copy the cars_db file to the Public Databases folder. These sample Butler database files will all have the suffix _db.

Click on the Cars Demo link. You should see the demo window, as shown in Figure 8.5. Note that you have a series of popup menus and text fields awaiting your input. By selecting several of the fields, you can extract portions of the database that match your search criteria.

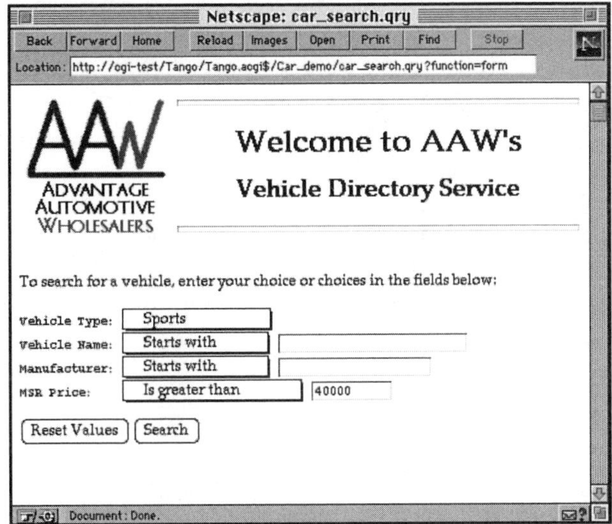

Figure 8.5 *The Tango cars demo allows you to search a database for cars that correspond to certain criteria. The information on the cars is stored in a Butler database.*

Select the various popup menus shown in Figure 8.5. These options are

Vehicle Type:	Sports
Vehicle Name:	Starts with (leave text field blank)
Manufacture:	Starts with (leave text field blank)
MSR Price:	Is greater than (40000)

Click on the Search button.

You will see a list of various database entries that match your search criteria, as shown in Figure 8.6. According to your search query, the results are displayed in an HTML table format. Note that the car model names are set up as hyperlinks. Clicking on one of the hyperlinks brings up one of the database entries, as shown in Figure 8.7.

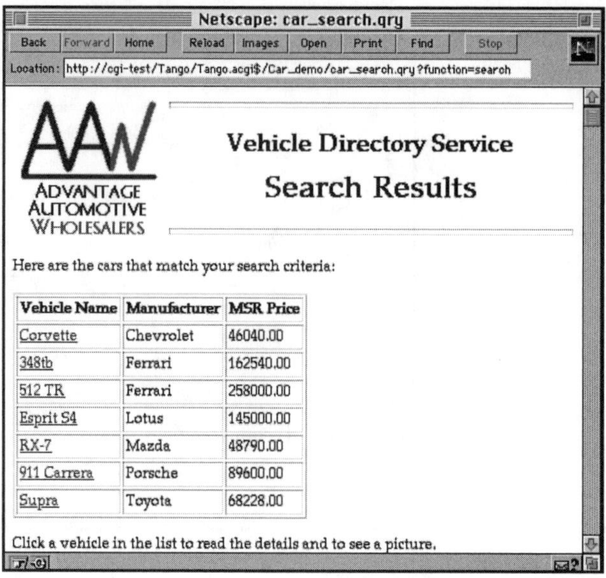

Figure 8.6 *Could you afford any of these? These database entries are returned by your search of a Butler database.*

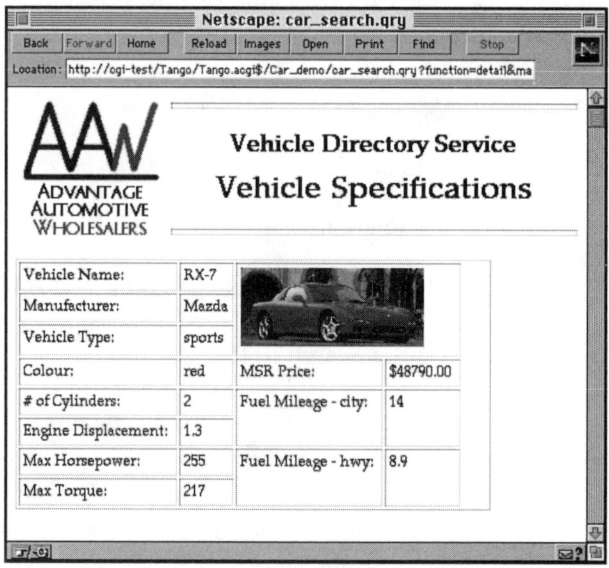

Figure 8.7 *The car of your dreams awaits you in a Butler database. This car matches your earlier search criteria. Note that you are able to call up both graphics and text as a result of the database search.*

Note that the database entry describing this car contains a variety of information. Furthermore, a picture of the car is included as well. This graphic might just as well have been a movie or even an audio file that you could have used to display a different types of files. You could even store alternative file formats for display using Netscape plug-in modules. You could construct a similar database using Butler SQL or any other ODBC-compliant system and use Tango to develop a Web-based front-end.

NOTE

See Chapter 9, "Beyond HTML," for more information on Netscape plug-in modules.

Seminar Demo

To run this example, look for the Seminar_db file in the Utilities folder inside the Seminars folder. Move, copy, or alias this file to the Public Databases folder. Go back to the Tango demo page and click on the Seminar demo link. A page similar to that shown in Figure 8.8 will appear.

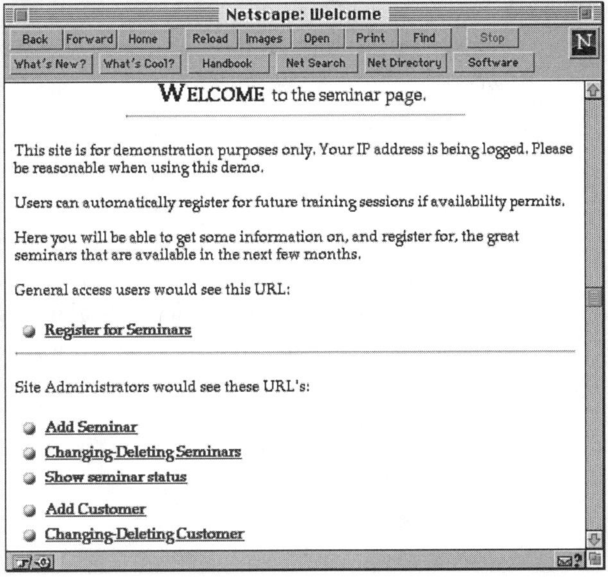

Figure 8.8 *Business seminar schedules can be posted on the Web using Tango.*

This page allows you to register and check the status of some hypothetical seminars. For further examination, click on the Show seminar status link. You'll see a window similar to that shown in Figure 8.9. You'll be shown a list of seminar subjects from which to choose. Click on the HTML link.

Figure 8.9 *Click on the seminar subject for the status you want to check.*

You should then see the HTML-related seminars layed out in a nice orderly HTML table, as shown in Figure 8.9. Each seminar is displayed with information regarding its location, date, time, sponsor, number of registrants, and the seminar capacity. All these data are fields in the Seminar_db Butler SQL database; you are using Tango to extract these fields and display them on a Web page.

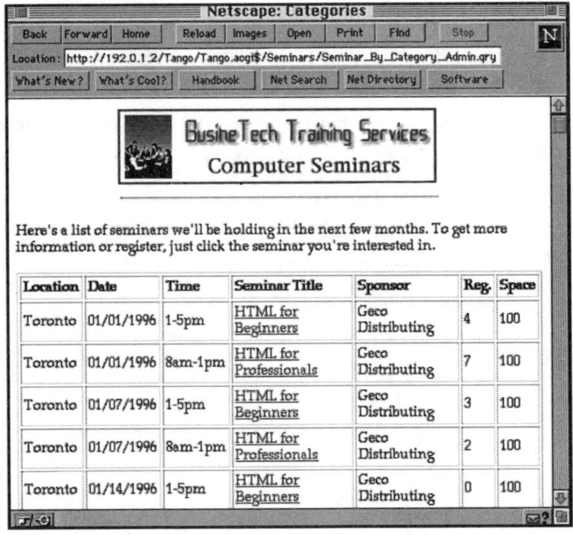

Figure 8.10 *Click on the various HTML seminars to find out their status.*

Finally, click on the top entry under the Seminar Title column, HTML for Beginners. As seen in Figure 8.11, you'll see another HTML table containing the names of people currently registered for that seminar along with data about the registrants.

Figure 8.11 *"What do you mean I'm not registered?"*

This example shows the power of sophisticated databases. You were able to store information on several different levels. On one hand, you were able to store information about the seminars; the Butler database contained information about the seminars such as the location, date, and sponsor. Even so, you were able to store and access information one level deeper. Information about the registrants, such as their name, their registration ID, and the date they registered, was stored in the Butler database. With the proper amount of programming and resources, you can embed several layers of information in your databases.

Guide to Using Tango

Tango is comprised of two elements: the Tango CGI and the Tango Editor. These two applications are the heart of the Tango interface. We'll learn how to use these two applications to build a Web-based interface to your databases.

The Tango CGI

The Tango CGI is a stand-alone multipurpose CGI application that works between your database and your WebSTAR server. The Tango CGI processes queries embedded in HTML documents created by the Tango Editor. Written in C++, the Tango CGI is asynchronous, multithreaded, and PowerPC native.

The Tango CGI works like any other CGI application that we constructed in Chapter 7. However, it's specialized to work with query documents constructed with the Tango editor. It's called in one of two ways. The conventional method is to embed the CGI call in a URL like this:

```
http://my.web.server/Tango/example/
query_doc?function=form
```

The other method works exclusively with WebSTAR. You can associate the Tango CGI with a user-defined action in WebSTAR Admin. In this way, you can specify a certain file suffix with a call to the Tango CGI.

NOTE

You'll note from the previous examples that when you run a Tango query, the Tango CGI stays active even after the search. This saves time, as the tango.acgi application will then not need to be re-launched each time a query is made. You can close the application by selecting it from the application menu and quitting it like any other application.

NOTE

See Chapter 4, "Macintosh HTTP Servers," for more information on WebSTAR's user-defined actions.

The Tango Editor

Using a tool like ButlerLink/AppleScript, you can build a customized CGI script to access your Butler databases. However, a tool like the Tango Editor offers you a graphical means of developing query documents that are interpreted by the Tango CGI. As mentioned previously, the Tango Editor works with several types of databases, whereas ButlerLink/AppleScript limits you to developing only AppleScript CGIs. The Tango Editor lets you do three main tasks:

- **Generate query documents.** These documents are configured within the Tango Editor so as to present an HTML page that prompts the user for search criteria.
- **Generate record list documents.** These documents display the results of a Tango search.
- **Generate record detail documents.** These documents display detailed information about records returned as a result of search queries.

These documents are created by the Tango Editor and are not strictly HTML. Instead, they are interpreted by the Tango CGI, which develops HTML and displays the results of the database queries via WebSTAR. Let's look at these individual tasks.

The Query Builder

Launch the Tango Editor and open the document Lesson 1 Builder in the lesson_1 folder. You should see a series of windows, as shown in Figure 8.12. Note that there are two windows displayed. Click on the maintable entry in the Database window; you should see the list of columns appear in the bottom window. The opposite window is the main Tango Editor window. To compile a query document, you drag the desired columns from the Database window over to the Search Columns window.

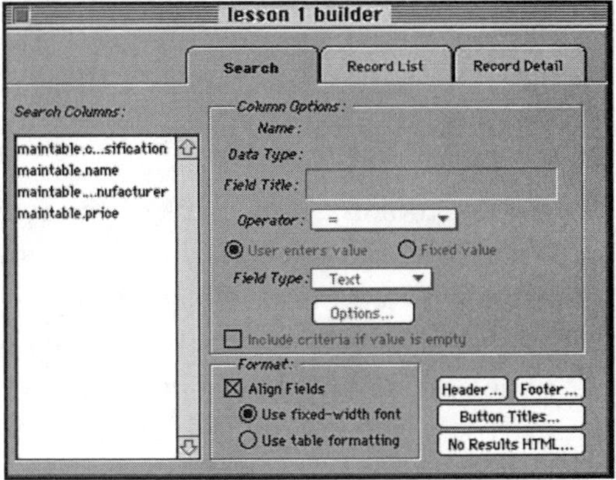

Figure 8.12 *The Tango Editor Search Query Builder offers a graphical interface for developing HTML pages that initiate database searches.*

In the Tango Editor window, you can then click on the various HTML options that you would like to include in your search query page. By selecting each column in the Search Columns window, you can specify the column title. You also can specify the manner in which the search criteria will be evaluated. The options in this window also tell the Tango CGI how to format the HTML fields in which the user enters the search criteria. You also can specify the page headers, footers, search button titles, and even the HTML text, telling the user that no results were found. You can even specify whether the search page is formulated using a fixed-width font or as an HTML table. Remember that on the HTML search page, each database column can be presented differently; simply reformat each column with different options within the Tango Editor.

Specifying the Search Results Page

While in the Tango Editor, click on the top button entitled Record List. The window should now appear, as shown in Figure 8.13. Once again, you can specify which columns from the database table are displayed in your search page. You also can specify how the information is formatted on the page. You can specify how many matches from the search should be returned. Once again, you can determine the HTML page headers and footers for the results page.

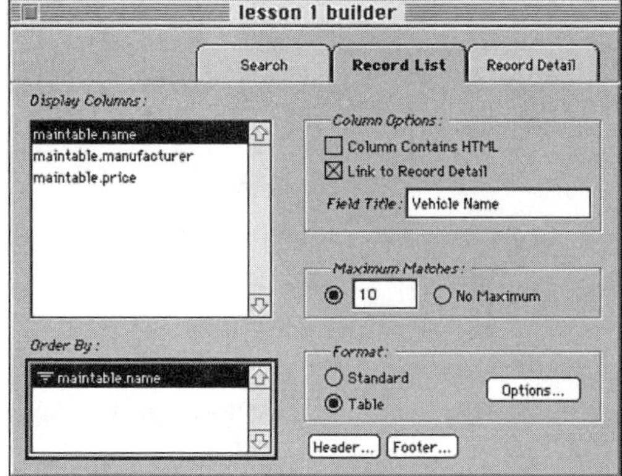

Figure 8.13 *Using the Tango Editor, you can specify the format of the HTML page that displays your search results.*

Giving More Detail on the Search Results

Given the results page that you've just specified, you may want to link in more information on the individual records returned on the results page. This is accomplished within the Tango Editor by clicking on the Record Detail button at the top of the window. You should see a window similar to that displayed in Figure 8.14.

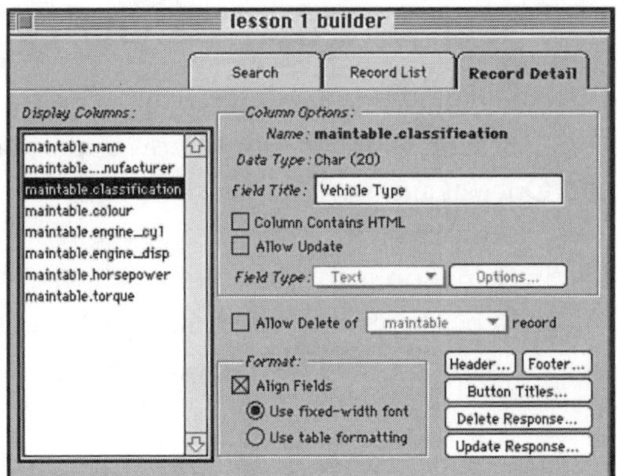

Figure 8.14 *Not only can you return results from a search query, but you also can display more information on each result.*

In the automobile classifieds demo (see the "Automobile classifieds example"), we noticed that once you received a series of cars that matched your search criteria, you were able to click on the individual entries and see an entire Web page devoted to that entry. This is what the Record Detail portion of the Tango Editor accomplishes.

Similar to the other Tango Editor environments, you can specify the way in which the different database records are displayed. This is a useful tool for giving your users more information about the database search results.

Query Documents

When you've finished your format specifications for your query, results, and resulting details, click on the File menu and select Generate Query Document. You'll be presented with a dialog box asking you where you'd like to store the query document. Enter a location that is accessible through a URL directed at your WebSTAR server. For example, you may want to locate your Tango query documents in a folder just inside of the WebSTAR folder.

In any case, you'll be presented with the actual URL in a dialog box similar to that in Figure 8.15. You can close the dialog box or copy the URL for pasting into a Web page. Remember that when initiating a database search, you don't use conventional URLs that point to HTML documents. Instead, the Tango CGI is launched and then interprets the query document named in the URL.

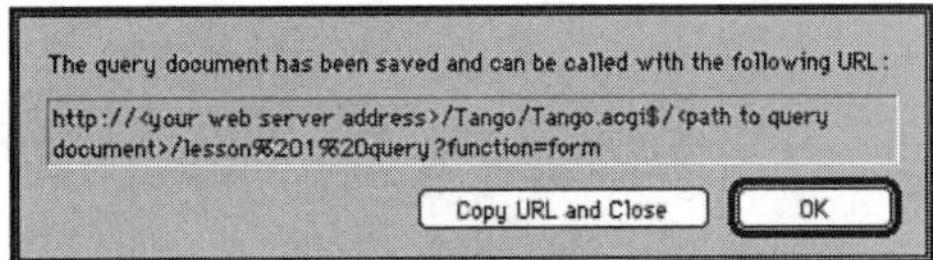

Figure 8.15 *When generating a query document, the Tango Editor will display that document's URL for you to incorporate in an HTML page.*

If you want even more control over the database query, you can edit the query document directly with the Tango Editor. Simply open a query document with the Editor and you'll see a set of windows similar to Figure 8.16. These windows depict the execution flow of your database search using graphical icons; the Action window details the types of operations you can develop in your search. By adding icons or modifying those in the query document window, you can customize the execution of your database search.

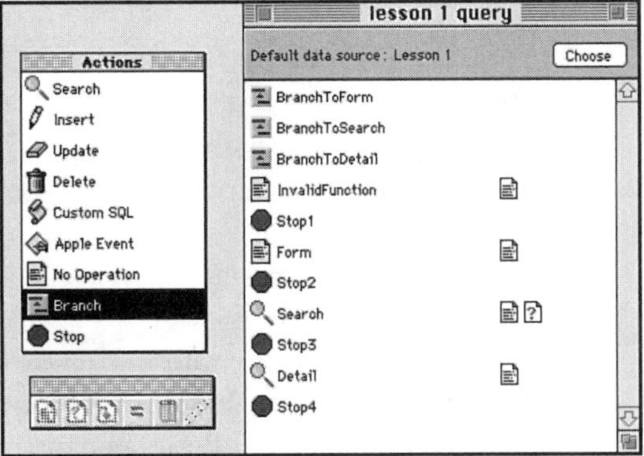

Figure 8.16 *The actions in the query document are executed in order, as shown. You can edit and even redirect the order of execution by modification with the Action icons.*

As mentioned in the beginning of this section, there are other databases available for the MacOS. Many tools exist that allow you to display the contents of these database on your Web pages. There are several CGI applications that offer forms-driven access to FileMaker Pro database files. The most popular FileMaker Pro CGI is ROFM CGI (formerly known as FMPro CGI) available at http://rowen.astro.washington.edu/.

Document Text Searches

Another powerful tool that you will want to make available on your Intranet is document searches. Think about it—most of the work done by your organization in the last few years is stored somewhere in electronic form. All the memos, reports, and technical papers exist scattered around on various desktop computers. You're forever locked out of the files on the computer belonging to the guy down the hall...simply because you don't know what's on his computer!

Imagine if all the text and word-processing files developed by your organization were now located in a central location or at least on a set of computers with network access. You would be able to search these holdings for relevant files. You could compile an online organizational library accessible not through file cabinets and librarians, but through your Intranet Web services.

Let's look at some of your options.

TR-WWW (http://www.monash.edu.au/informatics/tr-www.html) is a Web-based version of the Total Research document search application designed to work with the shareware HTTP server, MacHTTP. TR-WWW will also work with WebSTAR. Specifically, TR-WWW is a shareware text search and retrieval engine that you can use to search through text files for occurrences of text strings.

TR-WWW offers several advantages, the most beneficial of which is that your files do not need to be indexed. Many search engines require file indexing to speed up the search process. This entails setting up the files, or file descriptions, into a database or some structured file system, and running the search through that file system. As a result, you can just dump your files into a single directory and have TR-WWW scan them.

One disadvantage is that TR-WWW works only with text files. Therefore, your mounds of MS Word and WordPerfect documents are inaccessible to a TR-WWW search. Many people get around this short-coming by converting these types of documents to ASCII text, which requires some additional labor.

Installing and Configuring TR-WWW

TR-WWW is distributed as a fat binary, so it will take advantage of your Power Mac's faster processor. TR-WWW is very simple to set up. There are three elements to TR-WWW.

- ☐ **tr-www.cgi.** The actual search engine that works with MacHTTP. Like Tango, discussed in the "Introduction to Tango" section, it's a pre-written CGI application.
- ☐ **tr-www.prompt.** The file loaded into your Web browser used to initiate text searches.
- ☐ **tr-www.config.** A simple configuration text file.

Move all of these files into your Web server folder. You'll also nest a folder entitled Docs in this folder. This Docs folder will contain all of the files that you want to search. As you accumulate files that you want to search, just load them into this folder. For now, just load the sample Docs folder from the TR-WWW distribution. It contains several sample text files.

Once all the elements of TR-WWW have been moved into the Web Server folder, open a Web browser and insert the following string:

```
http://<your server>/tr-www.cgi
```

A search form page will return in the browser window. Scroll down and you should see the page as formatted in Figure 8.17. The page returned by the CGI is derived from the HTML code found in the tr-www.prompt file. You can customize the response returned by the tr-www.cgi by editing this file. To fully customize the response, you'll have to grab a Mac resource editor, such as ResEdit, and edit the STR resources in the tr-www.cgi.

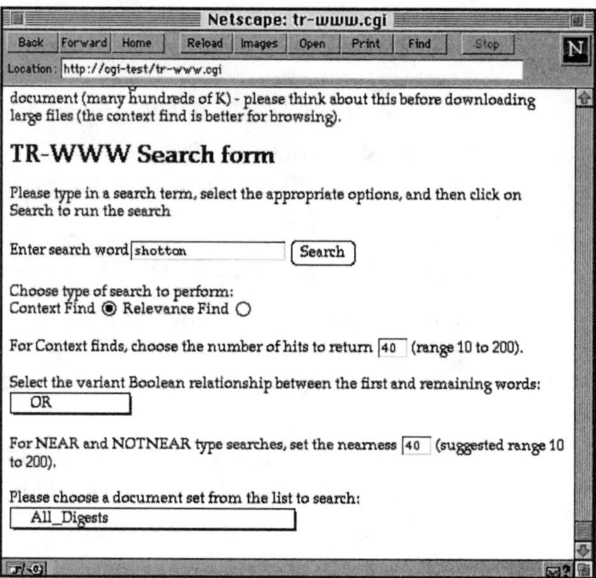

Figure 8.17 *TR-WWW offers several options to use in searching for documents.*

Note that users can specify several search options. First, you can specify whether the search is a context or a relevance search. A context search is one where the results depend on a relevance ranking—a file with a high relevance ranking usually contains several occurrences of the search string. A keyword search returns lines of text containing your search strings; clicking on the hyperlinked text returns the entire document.

You also can specify the maximum number of correct matches to return in the search. If your Docs folder contains many documents, this parameter will restrict the number of correct matches to your search.

TR-WWW gives you several ways to configure your search if your query contains multiple strings. Click on the popup menu to display the different Boolean operators. The function of these operators is described below:

OR	Returns logical union of your query strings.
AND	Returns logical intersection of your query strings.
PHRASE	Returns occurrences of your query strings where they appear side-by-side as in 'Power Macintosh' or 'Microsoft Word.'
NEAR	Returns occurrences of your search strings when they appear near one another. This nearness parameter is set at the bottom of the form.
NOTNEAR	Opposite of NEAR. Search strings cannot appear with in a certain number of words.

Below the popup menu, you'll see that you can set the nearness parameter. This parameter establishes the number of words that can separate multiple strings within a NEAR or NOTNEAR search.

Finally, you'll see that TR-WWW has assembled the contents of the Docs folder in a popup menu. This allows you to restrict the searches to certain files or embedded folders.

Clicking on the Search button at the top of the page executes the search and returns results similar to that found in Figure 8.18. The result in the figure corresponds to a context search; note that the actual lines of text appear in the browser window with the search strings hyperlinked to the actual document. Clicking one of the hyperlinks brings up the actual document, as shown in Figure 8.19. You can then jump down to the occurrence of the string or retrieve the file in its entirety.

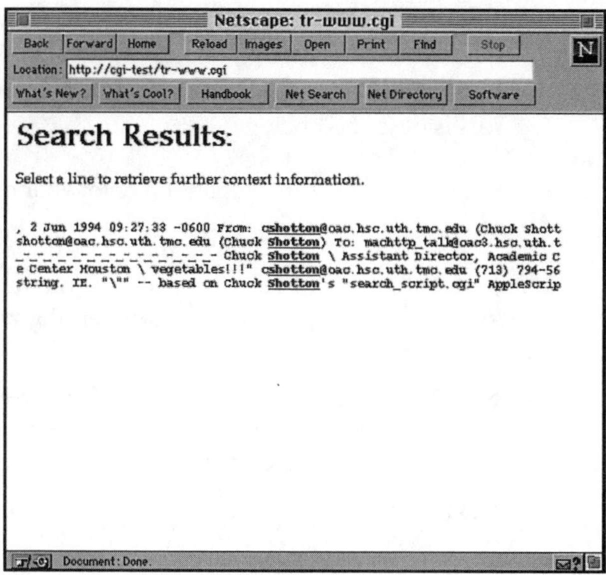

Figure 8.18 *A TR-WWW context search returns the actual lines of text in which your search strings appear.*

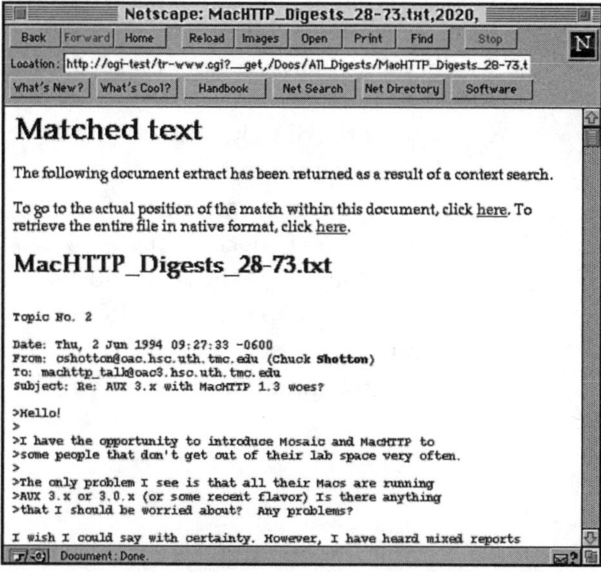

Figure 8.19 *The final result—you can view the file containing your search string or you can jump down to the search string itself.*

You can configure many of the search options that we've discussed so far. The search configurations are stored in the tr-www.config file. You'll find the default values for your TR-WWW searches contained in this file. The options listed in this file are well-documented and are an easy means of customizing a series of searches.

AppleSearch

AppleSearch (http://product.info.apple.com/productinfo/datasheets/ss/applesearch.html) is a search engine developed by Apple Computer. As a commercial software offering, it offers more functionality than that presented by TR-WWW. AppleSearch will search for files anywhere on a particular volume and will also search for files on computers accessible through a local network or on the Internet.

AppleSearch can search for documents on both Mac and Windows PCs. Furthermore, the application comes with a variety of filters so that it can search files of varying types including Microsoft Word, MacWrite, Microsoft Excel, WordPerfect, and many others. This is an important feature, as much of the work produced by your Intranet users is in files of these types. You are not limited to strictly text-only file searches when using AppleSearch.

Apple also produces the AppleSearch.cgi application. Like TR-WWW, AppleSearch.cgi (http://kamaaina.apple.com/) is an application that acts as an interface between AppleSearch and your HTTP server. As a result, you can integrate AppleSearch into your Web services using the AppleSearch.cgi.

MacSite Searcher

Blue World Communications' MacSite Searcher (http://www.blueworld.com/macsite/searcher/) is a competing commercial application to the AppleSearch/AppleSearch.cgi search tools. MacSite Searcher is based on custom Frontier scripts and FileMaker Pro. The application periodically indexes text files stored in a particular folder into a FileMaker Pro database. The MacSite Search Frontier scripts then interact with FileMaker Pro to search the files for particular strings in the database.

Summary

One of the most useful features you can offer your Intranet users is the capability to work with databases and search for documents. We've covered how you can accomplish these tasks using simple-to-use Web-based interfaces. Much of the difficulty involved with developing database applications and customized search applications is obviated through the use of applications like EveryWare's Tango as well as the TR-WWW document search tools. Working these tools into your Intranet will provide a potent and flexible capability to your users.

In Chapter 9, "Beyond HTML," we'll talk about some of the ways that you can supplement your Intranet Web pages with new formats and techniques beyond the conventional HTML and graphics files. We'll talk about PDF, RealAudio, VRML, Java, and other hot topics. Feel free to jump around in this book. Some chapters related to this current one include:

- Chapter 4, "Macintosh HTTP Servers," to learn about the different software you can use to set up World Wide Web services on your Mac.
- Chapter 7, "Writing CGI Scripts," to learn about writing scripts for your Web site. These scripts allow you to process data from HTML forms and return customized Web pages.
- Appendix C, "Perfecting HTML," to learn about some advanced HTML programming features as well as how to use some popular HTML editors, including Adobe PageMill and BBEdit.

Links Related to This Chapter

Claris	http://www.claris.com
ACI-US	http://www.acius.com
4th Dimension	http://www.acius.com/Pages/GUI/ACI_US/English/Home.html
EveryWare Development	http://www.everyware.com
Tango Mailing List	tango-talk-request@lists.everyware.com
ROFM CGI	http://rowen.astro.washington.edu/
TR-WWW	http://www.monash.edu.au/informatics/tr-www.html
AppleSearch	http://product.info.apple.com/productinfo/datasheets/ss/applesearch.html
AppleSearch CGI	http://kamaaina.apple.com/
MacSite Searcher	http://www.blueworld.com/macsite/searcher/

CHAPTER 9

Beyond HTML

In an environment that changes as rapidly as the World Wide Web, it's difficult to make predictions as to what lies in the future. This section, however, discusses several emerging technologies that will make their presence known on the Web. You'll need to keep abreast of these new areas, because these technologies can yield new and useful services to your users. For each topic discussed, you'll see how it could be incorporated into your Intranet.

PDF

The Portable Document Format (PDF) is a document format proposed by Adobe Systems, Inc. Much like HTML, it's seen as an alternative file format to HTML. This non-ASCII format describes a cross-platform means of viewing documents. The Adobe Acrobat Pro application lets you construct and add features to PDF documents, whereas the Adobe Exchange application enables you to print your documents from an assortment of word-processing and page-layout applications. Finally, Adobe has offered the Adobe Acrobat Reader as a freeware PDF viewer. This enables users from all major operating systems to view and print PDF files. An example of a PDF file as viewed with the Adobe Acrobat Reader is given in Figure 9.1.

NOTE

> Adobe also is the company that brought you the PostScript language. PostScript is a graphical description language that is used by printers and some display devices to express graphics. Adobe also developed Acrobat Distiller, which is a means of converting PostScript documents to PDF.

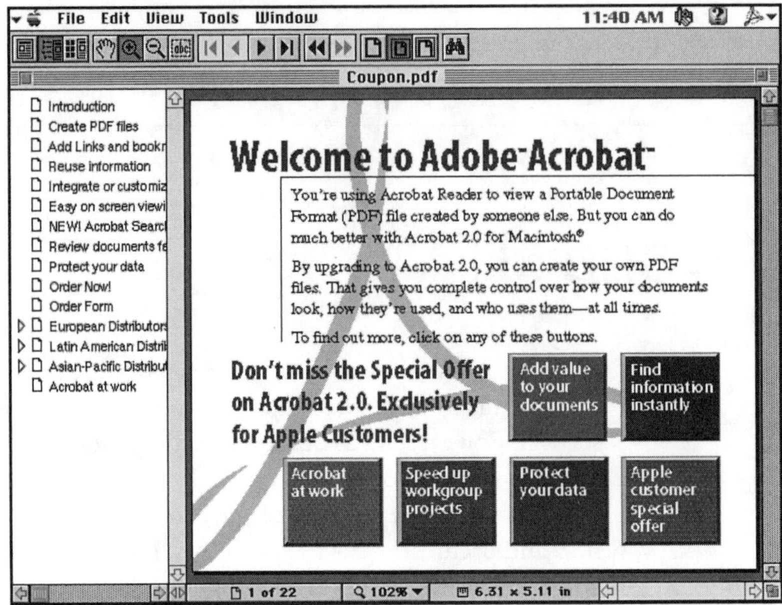

Figure 9.1 *The Portable Document Format allows more sophisticated formatting than does HTML.*

PDF allows several text-processing options not found in HTML, such as multiple columns, text flow around graphics, color, and font specification. Furthermore, Acrobat users can install annotations in the form of scrollable text boxes for workgroup applications. PDF files also can sport hyperlinks within the document; using the WebLink Acrobat plug-in, you can click and launch URLs within the PDF document.

NOTE 

> Grab a free copy of Adobe Acrobat Reader along with the Amber and WebLink plug-ins at http://www.adobe.com.

Because of the typesetting freedom allowed by the format, PDF files are frequently published on the Web using Acrobat with the Reader as a helper application. PDF files are even viewable with Navigator or Internet Explorer using the Amber plug-in, described in the section "Amber" at the end of this chapter. You may want to serve PDF files for documents that cannot be accurately rendered in HTML. An example of such a case is a newsletter, company brochure, or any document that uses formatting not available in HTML.

RealAudio

RealAudio, by Progressive Networks, is a means of broadcasting high-quality audio transmissions over the Internet. Although it seems like an esoteric use of the Internet, RealAudio sites have proven to be very popular. Applications include music concerts, sports and news broadcasts, and real-time conferencing. RealAudio 2.0, which was introduced in early 1996, can produce FM-quality audio, even over a 28.8 modem connection; AM-quality sound can be transferred to a computer with a 14.4 modem connection.

RealAudio employs a client-server architecture and sophisticated compression techniques to broadcast live and archived audio data to multimedia computers with Internet connections. The following are the three major components of the RealAudio system:

- **RealAudio Server.** The server delivers live and archived audio over TCP/IP networks to multimedia computers. The Macintosh port of the RealAudio server works with the MacHTTP and WebSTAR servers; a Power Mac is required.
- **RealAudio Encoder.** This is required to compress audio files into the RealAudio file format. The Encoder has the capability of compressing audio files directly, or it can compress live audio feeds for streams fed into the RealAudio server.
- **RealAudio Player.** You need this freeware utility to listen to real-time audio from a RealAudio server.

NOTE

Check out information about the RealAudio system at http://www.realaudio.com/products/ra2.0/. You'll be able to download free copies of the RealAudio player.

The RealAudio server publishes the audio data in streams. The number of streams handled by the server is dictated by the speed of its connection to the Internet. These streams can be multiplied by a splitter across the Internet to reduce bandwidth requirements on the RealAudio server.

As far as the Web server is concerned, it doesn't know that it's fielding a request for a RealAudio transmission. A hypothetical RealAudio request over the Web probably goes like this:

> Browser: "Hey, my user wants to look at this URL. It has a funny suffix, ra, I wonder what that means? I'll send it up to the server."
>
> Server: "Oh yeah, that thing! I don't even know what RealAudio is, but this link has some information here. I'll pass it on to its helper application. Now leave me alone."
>
> Browser: (to RealAudio Player) "Here, this is for you."
>
> RealAudio Player: "Oh boy! A request for a RealAudio stream. How exciting! Let me contact the RealAudio server mentioned in the link and tell it to play this particular stream for this particular time. Man, this is great! I just need to tell the RealAudio player something about the computer on which I live."
>
> RealAudio Server: "I'm there, dude. Let me start up this stream but before I do, let me see how fast your connection is. 28.8? Great, here's the stream he wants. It's a live feed, so I need to start compressing the data as it leaves my box. Here it goes."
>
> RealAudio Player: "Okay, here it comes. I know I have the Mac SoundManager extension here onboard with me so it'll figure out how to let the user hear this. Man, I love this job!"

You may want to serve RealAudio feeds, or you may want to serve archived sound in RealAudio format. Whichever you choose, you will need to configure your server with enough network bandwidth and disk space to cover your load. Progressive Networks states that an hour-long FM-quality transmission requires 8 MB of disk space.

One possible application of RealAudio is to use your server as a means of broadcasting real-time conferences; unless you plan to couple that with real-time video conferencing, it's hard to see RealAudio's advantage over conventional teleconferencing. The FM-quality sound is more valuable for music transmission. Even so, the RealAudio service is an emerging technology that is a really interesting solution in search of a need that you might have.

VRML

The Virtual Reality Modeling Language (VRML—rhymes with thermal) is a draft specification for a language that can publish three-dimensional data over the Internet. As HTML enables you to construct a two-dimensional publishing metaphor for graphics and text, VRML is a separate language designed to extend the metaphor to a third dimension. With Netscape and HTML, you meander across a page and click on links and graphics as you see fit; a VRML browser allows a hypothetical third-dimension to be traversed as well. Instead of two-dimensional imagemaps, VRML browsers have hallways that can be traversed much like you would in a virtual reality simulation. Information can be displayed from a variety of three-dimensional perspectives instead of the rigid display defined by your two-dimensional Web browser.

Whereas you jump from page to page using HTML, VRML users jump between "worlds." These worlds can be configured with various VRML editors. Loading a world over the Internet requires not much more time than a large graphic does using HTML. It's possible that three-dimensional graphics will become more prevalent in the Mac environment with the recent release of QuickDraw 3D, a new 3D-rendering technology (available at http://qtvr.quicktime.apple.com/). Apple has released QuickDraw 3D for Windows as well.

Programming in VRML is analogous to programming in HTML. The three-dimensional interface leads to new possibilities in information publishing. If you have ever played DOOM or Marathon, you've seen some of the applications of three-dimensional graphics under the MacOS. As you explore other VRML worlds, you can think of ways that you can use the three-dimensional metaphor to present information to your users. Examples of this metaphor can include a virtual reality implementation of a library; users can navigate through virtual stacks to browse some of the library selections.

Several VRML editors and browsers are available for the MacOS. Virtus Corporation sells Walkthrough Pro, a VRML editor, and Voyager, a VRML browser. Strata Corporation sells StudioPro Blitz, which supports QuickDraw 3D. Both Voyager and StudioPro Blitz are VRML browsers in their own right, but can be configured as Netscape VRML helper applications.

Java

The computer industry does a poor job of predicting the next big thing. When you think of events that have taken the computing industry by storm, such as the Macintosh, the Internet, and the Web, they usually have come unheralded and by surprise. In contrast, things that the industry heralds as significant never really live up to their promise; examples of this are the Ada computing language, Apple's Newton, Microsoft Bob, and Windows 95. Java may be the first event to buck this conventional wisdom. Despite all the hype it has received in recent months, many experts predict that Java will revolutionize not only the Web, but the computing paradigm as we know it.

Caffeinating the Web

Java was developed at Sun Microsystems, as a possible means for the Unix workstation manufacturer to venture into consumer electronics software. As originally conceived, Java would operate such devices as light switches, microwave ovens, television box tops, and other mundane devices. The intention was to build a language that was as efficient as C++ but much more reliable. Sun's consumer electronics initiative failed at the same time that the Mosaic browser was introduced. All of a sudden, Sun found another use for Java.

The idea behind Java is simple. For an application to run, it must first be translated from a programming language such as FORTRAN or C++ into a computer's native machine code. This process is time-consuming and needs only to be done once. As a result, applications are compiled and delivered to the desktop in some manner whether it's by hard drive, CD-ROM, or network. The problem with installing an application built from compiled code is that it's a one-time operation; to develop a robust application, you have to pile everything but the kitchen sink into the program. Anyone who has waded through a 30+ disk installation of Microsoft Office can attest to this. Furthermore, different compilations have to be created to run on a variety of computing platforms, often with a nontrivial amount of rewriting.

Java gets around this by using an interpreted approach to code-building. Interpreted code operates much slower than compiled code. However, Java applications, or applets, are much smaller than conventional applications. These Java applets are sent down the Internet to do small specialized tasks. A commonly cited example of this is a payroll time sheet built into the Web. You can take a payroll form and build it with HTML forms commands. To interactively calculate billable hours and tally personal leave like a spreadsheet, you would have to write a cumbersome CGI script that would exchange data with the HTTP server, do the calculations and reload the entire page with the updated results. In contrast, a Java applet would be built into the page just like ordinary HTML. A Java-aware browser would run the applet and perform the necessary spreadsheet-like calculations on the client computer. Other Java applications include real-time stock ticker Web pages, animation, Web pages with rudimentary word-processing capability, and many others.

Using Java in your applications improves your server performance. Whereas CGI scripts place an extra load on your server (some Internet Service Providers forbid you from using developing CGI scripts for this very reason), Java applets run on the client computer. Despite the fact that Java applets run on your browsing computer, these applets have a limited capability to affect the user's machine, making Java virtually virus-proof.

Netscape, Java, and HotJava

Netscape has worked closely with Sun to obtain support for Java within the Netscape Navigator browser. Alternatively, Sun also is developing a new browser known as HotJava. In contrast to Netscape, HotJava will be intertwined with Java to produce a more interactive browser. If a conventional browser encounters an image file format it does not recognize, for example, it throws the problem back at the user. HotJava, on the other hand, will not only download the image, but also the specification, written in Java, for handling the image file type. Granted, this will occur in Java-capable browsers but it's likely that HotJava will always be a more robust and flashier browser for reading and downloading Java applets. HotJava requires less dependency on helper applications and plug-ins than do conventional browsers.

A $500 Java Box?

Many experts predict that Java may mean the end of Microsoft's desktop hegemony. By sending cheap applets down your browser, it would no longer be necessary for you to have a word-processing application that takes up 30 MB of hard drive space. A word-processing applet would come down to your computer and evaporate as soon as you finished using it. Need a spell checker? Summon an appropriate applet and then send it packing when you're finished with it.

With a fast enough network connection, Java applets would obviate the need for expensive desktop applications. In fact, some experts say that operating systems would become obsolete. Your future computer may be a $500 box that does little more than connect you to a Java server through a very fast network.

As you can imagine, Microsoft disagrees with this vision of the future. They responded to the Java threat with a similar language known as Visual Basic. Visual Basic also contains a programming language and an interpreter similar to C++. Surprisingly, Microsoft has acknowledged Java's popularity by announcing support for Java in its new Web server and browser software.

Java and You

Of all the emerging technologies mentioned in this section, Java is probably going to most affect you as a WebMaster. It may actually turn out to be one of the lone heralded revolutions in computing. The Java/HotJava paradigm is one that you should be looking to adopt in your server.

JavaScript

JavaScript is similar to Java, but without Java's more sophisticated C-like type checking and static typing. Furthermore, JavaScript isn't really built for graphics—it's not multithreaded, and it can't be extended to create new data types like Java. JavaScript is supported by Netscape Navigator. Inasmuch as Java may have applications beyond Navigator, JavaScript is designed to work inside an HTML page as a run-time configurable option. JavaScript actually is embedded into the HTML code, whereas Java applets are compiled and accessed by the server and are distinct from the pages that call them.

NOTE 

> For more information on programming with JavaScript, see *JavaScript for Macintosh* by Hayden Books.

Whereas Java is descended from C++ and other languages that strongly support object-oriented design, JavaScript belongs to the same class of smaller, dynamically typed scripting languages such as AppleScript, HyperTalk, and dBASE. These types of scripting languages offer more appeal to less-experienced programmers who appreciate the more comprehensible syntax, specialized features, and the freedom from having to deal with object classes and inheritance.

JavaScript also supports event handlers. For example, you would be able to execute a script or function by having the user click on an area of the browser window or even move the mouse to that area. Because JavaScript is an interpreted language, complicated tasks run more slowly and are better executed using Java applets.

However, JavaScript is ideal for simple tasks that extend beyond the capabilities of your HTML and would normally require sophisticated CGI scripts.

Netscape Plug-Ins

The Netscape plug-in architecture enables third-party developers to create modules that extend the functionality of the Navigator browser. Within the Navigator context, the plug-in allows the browser to display a file for which there is no native MIME definition. A plug-in registers its MIME-type definitions when the Navigator is launched; other than disk space, the plug-ins consume little or no system or application resources.

NOTE

The concept of plug-in modules is not new to the software industry. Adobe Photoshop has plug-in modules to enable users to install different types of graphics filters and effects.

Navigator plug-ins are used to extend the functionality of the browser. For example, when Navigator is sent a GIF file from a Web server, it displays the GIF image within the browser. The same can be said for JPEG images. The code that tells Navigator how to display these images is resident within the application. All a plug-in does is tell Navigator how to display files of certain MIME types. Essentially, the plug-in creates a partition or subwindow within the browser window to display a file of a certain MIME type.

Netscape distributes the plug-in Application Programming Interface (API) free-of-charge; as a result, Navigator plug-ins started to appear shortly after version 2.0 of the browser was released. Given the open plug-in architecture, there are virtually no limits to the types of files that you can display within your browser window. As an Intranet administrator, you should be cognizant of the types of files that members of your organization may want to view within Navigator. For example, engineers doing computer-aided design (CAD) work on high-end workstations may desire to keep a database of CAD drawings accessible through Web pages. Using pre-Netscape 2.0 technology, you could develop a Web front end to the database and have the engineers download the drawings to their workstations or desktop computers. However, using the Navigator plug-in API, you could develop an online CAD drawing viewer; in this manner, users could access files from the database using a Web interface and view them within the browser window before downloading them into a CAD application. At the rate that plug-in modules are being developed for Navigator, there's a good chance that most of the file types you work with are represented in the Netscape plug-in index.

Plug-In Architecture

Plug-ins can have three types of operation: hidden, full-page, or embedded. A *hidden* plug-in, like the RealAudio plug-in, runs in the background, and the effects are not visible to the user. An example of a hidden plug-in would be a sound player that plays sounds in the background. A *full-page* plug-in fills the browser window with the downloaded file. An example of that would be a PDF or CAD drawing file that would be viewed and manipulated within the browser window. Finally, *embedded* plug-ins incorporate the downloaded file into the HTML code much like GIFs and JPEGs are displayed alongside text. In each case, the browser interface remains the same. Users can use the familiar Back and Forward keys and have access to bookmarks and link history.

Several types of plug-ins have been made available to the Netscape user community. The plug-ins display popular file formats, but other than time and money, there is nothing to prevent you from developing plug-in modules that display more arcane file types than are actually relevant to your organization.

NOTE

A directory of current Netscape plug-ins is available at http://home.netscape.com/comprod/products/navigator/version_2.0/plugins/index.html.

Shockwave

One of the splashiest plug-ins to hit the Navigator user community is Shockwave. Shockwave for Director is a way to package and play Director movies over the Web. Macromedia Director enables you to construct animated multimedia presentations. Shockwave for Director actually consists of two applications: Afterburner, which is a means of compressing Director files for faster Web transit, and the Shockwave Netscape plug-in, which allows you to display Director files in a window inside a Navigator window.

Shockwave can allow some degree of interaction with a Director file. Figure 9.2, for example, shows how a user within Netscape Navigator can interact with a Director file to play the venerable game of Tetris. In this manner, a number of applications can be developed for the Web. Another example is the use of courseware. Courses that currently reside on videotape can be transferred to Director files, compressed using Afterburner, and downloaded to a student's computer using Navigator and the Shockwave plug-in. The user would be able to start, stop, pause, and repeat sections of the course simply by using built-in Director controls.

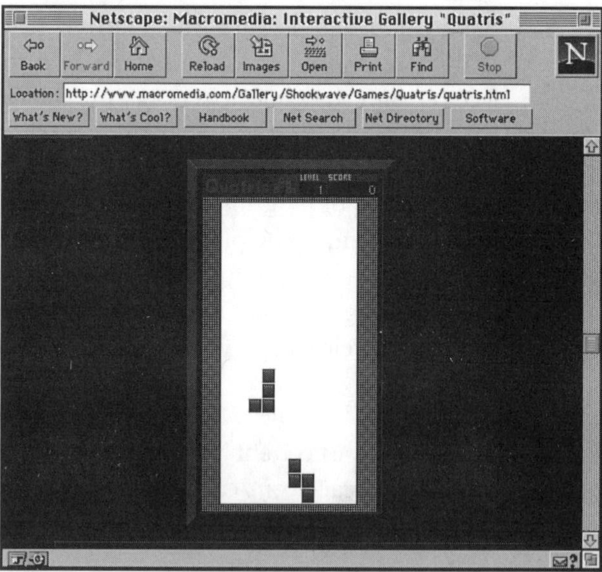

Figure 9.2 *A Tetris-like game can be set up inside Netscape using the Shockwave for Director plug-in module.*

Macromedia also plans to develop a hypertext version of Shockwave. In this manner, you will be able to link Web pages to certain areas of a Director file. Going back to the courseware example, a Director developer would be able to code certain parts of the presentation with links. To get more information on a subject, a user can click on an area within the movie that is associated with a certain URL. The movie pauses, and the link manifests itself within the Web browser.

QuickTime

By the time you read this, Apple will have developed a QuickTime plug-in that enables you to display QuickTime movies within a Netscape window. This plug-in is similar to Macromedia's Shockwave, except that QuickTime is a more prevalent movie format on the MacOS and even Windows platforms. This plug-in enables many of the same movie controls as do the rudimentary video players.

Amber

Amber is the code name for a PDF viewer plug-in module from Adobe. The PDF format is growing in popularity, mostly because of the ubiquity of the cross-platform Adobe Acrobat Reader applications. Using Amber, you can examine PDF files within Netscape. Documents viewed with the Amber plug-in will be interactive; clicking on a section of the document will bring up another page in the browser window.

Popular Plug-In Modules

As stated before, a plug-in can be developed to allow a file of almost any type to be displayed within Netscape. VRML plug-ins are becoming popular; these modules enable you to access VRML worlds from within Netscape. There are also plug-ins that enable you to view Microsoft Word and Excel documents. Progressive Networks has a plug-in enabling you to listen to RealAudio streams from within your Web browser. There are also MacOS plug-ins that enable you to convert the contents of a browser window to speech.

The future will bring only more sophisticated plug-in modules that promise to extend the functionality of Netscape Navigator (and presumably other browsers) to levels we can hardly imagine today.

Summary

There's more to the Web right now than just HTML. New capabilities are constantly developed for the Web browsers. This chapter discussed some of those new capabilities.

This is the last chapter that discusses Web-based applications for your Intranet. The rest of the book looks at some of the Intranet services you can provide outside your Web service. Chapter 10, "FTP Services," talks more about providing FTP services. If you want more information regarding the topics discussed here, see the following chapters:

- Chapter 4, "Macintosh HTTP Servers," to learn how to set up HTTP servers on your Macintosh.
- Chapter 5, "Managing Your Intranet Web Services," to obtain tips on efficient Web server management. These tips are relevant to your Internet Web services as well.
- Chapter 6, "Creating an Efficient Web Site," to learn about ways that you can develop a Web site that is easy to browse. Once again, the topics discussed in this chapter are relevant to your Internet Web services.
- Chapter 7, "Writing CGI Scripts," to learn about writing scripts for your Web site. These scripts enable you to process data from HTML forms and return customized Web pages.
- Chapter 13, "Intranet Server Security," to learn how you can configure hardware to provide secure transactions within your Intranet and out to the Internet.
- Chapter 14, "Sample Intranet Applications," to learn how you can apply some of the technology we've discussed in this book.

Links Related to This Chapter

Adobe, Inc.	http://www.adobe.com
RealAudio	http://www.realaudio.com/products/ra2.0/
RealAudio Server	http://www.realaudio.com/prognet/serrel.html
QuickTime VR	http://qtvr.quicktime.apple.com
The VRML Repository	http://sdsc.edu/vrml/
VRML Overview	http://www.caligari.com/lvltwo/2vrml.html
Virtus Corp.	http://www.virtus.com
Strata Corp.	http://www.strata3d.com
VRML Mailing List	www-vrml@hotwired.com
Java Home Page	http://java.sun.com
JavaScript	http://home.netscape.com/comprod/products/navigator/version_2.0/script/script_info/index.html
JavaScript Index	http://www.c2.org/~andreww/javascript/
Java Usenet	comp.lang.java
	comp.lang.javascript
Netscape Plug-in Index	http://home.netscape.com/comprod/products/navigator/version_2.0/plugins/index.html
Shockwave	http://www.macromedia.com

CHAPTER 10

FTP Services

At this point, you should have a thorough understanding of the Web and what is involved in running successful Web services on your Intranet. The latter portion of this book will deal with other protocols and issues of constructing a Mac-based Intranet. The second half discusses the File Transfer Protocol (FTP) and how you can implement an FTP server on your Mac. This section discusses how FTP can be a vital element of your Intranet server.

Fundamentally, your Intranet is designed to move information between computers, whether those sites are down the hall or across the planet. With the Web, you employ HTTP as a mechanism for transferring data between a Web server and your Web browser; the Web browser interprets the data and displays the appropriate files in the browser window. A more direct means of transferring data between computers is through FTP. Unlike HTTP, its more glamorous cousin, FTP has been around since the early days of the ARPAnet. It was designed to transport large amounts of data between remote sites.

Because the earliest users of FTP were computer scientists, programs that use FTP were designed with nonintuitive interfaces. Several Macintosh FTP applications utilize a more graphical interface employing icons, menus, and drag-and-drop. It was not long after FTP clients were developed for the Macintosh that FTP server applications began to appear. This chapter discusses some of the issues related to setting up an FTP server on your Mac. These topics include the following:

- How FTP works
- Using NetPresenz as an FTP server

- □ Using InterServer Publisher as an FTP server
- □ Organization of your FTP server

What Is FTP?

In the old days, when you had a few megabytes of data to transfer to a colleague across the country, you needed to make a physical copy of the data and deliver it through conventional means. This meant you had to ask your system administrator to copy the data to some storage medium, usually a magnetic tape, and then hand-carry it across campus or ship it through the regular mail. Internet users have become spoiled, as they now transfer files over the Internet and measure data transfer in thousands of bytes per second. Using FTP you can transfer large files between computers, regardless of their geographical distance.

FTP is a TCP/IP protocol much like Telnet. Whereas HTTP is a nimble protocol designed to transfer data using relatively short connection times, FTP can quickly transfer large amounts of data using lengthy connection times. With HTTP, a server responds to a browser request by sending the appropriate files and closing the connection as quickly as possible. In contrast, FTP users can browse the directories of an FTP server and transfer multiple files at their discretion.

FTP has a use within your Intranet. You can set up a site that's accessible to all your users. On this site, you can store software, documents, or other files useful to your users. Your Intranet FTP site can complement your Web services by making files available that are too large and cumbersome to be distributed by a Web server.

FTP is a client-server protocol much like HTTP and Telnet. An FTP session is similar to a Telnet connection; FTP servers listen for FTP traffic on port 21. To log in to an FTP site, you need a user account and password. With adequate privileges, FTP users can download and upload files, create folders, view text files, and even delete files. The main difference between FTP and Telnet sessions is that you cannot execute processes inside an FTP session.

FTP supports data transfer in all file formats. You can download binary and text files with equal ease. Not only can you serve PostScript or ASCII text files, but also you can serve software applications and operating system patches. Unlike HTTP, an FTP server does not need to know what type of file it's serving—it just needs to know the desired file format.

One weakness of using FTP is the lack of navigation aids. Cruising through FTP server directories is much like moving through a Unix or DOS directory system. Except for the file name, size, and creation dates, FTP does not transfer information about the file content or description. There is no easy way to change directories except through using the Unix/DOS-like cd command.

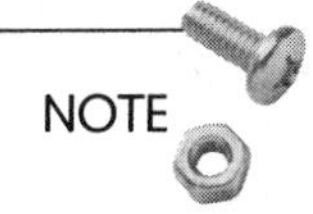

> Some FTP administrators provide a file that describes the files maintained in that directory. This file usually is called Readme or is given some name that puts it at the top of an alphabetical file listing.
>
> When running an FTP connection from a Unix computer, you can view text files, such as Readme files, using the little-known command `Get Readme -`. Macintosh FTP clients usually incorporate this feature through a pulldown menu option.

FTP Archives

An FTP server is analogous to a Web server. Instead of serving HTML files and graphics, FTP servers can maintain vast quantities of files in a variety of formats. These servers, also known as FTP archives, can store text files, graphics, or even software applications; these machines usually transfer files to the clients, and only in special circumstances do they receive files from FTP users. The FTP client application, in contrast to a Web browser, does not display the downloaded files. The client may decrypt or decompress these files after they've been downloaded, but FTP does not utilize or interpret the file the way a Web client displays HTML or graphics images.

Your Intranet FTP site can be used as an archive similar to the way FTP sites are run on the Internet. Depending on the size of your Intranet, you'll probably see less traffic than the major shareware archives, but you'll be able to adopt much of the same administrative techniques used by these archives. Later in this book, we'll talk about how you can integrate your FTP and WWW services (see Chapter 14, "Sample Intranet Applications").

Anonymous FTP

If your Intranet is small, you can just dole out individual accounts to your users; they can access your FTP servers much like they would log in to a normal Telnet session. It might be impractical for FTP site administrators to distribute user accounts for the hundreds of users who try to regularly download files from a particular site. For this reason, archive administrators enable anonymous FTP access so that users can visit the site and download files. Anonymous FTP users have restricted privileges and usually can do no more than navigate throughout the server directories and load files. File upload and deletion usually is not permitted.

The convention for anonymous FTP accounts is for the administrator to create an account with the user name "anonymous." Although passwords are not monitored by the server, users are obliged to enter their email address as a password. In one sense, anonymous FTP access provides a potential security hole for a server. Any time you give users computer access to an area they don't own, you run the risk that they could unintentionally, or intentionally, access material that they shouldn't be able to access. If your Intranet FTP site is accessible from the Internet, anonymous FTP exposes your site to possible aggressive hacking. Your best bet is to include innocuous public-access material on your anonymous FTP sites. We'll talk more about the security measures at your disposal in Chapter 13, "Intranet Server Security."

NOTE

On your Intranet, you may want users to enter their names, phone numbers, or employee IDs as their passwords; in this way, you'll be able to review the FTP logs and contact users when problems arise.

You can allow users to upload files to a specific directory. This directory would have suitable privileges to allow users to write files, but not to delete or even to see files in the folder. This allows users to collaborate on documents and transfer the finished products to a common area where a manager or supervisor can access them.

Remember not to use one of your real passwords as an anonymous FTP password. Unlike a Telnet session, a password from an anonymous FTP user is reported to the server administrator, and is therefore regularly seen by a human being. Some administrators use the anonymous password entries to maintain statistics on who accesses the site.

NOTE

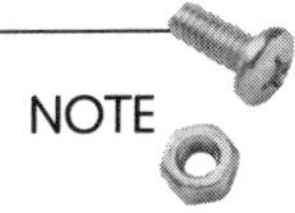

Both email and FTP are used to transfer information between computers. Email systems enable you to attach files to your messages. This is an easy way of sending documents to other users. So when should you use FTP and when should you use email to send files? The answer usually relates to the size of the files. FTP is geared toward sending large files over a network. Sending a 2 MB file to someone over email usually is an unwelcome surprise on the receiving end. On the other hand, users can always FTP a file to a common site and notify the recipient by email that a large file is waiting for them. The recipient can retrieve the file at leisure.

Intranet FTP Services

FTP can provide the backbone for providing file transfer capability to users on your Intranet. In many ways, FTP is a superior transport mechanism to MacOS File Sharing. For one thing, FTP is cross-platform, so Unix and Windows users on your Intranet will be able to access files. Furthermore, TCP/IP is a more robust protocol than AppleShare. For example, the Internet has never crashed and was originally designed to withstand a nuclear attack. In contrast, a crash on an AppleShare network usually takes out several Macs at a time.

As mentioned previously, TCP/IP is a means of transporting information over nodes on the Internet; in contrast, AppleShare is based on AppleTalk, which was designed primarily as a means of printing documents onto LaserWriters and ImageWriters. AppleTalk is a very inefficient and chatty protocol that requires a lot of network bandwidth to transport a small amount of information. Chatty network protocols usually allow traffic to flow back and forth several times between two nodes before a transfer is complete. This traffic is usually diagnostic in nature, meaning that the sender and recipient are constantly checking, during the transfer, on one another. This extra traffic slows down your file transfer.

Possible functions for FTP on your Intranet include the following:

- Storage of organizational reports, documents, and memoranda
- Archive of graphical images, photographs, or video clips
- Archive of site-licensed application software

Users in your organization can access your FTP server for the purpose of accessing files of the types previously described. The added advantage of modern Web browsers, such as Netscape and Mosaic, is that they double as FTP client applications. In this manner, your users can employ Netscape as a fully functional Intranet access client.

Using FTP on the Macintosh

FTP service has a long history under the Unix operating system. From the Unix command line, users can open an FTP connection to a remote computer and exchange files with the remote computer. Arcane commands, similar to Unix operating system commands, are required to navigate the remote file system.

FTP clients for the Macintosh were developed soon after the introduction of MacTCP. Previously, users had been forced to dial into bulletin boards and download the files by modem. With FTP clients running on Ethernet networks, suddenly you could download files to your Mac with a quantum leap in speed over modem speeds. Furthermore, the antiquated FTP interface needed to be updated to be more user-friendly for many Mac applications. Options that were previously driven by arcane command-line options were now available under the familiar pulldown menu paradigm.

Using capabilities under System 7, FTP clients on the Macintosh, such as Fetch and Anarchie, have blossomed in capability. Using AppleEvents, FTP clients can be launched from other applications such as text editors and newsreaders. Drag-and-drop capability has been added to FTP clients; with this feature, you can drag a collection of files to your client window and initiate an FTP transfer. Similarly, you can drag files off the client window onto your desktop, thereby transferring those files to your Mac.

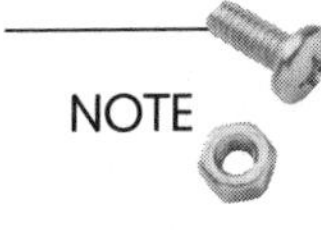

CD-ROM

> Using the Internet Config application and the ICeTEe extension, both provided in the NetPresenz folder on the Intranet CD-ROM in this book, you can define default applications for FTP, Usenet, and Web browsing among others. The ICeTEe extension enables you to double-click on any URL to activate the appropriate browser as defined in Internet Config. The URL has to appear in an editor that employs the MacOS TextEdit resource. Applications that use this resource include SimpleText and Eudora.

Many of the large FTP archives on the Net are running on large Unix machines. In contrast to the MacOS, FTP service is built into the Unix operating system; FTP connections are handled much like remote Telnet logins. In order to serve files through FTP on your Mac, you need to install an FTP server. These servers act like the HTTP servers described in Chapter 4, in that they respond to your FTP client requests. In addition to text and binary transfers, Mac FTP servers can serve files using the MacBinary format. The MacOS stores file information in the data and resource forks; the MacBinary file format allows an FTP server to transfer both sets of information, thereby preserving the integrity and usefulness of the transferred file.

Two FTP servers in use for the MacOS are NetPresenz by Peter N. Lewis and InterServer Publisher by InterCon Systems Corporation. Both applications are multi-protocol Intranet servers in that they can distribute files using WWW, Gopher, and FTP. This is an advantage because you will likely implement WWW and FTP services on your Intranet. These applications give you an integrated means of serving these protocols; otherwise, you will need to implement a separate WWW server and FTP server application. To run both applications, you will need System 7 as well as a properly configured version of MacTCP. It's recommended that you have at least 8 MB of RAM and sufficient hard drive space to contain all the files you want to serve.

Using NetPresenz

NetPresenz is a shareware implementation of an FTP, Gopher, and Web server. In its original incarnation, NetPresenz provided only FTP service, but Gopher and later Web services were added. NetPresenz 4.0.1 is Power Mac-native and is compatible with Open Transport, according to Peter Lewis, the program's author.

Installing NetPresenz

NetPresenz 4.0.1 is found on the CD-ROM in this book. Drag it over to a desired folder on your hard drive. If you have not already started Internet Config on your Mac, do so now. Internet Config is required for NetPresenz and is a good application to have running on your computer.

For the sake of simplicity, the discussion on using NetPresenz as a Web server was deferred from Chapter 4 until this point. NetPresenz's greatest utility is its FTP service; therefore I chose to include the full discussion of the application in this chapter.

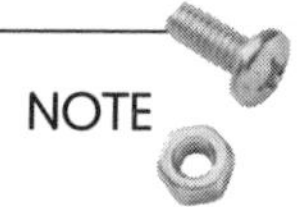

As with all shareware on the CD-ROM, purchase of this book does not fulfill your shareware obligations. If you use this software for more than a limited amount of time, you are obligated to pay your shareware fee.

Creating MacOS User Accounts for Use by NetPresenz

To assign user privileges, NetPresenz makes use of the accounts established under System 7's AppleShare hierarchy. For this reason, you'll need to have File Sharing turned on. If File Sharing has not been enabled, then open the Sharing Setup control panel, as shown in Figure 10.1. Enter the name and password of the computer's administrator. Enter the Macintosh name as well.

NOTE

> The computer name in the Sharing Setup control panel is only for the benefit of AppleShare users; this name does not affect your IP node registration.

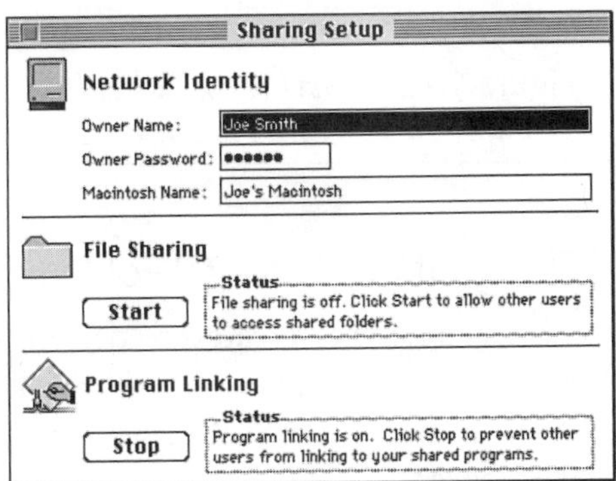

Figure 10.1 *File sharing is enabled using the Sharing Setup control panel.*

Now open the Users & Groups control panel. This control panel enables you to add user accounts so that other Mac users can access certain parts of your disk drive. NetPresenz uses this account structure to enables users to set up FTP connections to your Mac.

To add a user, click on the File menu and choose New User. An icon similar to the faces shown in Figure 10.2 will appear. Type the user's name in the field below the icon and double-click on the icon. A dialog box will appear, prompting you to enter the user's password (see Figure 10.2). Click on the appropriate checkboxes to allow the user to connect to the server and to change his or her password. Repeat this procedure for as many users as you need to define.

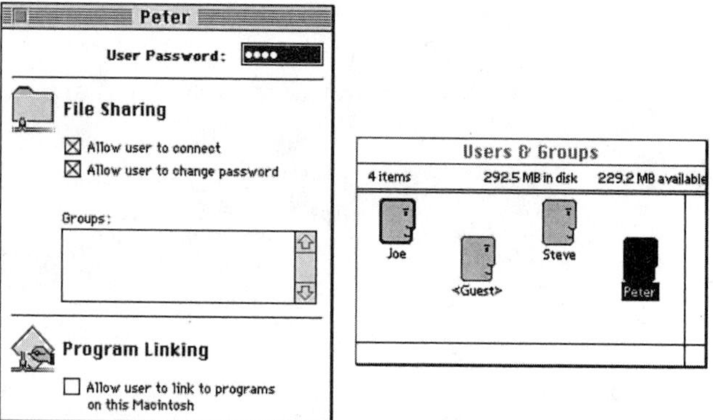

Figure 10.2 *NetPresenz uses the accounts setup in the Users & Groups control panel to enable FTP access.*

Designating Your FTP Folder

Now you need to create a folder on your hard drive from which you want to serve files via FTP. Click on the File menu, dragging down to Sharing. A dialog box similar to that shown in Figure 10.3 will appear.

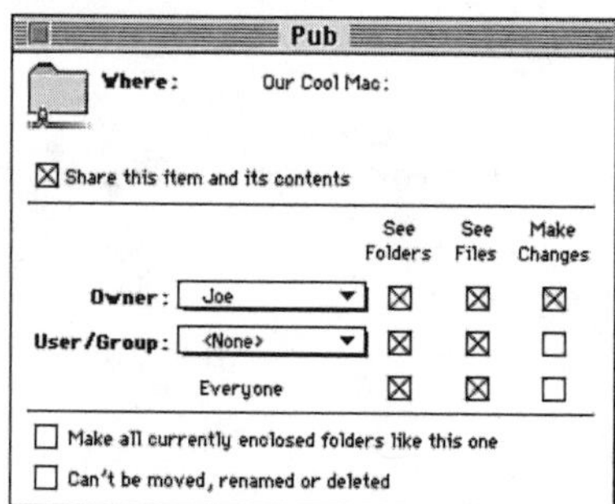

Figure 10.3 *You can set the file sharing preferences to configure NetPresenz access.*

As the Owner, you'll want to allow yourself privileges to see folders and files and to make changes; check these boxes accordingly. Next, assign privileges to the various users you have defined by scrolling through the User/Group popup menu and selecting the users and their privileges accordingly. For guest or anonymous FTP access, you will almost certainly not want to check the Make Changes box. NetPresenz enables anonymous FTP users with whatever privileges you supply guests under File Sharing. Therefore, if you allow your guests to make changes, any anonymous FTP user can add or delete files and folders within the folders you have defined.

NOTE 

You can enable groups of FTP users with the same privileges by creating a File Sharing group under the Users & Groups control panel. For folders like the Pub folder, you can set similar privileges for all non-anonymous FTP users.

Finally, you can check the box entitled Make all currently enclosed folders like this one, if that is indeed what you want. All the privileges that you specify in a root folder then get carried down to a nested folder, unless you define that nested folder differently. For this reason, you will need to be careful when checking this box on any folder on which guest users have write privileges.

Repeat the above procedure for all folders that you want to open for FTP access. User folders can exist anywhere on your Macintosh desktop, but associated users must have the proper privileges. For example, assume you have a folder entitled Pub and there's a folder named Steve inside. You want to name Steve, the folder, as the root directory for Steve, the user. You must allow Steve the user privileges to get inside Pub folder. The File Sharing privilege arrangement can be difficult to understand, so when you get NetPresenz up and running, you will likely need to test your guest and user privileges.

Configuring NetPresenz for User Access

At this point, you are ready to start FTP service on your Mac. NetPresenz actually is configured by the NetPresenz Setup application. Before launching NetPresenz Setup, double-click on the

NetPresenz application to start the FTP service. The NetPresenz access log should appear. Now that the NetPresenz application is up and running, you have officially opened your doors to the Internet. Double-click on the NetPresenz Setup icon to launch the application.

Upon opening the NetPresenz Setup application, you will see a configuration panel, as shown in Figure 10.4. By clicking on the various icons, you can configure security for FTP, WWW, and Gopher services provided by NetPresenz. Let's start by talking about FTP security.

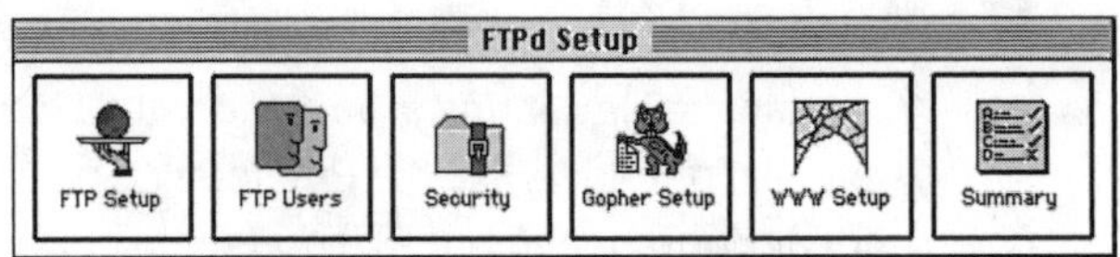

Figure 10.4 *You can customize FTP, WWW, and Gopher privileges to your server with the NetPresenz Setup configuration panel.*

Setting Up FTP User Privileges

Clicking on the FTP Setup icon in the configuration panel brings up the display shown in Figure 10.5. This display is separated into three sections: Privileges, Miscellaneous, and SIVC. In the Privileges section, you see that there are three types of users: Owner, Users, and Guests. Each of these user types has four different types of access: None, Read Only, Upload, and Full. Access privileges are configured by using the popup menus located beneath each of the three types of users. The FTP users and privileges are defined in Table 10.1.

Table 10.1 *FTP Users and Privileges Definition*

Types of Users	
Owner	Owner of machine as defined in the Sharing Setup Control Panel.
User	Anyone with user privileges defined in the Users & Groups control panel.
Guest	Someone who accesses the server through anonymous FTP.

Privileges	
None	User has no access.
Read Only	User can navigate through folders and download files but cannot transfer files to server.
Upload	User can download and upload files to server but cannot overwrite or delete existing files or folders.
Full	User has full run of the system. User can add, delete, and rename files and folders.

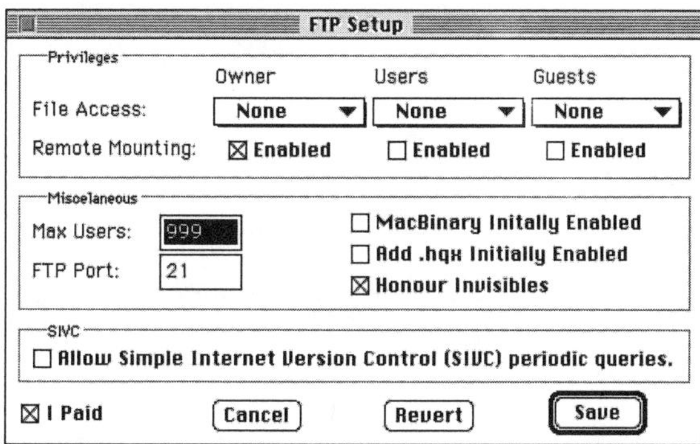

Figure 10.5 *You can specify access privileges as well as other miscellaneous settings with NetPresenz Setup.*

NOTE

> You have to assign privileges to all your users as a unit. For example, you cannot let one user have Upload capability and another user have Full access.

Ideally, you will want to enable the Owner to have full access to the server; click Full for Owner privileges. Often, you'll want users with accounts on your machine to be able to upload files; if so, give the Users class the capability to upload by selecting Upload from the pop-up menu. Finally, you will want Guests to be able to download files, but not be able to change anything on your server; therefore, assign Guests the Read Only privilege.

Assigning Home Folders

Like out-of-town guests, you need to find room for FTP users once they stop in for a visit. When users log in, they will have initial access to a folder that you specify. Clicking on the FTP Users icon in the NetPresenz Setup configuration panel enables you to specify at which points in your file system different users start out. A dialog box such as that shown in Figure 10.6 will appear.

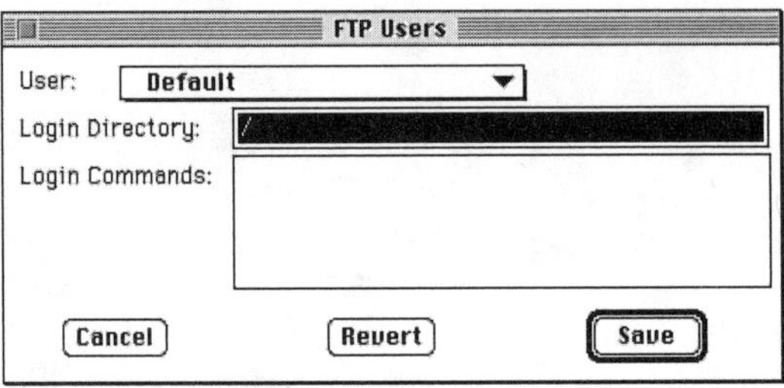

Figure 10.6 *You can set home folders for your FTP users in NetPresenz.*

You can specify login directories for the following types of users:

- **Default.** This specifies all users including the Owner, all defined Users, and Guests.
- **Owner.** This specifies the administrator's home folder.
- **User (Default).** You can specify one default directory for all your defined Users.
- **Guest.** Guests can start out in a specific directory.
- **Individual Defined Users.** Your defined Users can each have a default login directory.

The above options are all available in the pulldown User menu shown in Figure 10.6.

To specify the login directories, you need to enter the path leading to the desired folder. The folder names need to be delineated with the forward slash (/). On your desktop, for example, you might have a public folder called Pub. In Pub, you might have a folder named Steve, and you'd like to designate that folder as the login directory for a user named Steve. You would scroll down the User popup menu until you got to Steve's name. In the Login Directory field, you would enter /Pub/Steve. Steve would need to have access to the folder Pub.

NOTE

There is no limit to how far down a folder tree you can locate a login directory. The first folder that you specify in the Login Directory path has to be the highest folder in the tree that's accessible by the User.

In addition to defining the directory tree, you also can define commands that are executed upon the user's login. These need to be standard FTP commands and will be discussed later in this section.

Securing Your NetPresenz Connections

You can override some of the File Sharing permissions you declared earlier using NetPresenz Setup. Click on the Security icon in the NetPresenz Setup configuration panel. A display much like that shown in Figure 10.7 will appear. This display is divided into four sections: General Security, Connection Sounds, User Restrictions, and Owner Restrictions.

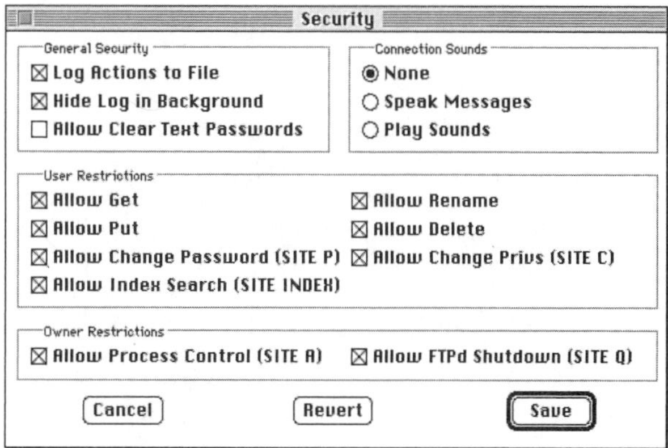

Figure 10.7 *NetPresenz Setup enables you to set the desired level of security you need for your FTP server.*

Under the General Security section, you can check three options. First, you can toggle access logging. Checking the Log Actions to File box causes NetPresenz to record file transfers to the access log. This log file is accessible when you launch the NetPresenz application, but we'll discuss it in more detail later. You can also hide the log in the background when NetPresenz is not in the foreground. Finally, you can prevent users from mounting AppleShare volumes that require clear text passwords.

NOTE

> The term *clear text passwords* describes the authentication method used by some AppleShare servers. These servers accept passwords using straight ASCII text, which can pose a security risk. Your system could be compromised through the use of *sniffer* programs, which record transmissions on the Internet.

In the Security interface, you also can specify if you want some sort of signal when connections are established with your server. You can tell NetPresenz to speak messages when users log on and off or when you launch or shut down NetPresenz. This is useful if the server resides within earshot of your office. As an alternative to having NetPresenz speak to you, you can check the Play Sounds button to have NetPresenz beep when users log on and log off.

The check boxes in the User Commands section detail the type of control that you can exercise over defined FTP users. The controls can be summarized as follows:

Restrictions on FTP User Access

Checkbox	Description
Allow Get	Enables users with Read Only access to download files.
Allow Put	Enables users with Upload access to upload files.
Allow Rename	Enables the Owner to rename files and folders.
Allow Delete	Enables the Owner to delete files and folders.
Allow Change Password	Enables all users to change their passwords.

Checkbox	Description
Allow Index Search	Enables users to search the server using SMNT commands.
Allow Change Privs	Enables users to change privileges of folders they own.

You also can place two restrictions on the Owner. You can allow the Owner to launch and close processes on the server. This would be advantageous if you had a script that you wanted to execute remotely. You could, for example, have Eudora check your mail on the server and then download the messages to your remote client. You also can enable the Owner to shut down the server remotely.

Miscellaneous FTP Configuration

You can apply a variety of miscellaneous customizations to NetPresenz. In the FTP Setup, you can set the maximum number of concurrent FTP users (refer to Figure 10.5). This number will have to be adjusted by reviewing performance of the server after it's been running a while. You are under the restriction of 64 simultaneous connections. To reserve MacTCP connections for other applications on your server, you may want to limit the number of maximum users to 40–50, thereby guaranteeing that other Internet applications will have connections available. You also can set the IP listening port. On the Internet, the standard IP port for FTP is 21. You may want to alter this port if your FTP server is not behind a firewall or some device that restricts access from the Internet. We'll talk more about security in Chapter 14, "Sample Intranet Applications."

NOTE

If you want to set up an experimental FTP server, set the port number to greater than 1024.

NetPresenz maintains the capability to transfer files using the MacBinary protocol. By checking the MacBinary Initially Enabled box, you turn on MacBinary as the default transmission method. Also, by checking the next box below, you can have NetPresenz convert files to a 7-bit text format using the BinHex algorithm before transferring them to the FTP client. Lastly, you signify whether you want the user to see invisible files in the server directories.

SIVC Duty

SIVC stands for Standard Internet Version Control (SIVC—pronounced "civic"). This protocol is used to allow applications to communicate with SIVC servers for the purpose of transmitting information on how and when the software is being used. Certain Macintosh applications are SIVC-aware, such as NetPresenz, Anarchie, MacTCP Monitor, and others. By checking the box in the FTP Setup display, you allow NetPresenz to periodically transmit information to a SIVC server; this transmission details such information as the server IP address, the software version, and other data useful for tracking the application usage. SIVC allows shareware authors to determine who is using the software and what versions are being used. This information, along with the rest of the SIVC data, enables authors to better gauge the distribution of their software.

NOTE 

> Clicking the I Paid checkbox returns a grateful response from the author. Try it.

Running NetPresenz in the Background

You can run NetPresenz in the background by clicking under the File Menu, in NetPresenz Setup, and dragging down to NetPresenz Background Mode. Choose the copy of NetPresenz that you want to run in the background and click the Background Only checkbox. When running in Background Mode, you will not be able to access, nor directly quit, the NetPresenz application. You will need to quit the file using the same process management application or through AppleScript. A simple AppleScript to do this is given here.

```
tell application "NetPresenz"
quit
end tell
```

Another ramification of running NetPresenz in the background is that you will not have access to the NetPresenz log file.

NOTE

For better performance on a machine that is a dedicated FTP server, run NetPresenz in the foreground. This will improve access and give you real-time access to the NetPresenz access log.

Remote NetPresenz Commands

NetPresenz accepts various commands designed to configure the server remotely from a command-line FTP session. Some of these commands are summarized in Table 10.2.

Table 10.2 *NetPresenz File Transfer Options*

Remote NetPresenz Command	Description
get 'file'	Get 'file' from server
get 'file'.data	Get the data fork of 'file'
get 'file'.rsrc	Get the resource fork of 'file'
put|get 'file'.bin	Put or get the MacBinary version of the 'file' effectively combining the data and resource file forks
put|get 'file'.hqx	Put or get the BinHex version of 'file'

Mounting Remote AppleShare Volumes

Not only can you access a remote Mac using NetPresenz, you can access all the available Macintosh computers on the remote computer's AppleTalk network. This is a powerful and potentially disastrous capability, giving anonymous FTP users from all over the world access to all the File Sharing-enabled computers on the remote local area network.

Using the FTP Structure Mount (SMNT) command below, you can mount a remote AppleShare volume.

```
quote smnt volume:server@zone:username:password
```

If you are attempting to access a server in the same AppleTalk zone as your NetPresenz server, you can use @* instead of @zone. If your username and password are the same as your NetPresenz account, you can leave them out. For example, you want to mount a volume entitled Public off a server entitled Steve's Mac. This server is in the same zone as your NetPresenz server, and you have the same user information on this remote volume as you do on the NetPresenz server. Your SMNT command would then be

```
quote smnt Public:"Steve's Mac"
```

To avoid bringing the wrath of your network administrator down upon you, I recommend disabling this feature unless your remote AppleShare volumes are tightly secured and controlled with guest accesses.

Other SMNT commands include those described in Table 10.3.

Table 10.3 *SMNT Commands Used on NetPresenz Servers*

SMNT Command	Description
quote site u	Display server's current usage statistics including available memory and connections, number of users, and so on.
quote site v	Display server's ongoing statistics including total number of logins, total bytes transferred, server up-time, and so on.
quote site s	Use short DOS-like file names.
quote site l	Use 31-character file names.
quote site h e|d	Enable|Disable adding .hqx file suffixes.
quote site q	Shut down NetPresenz process. Use with care.
quote site index 'string'	Search your NetPresenz server for files or folder names that contain string.
quote site p 'password'	Change your password.
quote site a list	Display list of running processes along with their creator codes.
quote site a oapp 'code'	Launch application with creator type code.
quote site a quit 'code'	Quit application with creator type code.

These commands can be entered from command-line FTP sessions, or they can be entered in certain ways using Mac FTP clients. Furthermore, these commands can be entered as initial login commands under the FTP Users display shown in Figure 10.6. This enables you to have certain commands executed when certain users log onto the server. An Owner, for example, may want the server statistics displayed when logging onto the system.

Displaying the NetPresenz Access Log

One advantage of running NetPresenz in the foreground is that you have access to the NetPresenz log. An example of this log is shown in Figure 10.8. Note that NetPresenz tracks when the server is shut down and started up. You also have records of when users log in, from what IP address the request originated, what password they used, and which files they downloaded.

NOTE

> Invalid accesses are logged as well. This is a good source of monitoring potential security problems with your server.

Log Window

```
12:04 PM 12/16/95 205.252.17.182 toa 15 log in Owner
12:05 PM 12/16/95 205.252.17.182 toa 15 get file MacTCP
12:06 PM 12/16/95 205.252.17.182 toa 15 log out Owner
1:45 PM 12/17/95 205.252.17.239 toa 16 failed login
1:45 PM 12/17/95 205.252.17.239 toa 17 failed login
1:46 PM 12/17/95 205.252.17.239 toa 18 log in Owner
1:46 PM 12/17/95 205.252.17.239 toa 18 log out Owner
12:17 AM 12/19/95 205.252.17.178 toa 19 log in Owner
12:18 AM 12/19/95 205.252.17.178 toa 19 get file smithers.gif
12:18 AM 12/19/95 205.252.17.178 toa 19 log out Owner
4:21 AM 12/19/95 193.101.168.34 fuchs@litef.de 20 log in Guest
4:23 AM 12/19/95 193.101.168.34 fuchs@litef.de 20 get file finalrep.zip
4:24 AM 12/19/95 193.101.168.34 fuchs@litef.de 20 get file FINALREP.ZIP
4:29 AM 12/19/95 193.101.168.34 fuchs@litef.de 20 log out Guest
9:30 AM 12/19/95 205.252.17.69 toa 21 log in Owner
9:31 AM 12/19/95 205.252.17.69 toa 21 get file mathematica.html
9:32 AM 12/19/95 205.252.17.69 toa 21 get file cleartaz.gif
9:33 AM 12/19/95 205.252.17.69 toa 21 get file Sears.GIF
9:34 AM 12/19/95 205.252.17.69 toa 21 get file mac.GIF
9:34 AM 12/19/95 205.252.17.69 toa 21 get file tm.gif
9:35 AM 12/19/95 205.252.17.69 toa 21 get file construction.GIF
9:35 AM 12/19/95 205.252.17.69 toa 21 log out Owner
3:55 PM 12/20/95 144.212.12.42 potvin@mathworks.com 22 log in Guest
3:56 PM 12/20/95 144.212.12.42 potvin@mathworks.com 22 get file FinalReport.ps
3:56 PM 12/20/95 144.212.12.42 potvin@mathworks.com 22 log out Guest
```

Figure 10.8 *You can track NetPresenz activity using the NetPresenz access log.*

Setting Up FTP Introductory Messages

You can display messages to users when they log in to your server. These messages can detail news about the server or conditions for its use. These messages may be different for anonymous FTP accesses versus Owner and User connections. In the NetPresenz application folder, there is a folder entitled Startup Messages. Three files reside in this folder, which can be edited with a text editor such as SimpleText. These files are named Guest Startup, User Startup, and Peter Startup. These files are displayed when the Guests and Users log into your server. You can change the name of Peter Startup to reflect the Owner's user account.

NOTE

As an alternative to residing in the NetPresenz folder, the Startup Messages folder can be stored in the NetPresenz Preferences folder.

You also can display messages to the users when they move into certain folders. The contents of a file with the name !Folder Info will be displayed when a user moves into that particular folder. These files are limited to 5 KB in size, so excessively large messages, such as directory listings, can be stored as files within the folder and referred to in a smaller !Folder Info file.

WWW Service

NetPresenz 4.0.1 provides HTTP services. To enable WWW access through NetPresenz, go to the NetPresenz Setup application and click on the WWW Setup icon. A dialog box, similar to that shown in Figure 10.9, will appear. You enable WWW service by checking the box at the top of the dialog box. You can specify the root directory for WWW service in the same way that we did for the different users. Furthermore, you can specify the TCP/IP listening port; as we discussed in Chapter 4, the default port for HTTP transactions is port 80.

NOTE

The default Web page for a directory under the NetPresenz hierarchy is index.html. For example, if someone sends a request to http://www.anyplace.com, a file entitled index.html that resides in the directory specified in the WWW Setup dialog box will be returned to the browser.

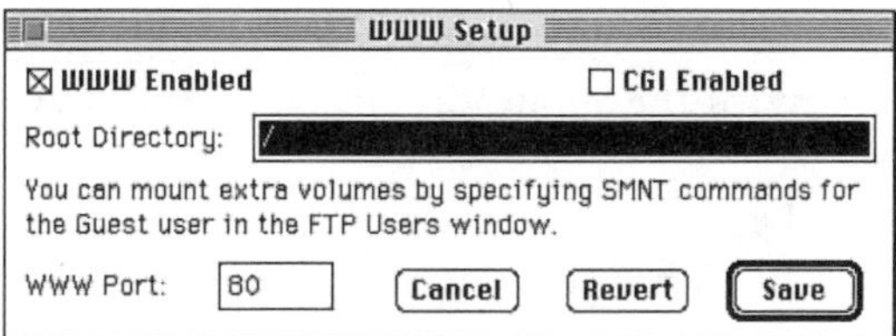

Figure 10.9 *NetPresenz offers rudimentary control of WWW services.*

NOTE

You can restrict and enable host accesses by IP address. However, this requires editing a resource in the NetPresenz file, or ultimately the NetPresenz Preferences file using a resource editor such as ResEdit. This is a messy way to perform a much-needed task, and I'm sure later versions of NetPresenz will use more straightforward ways to restrict IP addresses; so refer to the NetPresenz documentation for explanation of this process.

Using InterServer Publisher

Chapter 4 discussed using InterServer Publisher as a full-service Internet server. You can use Publisher as an integrated WWW, FTP, and Gopher server. This section discusses how to use Publisher as an FTP server.

Installing InterServer Publisher

In the InterServer Publisher on the CD-ROM, double-click on the InterServer installer icon. You'll be presented with the standard installer dialog box. You'll then be queried as to whether you want an Easy Install or a Custom Install. The Easy Install option will add a lot of ancillary software, such as a huge assortment of clip art, the HTML Pro editor, the graphics utility GraphicConverter, and InterCon's own Web browser, NetShark. If you do not already have a copy of MacTCP, you can install it now; if you have one but it's not as recent as version 2.0.6, the installer will replace your version. By choosing Custom Install, you can always pick and choose which features you would like to add. Select where you want the application installed and proceed with the installation.

Let's assume that you performed the full installation of InterServer Publisher. The installer inserted the InterServer Publisher extension into the Extensions folder of your System folder. Unlike other installations you may have run, you are not required to restart your Mac after the installation.

The InterServer Publisher extension does all of your WWW, FTP, and Gopher service. Four applications are used in conjunction with the extension. These applications are described here.

Application	Description
InterServer Publisher Setup	Initializes Publisher and configures WWW, FTP, and Gopher service
StartServer	Starts Publisher service
StopServer	Stops Publisher service
InterServer Log Viewer	Views access log window without using InterServer Publisher Setup

These four applications are all that you need to run your WWW server. Just double-click on the StartServer icon and you are ready to start publishing on your Intranet Web.

Using InterServer Publisher Setup

The InterServer Publisher Setup application is by far the most involved of all the ancillary applications you'll need to run to set up WWW services using InterServer Publisher. Double-click on the InterServer Publisher Setup icon to launch the application. If you have not launched the StartServer application, launching Setup will initiate this process.

The InterServer Publisher Configuration editor will appear on your desktop. It looks similar to the old pre-System 7 control panel arrangement, as shown in Figure 10.10; as in the figure, the Minimal configuration panel should be active. In the field marked General, you need to specify your server's node name. To enable your WWW service, simply click the box entitled Enable World Wide Web server. Presto! You've launched your Intranet Web service!

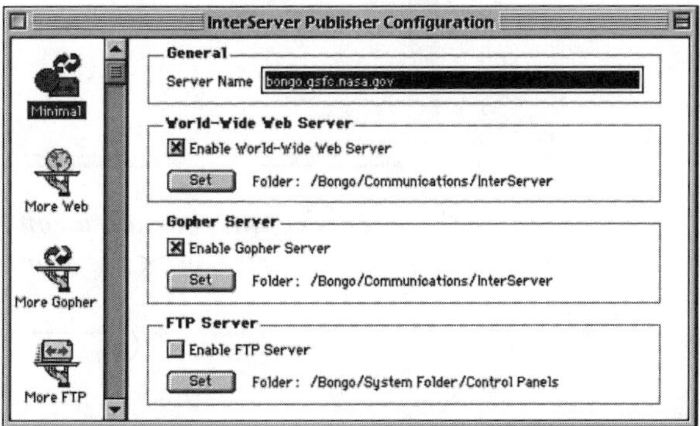

Figure 10.10 *The InterServer Publisher Minimal configuration enables you to customize important features of your Web services.*

To further configure your Intranet FTP server, you need to click on the More FTP configuration panel. In this panel, shown in Figure 10.11, you have additional parameters with which to customize your server. You can enter the maximum number of simultaneous FTP connections. Sizing this number higher enables more users to connect to your server but can slow down your FTP processing. This number will likely need to be adjusted after viewing the server statistics.

You also can specify the time that you want to hold open idle connections. Remember that the more connections you hold open, the fewer chances you have to handle other FTP requests. You will want to keep FTP sessions open for a little longer than you allowed for HTTP connections. Normal FTP connections consist of file transfer and navigation between folders. As a result, there may be idle connections as the user ponders navigation options. Despite the burden the FTP connections place on your server, it is advisable to keep idle connections open for as long as 3 to 5 minutes.

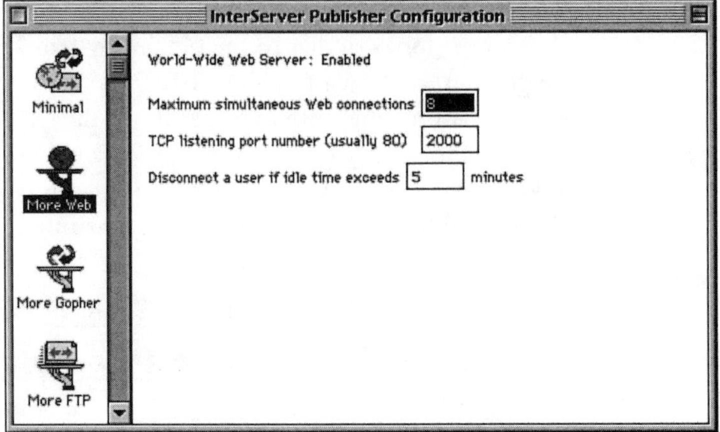

Figure 10.11 *Additional configuration of InterServer Publisher FTP services can be effected with the More FTP configuration panel.*

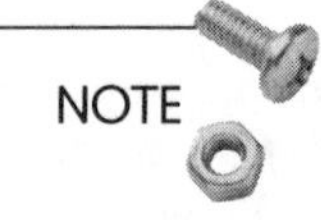

NOTE

Because of the limitation on the number of MacTCP connections, InterServer Publisher limits you to a total of 50 connections shared between your FTP, Gopher, and WWW servers.

Securing Your Server

You can use the InterServer Publisher Setup application to secure your server in the following ways:

- Specify domains and addresses to be allowed and denied access to the server
- Create user accounts and passwords
- Utilize security realms to restrict access to certain files and folders

Restricting Host Access

In the InterServer Publisher Setup application, click on the Host Access configuration panel. The display should look like Figure 10.12. You can enter the domain or IP address in the Web Allow or

Web Deny text fields. For example, to allow access only to members of the domain anyplace.com, you would enter @anyplace.com in the Web Allow field. Conversely, you could deny access to the entire domain by entering @anyplace.com in the Web Deny field.

You also can specify subnets that you want to restrict or enable access to your server. Entering the string 128.184.22 in the FTP Deny field, for example, restricts any address in the 128.184.22.xxx subnet. Entering any domain in the FTP Allow field, although leaving the FTP Deny field empty, enables only that domain to access the server. Conversely, entering any domain in the FTP Deny field, while leaving the FTP Allow field empty, restricts only that domain from accessing files on that server.

This is an important tool because it will enable you to restrict access to certain areas of your server. Even if your server is blocked off from the Internet, you may want to restrict access to your marketing data from anyone outside your marketing department. By locating your marketing department behind a subnet, as discussed in Chapter 2, you can restrict all other subnets within your Intranet from this part of your FTP site.

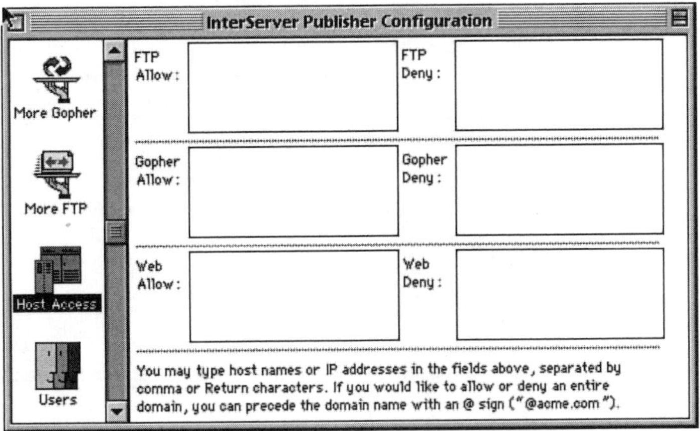

Figure 10.12 *The Host Access configuration panel enables the InterServer Publisher Setup application to restrict or enable access based on the user's Internet address.*

Adding Users to Your Server

You not only can restrict or enable access by domain, but you also can customize the privileges of individual users. Users with similar privileges are grouped into realms; members of realms have access to certain files and folders. Before we talk about realms, we need to learn how to add users to the system so that we can create realms.

Scroll down the left side of the Setup application and click on the Users configuration panel. A dialog box similar to that shown in Figure 10.13 will appear. In the top right of the window, there are three buttons: New, Rename, and Delete. Click on New to create a new account. A New dialog box will appear and you can enter the user name. Click OK to close the New dialog box. Back in the Setup application, you can enter a password for this new user. Note from Figure 10.13 that the password field is blocked, but unfortunately there is no password verification scheme. You then enter a case-sensitive password for the user. Once you have accumulated enough user accounts, you will be able to change the user names or even delete accounts using the Rename and Delete buttons.

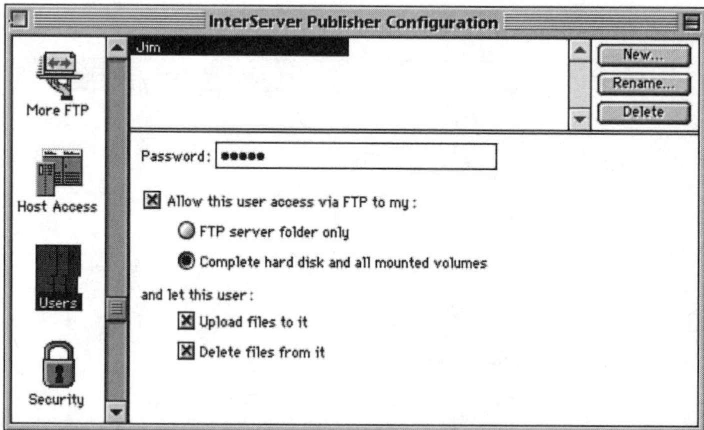

Figure 10.13 *Security realm user accounts can be created using the Users configuration panel.*

The bottom half of the dialog box in Figure 10.13 specifies FTP user privileges. Using the radio buttons and checkboxes in this dialog box, you can enable the user to access the entire hard disk or just the folder specified in the Minimal configuration panel. You also can specify whether the user can upload files to the server or delete files from the server.

Creating Security Realms

After you have accumulated a stable of potential users, you can arrange them into secure realms. Attributes of these realms can be configured to permit all the relevant users to access certain parts of the file system. After privileges have been assigned to a realm, members of that realm can access files that contain certain keywords. These realms are constructed using the Security configuration panel.

Using realms, you can allow InterServer Publisher to restrict access to your system. This is useful to restrict access to information such as personnel files or some data that needs to be accessed by people from different subnets. InterServer Publisher allows you to restrict access from users from different subnets, but if your intended users are sprinkled throughout your Intranet, you'll need to construct security realms to provide needed security.

Upon clicking on the Security configuration panel, as shown in Figure 10.14, you will see a list of user accounts that you have created. Once again, there are three buttons in the upper right of the dialog box. In order to create a new realm, click the New button. You'll be prompted for the name of the new realm. Enter the name and click OK.

Members of a particular realm can access files that contain a certain string. For example, if the access keyword for a realm is "financial," members of that realm will be able to access any file or folder whose name contains the string "financial." By selecting a realm in the Security configuration panel, a field opens up in the middle of the dialog box into which you can enter a realm keyword. In the user list field at the bottom of the page, you can add users to the realm by clicking on the column to the left of the user names. You can create several realms in this manner. As expected, you can rename and delete realms using the appropriate buttons in the upper right of the dialog box.

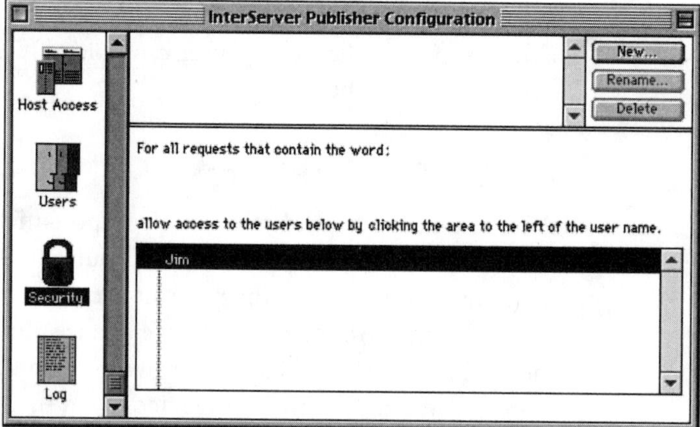

Figure 10.14 *Using the Security configuration panel, you can create realms that allow access to restrict folders or files.*

Maintaining an Access Log

InterServer Publisher enables you to record a log of WWW, FTP, and Gopher accesses. The access history is written in a tab-delimited text file and the contents can be pasted into a spreadsheet such as Microsoft Excel or a database such as FileMaker Pro. As users access your server, pertinent information is written to the log file. You can manually archive versions of the log file or have archives created automatically. Furthermore, InterServer Publisher enables you to view the log remotely.

Configuring Your Log Characteristics

Click on the Log configuration panel in the InterServer Publisher Setup application. A dialog box similar to that shown in Figure 10.15 will appear. You can specify whether you want to archive the log file manually, have it done periodically, or have the file archived when it gets to a specific size. Your choices of periodic archiving are daily, weekly, monthly, or annually. Archiving your log file keeps the file size down and allows the individual archives to be small enough to be perused at a later date. Furthermore, if you want to view your log archives remotely, you can click the appropriate check box.

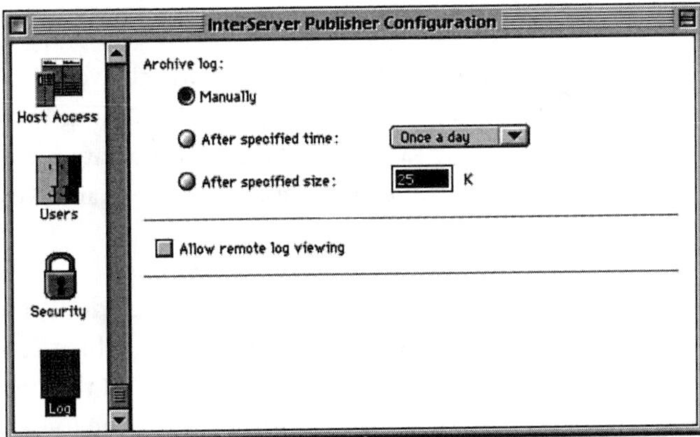

Figure 10.15 *Specify certain access log characteristics using the Log configuration panel.*

The InterServer Publisher log file can be viewed by clicking on the Setup menu and dragging down to Show Log File. The following access data will be displayed under each entry of the log.

Log Field	Description
Date	Date of access
Time	Time of access
Server Type	Type of access (Web, FTP, Gopher)
Status	Indication of successful transfer
Client IP address	IP address of client
Client Node Name	Alphanumeric IP address of client (if available)
Transfer Size	Number of bytes transmitted during request
Connection Duration	Duration of HTTP connection
Authenticated User Name	User's name if transaction was authenticated
Requested File	File requested by client
Additional Notes	Various information provided by the server

These fields are not configurable.

Archiving Your Log File

As mentioned previously, periodically you'll want to trim the size of your log file to prevent it from becoming too large. This is done by periodically saving your log to a separate file and clearing the log contents. You can maintain a series of archives to peruse your access statistics.

One way to archive your log file is to do it manually. First, double-click on the StopServer application, which causes InterServer Publisher to refuse new connections. Find the log file, named Current Log, and give it some other name. The log files are stored in the InterServer Publisher Logs folder in the Preferences folder found in the System folder. Then activate the StartServer application to restart your server. A new log file will be created.

If you enabled remote viewing of your access log, you can access the current log and any archives you have created. You can bring up the log page in a Web browser using the following URL:

```
http://your_server_address/.log
```

Your current log and any archive logs are available through hypertext links on the resulting Web page.

The InterServer Log Viewer is an application that you can use to view the current log, if you are running Publisher on the same Mac. It's a means of viewing the log file without having to open up the InterServer Publisher Setup application.

Administering InterServer Publisher

Now that you've learned how to configure InterServer Publisher, you need to learn how to administer the ongoing Web service. There are several tools and tips at your disposal.

Using the Status Window

The Status window is available under the Setup menu item under Show Status window. This window, shown in Figure 10.16, enables you to monitor current connections to your server. Each entry in this window details the following information: connection type (WWW, FTP, or Gopher), client address, server activity, and completed percentage of the request. At the bottom of the Status window, the number of available free connections for each protocol is displayed. You can close a connection by selecting a transaction and clicking the Close Transaction button at the top of the window.

Setting Up Your FTP Sharing Folder

Okay, you're almost there! It's time to start populating your FTP Sharing folder. In the InterServer Publisher Setup application, you specified which folder would contain your documents. This folder now becomes the root folder for your FTP server file system. Folders in this folder can contain FTP documents, provided they are indexed correctly in the FTP browser.

NOTE 

> You do not need to store BinHexed and MacBinary versions of files in your InterServer Publisher file system. If a user of an FTP client appends the hqx or bin suffixes to the desired file name, Publisher will send BinHex or MacBinary versions of the files.

Effective FTP Server Style

No matter which FTP server application you use, you'll be faced with some of the same issues in running an FTP server on your Mac. As always, you have to keep your audience in mind. Are your users interested in downloading applications or text files? Are your users primarily Mac users, or will Windows and Unix users be visiting your site? In this section, we will discuss some of the issues involved in running an FTP server.

File Formats

All the files that you will be serving can be classified into two formats: binary (or MacBinary) and text. Mac users will be happy to download applications from your server if they are stored in the MacBinary format. You could even serve Unix and Windows binary files, provided they are not stored in the MacBinary format. ASCII text can be stored for retrieval by an FTP client on any platform.

One thing you will want to do is compress your binary files, and sometimes even your text files. As an FTP administrator, you want to provide service to as many users as possible. This means that you'll want to reduce the amount of time that users spend downloading files. For this reason, you'll want to make your files smaller using various compression schemes. The most popular compression scheme used under the MacOS is made by Aladdin Systems StuffIt Deluxe. A StuffIt archive can be a significant fraction of the size of the original file; the degree of compression depends on the type of file. Self-extracting StuffIt archives are slightly larger than plain StuffIt archives.

Between a Macintosh file server and a Macintosh FTP client, it is not always necessary to encode files using the BinHex algorithm. BinHexing a binary file converts it from an 8-bit format to a 7-bit format. This is useful for transferring binary data along media that only support text transfer, such as electronic mail. BinHexing a binary file, such as a StuffIt archive, can significantly add to the file size. For this reason, it's important to evaluate on a case-by-case basis whether BinHexing a file is a useful means of storing the file.

NOTE

The file extension .sit denotes a file that has been stored in a StuffIt archive. The file extension .sea denotes a StuffIt self-extracting archive. You need a decompressing application, such as StuffIt Lite, StuffIt Deluxe, or StuffIt Expander to open a StuffIt archive. In contrast, a self-extracting archive works like its name suggests; some of the extraction algorithm is stored in the file itself so that double-clicking on the file causes it to uncompress itself.

Options for Storing Text Files

ASCII text is the ultimate cross-platform format. All operating systems can interpret ASCII text once they accommodate the different line-breaking mechanisms. However, a 100-page text document may not be useful served as straight ASCII text; a hard copy of such a document may be monotonous to read because there are no formatting or stylistic customizations. You need to determine whether in some instances you can store text files in alternative formats. The next most popular format would be PostScript. Serving a PostScript document enables the user to print it on a laser printer, thereby obtaining a more professional-looking document.

NOTE

> Macintosh users can create PostScript documents from virtually any application, providing the LaserWriter driver is version 8.0 or higher. When printing the document, the user is given the option of printing to a printer or PostScript document. This document is viewable or printable by users on other operating systems.

Another option is to convert the file to HTML. In this way, you can have your WWW server point to the file as well. Users can download the file for local viewing within a Web browser. The final option is to store the file in Portable Document Format (PDF) used by Acrobat Pro from Adobe Systems, Inc. The Acrobat Reader application is freeware and readily accessible through a variety of Web pages and the usual anonymous FTP archives as well as Adobe's home site. PDF is a cross-platform binary format; Windows and Unix users can read PDF files through their own versions of the Acrobat reader. The one drawback is that whereas the Reader is freeware, the Acrobat Exchange is not. You need the application to write and manipulate files in PDF.

Setting Up Mirror Sites

If your organization has many users, your server becomes very popular; so you may think about setting up a mirror site. A mirror site does not have to be halfway across the planet like some of the shareware archives maintain. Your mirror site can be located down the hall. Using a simple AppleScript or Frontier script, you can periodically transfer files from your main FTP archive to your mirror site(s). The script would run automatically, compare the file systems, and update the mirror site.

NOTE

If the two servers are on the same AppleTalk network, a useful way of doing this is to use an application like Qdea's Synchronize! or Synchronize! Pro (http://www.qdea.com). Synchronize! compares two volumes and copies missing files or the most recent file versions to the appropriate locations. Synchronize! Pro is slightly more expensive, and it allows you more advanced administration features, such as login and graphical displays, to manage your file synchronization.

Directory Structure

Unlike the Unix operating system, the MacOS is not efficient at handling file systems with large numbers of files. For this reason, your server performance will suffer if you maintain folders that store hundreds of files. A good rule of thumb is to limit your folders to storing 100 files. You can break up large numbers of files into smaller folders.

Summary

There's more to your Intranet than your WWW services. As sophisticated as your Web pages may become, your WWW service is only a part of your Intranet and will be supplemented by other services such as your FTP site. There will be many instances where you will need to archive documents and files within your Intranet. Setting up an internal FTP site enables you to provide a robust means of providing this data.

In Chapter 11, "Email Services," we'll look at yet another Intranet service that you can provide to your users. As always, feel free to skip to the following related chapters.

- Chapter 14, "Sample Intranet Applications," to learn about some services you can provide using the WWW, FTP, and email technologies discussed in this book.

- ☐ Appendix B, "Establishing an Internet Presence," to learn more about adapting or expanding your Intranet to provide services to the Internet.

Links Related to This Chapter

Fetch	http://www.dartmouth.edu/pages/softdev/fetch.html
Peter Lewis	http://www.share.com/peterlewis/
InterCon Systems	http://www.intercon.com
Aladdin Systems	http://www.aladdinsys.com
Qdea	http://www.qdea.com
Apple Mailing Lists	http://www.solutions.apple.com/apple-internet/

CHAPTER 11

Email Services

Perhaps no other service you provide on your Intranet will be used more heavily than your electronic mail, or email, services. When your office network goes down, the first complaint you'll hear from your users will be that they can't check their email!!! Whether they're kicking a message down the hall or across the planet, email has become in recent years a lifeline of communication in the workplace. With so many domestic users signing onto commercial online services, email has become a familiar part of many people's lives.

Providing email in the workplace has never been easier, and there are several useful email servers for the Mac. In this chapter, the basics of email administration will be covered. Some of these topics include the following:

- A discussion of how email works on the Net
- Some of the protocols used to get mail from one place to another
- A brief look at some commercial and freeware email servers for the Mac
- Installing and running the Apple Internet Mail Server
- Email clients for your Intranet users
- Good administration tactics for your email service
- Using and operating mailing lists

In addition to discussing terminology, use of several software applications will be reviewed. As with software covered in previous chapters, my intent is to make this review as informative as possible without parching your throat on technobabble. Readers of this book are likely computer experts who plow into software only looking at the manual as a last resort. This book is by no means a software manual, but is designed to introduce you to those features of the program that you require to get up and running as soon as possible. Unfortunately, these software primers therefore will be drier than the rest of the book, but would you really rather be reading the documentation?

NOTE

See Que's *Using Internet E-Mail* for a more in-depth discussion on email and its use on the Internet.

How Email Works

For years, Internet users have used email to transfer messages and files across the country as a fast and inexpensive alternative to conventional methods of communication. Only in the last few years has email become commonplace in the work environment. Email has transformed the traditional office hierarchy; mailing your boss's boss's boss is no more difficult, though potentially disastrous, than sending a message to your officemate. I routinely receive mass mailings from my boss, whereas a few years ago, my coworkers and I would have received a hard copy memo in our mailboxes. Furthermore, office email goes a long way to beating the "sneaker net" syndrome. In the brief interval between widespread PC usage and corporate email usage, users would commonly walk files over by floppy disk from computer to computer; email applications enable you to transfer files along with messages across the hall as well as across the country.

Your email server will be the most heavily used portion of your Intranet services. You'll need to establish a reliable server that can transfer large amounts of data, depending on the size of your Intranet, without a lot of intervention on your part. Unlike FTP and Web services, which require constant updating and tweaking, email should be a "start-up-and-forget" service, meaning that other than adding users, you shouldn't be paying a lot of day-to-day attention to your administration.

Like other Internet/Intranet services, email is a complicated service that has an increasingly friendly user interface. In the early days of email, users corresponded with one another on mainframes using arcane command-line editors. Now, many commercial email packages exist that shield users from the inner workings of mail. However, let's take a brief look at the mechanisms used to transfer mail down the hall and across the planet.

Simple Mail Transfer Protocol

Simple Mail Transfer Protocol (SMTP) is one of the oldest members of the Internet protocol family. This protocol is used to route mail messages between hosts on the Internet. Users of local area networks, such as an AppleTalk network, use other protocols to disperse mail, but SMTP is a standard that enables you to communicate with other users not inside your LAN.

Your users will likely never need to worry about the intricacies of SMTP because your server will handle the intricacies of the protocol. Specifically, your server will employ some sort of mail transfer agent (MTA) that utilizes SMTP and other associated mail protocols to send your messages to other hosts. On Unix hosts, the sendmail application is a popular MTA, and your Mac server will employ a similar method of working with SMTP.

Referring to a time-worn analogy, it's illuminating to think of SMTP as the postal service that actually takes your letters and moves them either across the country or across the street. Much like your Internet email, your post office mail moves between various stops or other post offices before reaching its final destination; your email moves between various hosts, often in a geographically zig-zagged pattern, to get to its final destination. Your email server's MTA is much like the mail carrier who picks up mail from your mailbox and brings it to the local post office.

MTAs are important links in your email messaging process for the same reason that you don't personally deliver your letters and bills across town. Can you imagine driving a half-hour to the electric company's offices to drop off your bill only to find out that the office had closed a few minutes earlier? You'd have to repeat the drive the very next day. Similarly, your mail recipients may not be able to receive your mail for a variety of reasons—their server is down, their network is down, and so on. Rather than have a user's email client repeatedly try to make the connection, the server's MTA repeatedly tries to connect to the recipient's mail server until it's successful. After a specified period of time, the MTA throws up its hands and tosses the message back to the user with some form of diagnostic whining.

Many commercial mail programs use different protocols to exchange mail through local networks. However, these applications use *gateways* to transfer mail across the Internet; larger Intranets use gateways to move mail between LANs. These gateways are usually stand-alone computers that transfer the message from the proprietary mail protocol into SMTP. Gateways represent another hop in your messages' journey to their destinations.

The Post-Office Protocol

The Post-Office Protocol (POP) is another standard protocol like SMTP. Whereas SMTP is designed to package messages and move them out along the Internet, POP provides a medium for users to download mail to a local computer from an SMTP server. Many email clients for the Mac such as Eudora and Netscape Navigator, as well as Windows, incorporate POP service.

Once again revisiting the post office analogy, a POPmail client is similar to a post office box. If you're used to getting your mail at the post office, a post office box is a means of obtaining mail when the office is closed. Similarly, it may be expensive or prohibitive for you to keep your personal computer running all the time to accept messages. POP is a means of querying an SMTP host and then downloading the messages you have received to your computer. A diagram of this process is shown in Figure 11.1.

Mail clients that use POP provide ready access to the SMTP server without the hassle of remotely connecting to the server through a Telnet session. There is a popular POP server application that runs on Unix machines; in these cases, using a POP-aware mail client, often referred to as a POPmail client, enables you to retrieve your mail without having to Telnet or remotely log on to the Unix workstation. Similarly, the Mac makes an excellent POPmail server platform.

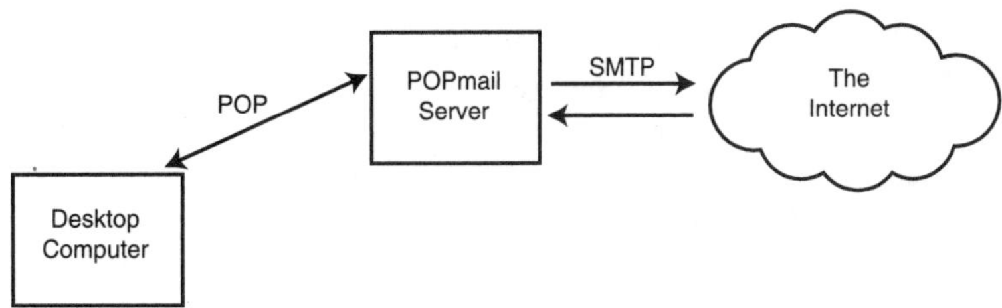

Figure 11.1 *Desktop computers send and retrieve email via SMTP through interaction with POPmail servers.*

One advantage to the POPmail system is that users are primarily responsible for managing their mail traffic. Unlike strict SMTP mail systems where messages collect on the server ad nauseam, POPmail systems enable users to download their messages to their personal computers. You therefore will not need an inordinate amount of disk space to store users' mail on your POPmail server because it's downloaded on a continual basis. Hence, an older Mac with a modestly sized hard drive will make an ideal POPmail server.

Commercial Email Servers

The emphasis of this chapter will be on POPmail servers and clients. POPmail has many advantages as an Intranet mail system. However, there are several commercial alternatives to POPmail upon which you may want to base your Intranet mail services. With commercial email packages, you are locking yourself in to more than just a mail client. These applications also use proprietary mail formats to communicate between the server and the client. Some of the major commercial email systems are discussed briefly here.

CE QuickMail

CE Software's QuickMail, having been available for several years, is one of the oldest Macintosh email systems. The latest version of QuickMail, version 3.5, offers such features as drag-and-drop message creation, attachment handling, and a sophisticated message rules definition. The message rules enable you to deflect incoming messages into different folders based on the information in the various mail headers. For example, you could have all mail from joe@anyplace.com that contains the subject Financial Data relegated to a folder entitled Joe's Financial Data.

Execution of these rules is the responsibility of the QuickMail server; this capability requires a fair amount of server RAM. The client requirements are fairly modest and QuickMail caters to both Macs and PCs.

Quarterdeck Mail

Quarterdeck Mail has a long and tortuous history. Quarterdeck Mail was formerly known as Microsoft Mail, which was an original part of Microsoft Office. As a result, Quarterdeck Mail works within several Microsoft applications such as Word and Excel. As with QuickMail, you can run the server application on a Mac. Mac users of Quarterdeck Mail can exchange mail with Windows users using a separate gateway application.

Lotus cc:Mail

Lotus cc:Mail is yet another cross-platform mail application. In contrast to the other applications, there is no server available for the Mac, so you will need an Intel-based PC to run the post office. cc:Mail is quite popular within corporate Intranets. However, the mail protocol is proprietary; so like the other commercial systems, it is difficult to read your mail with alternate mail clients.

cc:Mail offers sophisticated rules execution much like QuickMail. Because cc:Mail was developed primarily under Windows, the Mac client has historically trailed behind in terms of features and performance. One advantage to cc:Mail is its integration into applications such as Lotus Notes.

Using Apple Internet Mail Server (AIMS)

Setting up POPmail on your Intranet has many advantages over commercial mail systems. POP is an open and standardized protocol; even though you may be running a certain type of POPmail server, your users can operate a variety of POPmail clients such as Claris Emailer, Eudora, or even Netscape Navigator. POPmail servers are usually free, and the clients are likewise inexpensive. As POP works with SMTP, there is no need for a special gateway to the Internet as is the case with some commercial mail systems.

One popular POPmail server for the Mac is Apple Internet Mail Server (AIMS). Formerly released as MailShare, AIMS has been acquired and is now distributed by Apple. In addition to working with POP and SMTP, AIMS supports many advanced features in conjunction with POPmail clients like Eudora.

Currently, AIMS 1.1 is in beta testing, so AIMS 1.0 will be covered in this section. The chief difference between the two versions is that AIMS 1.1 is Open Transport-compliant. This means that your mail server will not be subject to the 64-stream limit imposed by MacTCP. For high-volume mail systems, this can prove significant.

Installing and Launching AIMS

AIMS is available on this book's CD-ROM. To install AIMS, simply drag the application over to a suitably located folder on your hard drive. In order to run AIMS, you'll need to be running System 7.0 or later and MacTCP 1.1.1 or later; however, the latest OS and MacTCP versions are highly recommended.

As powerful as AIMS may be as a POPmail server, it is surprisingly simple to configure. Let's start by double-clicking the AIMS application icon. Upon startup, AIMS will attempt to find out the node name of the host computer. You can see this happening as the Debug window opens on startup; a typical Debug window is shown in Figure 11.2. The Debug window gives you a record of your AIMS transactions. You have other logging options within AIMS, but the Debug window enables you to view the status of the server as well as possible error codes. Furthermore, you can record the Debug window contents to a file using the Capture to file option under the Debug menu.

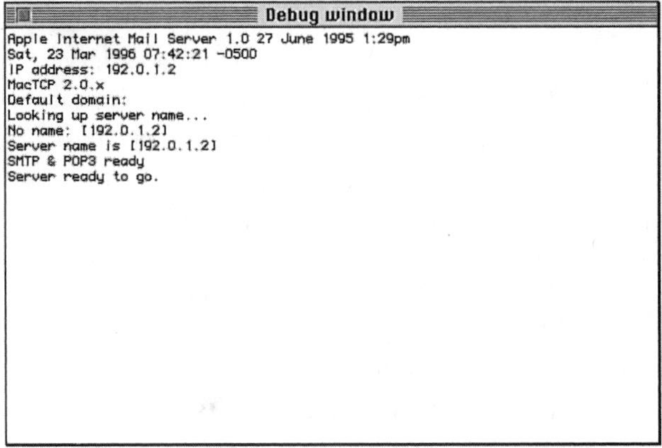

Figure 11.2 *The AIMS Debug window enables you to keep tabs on your POPmail server. You can even record the contents of the Debug window to a file for further inspection.*

Setting AIMS Preferences

You can configure some of the AIMS connection and configuration preferences using the Preferences option under the Server menu. The Preferences dialog box will be similar to Figure 11.3.

AIMS offers three types of services: POP3, SMTP, and Password services. POP3, also defined as an Internet standard, is supported by AIMS and Eudora. Because your server also handles incoming and outgoing SMTP traffic, you can configure the number of connections required. The Password service enables users operating mail clients like Eudora to alter their passwords without having to bug you.

MacTCP enables you to maintain 64 simultaneous IP connections or streams. These streams convey all types of Internet traffic, including Web and FTP transactions. AIMS gives you the ability to reserve some of those streams for your mail server operations. Keep in mind that AIMS 1.1 and later versions will be Open Transport-compliant; the number of streams available to your Intranet applications will be limited only by your processor and RAM availability.

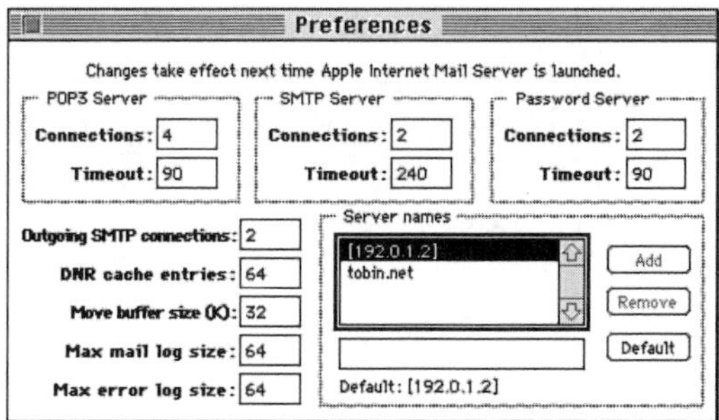

Figure 11.3 *AIMS allows you to set many options regarding your AIMS services, such as IP connectivity and mail server definition.*

As seen in Figure 11.3, you can reserve a number of your server streams to the various AIMS servers; furthermore, you can configure the timeout allowances (in seconds). POP3 connections are established when your users check or download mail from your server. SMTP connections are established with remote hosts for the purposes of sending or accepting mail via SMTP. The Password server enables users to change their passwords without your involvement. This service requires a special IP stream just like your other services.

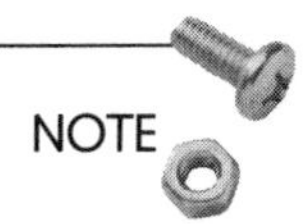

NOTE

If you want to deny a service, such as password modification, just set the number of connections to zero.

There's no formula that you can use to determine the number of connections you need for your Intranet. Generally, the larger your user base, the more simultaneous connections you'll need to reserve for AIMS. Your POP traffic will likely be pretty constant; mail clients are often configured to periodically check the mail server for new mail. I have my copy of Eudora checking my POP server every five minutes. If hundreds of users have their mail clients pop on to your server every few minutes, you'll have to reserve a larger number of connections.

> Moreover, if you assign more connections, you'll need to reserve more RAM for AIMS. Nominally, the application needs a minimum of 1 MB, but you'll have to increase that if you want to serve more users.

There are other preferences you can set within this dialog box. Of the SMTP connections reserved for AIMS, you can set the maximum number of outgoing SMTP connections. AIMS stores outgoing messages in a queue; the more connections reserved for outgoing mail messages, the smaller this queue will generally become.

You can set the number of DNR cache entries within this dialog box. Both MacTCP and OT use a domain name resolver (DNR) that allows Internet applications to transfer IP addresses, such as www.anyplace.com, to a more readily accessible format. Even though the process takes little time, AIMS circumvents this lookup by caching the most frequently used domain addresses used by your site. This caching reduces the load on your domain name server.

> For more information about how your Intranet services use domain name services, see Chapter 12, "Providing Domain Name Service."

By altering the size of your Move buffer, you can optimize AIMS' management of large mail files. Frequently, your users may want to send attachments over the Internet. These attached files can consist of MS Word files, graphic images, spreadsheets, or any other document. Such attachments can be large and are included in your mail message; increasing the size of your Move buffer in the Preferences dialog box optimizes handling of such large messages.

We'll talk about the AIMS mail and error logs later in this section; these logs allow you to review various server status messages. However, AIMS performance decreases when the size of the logs becomes large. For this reason, you can configure the maximum size of these logs in the Preferences dialog box. When the logs reach this predetermined size, AIMS throws away old messages, thereby reducing the log file sizes. You'll have to set the log file size after observing AIMS' performance after some time.

Finally, you can configure the server addresses to which AIMS will respond. For example, your mail server may have the address mail.anyplace.com. Therefore, Joe Smith may receive mail using the hypothetical address joe.smith@mail.anyplace.com. For the sake of simplicity, Joe may want to have his mail sent to the more abbreviated address, joe.smith@anyplace.com. You can enable this by entering the different server addresses to which AIMS will respond.

As soon as AIMS is launched, it will look up the server address. You can enter additional names by which you want the server to be known in the Server Names box. You also can redefine a different default server address. By entering anyplace.com into the Server Names box, you allow users to accept mail with the same account name using that abbreviated address.

Adding and Deleting Users

Now that you've configured AIMS to your specifications, it's time to start adding users to your server. Go up to the Server menu and choose Account information. A dialog box similar to that shown in Figure 11.4 should appear. There should already be two users defined: <any-name> and Postmaster. The account <any-name> is like a dead-letter office for your mail server. Mail addressed to your server with an incorrect user name will be forwarded to this user account. Normal mailers bounce the misaddressed mail back to the sender, but AIMS allows you to retrieve and possibly respond to the sender. The Postmaster account has more privileges than other user accounts. Furthermore, this account is somewhat of a standard on the Internet. For example, if you needed to get a mail address of someone you know who works at UFaxIt software, you could take a guess by sending mail to postmaster@ufaxit.com. The chances are good that UFaxIt's mail server similarly has a default account named Postmaster. This account is useful in that your server may have successive administrators as personnel turns over. The Postmaster account is not fixed to one person and can be accessed by the relevant user.

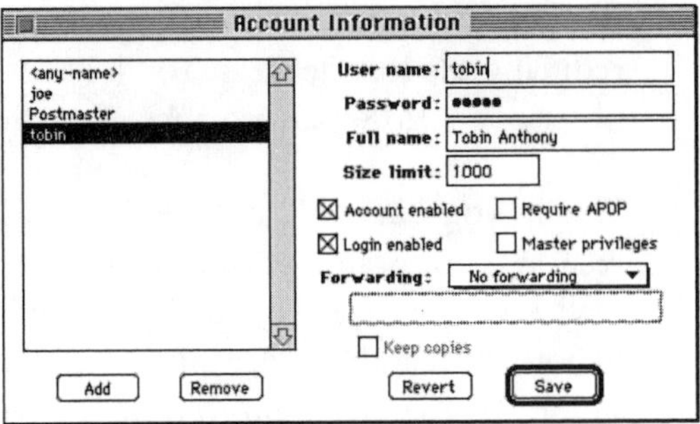

Figure 11.4 *AIMS allows you to add mail users and also to set various options for each user.*

To enter a new user, enter the user's account name, a password, and their real name in the upper-right fields of the User Account dialog box. You also can set the maximum size of the user's mailbox file on the server. This prevents a huge amount of mail from accumulating in the user's server partition.

Typical precautions should be made in selecting the user's password. One practice is to assign a password that is the same as the user's account name. This is frequently done and is therefore a security risk if the user does not immediately change his or her password. A safe means of assigning passwords is to create an obscure alphanumeric combination and relay that to the user, either personally or via a phone call. Do *not* send the password in a mail message.

You also have several options to assign to each user account: Account enabled, Login enabled, Require APOP, and Master Privileges. By checking a user's Account enabled and Login enabled boxes, you allow the server to accept that user's mail and you allow that user to retrieve mail with a POPmail client. Depending on the forwarding options we'll discuss in Table 11.1, you may want to leave one of those boxes unchecked.

APOP is a protocol that provides more password security than straight POP. This option should be checked if your Intranet mail clients support APOP as does Eudora. As of yet, AIMS does not have a remote administration package; when one becomes available, a user with Master privileges will be able to perform sophisticated administration from a remote site.

AIMS allows you several options in forwarding users' email. Click on the Forwarding popup menu to see these options (outlined below).

Table 11.1 *AIMS Mail Forwarding Options*

Forwarding Option	Description
No forwarding	Default option that lets mail accumulate on server for retrieval by user.
Forward to	Forwards mail to user. The address can be on the server or on another host.
Save as archive	Saves mail in a file using a Unix/Eudora format. File name is entered in text field below.
NotifyMail to	Sends message to NotifyMail client. Client's address is entered in text field below.
NotifyMail to last IP	Same as above except that the message is sent the last IP address from which the user checked their mail.
Mailing List	Sends mail to a mailing list. Location of text file containing mail addresses is entered in the text field below.

NotifyMail is a Mac extension that listens for a message from a POP server. When NotifyMail receives this message, an alert is sounded and the user is notified that mail is waiting to be retrieved on the server. NotifyMail works even when the POPmail client is not active. NotifyMail is available on this book's CD-ROM.

When you have the user configured correctly, click the Save button and the user information is stored. Similarly, you can remove users by highlighting their names and clicking the Remove button. You can remove any account except for the Postmaster and the catch-all <any-name>.

Routing Mail through Other Hosts

You may have occasions to route your mail through other hosts. For example, if your mail server is part of a larger Intranet, your company may want to route all mail to the Internet via a single location for logging purposes. Most sites will not use this feature, but it'll be discussed here just in case.

Click on the Server menu and choose the Sending setup option. A dialog box will appear that is similar to Figure 11.5. You enter the domains you want to remap into the Domain field; the asterisk (*) is a wildcard character and will match anything. By entering only an asterisk in the field, you will match all possible domains expressed in the users' mail messages.

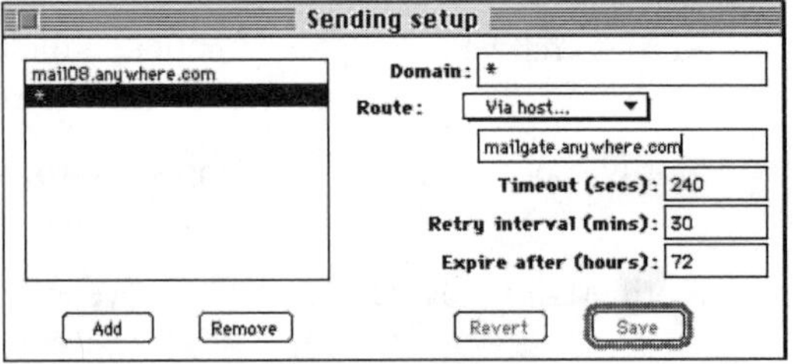

Figure 11.5 *AIMS allows you to route mail from your server through another host using the Sending setup option.*

You can route the messages either through another host or to a file. By selecting Via host from the Route popup menu, you tell AIMS to route mail to the address that you enter in the subsequent text field. By selecting Save as files, you will be able to save these messages into the file at the location you enter in the subsequent text field.

Also in this dialog box is information regarding how mail should be sent from the server. These fields are the only pieces of information typically altered by the administrator. You can set the timeout, retry, and message expiration limits.

The AIMS Outgoing Message Log

As with any major Intranet service, you'll want to have tools to troubleshoot and diagnose problems. AIMS provides several such logging tools. The Debug window was introduced at the beginning of this chapter; the other logging tools include the Outgoing Mail, Mail, Error logs and the Connection Statistics window.

An example of the Outgoing Mail log is shown in Figure 11.6. This window lists those messages that have not been delivered for some reason. If the recipient's mail server is down, AIMS will periodically try to resend the message; this retry period is set in the Sending setup dialog box. For each outgoing message, this dialog box lists the addressee, the size of the message, the time it arrived back at your server, and the time that AIMS will retry to send the message.

Figure 11.6 *The Outgoing Mail window allows you to monitor those messages waiting in the outgoing queue.*

The AIMS Mail Log

The AIMS mail log gives you a record of all mail moving in and out of your server. As shown in Figure 11.7, the Mail log contains information about who sent the message, to whom it was addressed, the size of the message, and the date it was sent or received. As seen in the figure, the sender's address is on the same line as `from` in the Kind column; the addressee is on the same line as `to`. If the message was sent successfully, the addressee is listed on an additional line along with the message size, the keyword `sent`, and the date of transmission.

Mail log

Address	Size	Kind	Date	Message ID	Internet address
Marilyn.Hostetter@gsfc.nasa.	770	sent	Fri, Mar 15, 1996 6:40:08 PM	v02130502ad6fb0418d79@[128.183.61.21	128.183.7.22
Rodney.V.Coleman.1@gsfc.na	1360	from	Fri, Mar 15, 1996 6:44:27 PM	v02130503ad6fb09aa282@[128.183.61.21	128.183.61.211
Philip.L.Petry.1@gsfc.nasa.go		to			
Philip.L.Petry.1@gsfc.nasa.go	1360	sent	Fri, Mar 15, 1996 6:44:29 PM	v02130503ad6fb09aa282@[128.183.61.21	128.183.7.22
Rodney.V.Coleman.1@gsfc.na	1405	from	Fri, Mar 15, 1996 6:45:24 PM	v02130504ad6fb163d198@[128.183.61.21	128.183.61.211
Jeffrey.C.Barnes@gsfc.nasa.		to			
christopher.austell@gsfc.nas		to			
rodney.coleman@gsfc.nasa.go		to			
rodney.coleman@gsfc.nasa.go	1405	sent	Fri, Mar 15, 1996 6:45:28 PM	v02130504ad6fb163d198@[128.183.61.21	128.183.7.22
christopher.austell@gsfc.nas	1405	sent	Fri, Mar 15, 1996 6:45:30 PM	v02130504ad6fb163d198@[128.183.61.21	128.183.7.22
Rodney.V.Coleman.1@gsfc.na	1813	from	Fri, Mar 15, 1996 6:45:30 PM	v02130504ad6fb163d198@[128.183.61.21	128.183.44.60
rwonyma@pop710.gsfc.nasa.		to			
Jeffrey.C.Barnes@gsfc.nasa.	1405	sent	Fri, Mar 15, 1996 6:45:32 PM	v02130504ad6fb163d198@[128.183.61.21	128.183.7.22
Rodney.V.Coleman.1@gsfc.na	1086	from	Fri, Mar 15, 1996 6:51:41 PM	v02130500ad6fb2f830bc@[128.183.61.211	128.183.61.211
xrgx26b@prodigy.com		to			
xrgx26b@aol.com		to			
Rodney.V.Coleman.1@gsfc.na	1378	from	Fri, Mar 15, 1996 6:52:32 PM	v02130501ad6fb3173815@[128.183.61.21	128.183.61.211
James.V.Geiger.1@gsfc.nasa.		to			
James.V.Geiger.1@gsfc.nasa.	1378	sent	Fri, Mar 15, 1996 6:52:35 PM	v02130501ad6fb3173815@[128.183.61.21	128.183.7.22
Rodney.V.Coleman.1@gsfc.na	2360	from	Fri, Mar 15, 1996 6:55:29 PM	9602158269.AA8269448S5@comail.gsfc.na	128.183.72.22
jgeiger@pop710.gsfc.nasa.go		to			

Figure 11.7 *The AIMS mail log gives you information on which mail comes in and goes out of your server.*

The AIMS Error Log

An example of the AIMS error log is shown in Figure 11.8. In addition to the mail server startup and shutdown times, AIMS records error messages in this log. Some of the causes that result in error messages include the following: a failure to startup MacTCP, the SMTP connection timed out, the addressee's domain is not recognized, and so on. These error messages are fairly self-explanatory.

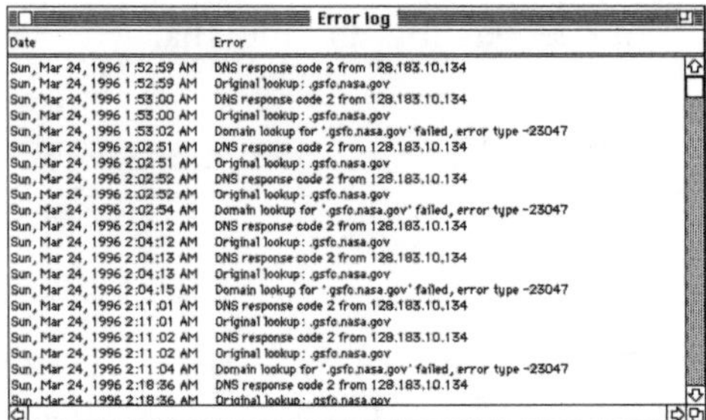

Error log

Date	Error
Sun, Mar 24, 1996 1:52:59 AM	DNS response code 2 from 128.183.10.134
Sun, Mar 24, 1996 1:52:59 AM	Original lookup: .gsfc.nasa.gov
Sun, Mar 24, 1996 1:53:00 AM	DNS response code 2 from 128.183.10.134
Sun, Mar 24, 1996 1:53:00 AM	Original lookup: .gsfc.nasa.gov
Sun, Mar 24, 1996 1:53:02 AM	Domain lookup for '.gsfc.nasa.gov' failed, error type -23047
Sun, Mar 24, 1996 2:02:51 AM	DNS response code 2 from 128.183.10.134
Sun, Mar 24, 1996 2:02:51 AM	Original lookup: .gsfc.nasa.gov
Sun, Mar 24, 1996 2:02:52 AM	DNS response code 2 from 128.183.10.134
Sun, Mar 24, 1996 2:02:52 AM	Original lookup: .gsfc.nasa.gov
Sun, Mar 24, 1996 2:02:54 AM	Domain lookup for '.gsfc.nasa.gov' failed, error type -23047
Sun, Mar 24, 1996 2:04:12 AM	DNS response code 2 from 128.183.10.134
Sun, Mar 24, 1996 2:04:12 AM	Original lookup: .gsfc.nasa.gov
Sun, Mar 24, 1996 2:04:13 AM	DNS response code 2 from 128.183.10.134
Sun, Mar 24, 1996 2:04:13 AM	Original lookup: .gsfc.nasa.gov
Sun, Mar 24, 1996 2:04:15 AM	Domain lookup for '.gsfc.nasa.gov' failed, error type -23047
Sun, Mar 24, 1996 2:11:01 AM	DNS response code 2 from 128.183.10.134
Sun, Mar 24, 1996 2:11:01 AM	Original lookup: .gsfc.nasa.gov
Sun, Mar 24, 1996 2:11:02 AM	DNS response code 2 from 128.183.10.134
Sun, Mar 24, 1996 2:11:02 AM	Original lookup: .gsfc.nasa.gov
Sun, Mar 24, 1996 2:11:04 AM	Domain lookup for '.gsfc.nasa.gov' failed, error type -23047
Sun, Mar 24, 1996 2:18:36 AM	DNS response code 2 from 128.183.10.134
Sun, Mar 24, 1996 2:18:36 AM	Original lookup: .gsfc.nasa.gov

Figure 11.8 *The AIMS error log can help you determine reasons why certain messages were not transmitted.*

Monitoring AIMS Connection Statistics

One useful tool is the Connection Statistics window, which tells you how many current POP, SMTP, and Password connections are active with your server. These numbers are compared with the maximum values that you set in the AIMS Preferences and can be used to determine whether your maximum values are set too low or too high. A sample Connection Statistics window is shown in Figure 11.9.

Connection Statistics

	Current	Maximum
POP3 Server:	0	0
SMTP Server:	0	0
Password Server:	0	0
SMTP Outgoing:	0	0%

Figure 11.9 *Using the Connection Statistics window, you can see how your traffic compares to the limits you've set in the AIMS Preferences dialog box.*

POPmail Clients

It's time to look at the other end of your Intranet email services—your POPmail client. The advantage of basing your email system on an open standard like POP is that you have a choice of mail clients to distribute to your users.

Eudora

Eudora is one of the oldest POPmail clients for the Mac. Originally developed by Steve Dorner as a freeware mail reader, now Qualcomm Inc. supports and distributes both freeware and commercial versions of Eudora. Eudora Lite is freely distributed as both a Mac and Windows POPmail client. Eudora Lite enables you to connect to a POP3 server, retrieve and send email. Eudora Pro has the same capabilities as Eudora Lite and then some. For example, you can filter messages based on the message header or mail contents. These messages can be redirected into a series of mail folders. Moreover, Eudora Pro comes with different encryption methods including MIME, BinHex, and uuencode; Eudora Lite works only with BinHex. The uuencode encryption works with Unix mail programs as well as Mac/PC mailers. Figure 11.10 shows a typical mail message viewed with Eudora Pro.

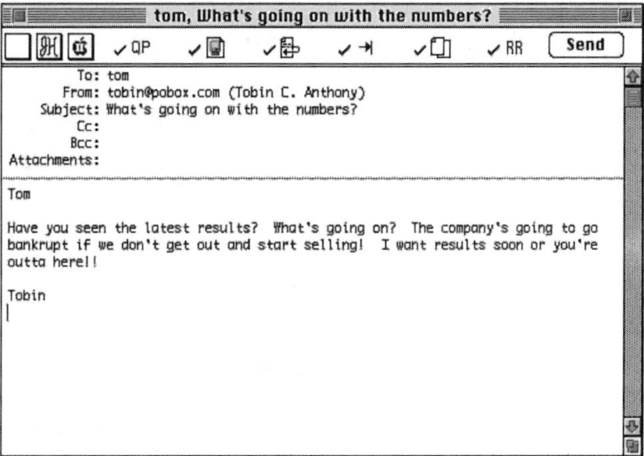

Figure 11.10 *Eudora Pro is a popular and functional POPmail application.*

NOTE

Eudora Lite is extremely popular with Mac and Windows users and is often distributed to customers of Internet service providers. If you are looking to reduce your Intranet software costs, you can always distribute Eudora Lite to those users who won't necessarily make use of the advanced capabilities of Eudora Pro.

Netscape Navigator

It's hard to picture what the Web would be like without Netscape Navigator. In addition to using it to browse the Web, you can actually use it as a POPmail client. Figure 11.11 shows a message being sent with Navigator. Although Navigator doesn't have quite the functionality that Eudora has, it's tightly integrated with the browsing environment. As a result, it's a snap to email Web pages, URLs, or files to anyone down the hall or through the Internet. Chances are that Navigator is liberally distributed throughout your Intranet anyway; many large companies with substantial Intranets have purchased site licenses of the application. As a result, many of your users may already have a useful POPmail client on their desktops.

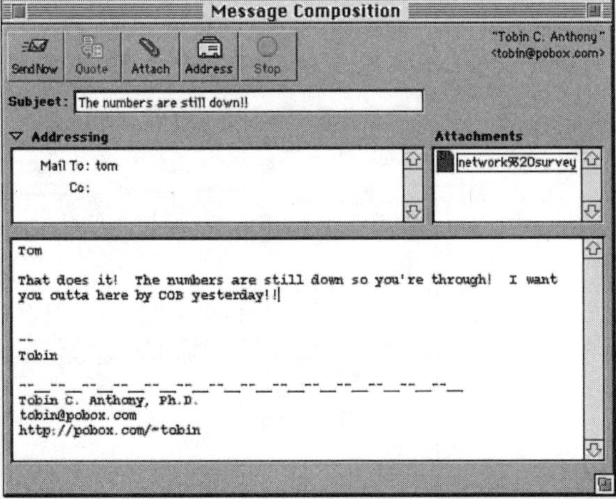

Figure 11.11 *In addition to browsing the Web, Netscape Navigator allows you to send and receive mail via POP. Note the attached file included in this message.*

Claris Emailer

Claris Emailer is a relative newcomer to the POPmail scene, but it is loaded with features. You can use Emailer to send and receive mail through POP as well as most of the online services such as America Online, CompuServe, and Prodigy. Emailer allows you to store all your message in one address book regardless of which mail server or online service you use. In addition to MIME support, Emailer allows you to Stuff your attachments with Aladdin Systems' StuffIt technology. Emailer has become a popular email program for Mac users on the Internet, but it's utility as an Intranet application is hampered by its lack of a Windows version. Figure 11.12 shows a typical message composed in Claris Emailer.

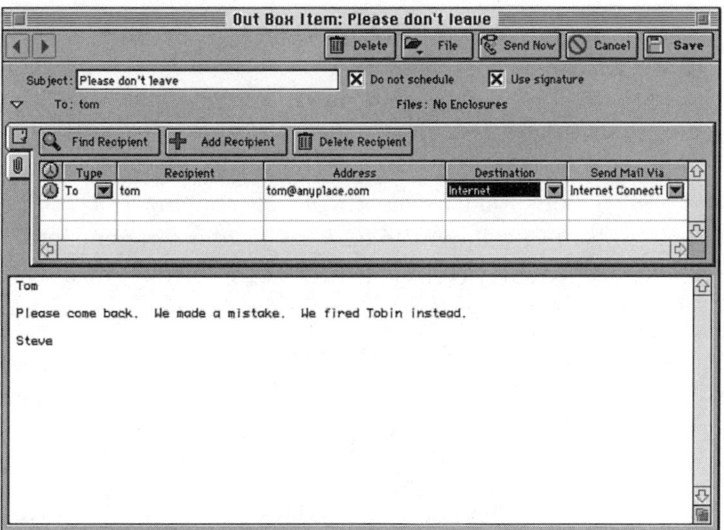

Figure 11.12 *Claris Emailer allows you to use email via POP, America Online, CompuServe, and other systems—all with one package.*

Administering Your Email Service

Well, you have the tools in place. You have the server and you've distributed your email clients. You've got AIMS up and running and you're watching the mail log fill up with messages that are the lifeblood of your Intranet, if not your entire company. Let's cover some administration tips so you can make your service that much more efficient and reliable.

Backing Up Your Server

As is the case with all computers, regular backups are essential. In some sense, POPmail users are less affected by server crashes, because their mail is downloaded periodically to their desktop computers. However, for users who are unable to check their mail for a few days, a server crash will eliminate the stored mail; so the users won't be able to retrieve that mail.

Daily backups would go a long way to ensure that these messages would never be lost forever. Weekly backups are almost as good, but you have less chance of retaining a slew of unread messages. You will want to back up all your different Intranet servers, but you'll need to pay special care to your email server. No other loss of data is going to elicit a mass riot among your users like the loss of a few days' worth of mail.

Providing Enough File Space

Most text-based email messages take up 3–5 KB of file space. Let's assume that a user will receive an average of 20 messages each day. Let's assume that two of those messages include a 100 KB file. At the worst case, each user therefore accumulates roughly 300 KB of mail each day. That means that this average user accumulates 3 MB of mail over a ten-day period; this is the length of time that a user will be gone on a week's vacation from the office. To prepare for worst-case disk usage, you'll need to allot around 3 MB of disk space for each user. This is not as bad as it seems with disk space running for 30 cents/megabyte. Each user's mail will cost you a dollar in disk space. You can easily store mail for 300 users on a 1 GB drive. Remember that your usage conditions may be different, so your mileage may vary.

Using Mailing Lists

Another service that you can offer on your Intranet is *mailing lists.* A mailing list was discussed previously in this chapter in the section "Adding and deleting users" in conjunction with the AIMS software. For the uninitiated, a mailing list allows users to blast email to many other users by directing mail towards a single address. Hence, mail directed to project_x@anyplace.com can be re-directed to multiple users; these users can be within the same domain or elsewhere out on the Internet.

NOTE 

AIMS and other mail servers offer a rudimentary mailing list capability, but software that manages stand-alone mailing lists offers users more functionality.

There are thousands of mailing lists circulating on the Internet. Discussion on these lists usually pertains to a certain topic; mailings on these lists are either moderated by a list manager or unmoderated allowing any list members to post whatever they want. Mailing lists are one step below Usenet newsgroups on the Internet food chain; many newsgroups started out as mailing lists.

Unlike newsgroups that are distributed by news servers throughout the Internet, mailing lists are operated through a central mail server usually operated by the list manager. Nowadays, sophisticated software is used to manage mailing lists that enables users to subscribe or unsubscribe to the list without assistance from the list manager. There are other sophisticated features found in modern mailing lists that will be discussed later in the section dealing with Macjordomo, a mailing list manager for the Mac.

NOTE 

Nothing irritates folks on the Net more than getting *spammed.* Spamming occurs when someone sends mail to a mailing list or newsgroup that is totally unrelated to the list or group charter. These postings are usually in the form of gratuitous articles or advertisements. For this reason, many Internet mailing lists accept postings only from list members.

Mailing List Uses for Your Intranet

The focus of this section will be on the use of mailing lists for your Intranet. If your organization is quite large, you may have groups of Intranet users who want to correspond with one another on a particular topic. You can use your Intranet email server to manage several different mailing lists. Let's talk about some potential uses for mailing lists within your organization.

Centralized Information Distribution

You or your management may want to distribute information via a mailing list. Information on this type of list would only be distributed from a centralized point. You or your bosses would be able to send mail to the mailing list address and have it distributed throughout your organization. You could restrict the list so that no other user could distribute mail through the list. Topics on this list could include memoranda, announcements, or policy directives.

Project-Specific Mailing Lists

If your Intranet consists of many different users, you can set up mailing lists similar to those circulating on the Internet. Members of projects or special interest groups can distribute information by using project-specific mailing lists. Messages could be sent by any member on the list to all the members on the list.

Special-Interest Mailing Lists

Similar to project-specific mailing lists, you may want to allow your users to set up lists that also include members outside your organization. You may want to have a mailing list relating to developments within your particular industry. For example, if your company is in the programming business, you may want to sponsor lists pertaining to topics that are not covered on conventional Usenet groups or other mailing lists. One drawback of this type of mailing list is that you are now drawing a good deal of attention to your Intranet. You cannot run a security check on each and every member of your list, so you are exposing your users to attention from people outside your organization. Sponsoring this type of mailing list could be a particularly bad idea if your company or group requires a high level of security.

Using Macjordomo

Macjordomo is a Mac-based mailing list server. The application's name is a play on the name of a famous and popular Unix list server known as Majordomo. Michele Fuortes, the program's author, insists that Macjordomo is not a Mac port of the popular Unix application and the applications only share a common name and function.

Macjordomo will work with any Mac- or Unix-based mail system, but it's specially configured to work with AIMS. Other than Macjordomo and an email server, you need only a POP address for each list you want to maintain and a POP administration address. This administration address is used by list members to subscribe and unsubscribe from the list. Because we've already discussed AIMS in this chapter, we'll concentrate on using Macjordomo in conjunction with AIMS.

Installing Macjordomo

Drag the Macjordomo folder from this book's CD-ROM to a spot on your hard drive. Macjordomo does not need to be in the same folder as AIMS. Double-click on the Macjordomo icon to launch the application.

Configuring AIMS to Serve Mailing Lists

As discussed in the section "Adding and Deleting Users," AIMS already supports routing mail through mailing lists. These mailing lists are static and require setup by the administrator. AIMS reads the file of mail addresses specified in the Account Information dialog box. Unlike conventional mailing lists, users have neither the authority nor the means to add or remove themselves from these mailing lists. To work with Macjordomo, you'll need to set up AIMS mailing list accounts.

If it isn't already open, launch the AIMS application. Within the Account Information dialog box, create one account for every list that you want to maintain. Let's create a list for workers involved with Project X. We'll call the list project_x and give it the password px096. Enter these in the text fields in the dialog box.

Create another list for list members to use to send commands to the list server. Let's give this account the name macjordomo and the password mac032. Finally, let's create an administrative account to which users can contact you, or the list administrator, with questions on the mailing list. We'll call this account listmom and give it the password mom301. The passwords are arbitrary but need to correspond to those used in Macjordomo.

Entering Mailing List Administration Data

Go back to Macjordomo, click on the Lists menu and drag down to Subscription List. A window will appear, as shown in figure 11.13. In the POP Address field, enter the subscription address; we have defined that to be macjordomo, so enter that name with the appropriate domain name. In this example, the domain is mail.anywhere.com, so enter macjordomo@mail.anywhere.com in the POP Address field. In the POP Password field, enter the corresponding password that you defined as mac032. For the SMTP field, enter the domain name of the POP server, mail.anywhere.com. If you did not want to use the AIMS POP server, you could enter another address; that mail server would have to be configured to accept mail from your mailing lists. For the Problems To field, enter listmom@anyplace.com as we defined earlier. Click the Accept Users Command button to allow subscriptions and list commands to be entered by users. Finally, in the Subscription Interval field, enter the period that you want mail to be checked in.

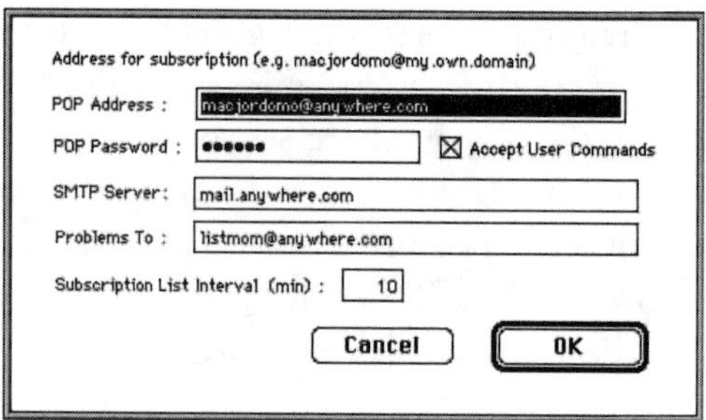

Figure 11.13 *Macjordomo allows you to define the list administrator and subscription list addresses. Users will use these addresses to subscribe or unsubscribe to the list or send mail to the list's administrator.*

Creating New Mailing Lists

Now that you have the administrative information entered, it's time to create new mailing lists. Click on the Lists menu and select New Lists. You'll be greeted with a window similar to that shown in Figure 11.14. In this window, you'll create the specifications for each list.

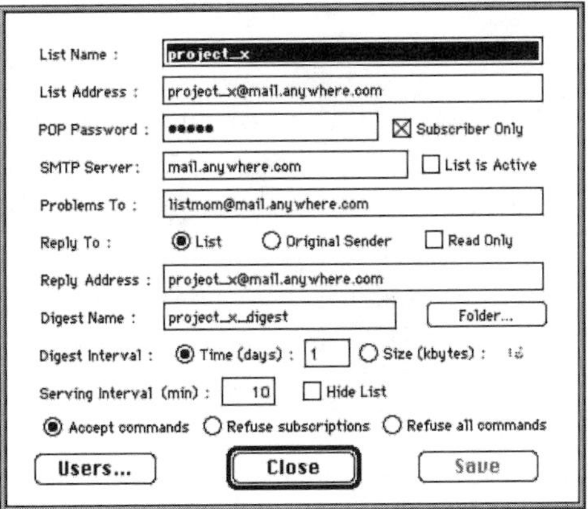

Figure 11.14 *Macjordomo allows you to configure many of the subscriber options available for a particular list.*

Enter the list name and list address in the respective text fields. As we decided on the list name project_x, enter that into the List Name field and append the server name to the list name, project_x@mail.anywhere.com, to insert into the List Address field. We decided on a list password of px096, so insert that into the POP Password field. Enter the POP server address, mail.anywhere.com, into the POP server address. For problems with this particular list, enter the address to which people should send mail; in this example, enter listmom@mail.anywhere.com.

Clicking on the Subscriber Only button enables only members of the list to be able to send mail through the list. This is useful in restricting unwanted mass mailings to your list. Clicking on the List is Active box activates the list.

Okay, here's where things get a little dicey. When using a package like Eudora, the message header consists of several fields. There are the To and From fields, which are self-explanatory; these detail the addresses of the email author and recipient. You'll also see the CC field and sometimes even a BCC field. These stand for carbon copy and blind carbon copy. Blind carbon copy recipients don't see any other names in the message header except for the author and the recipient. When receiving email from mailing lists, you'll see an extra field in your email messages entitled Reply To. The Reply To field contains the address to which the reply to the mail should be addressed.

The next few fields deal with how Reply To directs list messages. By clicking on the List button in the Reply To field, you are redirecting message replies to the entire list. For example, if you check the List button, someone reading a list message will see the list address in the Reply field. If you check the Original Sender button, the message author's address appears in the Reply To field; a response to this message will be directed to the author of the original email.

In the Reply Address field, you can either put the list address or a different address. If you insert a different address in this field, you can moderate the list contents. Mail will get sent to the account you specify; you can read and monitor the messages to regulate the content of the message postings.

By clicking the Read Only box, you prohibit the list address from showing up anywhere within the message. You may want to do this to restrict information about the list. In this case, you won't see the list address in the message's Reply To field. Instead, you'll see the address you've just entered in Macjordomo's Reply Address field. This can be the list manager's address or some other mail address.

Especially with high-volume mail lists, users may not want to receive mail message by message. Macjordomo can send the list mail in bulk. These bulk mailings are referred to as *digests*. Advantages of digests is that you only periodically receive one large message. The drawback is that the digest contains several different mail messages, and replying to an individual email deep inside the digest is not easy. You often have to manually cut and paste the author's address into a new field. List members can request to receive their mail in digest form by using some of the list commands we'll discuss shortly.

In any case, you can send messages by digest using Macjordomo. Simply enter a name for the digest in the Digest Name field; we'll use project_x_digest. Click on the Digest button to determine the location on your hard drive where you want to store the digest messages before they are sent out. Finally, you can specify whether you want to send the digest on a regular basis (that is, after a certain number of days) or when the digest file reaches a certain size. There are merits to both options, but you can choose only one.

You're almost finished configuring your first list, so hang in there. In the Serving Interval box, enter the amount of time that you want to send the list messages. Keep in mind that serving these messages generates a lot of SMTP traffic. You'll have to pick a time that works well with the list volume you expect.

Finally, the advantage of mailing lists through an application like Macjordomo is that your users can configure their list mail the way they want it...all without bothering you, the administrator. We'll talk more about the mailing list commands at your users' disposal in the following section, but it suffices to say that there are several commands that your users can embed in messages to the subscription address (in our example, this is macjordomo@mail.anywhere.com). By clicking on the Accept Commands button, you can allow users to use these commands to modify their personal list preferences. Similarly, you can refuse new subscriptions and any other command by using those respective buttons.

Modifying User Privileges

Okay, you've finished configuring the list. Now it's just a matter of getting users to join the list. Users can subscribe to the list themselves or you can create the user accounts yourself. To create new users, or to add yourself to the list, click on the Users button at the bottom of the dialog box. You will be greeted by a dialog box similar to that shown in Figure 11.15.

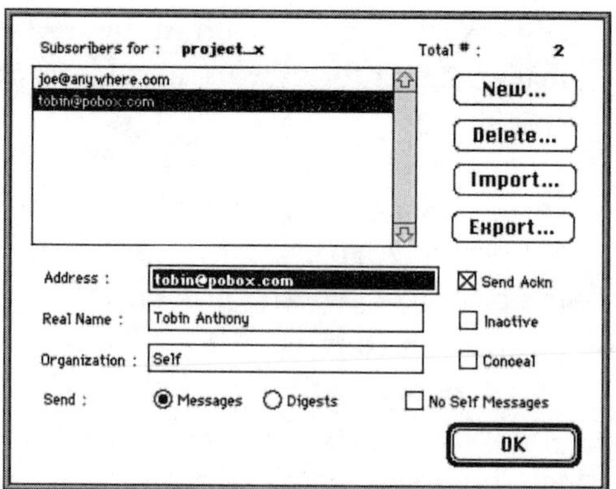

Figure 11.15 *Macjordomo lets you add users or modify the privileges of those users who have subscribed to the list.*

If your list is new, there won't be any users listed in the Subscribers field. Clicking on an existing name allows you to modify the user's mail address, real name, or organization. Similarly, you can alter the user's privileges by using some of the checkboxes shown in Figure 11.15. Clicking either the Messages or Digests buttons determines whether that user receives list mail via individual messages or by digest.

Clicking on the Send Ackn check box tells Macjordomo to send an acknowledgment message to this user whenever he or she sends mail to the list. Clicking the Inactive check box suspends the user's subscription. List members can ask Macjordomo to send them the names and address of all subscribers; clicking the Conceal check box hides the user's name from that list. Finally, users often see their own mail to the list sent back to them. Clicking the No Self Messages check box prevents users from having their messages sent back to them.

You can import or export users from text files by using the Import and Export buttons. The user names and addresses are stored in these files, which can be then exported to other POPservers for use with static AIMS mailing lists. You also can delete users by using the Delete button. Adding users is accomplished by clicking the New button; this brings on a dialog box, as shown in Figure 11.16. The fields are virtually identical to those shown in Figure 11.15

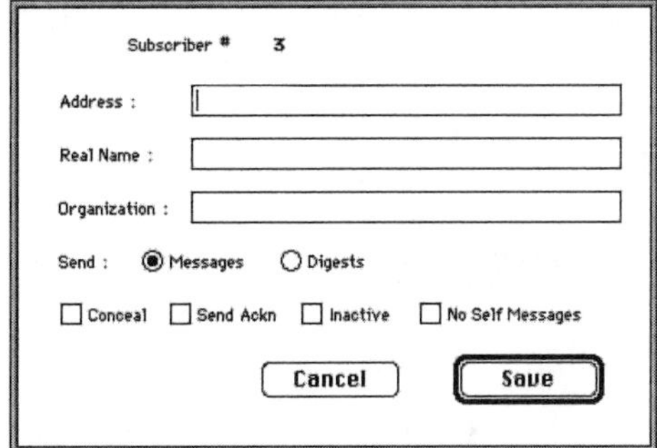

Figure 11.16 *Macjordomo allows you to manually enter subscribers to your list...if you really want to do so.*

Macjordomo User Commands

Congratulations! You've configured your first Macjordomo list. Repeat the above directions as necessary for each list you maintain. The advantage of maintaining a mailing list using Macjordomo, as opposed to a static mailing list through AIMS, is that your users have several commands at their disposal. The commands need to be sent in the body of a mail message that is directed at the Macjordomo subscription address (macjordomo@mail.anywhere.com in our previous example). All these commands return some sort of message to the user; this response is either a benign acknowledgment or a response to the user's command. These commands are summarized below; the underlined portions of the commands are shortcuts to the commands:

subscribe list_name your_first_name your_last_name	subscribes user to list_name mailing list
unsubscribe list_name	subscribes user to list_name mailing list
list	details all the lists served at this site
review list_name	returns a list of users currently subscribed to the list_name mailing list
help	returns a help message describing these commands

get list_name file_name	retrieves file_name stored in digest folder
index list_name	returns list of files that can be retrieved using get
search list_name search_string	searches files in digest folder for occurrence of search_string
info list_name	returns info on list (provided with the Edit Info command discussed below)
set list_name option	option consists of the following list options
ackn	returns acknowledgment when you send mail to the list
noackn	no acknowledgment is sent [default]
conceal	conceals your name and address from a review command
noconceal	opposite of conceal [default]
active	activates your subscription [default]
inactive	inactivates your subscription—different from unsubscribe
digest	request for list mail to be sent as digests
mail	request for list mail to be sent individually [default]
repro	authors get copies of their own messages
norepro	authors do not get copy of their own messages [default]

Editing Response Info

Macjordomo allows you to modify the response messages sent back to the user. Click on the Special menu and select either Edit Generic Messages or Edit List Messages. You'll be able to modify a variety of the types of messages returned to the user, when making any of the requests mentioned in the previous section. In addition, Macjordomo keeps logs of the errors and mail transactions. You can view these logs by clicking on Special and selecting Show Log or Show Errors.

ListSTAR

Macjordomo is an excellent solution for most of your simple mailing list needs. However, you may desire a more robust and configurable mailing list capability. ListSTAR, distributed by StarNine Technologies (now a subsidiary of Quarterdeck Corp.) who also develops WebSTAR, allows you to offer sophisticated and highly customizable mailing list services that rival those offered by Unix mailing list server applications. ListSTAR actually comes in four different flavors; there's a version that works with CE QuickMail, Quarterdeck Mail (formerly Microsoft Mail), SMTP, and POP. To keep with the theme of this chapter, we'll look at ListSTAR/POP.

NOTE

ListSTAR/SMTP doubles as an SMTP server so you don't need to run ListSTAR in conjunction with a separate mail server as you do with the QuickMail, Quarterdeck Mail, and POP versions. ListSTAR/POP allows you to operate over dial-up connections, but you need to configure POP accounts for ListSTAR. In contrast, ListSTAR/SMTP functions as a mail server, so you do not need separate mail accounts.

NOTE

When should you use ListSTAR over Macjordomo? Both applications give mailing list users a great deal of capability to customize their personal mailing list preferences. However, ListSTAR uses sophisticated rules that can be configured to provide a variety of services to users. You can respond to a request based on text contained in a mail header; while Macjordomo gives you a set of predefined responses to return to the user, ListSTAR allows you to customize the types of mail actions. Furthermore, ListSTAR can run AppleScripts that can execute sophisticated functions.

For example, the AutoResponder script directs ListSTAR to mail the files to mailing list subscribers. The user fills in responses on a form generated by the script; ListSTAR interprets these responses and, through Apple events, mails the selected files back to the user.

continues

ListSTAR also uses *regular expressions* to set up rules. Regular expressions are popular in many Unix applications and in text-processing software on other operating systems. With regular expressions, often referred to as regexps, you can establish search criteria that match characters, numbers, and other alphanumeric sequences. Regexps greatly expand your ability to set up rules to provide sophisticated user services.

As Macjordomo is offered as freeware, you get a lot of bang for no bucks. However, if you want to offer more sophisticated mailing list capabilities, you may want to pony up the extra cash for ListSTAR.

ListSTAR Rules and Services

The flexibility that you get from ListSTAR comes at the cost of a complicated user interface. The ListSTAR documentation is comprised of over 130 pages of Adobe Acrobat documentation. I can't hope, nor it is my intention, to reproduce the documentation here in this chapter; however, I would like to give you a flavor for how mailing list services can be constructed using ListSTAR.

Double-click on the ListSTAR Server icon; you'll see the ListSTAR services window appear, as shown in figure 11.17. A ListSTAR service is defined as a series of ListSTAR functions. A service could be a mailing list delivery, an email-on-demand service, an administrative service, or some sort of specialized service that you've concocted. ListSTAR services can be differentiated into two categories:

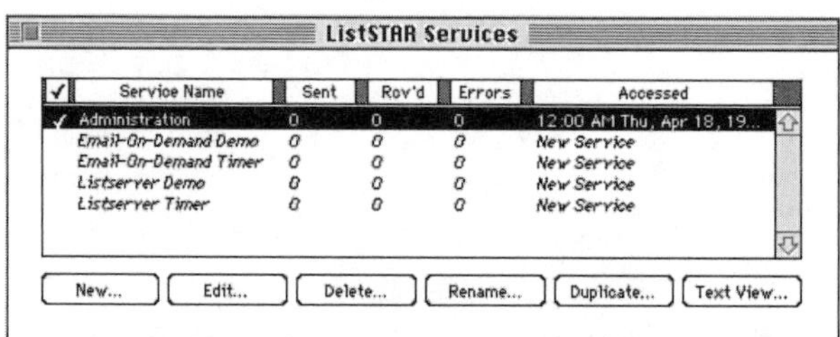

Figure 11.17 *The ListSTAR Services window contains all the different mailing list services that you can offer.*

- **Mailer services.** These services process email requests and serve mail to list users.
- **Timer services.** These types of services occur at certain predetermined times. An example of a timer service is one that combines a day's worth of list mail for compilation and distribution as a digest. Digests are mailed out to list members on a periodic, often daily, basis. Administrative services, such as message log purging or formatting, are also examples of timer services.

Configuring Timer Services

If you've installed ListSTAR correctly, you'll see the list of available services, as shown in Figure 11.17. Let's take a look at some of the administrative services already defined. Select the Administration entry in the Services window and select the Edit button (you also can double-click the entry to edit it). You should see a window like that displayed in Figure 11.18. This window allows you to edit the rules that define your administrative services.

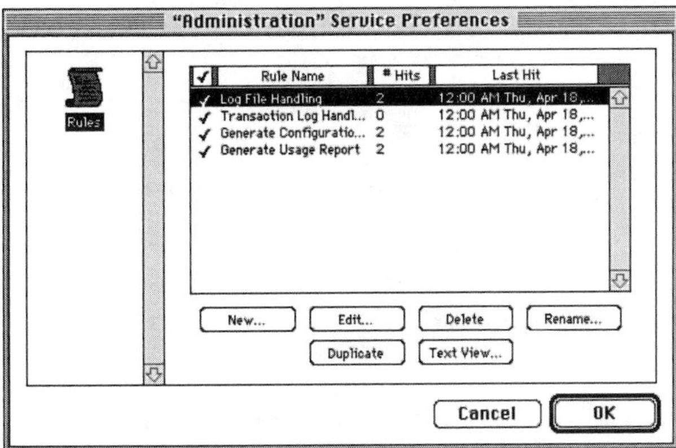

Figure 11.18 *You can edit or define rules that comprise your administrative ListSTAR services.*

Note that there are four default rules that comprise your administrative ListSTAR services. Let's work on the Log File Handling rule; clicking on this rule and clicking the Edit button brings up the rules editor, as shown in Figure 11.19. Note that you can customize four types of preferences for this rule: Timing, Admin, Miscellaneous, and Comment. By clicking on these preference icons at the left of the window, you can bring up the particular options for those topics. As the Administrative services are timer services, you are given the option as to when you want the rule to be executed. The timing preferences are shown in Figure 11.19. Note that you can set the time and frequency that the rule is executed. You can direct logging messages to a certain file, and you can even execute an AppleScript that you've created for a particular purpose.

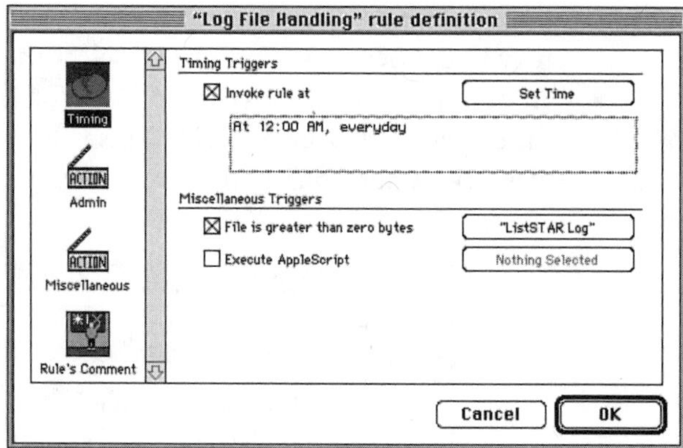

Figure 11.19 *Once in the rules editor, you can customize several of the rule's preferences. For timer services, the timing preference is the default entry in the editor.*

Figures 11.20 through 11.22 detail the options for configuring the administrative and miscellaneous rule configurations as well as a comment that you can install to describe the rule. Note that in the administrative configuration (see Figure 11.20), you can specify the actions that you'd like ListSTAR to perform. For example, you can clear various logs, such as message or error logs, and even have ListSTAR send you email when this occurs.

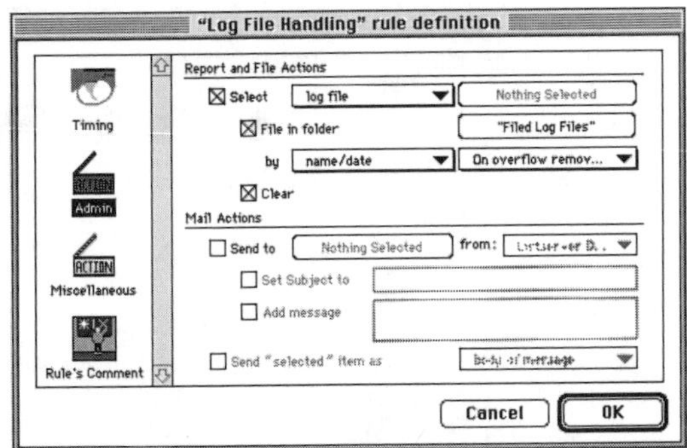

Figure 11.20 *You can specify some miscellaneous rule preferences in this editor.*

Note that in Figure 11.21, you can have an AppleScript executed when a rule is executed.

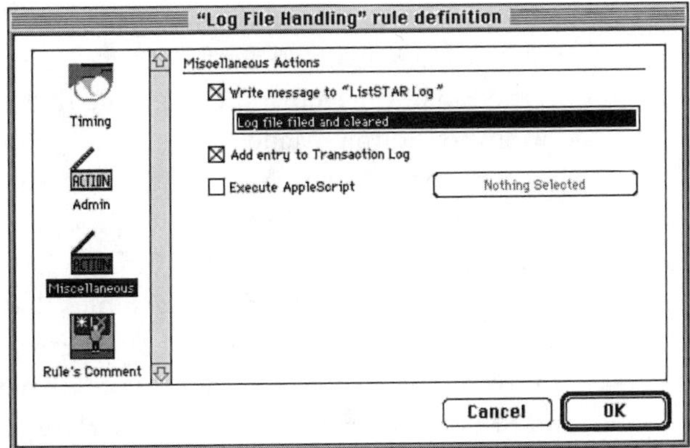

Figure 11.21 *You can specify some miscellaneous rule preferences in this editor.*

Finally, you can install a comment to remind you why you created this rule.

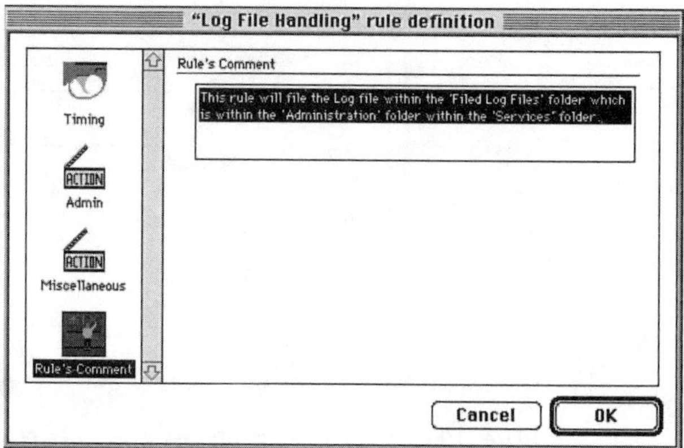

Figure 11.22 *In case you forget what this rule does, you can install comments in the editor to remind you.*

Configuring Mailer Services

Let's go back to the Services window (shown in Figure 11.17) to look at what's involved configuring a Mailer service. Double-click on the Email-on-Demand Demo rule. Note that you have more options for editing Mailer service rules than you do when editing a Timing service (refer back to Figure 11.18). With a Mailer service, you are directing the ListSTAR to process some mailer function. Each Mailer service configured in ListSTAR requires its own POP account. The ListSTAR Server assumes that it has exclusive access to this account and deletes mail messages received into the account as it reads them. For this reason, you'll have to define both a POP and SMTP account for the Mailer service, as shown in Figure 11.23.

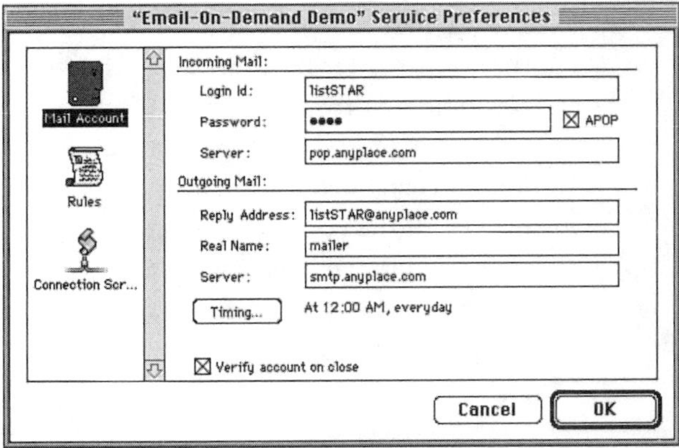

Figure 11.23 *Mailer services require POP and SMTP mail access.*

This particular Mailer service, included as a demo in the ListSTAR distribution, handles email on-demand. This particular service is comprised of several rules as shown in Figure 11.24. These rules are actually activated in the order that they are listed in the figure—the top rule, Mailer Daemon Mail, is evaluated first in the sequence. If the incoming mail message matches the rule conditions, referred to as *triggers*, the actions specified in the rule are carried out. If not, the next rule, Send Desired Recipes, is evaluated.

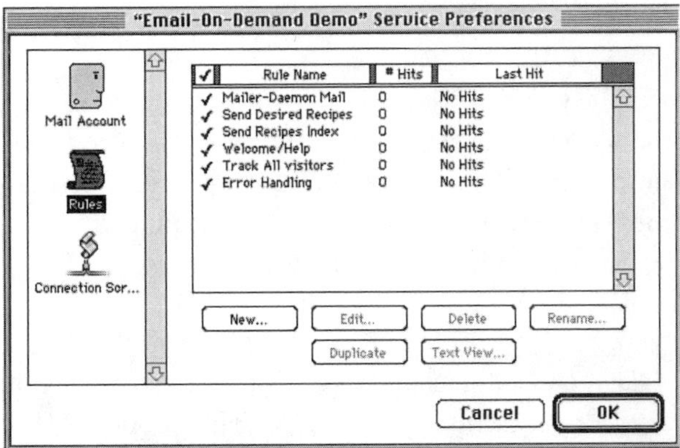

Figure 11.24 *ListSTAR services can be comprised of several different rules.*

Select the first rule and click on the Rules icon in the left-hand side of the window. This will bring up the display shown in Figure 11.25. The first two icons on the left-hand side of the window, Content and Address, represent the rule triggers. These triggers represent certain conditions which, in this example, are evaluated against both the content and the address of incoming messages. Incoming messages that match the trigger criteria cause certain actions to be taken. These actions are listed under the Reply and Mailing-List icons.

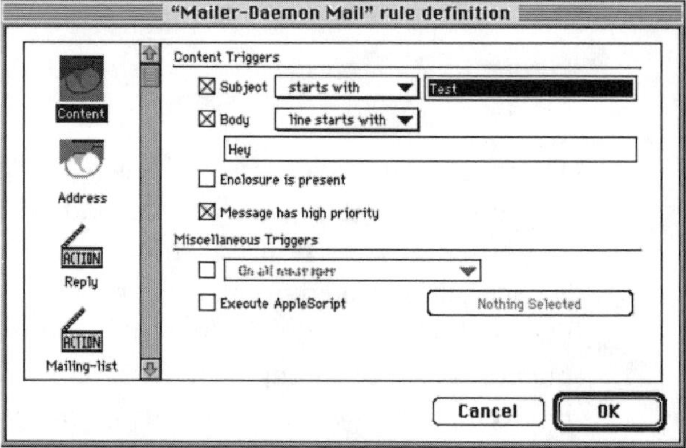

Figure 11.25 *You can define both triggers and actions associated with various service rules.*

Finally, you can issue connection scripts that can be executed when the service logs in and out of the POP server. These scripts are just simple AppleScripts that execute predetermined tasks. You select the AppleScripts after selecting the Connection Scripts icon on the left, as shown in Figure 11.26.

NOTE

ListSTAR connection scripts can be used to dial in to and out of commercial Internet providers. Your Intranet will likely have a much faster and more direct connection between your ListSTAR server and your POP server, so you may not need to use connection scripts in your services.

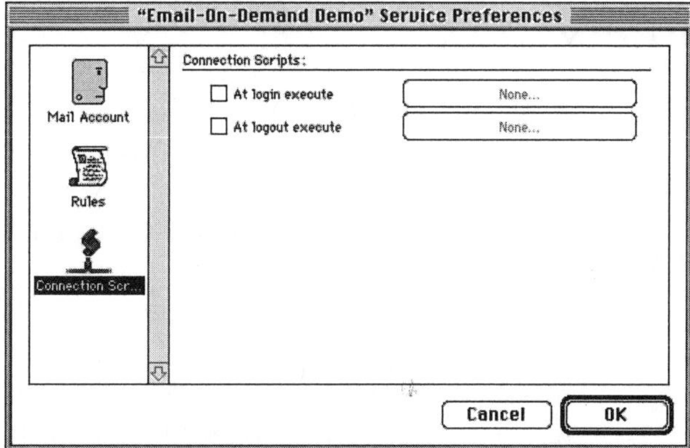

Figure 11.26 *ListSTAR allows you to execute AppleScripts when your services start up and also when they commence processing.*

Address Lists

Now that you've seen how ListSTAR responds to certain tasks and mailing list requests, it's time to take a brief look at how ListSTAR manages address lists. Clicking on Windows and selecting Address Lists brings up the window in Figure 11.27. You can create and edit lists, add users, and get info on the lists themselves. This editor is very simple to use and is very similar to the method used by Macjordomo.

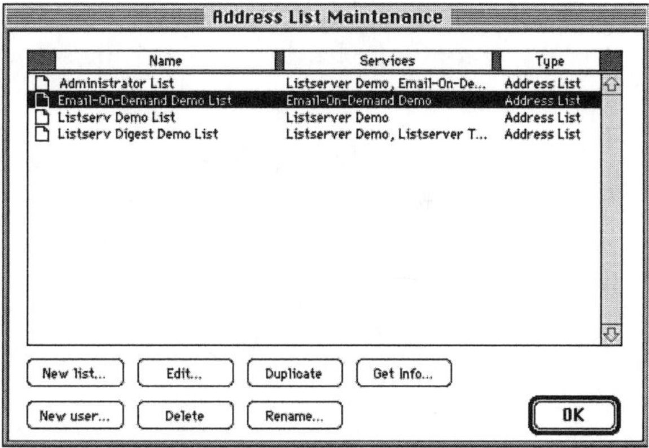

Figure 11.27 *ListSTAR provides an easy means of adding and editing mailing list user privileges.*

Summary

AIMS and Macjordomo, or AIMS and ListSTAR, provide a potent combination for you to use to manage your Intranet email services. Email will likely be the lifeblood of your Intranet. You'll be able to supplement your email services with a mailing list capability. Mailing lists will allow your users to communicate with one another in an informal but effective manner.

Macjordomo and ListSTAR represent two useful Intranet services. Much like the "fax-on-demand" that many companies have instituted for their customers, you can use these applications to offer an "Email-On-Demand" feature for your Intranet users. Not only can they use mailing lists to communicate with one another, they also can obtain specific information from the mailing list server itself. Macjordomo offers a great deal of functionality for a freeware application. ListSTAR, however, provides a powerful tool with which you can manage your Intranet mailing lists. Through the comprehensive Mailer and Timer services, as well as AppleScript support, you can further customize your mailing list services to support your Intranet users.

In the next chapter, we'll talk about providing domain name service to your Intranet. If you want to look elsewhere, see these other chapters:

- Chapter 13, "Intranet Server Security," to learn how you can configure hardware to provide secure transactions within your Intranet and out to the Internet.

- Chapter 14, "Sample Intranet Applications," to learn about some services you can provide using the Web, FTP, and email technologies discussed in this book.

Links Related to This Chapter

AIMS home page	http://www.solutions.apple.com/products/AIMS/default.html
Qualcomm, Inc.	http://www.qualcomm.com
Netscape	http://www.netscape.com
Claris Emailer	http://www.claris.com
Macjordomo	http://leuca.med.cornell.edu/
StarNine	http://www.starnine.com
Usenet	comp.mail.eudora.mac comp.sys.mac.comm

CHAPTER 12

Providing Domain Name Service

Did you ever wonder what happens to an envelope when you drop it in the mailbox? Oh sure, you put a ZIP code on it and that does the trick, but what's a ZIP code, anyway? It's the same thing with using the speed-dial buttons on your telephone. You call your mother using a special button. It's kind of like magic—every time you punch that same key, your mother answers. You probably don't even remember her real phone number anymore.

People are reaching the same sort of complacency when it comes to the Internet. Think about it. You put an address into a Web browser and lots of pictures and text appear. It's the same thing with email. Sending mail to an address like steve@aol.com now seems familiar. Have you ever wondered how that works? I mean, how do mail and Web requests get to aol.com anyway? Now that you mention it, what does aol.com mean?

One important part of the Internet is the Domain Name System (DNS). DNS is the structure that allows mail to be sent, Web browsers to work, and many other wonderful things as well. You'll need to have access to domain name service not only to access the Internet, but also as a shortcut for users on your Intranet as well.

Still too abstract? No problem, we'll cover the important parts of DNS one step at a time. These topics include the following:

- A brief introduction to Internet domains
- A brief introduction into how domain name servers work
- A look at domain name servers for the Mac

An Introduction to DNS

Your computer's domain name doesn't mean much to other computers. When sending IP traffic, computers really care about your 32-bit IP address. That's the long numerical listing; that is, 128.183.44.89. Computers are perfectly happy to converse according to IP address. However, speed-dial buttons are put on your phone because you can store only so many numbers in your head at any given time. Similarly, you're not going to be able to remember too many IP addresses. I've been using the Internet for years and I can only remember my Mac's IP address and maybe my local domain name server if I'm lucky.

For this reason, the convention has been to apply mnemonic names that correspond with the IP addresses. It's a lot easier to send mail to joe@abc.edu than to joe@128.83.102.31. Now you see the problem—*you* work with the alphabetic address, while your *computer* likes the numbers. You need something or someone that will interpret for you.

This is where the domain name server comes in handy. When your Web browser or email application sends out data with a particular host name, your computer needs to convert that host name to a particular IP address. This is a task that your computer usually does not handle on its own. With the millions of hosts on the Internet, your computer would take all day to send a simple mail message if it had to sort through an internal database each time. Think of how that would slow down Web browsing!

Like the old saying goes, "It's not what you know, but who you know." Net hosts are the same way. Your computer, when trying to send a POPmail message or any other type of IP data, sends out a message through its ***domain name resolver*** (DNR). The DNR then sends a message to a domain name server. This domain server also doesn't have a larger Internet host database, but it can deconstruct the host address. If it needs to do so, it can query other domain name servers that it thinks might have the IP address of the desired destination host.

This is relevant for your Intranet even if your users are just sending mail and Web requests to computers on your private network. Just as on the Internet, your users' computers won't know how to access www.anyplace.com without an IP address. You'll need to provide them with domain name service to make all this work. Before you go any further, take a look at the hierarchy of the Internet domain name system; this will give you a better understanding of domain name service for Net traffic within and outside of your Intranet.

The Domain Name Hierarchy

Figure 12.1 shows a portion of the Internet domain name hierarchy. In the early days of the Internet, there were only a few domains available to users; this stems from the fact that most Internet users at the time were cloistered in a finite number of institutions: government, the military, universities, and so on. Currently, domains are organized either by organizations or geographically.

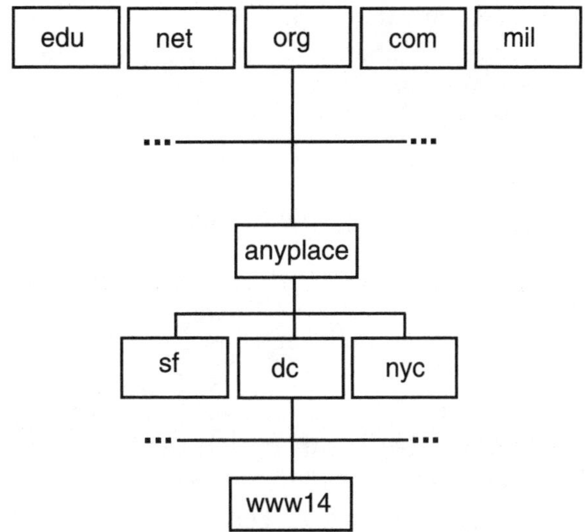

Figure 12.1 *The Internet domain hierarchy—your domain name server skims down this chain until it finds the address for a desired host.*

These domains contain subdomains (and so on) down the chain. As a result, you can describe an actual computer host name using a series of domain names and subdomain names. The domain name usually is associated with the type of organization. The organizational domains can be described as such:

com	Used by commercial organizations.
edu	Used by colleges and universities.
gov	Used by government agencies.
net	Used by network providers (although many nowadays use com).
mil	Used by the military.
org	Used by non-profit organizations or anyone that doesn't fit into the above categories.

For example, a Web server at Anyplace Corporation, Washington DC, might have the host name www12.dc.anyplace.com. Deconstructing this address, we can tell the following about the host computer:

- ☐ The host lies within a commercial outfit
- ☐ The computer belongs to Anyplace Corp.
- ☐ The computer's located in Anyplace's DC office
- ☐ The computer's host name within the organization is www12

These domains describe organizations in the U.S., but there's a lot of Internet activity outside the U.S. Users outside the U.S. are assigned a two-letter domain that corresponds to their country of origin. The naming convention for the subdomains is similar for U.S. hosts.

NOTE

The country domains are standardized, and a listing is available at ftp://ftp.isi.edu/in-notes/iana/assignments/country-codes.

Going back to domain name servers, say that you are on a personal computer trying to access a hypothetical and imaginary Web site at www12.dc.anyplace.com. Your personal computer's DNR will send a message to your local domain name server. Your domain name server will try to find out the IP address of your desired host.

Iterative and Recursive Queries

There are two types of responses that your server can provide: recursive and iterative. A *recursive* DNS query returns the actual address of the desired host, regardless of how many other servers need to be queried. In contrast, an *iterative* query just passes the buck; the domain name server receives a response containing the address of another server that might know the correct IP address.

A recursive query might go something like this:

You	Okay, here goes. I want to see what's on www12.dc.anyplace.com. I've got Navigator running, so I'll just click on this link...here.
Your computer	Okay, www12.dc.anyplace.com. I wonder what he means by that? I sure don't know. I'll just pass this on to the domain name server identified in my copy of MacTCP.
Your domain name server	Okay, I've got to look for an address in the com domain. Hey, you! You're a com domain server, can you help me out?
com server	Well, let me take a look. Yeah, anyplace is one of my subdomains. Let me pass that on for you.

anyplace server	Um, let me see. Yeah, dc's in my domain. Let me pass you on.
dc server	Hold on a minute. I manage this domain. Let me check my tables. Oh yeah, www12's address is really 192.0.1.12. Did you get that?
anyplace server	Got it.
com server	Got it.
Your domain server	Got it, and thanks everyone! Let me pass this on to my user.
Your computer	Oh, so that's who that is. Okay, I'll just send out an HTTP request to 192.0.1.12. Boy, I sure hope it's a Web server!
You	Gee! What a boring Web page.

Now an iterative query might go something like this:

You	Okay, here goes. I want to see what's on www12.dc.anyplace.com. I've got Netscape running, so I'll just click on this link...here.
Your computer	Okay, www12.dc.anyplace.com. I wonder what he means by that? I sure don't know. I'll just pass this on to the domain name server identified in my copy of MacTCP.
Your domain name server	Okay, I've got to look for an address in the com domain. Hmmm. No one's answering. How about you? Do you know where I can find this address?

Server #1	Nope, I sure don't know. Try Server #2.
Your domain name server	Okay. Hey, Server #2, can you tell me where I might find this address?
Server #2	Nope, I sure don't know. Try Server #3.
...and so on...	
Server #7	Hmm, yeah, I've got that in my files. The address is 192.0.1.12.
Your domain name server	Hey, it's about time. Thanks a lot.
Your computer	Zzzzzzz...huh? Well, that took a little longer than usual. Oh, so that's who that is. Okay, I'll just send out an HTTP request to 192.0.1.12. Boy, I sure hope it's a Web server!
You	Gee! What a boring Web page...and it took a long time to load!

The difference between an iterative and a recursive query is that with the iterative query, the name server had to run several queries back and forth until it found a server that could respond to the request. Your name server can handle both types of queries depending on how successful it is at finding a server than can respond correctly.

Caching

A domain name server will store answers to queries in a cache. This saves a bit of time, in that the server just refers to the cache file rather than send out a request on the Internet. Sometimes cache files save the server time even if they store a portion of the address. In the previous example, if you had tried to look up an address in another commercial organization (that is, still in the com domain), your server would have the address of a com domain router, saving that much more time in a query. Many servers date the cache elements so that they expire after a certain amount of time. This precludes the server from using outdated addressing information.

NOTE

> Domain name resolvers, such as the one built into MacTCP, also cache requests. If you're still running MacTCP, look in the System folder for a file called MacTCP DNR. You won't be able to read it, but it's a cache file containing frequently accessed domain names.

Providing DNS on Your Intranet

Your Intranet users primarily will require DNS to access hosts out on the Internet. However, they will also need to have some way of resolving hosts within your Intranet. As a result, the DNS you provide to your users will be the linchpin of your Intranet—a service they cannot do without. This section looks at some of the concerns you'll have as a DNS provider.

The Mac's Missing Link

The Macintosh has provided IP client services for several years. There have been FTP and Web servers for some time now. Domain Name Service is a relative newcomer to the Mac IP server family, and it's a welcome one. Using some of the products discussed later in this chapter, you actually can provide DNS on the Mac, rather than relying on a Unix host as in the past.

You'll need a dedicated name server Mac within your Intranet. This computer does not need to be a high-end Power Mac, but it should be able to handle the traffic load presented by DNS requests from your Intranet users. As this machine will be dedicated, it will need to handle little else but serving domain name requests. Your name service, like your other IP services, will require a fast Internet connection more than it will require a fast microprocessor. Depending on the size of your Intranet, you may be fine using a 68030- or 68040-based Macintosh running one of the software packages discussed in the next section.

Primary and Secondary Name Servers

When the name servers go down in our office, the whole place shuts down. Without DNS, you cannot check email, browse the Web, or download files from an FTP server. This is because you most likely refer to these services by host names rather than IP address. Without DNS, your computers cannot resolve these names, and these services are then closed to you. Again, this is true even when accessing your Intranet hosts. The name server, therefore, represents a single point of failure for your Intranet.

One thing you can do is set up primary and secondary name servers. In this scenario, it's unlikely that both machines will go down at the same time, so your users will have access to DNS at all times. Many domain name resolvers, such as those used in MacTCP and Open Transport, allow you to declare multiple name servers for this very purpose. If the primary server goes down, your users' computers will refer to the secondary server for DNS requests.

Your primary server will maintain DNS lookup information for your Intranet hosts in files configured by your administrator. This server will field requests for host information from your Intranet users; it will also respond through use of cache files to queries from your users for addresses on the Internet. Your secondary name server will refer requests to your primary server while the primary server is working; however, the database and cache files can be periodically uploaded to your secondary name server to ensure that information is available to your Intranet if and when your primary service becomes unavailable.

Naming and Registering Your Domain

Your Intranet may already exist in a network that has a defined domain. You may be trying to set up an Intranet for your department at a large university. As academia was one of the vanguards of the Internet, there's an excellent chance that you already exist in a defined domain. If you're setting up shop in a Internet-free organization, however, you'll have to name and register a brand-spanking new domain. Before you register your domain name, you have to give it a name. By naming and registering your domain, you avoid the possibility of having 30 other people claiming the same domain name.

Host naming conventions were discussed earlier in the section "The Domain Name Hierarchy." The list of domains will give you an idea of where your organization fits into the hierarchy. Keep in mind that your domain name should be easy to figure out. Apple and Microsoft, for example, both use domains that are easy to remember (apple.com and microsoft.com). The same should be true for your organization. You want name recognition. Anyplace Corporation is going to be a lot more recognizable on the Net as anyplace.com as opposed to some other name.

If your organization is large, you may want to think about setting up subdomains. Many large organizations that are split into different parts of the country utilize subdomains. The National Aeronautics and Space Administration (NASA), for example, is a U.S. government agency. Therefore, all NASA computers should lie in the domain, nasa.gov. However, NASA is comprised of several field centers located throughout the country. Computers located in NASA's Johnson Space Center, in Houston, would then have the designation jsc.nasa.gov. In this way, the different field centers are served by different name servers. You may want to adopt a similar approach if your organization is scattered among remote sites.

Querying the InterNIC Domain Name Registry

After you've decided on a domain name, it's time to register it. The InterNIC project is a cooperative effort between AT&T Corp. and Network Solutions, Inc. Network Solutions handles the domain name registrations. After you've determined your domain name, you've got to check to see if anyone else is using it. You can do this from a Telnet session or using InterNIC's Whois Web interface, as shown in figure 12.2. You can get to this service at http://internic.net/cgi-bin/whois.

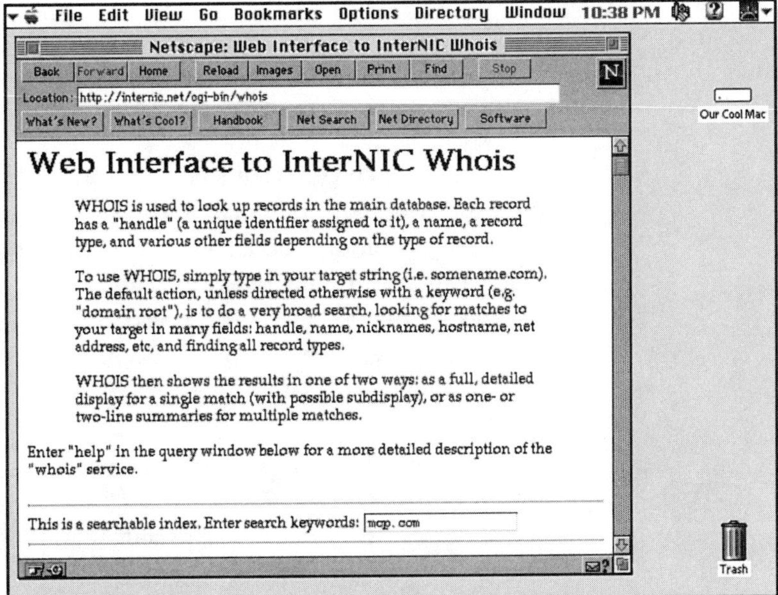

Figure 12.2 *InterNIC allows you to query the domain name registry to see if your dream domain name has been used.*

Let's take the Whois service for a spin. Entering mcp.com in the search field gives the following response:

```
Macmillan Computer Publishing (MCP-DOM)
  201 W 103rd Street
  Indianapolis, IN 46290

  Domain Name: MCP.COM

  Administrative Contact:
   Gold, Jordon (JG187) jgold@MCP.COM
   (317)581-3669
  Technical Contact, Zone Contact:
   Hoquim, Robert (RH159) robert@IQUEST.NET
   (317)259-5050 ext 505 ext. 505

  Record last updated on 01-May-95.
  Record created on 13-Oct-94.
```

```
Domain servers in listed order:

NS1.IQUEST.NET          198.70.36.70
NS2.IQUEST.NET          198.70.36.95
```

Here we see that mcp.com is indeed a registered domain. We find that there are two contacts: an administrative contact within the sponsoring organization, and a technical contact from the organization that is supporting the domain. We also see the host names and IP addresses for the domain name servers that manage the mcp.com domain. Had mcp.com not been registered, no such information would have been returned.

NOTE

Registering your domain name with InterNIC doesn't give you any legal rights to it. You can't register a name that contains a trademark and expect not to hear from the trademark's owner...or the owner's attorney.

Registering Your Domain Name with InterNIC

Registering your domain name with InterNIC costs $100 for a two-year subscription. It's easy to do, and InterNIC provides an easy-to-use Web form to register. The link for this form is given at the end of this chapter.

A portion of this form is shown in figure 12.3. You'll be queried for all types of administrative and technical contact information. You'll also need to provide the names and addresses of primary and secondary name servers that are responsible for your domain. Within a few weeks, your new domain name will be activated.

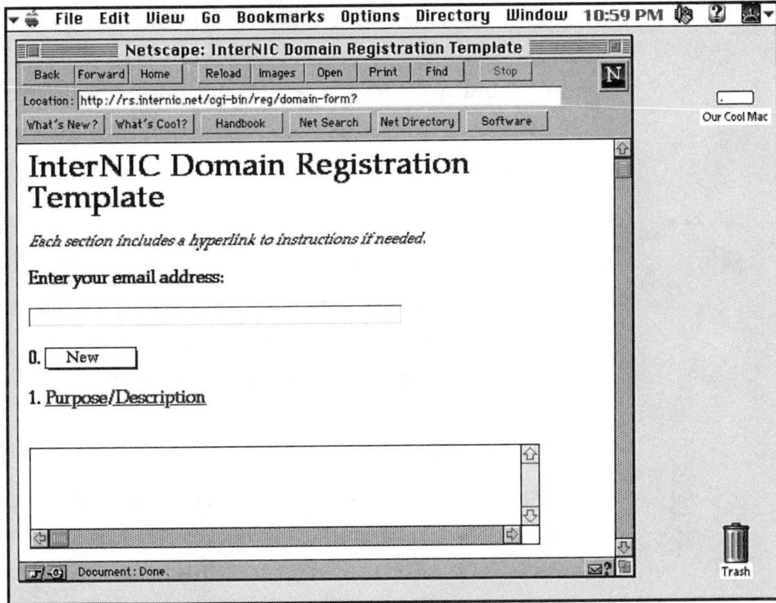

Figure 12.3 *You can register for a domain name with InterNIC's online forms.*

QuickDNS Pro

Now it's time to configure a domain name server. The first application we will review for your DNS is QuickDNS Pro from Men & Mice (http://www.menandmice.is), a software company in Iceland. Besides QuickDNS Pro, Men & Mice offer a shareware version, QuickDNS Lite; these versions are identical in every way except that QuickDNS Lite is a caching-only name server.

Installing QuickDNS Pro

Like WebSTAR and several other applications discussed in this book, QuickDNS Pro actually is comprised of two applications: QuickDNS Pro Server and QuickDNS Pro Admin. QuickDNS Pro is Power Mac native but will run on any machine from a Macintosh Plus or later. You'll need to be running System 7 as well as

MacTCP 2.0.6 or Open Transport. Allocate as much RAM as possible to QuickDNS Pro Server and at least 1 MB RAM to the Admin program. However, you'll get better performance and will be able to serve more domains with larger amounts of RAM allocated to the server.

You'll do better with a dedicated QuickDNS Pro server (or any dedicated Intranet server) if you only include the minimum number of apps you need to run the service. Therefore, get rid of any screen savers or other extensions as well that you won't need to run QuickDNS Pro.

Double-click on the QuickDNS Pro Server application. You'll be asked to enter a validation key. This key can be obtained from Men & Mice (see Note). When the validation key is accepted, you'll see a status window similar to that shown in figure 12.4.

As of this writing, Men & Mice provides 14-day evaluation keys at http://www.menandmice.com/cgi-bin/QDNSKeyForm. Permanent keys can be ordered through the company.

This status window details the following information:

Free memory Total amount of free memory available to the server. Increasing the allocated memory increases the size of the server's cache file.

Packets in	Total number of messages received.
Packets out	Total number of messages sent.
Requests in	Total number of requests received from your Intranet users' computers.
Requests out	Total number of responses to other servers' queries.
Replies in	Replies received from other name servers.
Replies out	Replies sent out to your Intranet users' computers.
Replies from cache	Total number of cached replies.

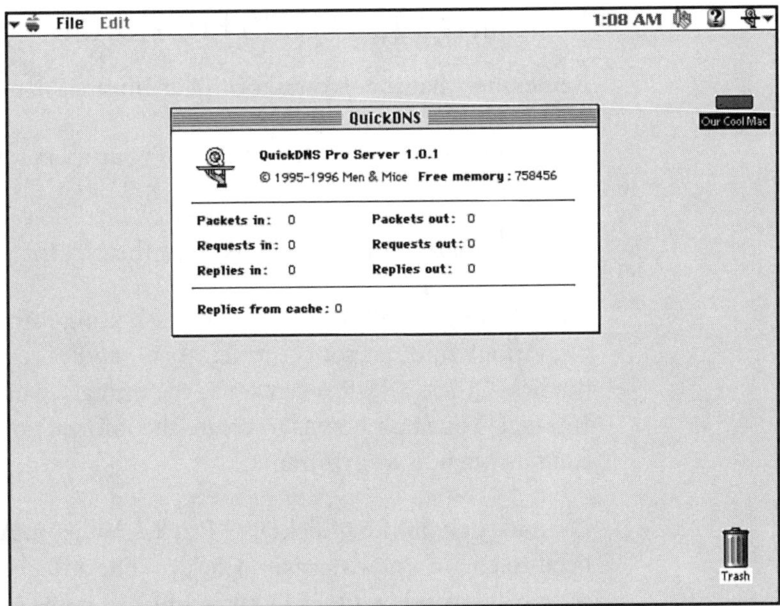

Figure 12.4 *QuickDNS Pro allows you to monitor the number of service requests handled by your server.*

Monitoring the status window periodically helps you decide if your server is handling the load of DNS requests. You can allocate more RAM to the application if the amount of free memory becomes low or if the number of cached replies appears to stagnate over time. As you can see, the most important features that you can add to your DNS server are RAM and network bandwidth.

QuickDNS Pro keeps server addresses of some important domain name servers stored in the server application itself. The server refers to these root servers for referral to some of the main domain servers. You'll also notice that QuickDNS Pro maintains an activity log. You can periodically check the log to troubleshoot any problems with your server.

Installing QuickDNS Pro Admin

Remember that the two tasks of your Intranet name server are to:

- ☐ Respond to name requests from your users for IP addresses outside your Intranet
- ☐ Respond to name requests from the Net for your domain

QuickDNS Pro will handle the first task using information regarding various Internet roots servers. As it handles recursive name queries, QuickDNS Pro can act as the primary name server for your Intranet. Your task now is to create the information that is served to users outside your Intranet.

Double-click on the QuickDNS Pro Admin icon. At this point you need to create a new domain. Click on File and choose New. You'll see a blank window titled Domain untitled.com. At this point, you would start creating records to correspond to your name server and other important server information. However, rather than create one from scratch, let's look at a demo domain folder that comes with QuickDNS Pro.

Close any open windows. Open the mydemocompany.com. file in the Example Domains folder. You'll see a window similar to that shown in figure 12.5. This is the domain data table used by QuickDNS Pro Server to respond to name requests. The table is comprised of several records. Before we look at how to set up the individual records, let's take a look at some of the table parameters.

Go up to Domain and select Get Info. A dialog box like that displayed in figure 12.6 will appear. This window allows you to specify information about the domain for other servers, but it also tells the QuickDNS Pro how to handle the domain information. Let's look at the different fields one by one.

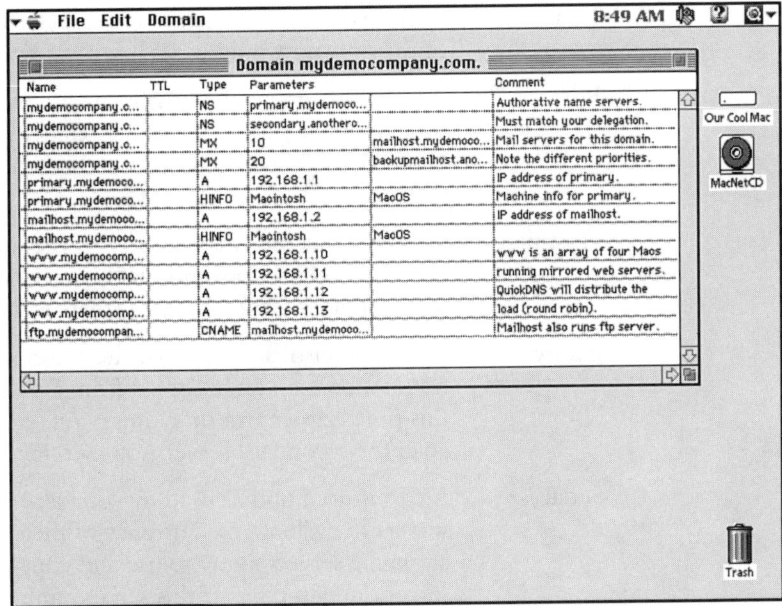

Figure 12.5 *You enter information about your domain hosts in a QuickDNS Pro domain table. This table is read by the server application and is used to respond to name queries.*

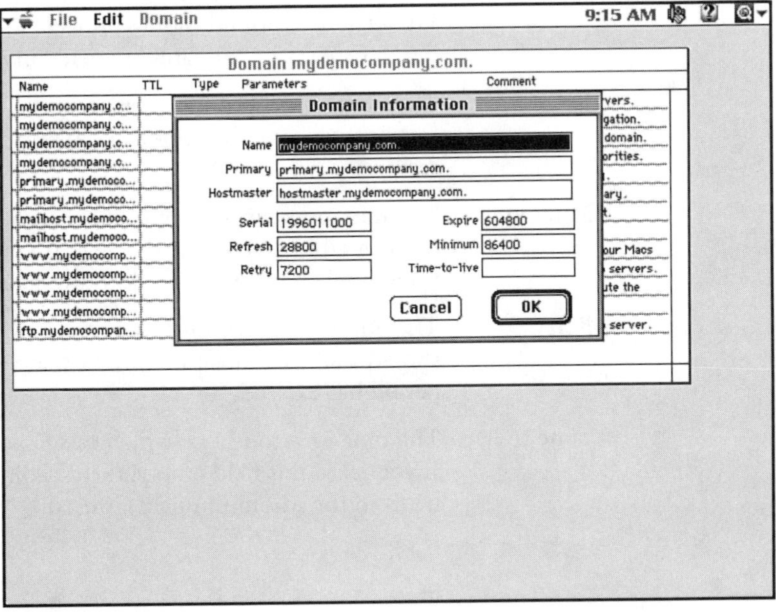

Figure 12.6 *You can enter a specific information regarding your domain in the QuickDNS Pro Domain Information window.*

Name	This is your domain name. It's displayed in the title bar of the domain window.
Primary	This field contains the host name of your domain's primary name server. Enter the relative host name; QuickDNS Admin appends the domain name you just created.
Hostmaster	This contains the email address of the domain administrator. Note: it's conventional to leave the dot instead of the standard @ after the hostmaster's mail account.
Expire	The number of seconds that the secondary server will honor a domain table copied from a primary server. If this time elapses and the primary server is not reachable, the secondary server stops serving this data.
Serial	An arbitrary number used by your secondary name servers to evaluate the currency of their data. Secondary name servers know to use and copy primary name server domain tables if this serial number is greater than the one in the table version they have. *This number should be incremented each time you modify the primary domain table.* Many administrators incorporate the revision date as a serial number using a date format of YYMMDD# where YY=year, MM=month, and DD=day. The pound sign (#) is used as a revision number in case several updates are made in one day.
Refresh	The number of seconds after which the primary server attempts to copy over domain tables from the primary server.
Minimum	The minimum amount of time, in seconds, that this domain table is viable. If this field is empty, the default value is taken from the Time to live field.
Retry	The number of seconds that the secondary server should wait to contact the primary server if the Refresh period has expired.
Time to live	The time in seconds for which this table remains viable. If you leave this field empty, the default value (the value from the Minimum field) is used.

NOTE

> Men & Mice has included an AppleScript which updates your domain table serial number. Look in the QuickDNS and AppleScript folder.

When you create your own domain table, store the information in the Primary data folder.

Resource Record Types

Now that you've defined the general server parameters for your domain, it's time to develop the actual records that your server will distribute. Looking back at figure 12.5, you see that there are variety of columns for each record of information. Each one of these records contains information about important hosts in your domain. These column headings are:

Name	Name of the particular host. Once you have the domain name defined, you can just use the host name. For example, if you insert only www in this field, QuickDNS Pro will append to domain name when you exit this field.
TTL	Length of time in seconds that this field should be cached by the name server requesting this record. Used to tell other servers the stability of the address. If left blank, this field defaults to the Minimum field described previously.
Type	This field contains record's resource type. See the list of resource record types below.
Parameters	Several of the standard resource record types have one or two parameters. These two fields contain one or more of those parameters
Comments	You can leave comments in this field for future referral.

There are many DNS record resource types used in various server systems. QuickDNS Pro uses several of them to define the types of resources in your domain. These designations are entered in the Type field described above. Also listed with each record type are the parameters required for each type.

SOA—Domain Information

The Domain Information (SOA) record contains essential information for your domain. Every domain has one Domain Information record. When a domain is created, QuickDNS Admin creates this record automatically for you and places default values in the record.

NS—Name Server

The NS record lists the authoritative name servers for your domain. Primary and secondary name servers should be entered in different records.

Parameter—The host name of the name servers.

MX—Mail Exchanger

The MX record contains information that can accept mail for a domain. You may have primary and secondary mail servers for each domain, but like the NS records, they should be listed on different lines. This record is important because it allows mail addressed to anyplace.com to be routed to a particular host.

Parameters—The first parameter represents the priority of the mail server. For example, a record with an MX parameter of 10 will be a higher priority than a mail server with a parameter of 20. The second parameter is the actual host name of the mail server.

A—Address

The Address record is the crux of all of domain name service. This record maps the name of an important host in your domain to an IP address. This is the important information that servers outside your Intranet will be looking for.

Parameter—The host IP address.

HINFO—Host Information

HINFO records are used to acquire general information about a host. The main use is for protocols (such as FTP) that can use special procedures when talking between machines or operating systems of the same type.

Parameters—One or two fields of information about the host, such as host platform and operating system.

CNAME—Canonical Name

The CN record is used to set up aliases between hosts. The example in figure 12.5 maps a mailing host to the same name as the FTP host. In this case, the main FTP server within the domain is run on the mail server as well.

Parameter—The real host name as denoted by a previous Address (A) record.

PTR—Pointer

The PTR records are used in developing reverse domains. More discussion on PTR records is found in the following section, "Creating a Reverse Domain."

Parameter—The actual host name corresponding to a reverse IP address.

TXT—Text

The Text record is used for additional comments. You can store up to 256 characters in this record. This record is often used to describe a server's physical location.

Parameter—Your text.

Creating QuickDNS Pro Domain Records

As seen in figure 12.5, the first thing to do is use NS records to define your primary and secondary name servers. After that, you'll want to define your primary and secondary name servers. Note that you have only defined the host names of these servers, so you'll need to define their IP addresses. This is really what the DNS is all about. You map the IP address to the host names using Address records.

For hosts that you've defined as mail and name servers, the addresses in the Name fields of the Address records must correspond with the names you've defined in the NS Parameter fields.

Similarly, you'll need to use Address records to map all the hosts in your domain. This is a very tedious process, as you'll need to update the table each time you register a new host in your domain. We will talk about security in greater detail in Chapter 13, "Intranet Security." However, you'll need to think about which servers you'll wish to expose to the Internet. You may want to list some public Web and FTP servers that may lie outside your firewall. Keep in mind that if you list hosts in your domain table that lie inside your firewall, they may still be inaccessible. Conversely, leaving a machine out of the DNS does not provide absolute security for that machine.

Load Balancing

You may want to share traffic load of a popular service, such as HTTP, among several computers. Apple Computer manages several of its Web sites in this manner. Requests made to one Web server domain (www.apple.com) are actually shunted to one of a set of computers. This is known as *load balancing*. QuickDNS Pro Server supports load balancing, as shown in figure 12.5. Note that in the domain table, several address records are used to map the same domain (www.mydemocompany.com) to four different IP addresses. QuickDNS Pro routes traffic to these Web servers in a round-robin fashion. This is an effective means of distributing heavy traffic load among several computers.

Creating a Reverse Domain

At times, your Intranet users, as well as your users on the Internet, will want to look up host names based on your servers' IP addresses. For this reason, you'll want to create *reverse domain* tables. For each domain table you create, you'll need a corresponding reverse domain table. Reverse domains map IP addresses to host names. This is done by using the PTR record discussed earlier.

For an example of reverse domain table, go back to QuickDNS Pro and open the 1.168.192.in-addr.arpa. file. This demo file is a reverse domain of the mydemocompany.com. example we just reviewed. Figure 12.7 shows what this sample reverse domain table looks like.

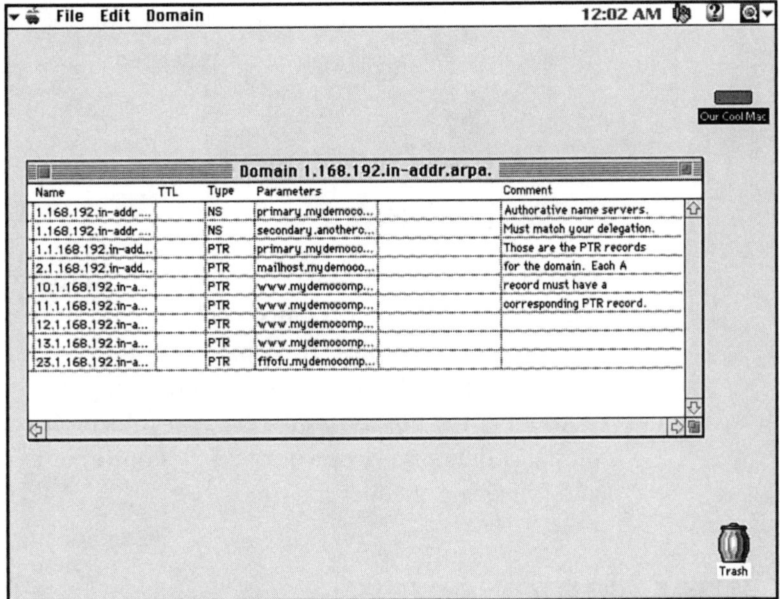

Figure 12.7 *Your reverse domain table will be comprised of NS and PTR records.*

Note that with your normal domain table, you had the host names in the Name fields and the IP addresses in the Parameter fields of the A records. With PTR records, you see that the reverse is true; the host name is in the Parameter field and the IP address is in the Name field.

NOTE

Along with the QuickDNS Pro distribution, Men & Mice has provided an AppleScript that creates reverse domain tables from existing domain tables (called Create Reverse Domains). To use this script, open all your domain data files with QuickDNS Admin and run the script. The script will locate every A record in your domains and update the corresponding PTR record. PTR records and reverse domains will be created as needed.

Importing Unix DNS Tables into QuickDNS Pro

QuickDNS Pro has some other useful administrative features. Most name servers are run on Unix machines that store domain information in ASCII text files. You can import these files and convert them to QuickDNS Pro domain tables using the Domain Compiler (located in the For Domain Text Files folder). It couldn't be simpler; just drag-and-drop your text files onto the Domain Compiler, and it'll create the files for you.

Other Name Servers

QuickDNS Pro is by no means the only MacDNS server. As Internet applications have proliferated on the Mac in recent years, DNS applications have sprung up within the past year. It's likely that more will be developed in the near future.

MacDNS

Developed by Apple, MacDNS is distributed as part of the Apple Internet Server Solution (AISS). AISS is a CD-ROM collection of popular commercial and shareware Internet server applications. Unfortunately, Apple does not sell AISS separately, and you can only obtain the CD by purchasing a Workgroup Server. There is a great deal of public pressure to change this, but as of this writing, MacDNS is not available through normal commercial or shareware channels. However, this may have changed by the time you read this.

NOTE

See Chapter 3, "Choosing Your Server Hardware," for more information on the Apple Internet Server Solution.

Unlike QuickDNS Pro, MacDNS functions as a caching-only server. While QuickDNS Pro also employs a DNS cache in addition to its primary and secondary name server capabilities, MacDNS only serves DNS entries from its cache file. This prevents MacDNS from acting as a primary name server. Furthermore, MacDNS performs no recursive DNS lookups. As a result, users' name resolvers need to make several queries before a host name is resolved.

MacDNS would be useful in an Intranet environment where not many DNS calls are made outside the firewall. If you are in an organization where DNS requests are made for hosts only within your domain, MacDNS's caching and iterative service would be suited for an Intranet domain name server. You could always have MacDNS point to a Unix name server for queries of Internet hosts.

MIND

Macintosh Internet Daemon (MIND) is the earliest DNS server for the MacOS. Originally named MacDNS, MIND is still in alpha testing as of this writing. It's intended to be a freeware domain name server. MIND apparently does not have the slicker graphical domain tables of QuickDNS Pro and MacDNS but relies more of the Unix-style DNS configuration.

Summary

Domain name service is a powerful and essential tool that you can provide for your Intranet community. This is true even if you choose not to expose your Intranet to the general Internet. Domain name servers running under the MacOS are now available and you have several options that you can use to provide this much-needed service to your users.

We're almost done with the hard stuff. In Chapter 13, "Intranet Server Security," we'll talk more about securing your Intranet and we'll discuss the prospect of insulating, or at least guarding, your network from the general Internet. If you wish to stick to issues more related to DNS, feel free to read one of the following chapters:

- Chapter 2, "Wiring Your Intranet," to learn more about networking terminology and other issues related to your network hardware.
- Appendix B, "Establishing an Internet Presence," to learn more about adapting or expanding your Intranet to provide services to the Internet.

Links Related to This Chapter

Domain Name Servers for MacOS	http://www.freedonia.com/ism/dns/dns.html
InterNIC Whois service	http://internic.net/cgi-bin/whois
InterNIC Domain Name Registration	http://internic.net/reg/reg-forms.html
QuickDNS	http://www.menandmice.is/QuickDNS
MacDNS FAQ	http://cybertech.apple.com/dns/DNS_FAQ.html
MIND Home Page	http://www.scriptweb.com/at/MIND/mind_info_news.html

CHAPTER 13

Intranet Server Security

Your Intranet is up and running. Users are downloading files, exchanging email, and checking Web pages every day. On your Intranet, you've provided all your users could need to do their jobs. The problem comes when they need to access locations outside your Intranet. Once you open that door to the Net, you unleash a Pandora's box of problems, concerns, and some potential headaches. Not only do you need to restrict sensitive information from accidental discovery by your users, you now need to worry about the hordes of Internet users knocking on your door.

You may not want to establish services geared toward the Internet. Home pages and FTP servers are nice public relations gestures, but you may neither have the time nor the resources to devote to them. By allowing your users to gain access to the Internet, however, you also are allowing the Internet to gain access to your users.

Luckily, you're running your system on the Mac. The MacOS provides fewer loopholes than Unix or other operating systems for undesirable elements to compromise. Still, the old saying goes, "An ounce of prevention is worth a pound of cure." This chapter discusses a few ounces of prevention including the following:

- The viability of the MacOS as a server platform
- How to determine the level of security you need
- A brief introduction to firewalls
- A brief introduction to SOCKS and Proxy servers

- How to protect against viruses
- How to encrypt your transactions

Advantages of the MacOS

The MacOS is primarily designed to be an operating system for the desktop computer. AppleShare is an extension of the MacOS for use in file sharing, but primarily the MacOS is designed to work between you and your software. The personal approach was revolutionary back when the Mac was introduced in 1984.

In contrast, the Unix operating system, upon which the majority of Intranet and Internet services currently are run, was designed as a multiuser system with remote access capabilities built into the operating system. Unix was developed around the dawn of the Internet, so the two have grown up hand in hand; for many years, Unix and the Internet were almost synonymous.

Unix was designed to allow users to connect to computers and workstations remotely. As a result, hackers are only a few ASCII characters away from logging on to a Unix workstation. Using Telnet, FTP, or email, hackers can attempt to insert a program on the Unix machine. If configured correctly, this executable can give users system-level privileges, assigning them freedom to wreak havoc on the system.

While the MacOS supports IP services through MacTCP, and recently Open Transport, these services are not native to the operating system. You selectively add these services to a Mac through third-party applications such as Web, FTP, and email servers.

NOTE

> Several Macintosh Internet companies sponsored a $10,000 security challenge. Challengers needed to obtain a line from a Web page that had been hidden using Maxum Software's NetCloak CGI application; the remainder of the page was visible to unauthorized users. After six weeks, no one was able to compromise the Web server. For details of this challenge, read the report given on http://www.forest.net/advanced/securitychallenge.html.

This is not to say that PC operating systems like the MacOS and Windows NT are impregnable server platforms. It's more likely that as hackers have honed their skills for years on Unix systems, loopholes in the MacOS server security have not yet been exploited. As MacOS servers become more popular and more prevalent, there may be incentives to uncover these loopholes. Possible security loopholes built into the Mac IP servers could be discovered more readily now that the applications are experiencing heavy use in Intranets and throughout the Internet.

Rest assured, that while not impregnable, the MacOS offers little opportunity for hackers to breach your Intranet. Many of the loopholes that exist within the Unix OS are not present in the MacOS. This is one reason for the popularity of the Macintosh as an Internet/Intranet server platform.

How Secure Do You Need to Be?

My brother and I had this tree house when we were growing up. You could enter the house by climbing a wooden ladder and undoing the combination lock on the door. The fact that the door was the only wall on the entire tree house didn't seem to bother us; except for some flimsy wooden railings, the rest of the tree house was exposed. Even so, we were sure that the big, shiny combination lock would keep out the unwanted neighborhood kids. However, we never had any neighborhood kids try to invade our tree house.

It will be a waste of your time to build a fancy and expensive security system if your security needs are minimal. Similarly, you'll be wasting more money and time if your security measures don't address the core loopholes of your Intranet. The first thing you'll need to do is determine the level of security that you'll need to use to protect your Intranet.

Know Your Enemy

So just who are you protecting your Intranet against? In some sense, you are protecting your system from accidents within your organization. Users can accidentally load FTP virus-infected applications to your FTP server. They can accidentally delete important data while connected to your Web server. These threats, however innocuous, are real and need to be dealt with appropriately.

The threats to your system from the Internet, however, are anything but innocuous. Unconstrained by geography, hackers from all over the world can attempt to access your system. Just recently, the FBI tracked down a hacker who allegedly broke into computers at a prestigious university. The hacker then allegedly used these computers as a jumping point to other systems on the Internet. This individual allegedly installed sniffer routines on various computers. Gaining access to these computers allowed the hacker to attempt to compromise other computers on the Internet. The big, shiny combination lock employed by the university failed to prevent the hacker from slipping around the side and past the flimsy wooden railings.

NOTE

A *sniffer* application is any application that records a user's keystrokes and relays them somewhere. Conceivably, a hacker could reproduce users' account names and passwords. One type of sniffer program appears to the user as a familiar login sequence. However, the user logs in only to be given a response that the system is down and to try again later. In reality, the system is up and the user's name and password have been stored in a file for use by the person who installed the sniffer program.

Hackers are the equivalent of the guys in your high school who spray-painted the school buses or flattened teachers' tires. While doing no major damage, they create a lot of havoc and make other people's lives miserable. They usually do it for the thrill of breaking into somewhere they shouldn't be. Even so, they leave your system vulnerable to others who may have specific desires to breach your Intranet.

In addition to thrill-seeking hackers, you'll need to secure your system from opposition if your organization is engaged in a competitive environment. This is true even if you work for a not-for-profit organization. For example, if your Intranet serves an academic department, you will want to secure the network from people interested in the department's research or financial activities.

Even if you totally isolate your network from the Internet, you'll still need to ensure some level of internal security both for and from your users. Typical Intranet security concerns include the following:

- Protecting sensitive personnel data
- Keeping users from accessing company management information
- Securing user's personal information from other users
- Isolating server applications from accidental disruption
- Protecting server data from accidental disruption

Most of your concerns deal with accidental interruption from users. However, if your organization is large enough or the information you store is valuable, you always run the risk of one of your users maliciously trying to comprise your network.

Even so, your most serious threats will likely come from outside your Intranet. By giving users email and Web access to the Internet, you expose your Intranet to interested parties on the outside. Some of the concerns you'll face when securing yourself against the Internet include the following:

- Denying your site as an Internet jumping point
- Protecting information sensitive to your organization
- Protecting your users' data
- Preventing malicious disruption to your Intranet services
- Protecting against introduction of software viruses to your system

There is virtually no way to establish a goof-proof security system for your Intranet. Similarly, unplugging from the Internet is about the only foolproof means of securing your Intranet from the outside. System administrators, regardless of how lax they might about security, don't want to see their network compromised by outside threats. The degree to which you guard against these types of threats is a tradeoff between the resources at your disposal and the viability of your services. The questions that you'll need to ask yourself when allocating your time and money to security provisions include the following:

- If this system is compromised, how much time and money will it cost to repair the damage?
- Is there sufficient time and money to put a system in place that minimizes the occurrence of a security breach?
- What will a security breach do to the users' confidence in the Intranet?

As I've said, system administration is a series of tradeoffs between risks and resources. You'll have to evaluate these tradeoffs as we discuss your technical options in the rest of the chapter. But that's enough philosophizing. Let's look at the options and tools you have at your disposal in securing your Intranet.

Securing Against Internal Threats

As mentioned previously, threats against your Intranet from your users are mostly benign. While it's unlikely that you will have to deal with hackers within your own organization, you'll have to provide some level of defense to prevent any intentional access of your system.

Quite honestly, the best way to reduce the possibility that a user will bring a server down is to restrict user access to that server. What users cannot touch, they cannot break. Generally, your Intranet will be based around the Web, email, and FTP services.

NOTE 

See Chapter 14, "Sample Intranet Applications," for examples of services that you can provide on your Intranet.

By restricting access to the Web servers, except through browser requests, you avoid the possibility that anyone will accidentally delete any of the server contents. You may chose to connect to your Web server either through FTP or through file sharing. Either way, you should remove all guest and anonymous access to the Web servers. Install one user account under the System 7.5 Users and Groups control panel. If you are using NetPresenz on your Web server, NetPresenz will adopt the file sharing user configuration for your FTP services. Hey, if you're really paranoid, remove the keyboard from the Web server after it's been configured. This will help prevent any accidental access.

In general, it's a risky business to allow HTTP and FTP traffic on the same computer. An aggressive hacker could upload a bogus CGI, which would then be executed by a browser request. Such a CGI script could create a new user account, or worse, remove data from the server. If you do need to provide FTP access to your Web server, use the FTP server's capability to restrict communication from only one other machine—your personal computer.

Your email server should have file sharing turned off. POP and SMTP traffic is transferred using MacTCP, so you can turn off file sharing. Your POPmail server is pretty resistant to data loss; remember that POPmail is transferred down to users' desktop computers, so few mail messages should be residing on the server for long periods of time.

See Chapter 11, "Email Services," for more information on POP servers and email service in general.

It's important to physically secure your Mac servers. Their simple desktop interface makes them much easier to navigate from the keyboard than Unix machines. As a result, you'll need to restrict physical access to the machines, or implement some sort of password access, if you want to guard against physical intrusion.

Securing Against External Threats

As discussed previously, your threats from outside your Intranet will not be as innocuous as those within your organization. You will have to outwit and out think these guys. We'll spend the next part of the chapter looking at software and hardware options you have in securing your Intranet from outside access.

Using Firewalls

In securing your Intranet, you have to make the tradeoff between reducing exposure to your Intranet and allowing your users the resources they need to get their jobs done. For example, pulling the plug on your Internet connection greatly reduces your odds of getting hacked; it also greatly reduces the chances that your users will be able to get their email out of the building—not to mention any work-related Web surfing.

Firewalls are one way of resolving your dilemma. Firewalls serve the same purpose as their namesakes. Real firewalls are comprised of heavy concrete or some other inflammable material: they prevent fire from spreading between buildings. Similarly, firewalls insulate your private Intranet from any kind of unwanted Internet traffic.

What Is a Firewall?

In the context of Internet traffic, the term *firewall* describes a system or group of systems that implements a restriction of data flow between two networks. In our discussion here, we'll be talking about restricting data flow from the Internet back into your private network. Firewalls are comprised of hardware and software solutions and work to restrict transactions as you permit. Unlike the real thing, Intranet firewalls allow traffic to pass back and forth between the Internet and your private network. Rather than a wall of concrete, I've heard of firewalls likened to a tinted glass window; you can see out, but no one can see inside.

Figure 13.1 shows a diagram of how a firewall would be implemented between your Intranet and the Internet. Information can get out of the Intranet so that your users can exchange email and Web traffic with Internet hosts. However, certain types of traffic get rebuffed at the firewall or are shunted to different types of computers. Let's cover the various types of firewalls that you can implement to work with your Intranet.

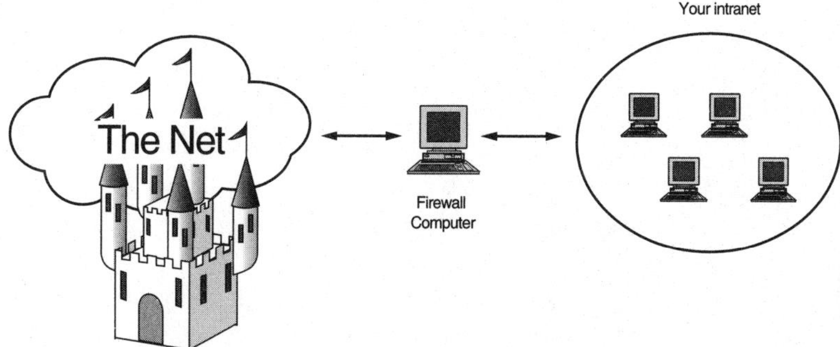

Figure 13.1 *The firewall computer sits outside your Intranet and filters incoming Internet traffic.*

Types of Firewalls

The type of firewall that you institute depends on the restriction that you want to place on traffic entering and leaving your Intranet. Luckily, your options vary from the very complicated and expensive to the reliable and inexpensive.

Single Bastion Host

Private networks like your Intranet often are likened to medieval castles. Your firewall is then analogous to the bastions where defenders of the castle repelled invaders. Therefore, computers involved in your firewall often are referred to as *bastion hosts.* In the configuration shown in figure 13.1, the bastion host obstructs IP traffic in both directions. HTTP traffic in and out of your Intranet is intercepted by the bastion host.

This can be problematic as IP traffic needs to be clearly transferred between client and host. As a result, the bastion employs software known as a *proxy* to communicate between the client and host. This proxy software does not work blindly and can restrict communication based on the Internet host IP address or other parameters. We'll talk more about proxy servers shortly.

Using Routers and Bastion Hosts

As discussed in Chapter 2, "Wiring Your Intranet," a router is a specialized piece of hardware that screens traffic between you and the Internet. Routers are getting more sophisticated with time, but their basic job is to block traffic based on IP port number as well as its source and destination. Routers can be used with bastion hosts to alleviate the traffic from flooding the bastion host. A diagram of this implementation is shown in Figure 13.2.

The router can permit some traffic to go directly to the Intranet. Web traffic, for example, typically travels on IP port 80. Your router can be configured to allow Web traffic to move uninhibited, unless you count the router, between the Internet and your network. Moving network traffic through the router is much more efficient than forcing it through a proxy server. Your bastion host still proxies some network traffic, but only a predetermined amount.

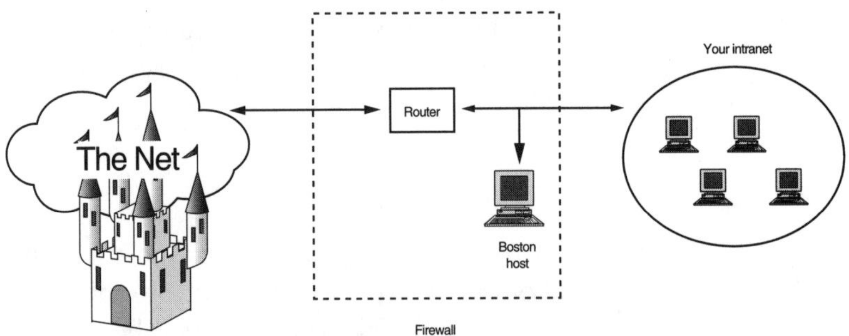

Figure 13.2 *Routers can expedite traffic flow through your firewall while maintaining your Intranet security.*

Multiple Bastion Hosts

With a single bastion host firewall, your traffic is slowed appreciably. Furthermore, if you want to set up public services, such as Web and FTP servers, you'll end up cramming a lot of network traffic through the firewall. For large organizations, this can be a problem.

Another option is diagrammed in Figure 13.3. Using multiple bastion hosts, you can spread the load between the firewall computers more evenly. These hosts do nothing but provide a specialized service. In the figure, you see that public Web and FTP servers exist outside the Intranet; much of the traffic between the Internet and your public servers never needs to filter into your private network. You can administer with those servers through a proxy server. Similarly, that proxy server can transfer FTP and HTTP traffic in and out of your Intranet. Finally, your email service lies outside your firewall but relays POPmail into your Intranet.

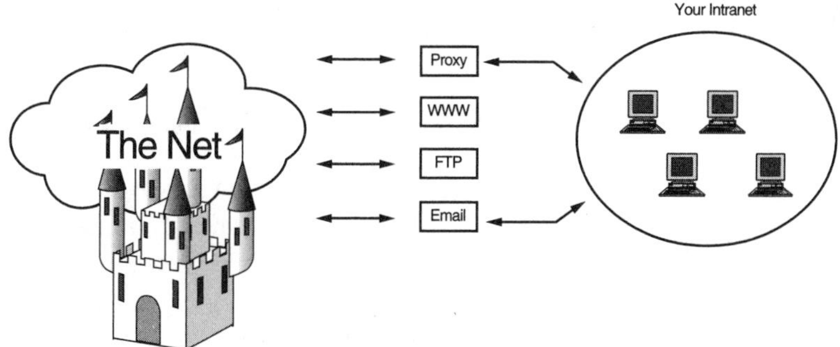

Figure 13.3 *Using multiple bastion hosts, you can spread the network traffic between several firewall computers.*

Your Firewall Hardware and Software

Your firewall is one of the few areas of your Intranet where the MacOS does not present the best solution. There are sophisticated proxy software solutions that run on small Unix-based machines. You should consult with a LAN administrator, as discussion in the area of Unix proxy software is outside the scope of this book. We will discuss basic proxy concepts and will also take a look at some SOCKS software for the Macintosh.

Basic Proxy Concepts

The main job of a proxy server is to accept or reject all IP traffic coming into an Intranet. Basically, the proxy server compares the traffic origin to a list of authorized addresses. A special type of proxy server, known as a SOCKS server, goes one step further. SOCKS software runs on the bastion hosts and monitors traffic entering and leaving the Intranet. SOCKS servers differ from regular proxy servers in that SOCKS servers only pass information that is accompanied by proper user authorization.

Applications on your users' desktop computers will have to be SOCKS-compliant, or SOCKS*ified*. Many Unix Internet applications are SOCKSified. Some Mac Internet applications work with SOCKS including Netscape Navigator and Peter Lewis's Anarchie.

Trying on SOCKS with Your Macintosh

Speaking of our good friend Peter Lewis, he has developed a rudimentary SOCKS server for the Mac. Named SOCKS, this application allows SOCKS records, embedded in network traffic, to pass once their source address has been checked against a list of permitted addresses. SOCKS has a rather crude interface; users have to edit SOCKS's CONF resource with a resource editor such as ResEdit. This resource contains a list of IP addresses and IP masks for SOCKS to check when validating network traffic.

The masks tell SOCKS which parts of the IP addresses are relevant. For example, you may have one address listed as 123.45.67.0 and the mask is 255.255.255.0. The SOCKS software will accept SOCKS records from any address in the range from 123.45.67.0 to 123.45.67.255. In this way, you can allow entire domains or subdomains access through your firewall. This is important if your organization has a remote site; you may want to allow users from the remote site to gain access to your Intranet. This would be accomplished by configuring the CONF resource to allow the subdomain, or subnet, access to the server. SOCKS also maintains an activity log for you to use to troubleshoot any possible security breaches.

You can set up a Mac, running SOCKS as a rudimentary firewall for your Intranet, much like was diagrammed in figure 13.2. The router would be configured to accept traffic on certain ports, such as those ports that transfer Usenet and email traffic, to your Intranet. All other traffic would have to be from SOCKSified applications and would be routed to the SOCKS server.

Protecting Your Transactions

Security within your Intranet is just as important as securing against threats from the outside. You may want to post Web pages that contain financial data or sensitive personnel issues. While HTML 2.0 allows you to set up authentication form fields, these measures are easily compromised by sophisticated hackers. You may or may not have to worry about this threat within your organization, but there are measures you can take to add more security to your Web transactions.

WebSTAR/SSL

The Secure Sockets Layer (SSL) protocol has been proposed by Netscape Communications to the Internet Engineering Task Force (IETF). SSL is a security protocol that provides privacy over the Internet. The protocol allows client/server applications to communicate in a way that prevents eavesdropping, tampering, or message forgery.

StarNine has introduced the WebSTAR/SSL, which provides secure Web transactions using the SSL protocol. This is a different version than the conventional WebSTAR we discussed in Chapter 4. WebSTAR/SSL works very much the same as conventional WebSTAR, except that the URL prefix https:// is used rather than http://. Netscape Navigator provides SSL support so that you can establish secure Web connections to your WebSTAR/SSL server.

Before you can use WebSTAR/SSL, you'll need to obtain a digital ID from VeriSign, Inc. VeriSign is a company formed by RSA Data Security, Inc. and other investors. RSA Data Security is a company that provides public-key cryptography solutions; the RSA public key encryption algorithm originated from this company. VeriSign distributes RSA-based digital signatures, or certificates, that act as means of authenticating mail messages and Web transactions. For more information on VeriSign and obtaining digital signatures for your WebSTAR/SSL service, look at VeriSign's home page at http://www.verisign.com. Netscape (http://www.netscape.com) also maintains a series of tutorials on Web-based encryption practices.

PGP

You also may want to encrypt your email while allowing other users to decrypt your messages. This can be accomplished with another encryption algorithm known as Pretty Good Privacy (PGP). PGP is a high-security cryptographic software application that enables people to exchange files or messages with both privacy and authentication. Only your intended recipients can read your messages. By providing the capability to encrypt messages, PGP provides protection against anyone eavesdropping on the network. Even if your data is intercepted it will be unintelligible to a hacker.

Furthermore, PGP provides the capability to digitally sign any file or message. PGP provides authentication and ensures the sender's identity.

PGP is based on the RSA encryption algorithm. Like RSA, PGP employs a dual key system. Whereas conventional cryptographic algorithms require a passcode or key to encrypt and decrypt a message, PGP users use one key to encrypt the data and a different key to decrypt it. Users often publish their encryption key, often called a public key, in email signature files or web pages. However, their decryption key, or private key, is kept private. These two keys work together; without the private key, encrypted data cannot be decoded.

As a result of this process, PGP is somewhat inconvenient to use. However, MIT distributes PGP for various platforms, including the MacOS. MacPGP is available from MIT's PGP home page; see the link at the end of the chapter. MacPGP is not included on this book's CD-ROM because of US export restrictions on PGP technology. You can obtain the software from the home page listed at the end of the chapter. MacPGP also comes with an AppleScript that allows you to send and receive encrypted mail using Eudora.

Summary

You can implement the most sophisticated firewall, set up the fastest SSL Web server, and distribute PGP to your users. However, none of these measures will bulletproof your Intranet without your having a firm idea how secure you want to make your network. You cannot protect against stupidity, so you will have to endow your users with the same secure mentality that you have. For example, your users should not distribute system passwords, bring in floppy disks from other systems, or exchange system information with people outside your Intranet. No matter how innocuous you think your network may be, it makes a wonderful and insidious jump point for a thrill-seeking hacker to exploit.

The next chapter, Chapter 14, "Sample Intranet Applications," discusses several customized applications that you can develop for your Intranet using a lot of the tools covered in the previous chapters. Before going to this chapter, you may want to go back and review some of the relevant chapters that contain material discussed in Chapter 14. Some relevant chapters include the following:

- Chapter 4, "Macintosh HTTP Servers," to learn about the different software you can use to set up World Wide Web services on your Mac.

- Chapter 7, "Writing CGI Scripts," to learn about writing scripts for your Web site. These scripts allow you to process data from HTML forms and return customized Web pages.

- Chapter 9, "Beyond HTML," to learn about some techniques to spruce up your Web site beyond just using conventional HTML and graphics. We'll discuss Java, RealAudio, and other cool topics.

- Chapter 10, "FTP Services," to learn more about setting up FTP services on your Macintosh.

Links Related to This Chapter

Mac Web Security Challenge	http://www.forest.net/advanced/securitychallenge.html
WebSTAR/SSL	http://www.starnine.com/webstarssl/webstarssl.html
VeriSign	http://www.verisign.com
MIT's PGP Home Page	http://web.mit.edu/network/pgp
RSA Home Page	http://www.rsa.com

CHAPTER 14

Sample Intranet Applications

At this point in the book, you have all the tools you need to establish a self-sufficient and productive Intranet. You've been introduced to many concepts and applications that you can adopt and utilize for your private use, and my hope is that you've been getting ideas to adapt many of these for your company's use.

This chapter will discuss some new types of applications that you can offer to your Intranet users. As Intranets are springing up all over the corporate world, developers are creating specialized products for this new market.

Other Intranet applications discussed here, however, are derived from the subject matter presented earlier, such as Web service, CGI scripting, and FTP service. As an administrator, you'll utilize the open environment of the Intranet to develop new and customized tools. You, or a team of developers under your direction, will construct Web pages, program CGI scripts, and develop sophisticated databases—all for the purpose of meeting specific needs within your group. The advantages of the applications you'll be developing arise from their open architecture and cross-platform accessibility. You'll be serving these programs from your stable of Macs, but you'll be able to service clients using a variety of operating systems.

You can add the following capabilities to your Intranet:

- Group scheduling to allow your users to set up meetings and allocate resources, such as conference rooms and multimedia equipment
- Videoconferencing, which is the next best thing to being there

- Bulletin boards to develop thread-based chat groups on your Intranet, allowing users to communicate and share information
- Ideas for Web-based management applications that you can develop

Group Scheduling

I'm sure you've encountered the frustrating situation that arises at the end of meetings when you're gathered around a table and trying to decide when to schedule the next meeting. It's difficult to coordinate schedules, especially when half of the people you need to be there aren't there. What's worse is that half of the people who are at the meeting probably forgot their personal calendars and have no way of knowing who's available at what time. After you've found a time that everyone can meet, you've got to find a room for the meeting. There's got to be a better way to do this, and there is; it's called *group scheduling*.

Group schedulers are like the personal calendar applications that you've probably used on your Mac for years; however, group schedulers are calendars that talk to one another over a LAN or even a WAN. You can propose meetings by having the scheduler select a time that all of the desired members are available. Some schedulers even allow you to incorporate the availability of resources such as conference rooms and overhead and projection panel displays.

Meeting Maker XP

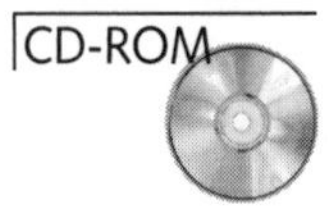

ON Technology's (http://www.on.com) Meeting Maker XP, or simply Meeting Maker, is a popular group scheduler application. Originally developed for the Mac, Meeting Maker is now a cross-platform application (hence the suffix XP) usable on the various DOS and Windows platforms, the MacOS, OS/2, and certain flavors of Unix.

Meeting Maker allows you to store offline versions of your personal calendar on personal digital assistants such as Apple's Newton, the Sharp Wizard, and even the Timex Data Watch!

Like a lot of the software discussed in this book, Meeting Maker is a client-server application. You run a Meeting Maker server on a spare Mac, PC, or Unix workstation. You then sprinkle Meeting Maker client applications throughout your Intranet. The Meeting Maker clients can work offline or connect to the server to do group scheduling. Let's take a look at some of the specific features of Meeting Maker.

Scheduling a Meeting

Setting up a meeting with Meeting Maker is a simple task. Figure 14.1 depicts a recently created meeting that was set up by clicking on a start time and dragging the mouse to the desired meeting end time. When establishing the meeting, a dialog box will appear similar to that shown in Figure 14.2. In this dialog box, you can fine tune the start time, duration, the frequency of the meetings.

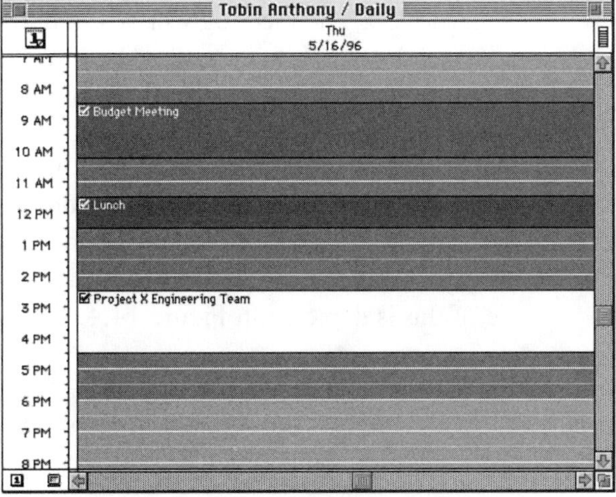

Figure 14.1 *Scheduling a meeting with a group scheduler like Meeting Maker can be done with a simple click and drag.*

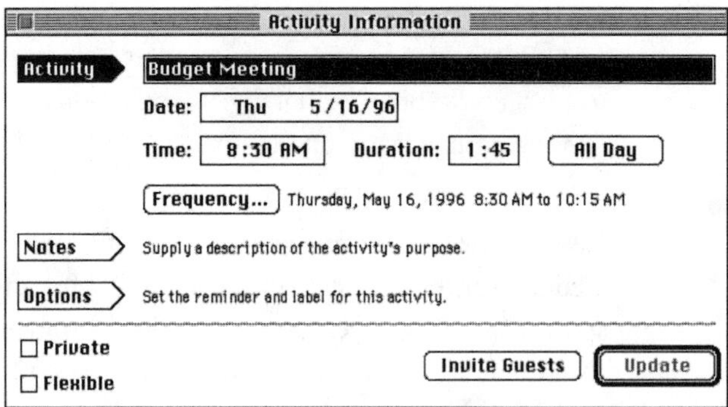

Figure 14.2 *Although you can create a meeting by clicking and dragging on the calendar, you can fine tune the start time, duration, and frequency of the meeting by using this dialog box.*

Inviting Guests to Your Meeting

Clicking on the Guests button enables you to invite a series of guests, by bringing up a dialog box similar to that shown in Figure 14.3. These guests are users like yourself who have accounts within the Meeting Maker server. All you need to do to invite guests is select their names and then click on Required or Optional buttons. After you send the request, guests will receive messages asking for their participation in your meeting; these guests can reply positively or negatively. The meeting will be established if all required guests can attend; refusals from optional guests won't prevent the meeting from being established.

Note that after you invite guests to your meeting, the tabs on the left side of the dialog box change names and new tabs appear. Now you can fine tune the scheduling of the meeting, and you can see how it appears on the personal calendars of your guests. An example of this is depicted in Figure 14.4.

NOTE

Clicking on your guest's names brings their personal schedule into the window in the Schedule dialog box.

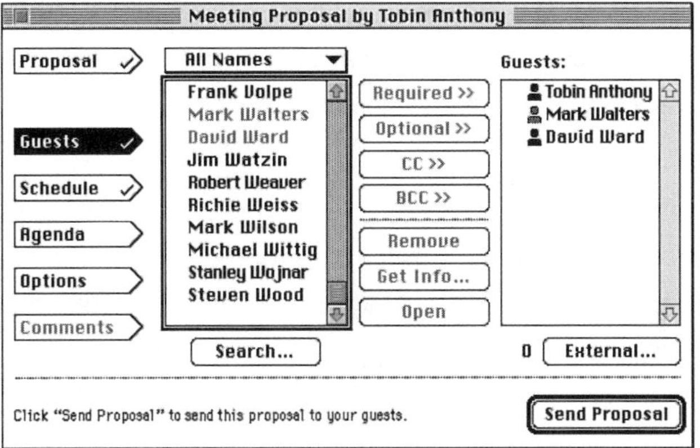

Figure 14.3 *You can invite other users, or optional guests, who have accounts on your Meeting Maker server to your meetings as required. Similar to email, you can notify guests of your meeting through carbon-copy or blind carbon-copy notificaion without actually inviting them.*

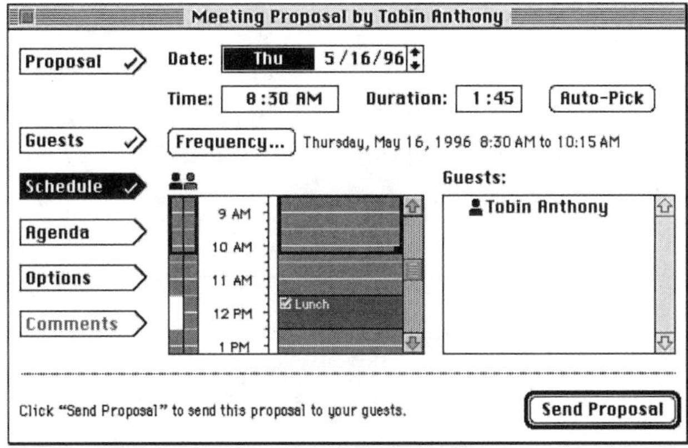

Figure 14.4 *After you've invited guests to a Meeting Maker meeting, you can graphically fix the meeting's schedule and duration and compare it to other guests' calendars.*

Customizing Your Meeting Request

You can include an agenda with your meeting request, as shown in Figure 14.5. You can include existing text files into your agenda, or you can save your agenda as a text file for future referral. Figure

14.6 shows some of the options you have in setting up meeting reminders and classification. If you're sitting at your desk while Meeting Maker is open, you can have Meeting Maker remind you of the meeting shortly before it is to take place. You can assign a predetermined time to be reminded of the meeting. Finally, you can specify what sort of label to fix to the meeting. Just like the System 7.5 Finder lets you fix colors and labels to icons, you can set up classifications and labels to differentiate between your meetings.

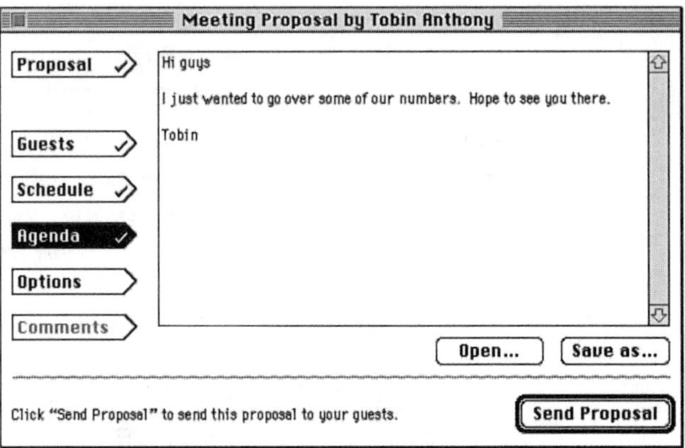

Figure 14.5 *You can include an agenda in your meeting requests. Instead of typing an agenda in this text field, you can include text from a file.*

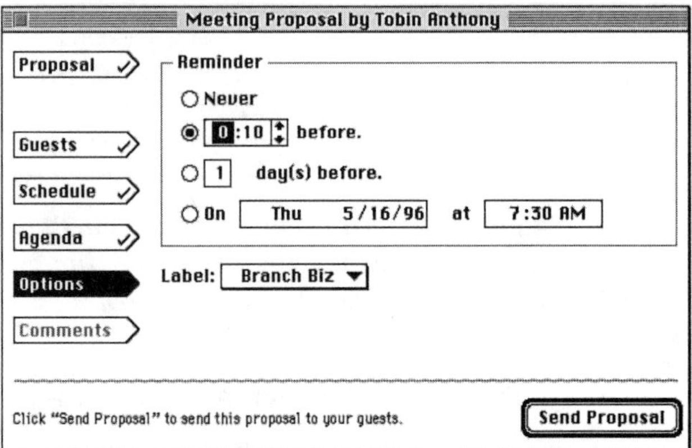

Figure 14.6 *Using Meeting Maker, you can customize your reminder options, as well as classify your different meetings according to pre-set labels.*

Sending the Proposal

When you've configured your meeting properly, you click the Send Proposal button. Your guests receive notice of the meeting if their Meeting Maker application is active. Recent versions of Meeting Maker actually incorporate notification through SMTP mail. This is relevant, as your users will likely check their email more often than they will their Meeting Maker application.

Other Meeting Maker Features

As many of your Intranet applications are based on TCP/IP, you'll be relieved that Meeting Maker does as well. Therefore you will not have to configure your hardware to distribute different network protocols. Furthermore, after you've established dial-in service for your Intranet, your users will be able to dial in from home or through remote sites.

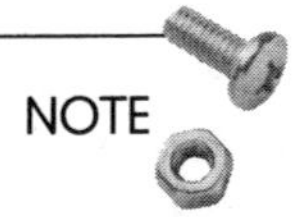

NOTE

> Meeting Maker also enables you to connect to a server via AppleTalk, but this means that in addition to your normal Intranet dial-in service, you'll need to configure service which allows your remote users to work with AppleTalk. See Chapter 2, "Wiring Your Intranet," for more information about Apple Remote Access.

Videoconferencing

I don't know about you, but on my job, I spend a good amount of time trying to explain things over the phone. I usually end up drawing a figure and faxing it to people on the other end of the phone. They end up sending back faxes, and I respond with even more faxes—all this eats up a lot of time.

Similarly, there are several conferences or meetings for which I've had to travel some distance. Sometimes the meeting lasts only a few hours—much less time than it took for me to travel there. That makes for an expensive meeting in terms of time and labor.

Many companies are looking at videoconferencing as an alternative to conventional travel for meetings. Videoconferencing actually is a big business nowadays. Few companies can sponsor videoconferencing inhouse because of the facilities required. Smaller companies usually contract out to special conferencing sites that provide reasonably high-speed audiovisual communication.

Depending on your network hardware, you can provide rudimentary videoconferencing services within your Intranet. With some additional inexpensive equipment, your users can videoconference across your Intranet and even beyond to the Internet. This section looks at one application that allows you to set up this unique form of telecommunication.

Videoconferencing with CU-SeeMe

CU-SeeMe is a freeware videoconferencing application distributed by Cornell University (available at http://www.cu-seeme.com). For several years, Mac and Windows users have been able to use CU-SeeMe to get video feeds from various video services on the Internet. CU-SeeMe also can be used, unlike a lot of the software discussed in this book, as a client-client application. With appropriate multimedia hardware, such as a video camera and microphone, you can send and receive audio and video over the Internet to other CU-SeeMe users.

NOTE 

> You can connect to NASA Select, NASA's video reflector service, at 139.88.27.43.

You can imagine the network bandwidth required to run CU-SeeMe over a small network. Many network administrators have banned videoconferencing products like CU-SeeMe from their networks. White Pine Software (http://www.wpine.com) has developed a commercial version of CU-SeeMe known as Enhanced CU-SeeMe, which is geared to be a better network citizen than the freely distributed CU-SeeMe. While your Enhanced CU-SeeMe is geared to run over a LAN, you can use the application to receive video transmissions with a 28.8 modem.

NOTE

> Alternatively, you can use just the audio capabilities of CU-SeeMe with a 14.4 modem. It seems somewhat counterproductive, however, to spend money on equipment for an Intranet just to let people talk through their computers.

Enhanced CU-SeeMe, which we'll refer to as CU-SeeMe for the remainder of this section, uses a special algorithm to compress and decompress the multimedia data. This is done without the need of special hardware such as audio-visual (AV) boards that would normally go into high-end desktop computers.

CU-SeeMe Reflector Services

One unique feature offered by CU-SeeMe is reflector service. This technology offers video broadcasts to concurrent users anywhere on the Internet or throughout your Intranet. Using a reflector server, you can serve multiple users (White Pine claims as many as 100) from a single server. This allows users on your Intranet to confer and collaborate, from remote sites, on shared documents and other media. You can concatenate, or daisy-chain, a series of reflector servers to provide wide-area broadcasting for large audiences.

While CU-SeeMe reflector software is available on several Unix platforms and Windows NT, it is not available for the MacOS as of this writing. The reflector service offers a client-server approach to wide-scale videoconferencing.

Hardware Required for CU-SeeMe

As mentioned earlier, CU-SeeMe is a peer-to-peer videoconferencing tool. Therefore, you'll need to provide the necessary hardware for your users to utilize the software. As of this writing, CU-SeeMe runs under Windows and Windows 95 as well as on 680x0-based Macintosh computers and Power Macs. Your PC clients will need an 8-bit sound card with a microphone input. They'll also need microphones and video cameras; I'll talk about the video cameras later. For your Mac clients, CU-SeeMe only requires System 7; however, it also requires software distributed with System 7.5. The

Mac's onboard audio and video hardware are sufficient to run CU-SeeMe. Microphones are included with most late-model Power Macs; your 680x0-based Mac users most likely have microphone jacks but may not have had microphones bundled with their machines.

If your company maintains a stable of video camcorders, such as the ones commonly found in electronics stores, you can use one of these for sending video and audio. However, both your PCs and Macintosh computers will need special AV cards to work with your camcorders. Another innovative and inexpensive solution is Connectix's QuickCam and Color QuickCam. The QuickCam is a no-frills video camera that unobtrusively sits on top of your monitor; the Color QuickCam, which displays and sends 24-bit color, is more expensive than the black-and-white QuickCam. You just point the camera in one direction, plug the other end into the serial port of your Mac or PC, and start broadcasting. You don't get the resolution and controls that you'd find on a more expensive camcorder and video card system, but at $300, even the Color QuickCam is an affordable plug-and-play videoconferencing tool.

Using CU-SeeMe

Double-click on the CU-SeeMe icon. You should see an array of status indicators similar to that shown in Figure 14.7. You'll be asked for the name of your local window; this name will be shown on other users' displays. If you have a video source hooked up, you'll see the output in the local window. The Audio window contains controls on your microphone and on your speaker. You can modulate the input level of your microphone and the volume of your speaker output.

Now it's time to videoconference. First, connect to another user. Hopefully, you've made arrangements with another user to set up a videoconference. In the conference menu, select Connect.

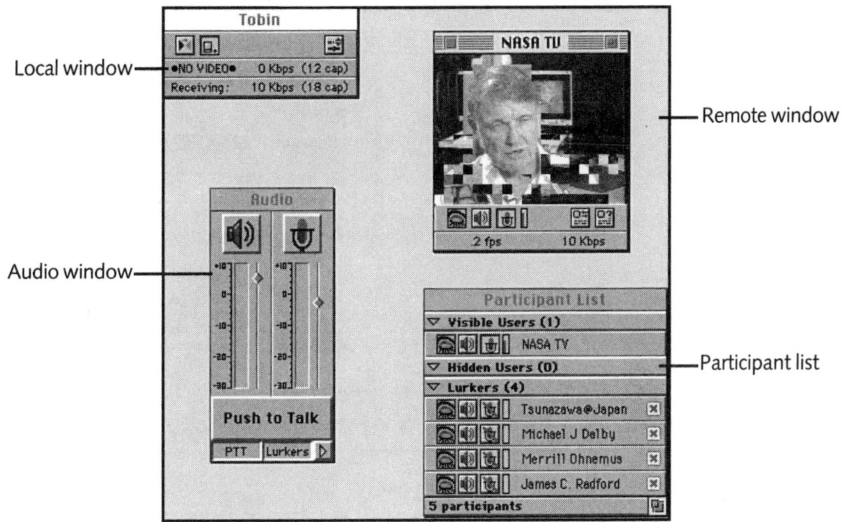

Figure 14.7 *It's the next best thing to being there. CU-SeeMe gives you several displays with which to control your audio and video processing.*

A dialog box pops up similar to that displayed in Figure 14.8, and it asks you the IP address of the remote user with whom you wish to conference. Enter the IP address and the conference ID. The conference ID should be zero, unless you intend to restrict other users from connecting. If they're running CU-SeeMe, your designated users will receive an alert message that you're trying to conference. At that point they can either accept or deny your request to conference. Once the conference is accepted, you'll be able to see and speak to one another providing you both have checked the I Will Receive Video box (shown in Figure 14.8). You'll have to adjust your brightness and contrast controls on the window's slide bar.

If you have set up a reflector on a Unix or Windows NT server, you can enter that server address. Now you can really restrict other users by issuing a non-zero ID. You'll be able to display up to eight other windows. You can select the users from the Participant list window. You'll be able to receive video from any participant who does not have an 'X' by his or her name. These users are known as lurkers. You may wish to establish a conference with lurkers who may not be able or may not desire to display video.

Figure 14.8 *Enter the IP address of another user running CU-SeeMe to initiate a conference request.*

White Pine has included a list of preconfigured reflectors, as shown in Figure 14.9. Just click on the Conferences menu and select the Connect To sidebar. You can edit the names and IP addresses of these services, and even add new listings, by dragging on the Edit menu down to the Edit Preferences sidebar.

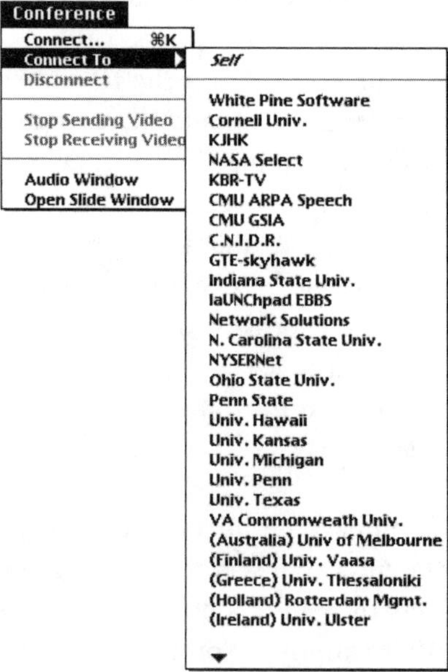

Figure 14.9 *White Pine offers a list of preconfigured video reflector services for you to sample.*

NOTE

Connecting to the NASA service enables you to receive NASA Select, which is NASA's public relations cable channel. Several of the preconfigured servers reflect NASA Select.

Using CU-SeeMe as a Web Browser Helper Application

You actually can launch CU-SeeMe from a Web browser. To do this, you need to configure the Web server and browser to interpret a certain MIME type as a CU-SeeMe application. If you are running MacHTTP, enter the following lines in the MacHTTP.config file.

```
TEXT .CU * * application/x-cu-seeme
TEXT .CSM * * application/x-cu-seeme
```

These lines mean that you will need to use the cu or csm prefixes on your configuration files. Second, configure your Web browser to launch CU-SeeMe when receiving a file of MIME type application/x-cu-seeme.

NOTE

In addition to configuring your Web server with the new CU-SeeMe MIME type, users will have to configure Navigator or any of the other browsers in order to launch a videoconference via the Web. It's a good idea to post instructions on your Web page detailing how to configure the major browsers (Navigator, Internet Explorer) with this MIME type.

Now create a file called test.csm. The following lines need to be in this file:

```
server_address
conference_id
file_options
```

The file_options variable can contain a variety of options. Look in the Web launch file in the CU-SeeMe distribution folder for a complete list. However, a simple test.csm file could be set up as

```
192.80.72.4
0
```

Accessing this file through a Web browser would then launch CU-SeeMe on White Pine's public reflector service.

You could link a series of CU-SeeMe files to a Web page associating them with different reflector servers. This would be one way that you could establish an easy means of setting up videoconferences. Telling coworkers to access a (hypothetical) URL http://www14.anyplace.com/CU-SeeMe/conf1.csm at a certain time would enable them to launch CU-SeeMe at the same server for a predetermined videoconference.

Bulletin Board Software

People congregate around electronic discussion groups, just as they do around the bulletin boards in your company's hallways. For many years, Usenet has been a popular forum for the exchange of ideas and concepts. Many organizations supplement their normal Usenet feed with local newsgroups pertaining to local interests. Running a Usenet server is problematic, as the sheer volume of traffic can amount up to 500 MB per day. You need a fast network connection and an abundance of disk space to accommodate a newsfeed. You also need a Unix workstation; there are no Usenet servers for the MacOS as of this writing.

Another alternative to the conventional Usenet feed is Web-based bulletin board software. Users can track discussion groups and individual postings, much as they do with Usenet. However, with a Web browser interface, users can click View More Information about the author and activate links inside the messages. Furthermore, running a Web-based bulletin board solution obviates the need for running a Usenet server.

Web Crossing

There are many Web-based bulletin board applications for the MacOS, but we'll talk about one in particular in this section. Web

Crossing (WebX) is a Web-based bulletin board application which functions much the same as a Usenet newsreader. As it's actually a CGI application, Web Crossing runs on your Mac in conjunction with WebSTAR or MacHTTP. For the sake of discussion, I'll assume you're running WebSTAR, although the same instructions are applicable if you run MacHTTP. You'll get almost the same functionality from running Web Crossing with MacHTTP as you would with WebSTAR, except that MacHTTP will not let Web Crossing display images of the message authors.

Web Crossing actually runs like a BBS system with an administrator who can modify user preferences and login information. Users login to the system, which provides a measure of security. Like Usenet, discussion folders can be formed based on certain topics. Web Crossing also allows the user to edit and/or delete the message after it's been posted. This is one advantage of WebX over conventional Usenet.

Installing and Configuring Web Crossing

Double-click on the WebX icon. Web Crossing uses a different installer setup than most of the applications that we've used in this book. When inside the installer, drag the WebX icon to the hard drive icon to unpack the software.

Once the software has been installed, find the Web Crossing folder and move it to the desired location. Take the Images folder and move it to your WebSTAR folder. If you already have an Images folder, rename the WebX images folder to something else. When you initialize WebX for the first time, you'll be queried as to the exact location of the folder.

Make an alias of the WebX application and put it with the rest of your CGI scripts and applications. Now enter the following URL

```
http://<your server name>/<your CGI path>/WebX
```

to start up WebX. WebX will lead you through a set of pages designed to customize the application. You'll be queried for the actual location of the WebX images folder, as shown in Figure 14.10.

You'll reload this page until the test graphics become visible, as they are in the figure. WebX uses these images throughout the bulletin board. These images represent buttons that perform certain functions, such as creating a new message, creating a new discussion topic, emailing the sysop, and other actions.

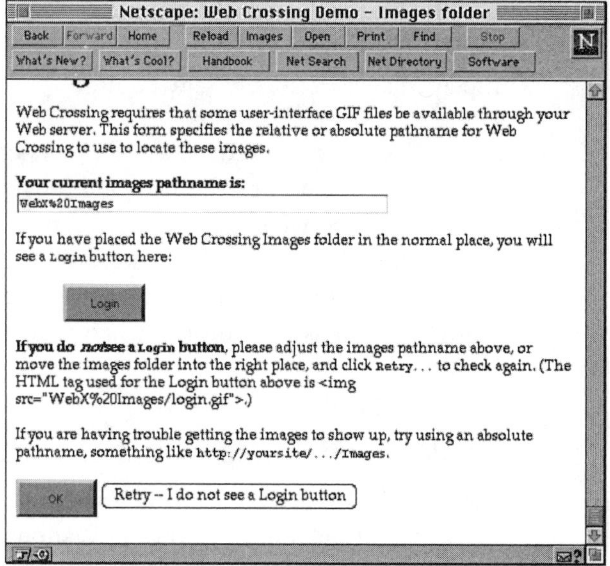

Figure 14.10 *When entering the location of the WebX images folder, don't forget to include special character codes for spaces and non-standard characters.*

In the following pages, you'll be asked to set preferences for the root account, which WebX refers to as *sysop*. You'll be asked for your email address. WebX will provide it to users who want to contact you with problems or lost passwords. Similarly, you'll be queried for the sysop password that you'll need in order to configure system and user parameters.

NOTE

If you login to WebX as sysop, you'll see an extra button at the bottom of the page labeled Control Panel. Clicking on this button yields a great deal of documentation as well as a wide variety of options that you can use to customize the appearance and operation of the bulletin board.

After you've finished configuring the sysop privileges, you'll be able to add users. This actually can be done by the users themselves, as demonstrated in Figure 14.11. WebX will ask for user information such as email address, descriptive text, home page URLs, and even a snapshot of the user. This snapshot can then be appended to each message posted by the user.

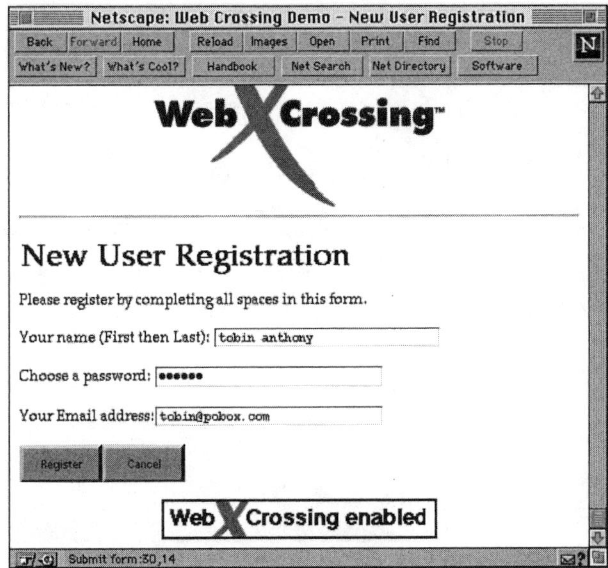

Figure 14.11 *Users must register with WebX before reading or posting new messages.*

Creating Messages with WebX

To create a new discussion group, simply click the Add Folder button. You'll be queried for the folder name and a description of the discussions to be contained in the folder. A WebX *discussion* is analogous to a Usenet *thread*; threads and WebX discussions contain messages of similar content. Once a new folder is established, it can be populated with discussions. You can begin to create a message by clicking the Add Discussion button at the bottom of the Web page. Then add the discussion title and descriptive text in the respective text fields.

After you've created a discussion, you can start posting messages to it. As shown in Figure 14.12, you can create a message using an HTML text field. WebX allows you to use plain text to construct the message; however, you can also include parts of previous messages and even HTML. This is important since you'll then be able to embed hyperlinks in your messages.

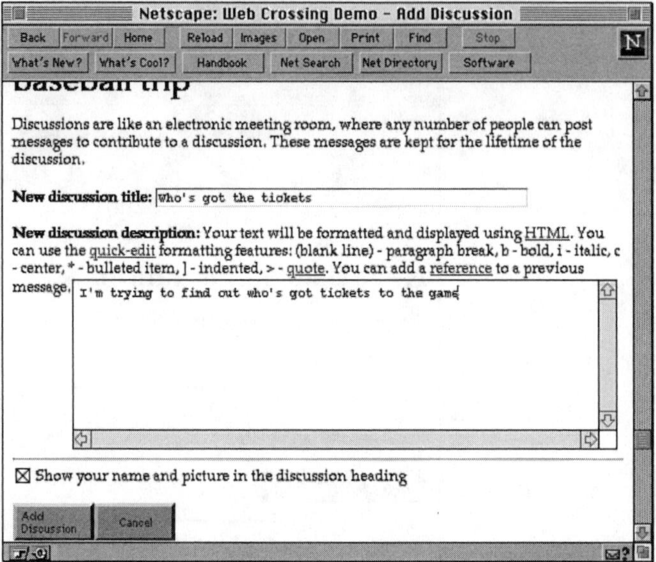

Figure 14.12 *You can post messages using the simple text field. However, you can add special characters and even HTML to your messages.*

Figure 14.13 shows the results of a posted message. WebX displays the author's picture next to the text, if the user preferences have been configured to do so.

Figure 14.13 *Images of the smiling message author can accompany the messages. Clicking on the author's image brings up a page filled with personal information about the message author.*

Specialized Web-Based Intranet Applications

The three applications discussed in this chapter are commercial offerings that you can use to supplement more open services on your Intranet. Many of the applications that you develop for your Intranet may be home-grown. You have several tools at your disposal in terms of HTML, CGI scripting languages, Java, JavaScript, database languages, and others. Many of these tools are both cross-platform and adhere to an open architecture. You'll be able to exchange applications with server administrators running the MacOS and other platforms.

In this section, I'd like to get you thinking about some of the products you can develop for your Intranet. Sure, you're limited by the rudimentary typesetting capabilities of HTML or the simplicity of JavaScript, but these tools will mature with time; hopefully, you'll be able to adopt new technologies as they develop.

I'm not going to go into the specific development of these products. I'll leave the HTML, CGI, and Java development up to you and other texts which can go into greater detail. Please refer to the preceding chapters or the appendices for more specific detail.

Timecard System

Companies and organizations have struggled with the concept of online forms for several years. Until recently, there was no viable standard with which you could replace office paperwork with electronic equivalents. The problems stemmed from reliability and lack of cross-platform solutions.

The forms capability in HTML offers you a rudimentary means of providing online forms. HTML 3.0 will offer more flexibility in this area. The basic idea with an HTML forms-based application is for you to do the following:

- Provide a cross-platform means for the user to enter data
- Process the data internally
- Relay the data to a person or database in a format where it can be implemented or archived

This list should describe virtually any online system that you develop.

For a timecard system, you're looking for the employees to be able to do the following:

- Enter their hours and associate these hours with certain charge numbers
- Be able to see the total charges for each pay period

- ☐ Process the data internally so that the charges are accumulated according to your bookkeeping methods
- ☐ Transport the processed time charges to the administrative staff
- ☐ Allow that person to review the time charges before further processing to personnel involved with your group's payroll

Now take a look at how you can develop these individual steps.

Developing the Online Timesheet

You'll need to develop an HTML form which is flexible enough to have enough text entry fields for the different days in your pay period and be able to track them according to charge numbers. As your users may have multiple charge numbers, you'll have to accommodate a varying number of charges.

You can develop this form by using a series of HTML FORM statements. It's a tedious but straightforward exercise in HTML programming, but one that is made easy with an editor like HTML PageMill (see Appendix C, "Perfecting HTML," for a discussion of Adobe PageMill). There are several ways you could do this, but one option is to establish a small text entry field for each day for each charge number. For example, if you have 10-day pay periods and a user is charging time to three different tasks, you'll need at least 30 different text fields. You may want to allow the capability to charge personal and sick leave in addition to overtime, compensatory time, or time worked on the weekends.

You'll also need to provide a *digital signature capability* to prevent fraudulent time sheets. This capability can be provided using WebSTAR/SSL, as mentioned in Chapter 13, "Intranet Server Security." WebSTAR/SSL provides you with a means to incorporate digital signatures with your Web pages. You can review this technology to understand how to secure your timesheet transactions. However, a user will need to be able to enter a digital signature somewhere on the form to provide verification. Furthermore, you may wish to add additional signature capabilities for supervisors.

No Mac-based browsers support user-certificates yet, although Navigator might support this feature by the time you read this. A user-certificate is necessary for this kind of authorization. For more information on user-certificates consult VeriSign's home page (http://www.verisign.com) or read Chapter 13, "Intranet Server Security."

Accumulating the Charge Data

Depending on how your organization works, you'll want to formulate the employees' charge data in several ways. Let's assume that you want to sum the work hours by charge number. There are two ways to do this—the easy way or the cool way. Let's look at the easy way first.

You can develop a Frontier, MacPerl, or AppleScript CGI script to do the simple addition of work hours for each charge number. Frontier might work best, as you can express the hours worked each day as an element in an array. The user enters the data and presses a Submit button of some kind. The array elements would then be summed and presented back to the user in another HTML page. The user then reviews the data and presses another Submit button to pass the data on to an administrative aide. If the data were entered incorrectly, the user could move back to the time sheet to correct the error.

The cool way to do this would be using Java. You could develop a Java applet which would automatically sum the hours worked and present them on the same page. Much like a spreadsheet, as the user entered the hours, a running sum would be kept at the end of the row. This would obviate the need for a CGI script to process the data and return it through another HTML form for the user's inspection. Using Java, the code would do all the arithmetic that you would have had to program a CGI script to do in the above paragraph. This saves you connection and processing time and reduces the load on the server. You'll still need a CGI script to move the data to the next step along the process.

NOTE

> JavaScript may be more appropriate for this timecard example than Java. JavaScript offers a more direct means of accessing form entries.

For more information on working with Java, see Hayden Book's *Teach Yourself Java in 21 Days for the Macintosh.*

Packaging the Data

You'll need to sum the data up by charge number. If you took the conventional CGI route, you've already summed the data when the script presented the data for review by the user. With the JavaScript applet approach, the summed work hours are displayed in certain HTML text fields.

Transporting the Data to a Third Party

Someone should review this data for accuracy or verification. This could be accomplished by developing a CGI script that takes the time charge data and inserts it into a mail message directed toward that user's supervisor. There are ample MacPerl, Frontier, and AppleScript CGIs which expedite data-to-email conversion. One problem with doing this by email is that you'll need to encrypt the data and enable the supervisor to attach a digital signature. This can be done but it requires the use of Eudora and MacPGP.

Another way would be to package the data within a Butler SQL database and develop HTML forms pages using Tango. In this way, you could avoid doing any of the SQL or HTML programming necessary to align the data into online forms. Supervisors could periodically peruse a secure Web page that maintains all the different employee time charge data. Digital verification could be afforded to each entry as a means of authorizing that employee's time charges.

Cutting Paychecks

After the supervisor has authorized the employee's time sheets, that data could be emailed to a payroll processing staff member.

Alternatively, it could be displayed using another secure Tango-derived Web page. Your next challenge would be to develop an interface between either the secure email or the secure Web page and your payroll processing software. There's a good chance that if you're using a third-party payroll software package, the vendor may have a solution for you to implement with your Intranet services.

Document Archives

Another mundane but vital resource within your organization is a document library. I'm sure that memoranda and technical reports are stored somewhere in a deep dark recess of your building, with a disgruntled librarian guarding the contents. However, there are solutions that you can incorporate which allow you to make much of documentation available online.

If your organization is modern enough to be interested in setting up an Intranet, there's a good chance that much of the paperwork your group has generated over recent years is available in electronic format. Many of these documents may be in a cross-platform format such as FrameMaker, PDF, or MS Office. These documents could then be stored in a Butler database and accessed by using Tango-derived Web pages. Butler SQL can store elements as large as your largest documents (2 GB of data), and you're limited only by your peripheral equipment such as hard drive space.

Your group librarian would then take the documents, incorporate them into a Butler database, and then update the Tango interface to make them accessible online. You would have to provide for several fields of information so that you could perform searches of the databases. Although we covered text searching with TR-WWW in Chapter 8, "Databases and Document Searches," many of your documents will not be comprised of strict text. You could use AppleSearch to search through the documents, but for large libraries this could be a cumbersome proposition. Furthermore, many of your documents might be composed of graphics, which have no text to search. For these reasons, you'll need to add extra fields in your Butler database to accommodate searchable criteria such as authors, keywords, and other relevant information.

Software Archives

Another related service you can provide is in the area of software archives. Many large organizations have some archives of site-licensed or inhouse software for use by their employees. You can set up an FTP server that works in conjunction with your Web services. If users want to download a new version of an application, they could step through a verification process on a Web page. The final result would be for the users to receive the file by initiating an FTP connection through clicking on a Web page link. You could even develop a simple CGI script that tracks the usage and download activity of the server.

Summary

The number and types of applications that you can write for your Intranet are limited only by your resources and your imagination. The Web, Java and JavaScript, CGI scripts, and other tools offer you a great deal of flexibility in developing applications that your organization can use. With the Intranet market heating up, the future will undoubtedly bring new and different tools that you can use to create even more specific utilities for your Intranet.

You've learned enough about programming and hardware to at least learn how much you don't know about setting up an Intranet. There's a great deal more to learn, and you'll learn it by charging ahead, setting up servers, and creating your own Intranet utilities. Feel free to go back and visit any of the preceding chapters to review any topics or discussion. In the appendices, we'll talk about some of the software included on the book's CD-ROM as well as other ancillary issues. Specifically, you can read the following appendices:

- Appendix B, "Establishing an Internet Presence," to learn how to convert or adapt your Intranet skills and resources to publish Web pages and establish FTP sites that are geared toward the Internet community.

- Appendix C, "Perfecting HTML," to learn about some advanced HTML programming features as well as how to use some popular HTML editors, including Adobe PageMill and BBEdit.

Links Related to This Chapter

ON Technology	http://www.on.com
White Pine Software	http://www.cu-seeme.com
Connectix	http://www.connectix.com
Lundeen & Associates	http://www.lundeen.com

CHAPTER 15

Summary

The Intranet concept has the capacity to change your way of doing business more than any single advance since the personal computer. You now have the tools and knowledge to create customized applications by using open technologies that will fulfill the long-heralded promise of the paperless office. In fact, you can add services, such as database access and document searches, that really have no parallel in the conventional office environment.

In contrast to the horrendous press Apple has been getting at the time of this writing, the Mac platform is going to be around for a long time. The wealth of Intranet applications available for the MacOS is staggering. The ease-of-use that makes the Mac so near and dear to all our hearts has allowed millions of users to move out and conquer the Internet. As we stand on the threshold of the age of the Intranet, we can see by the versatility of the tools covered in this book that the Mac will be a player in this new paradigm as well.

I hope this book put a lot of pieces together for you. It's unlikely that you were able to absorb all the material presented here, but extensive information was given to point you toward the resources you may need to master the software described in this book. As the environment described in this book changes so rapidly, you'll need to keep abreast of the new technologies to provide the highest quality service to your users, while still making your Intranet an essential yet fun place to be.

And isn't that what this is all about?

APPENDIX

What's on the CD-ROM

At the end of almost every chapter in this book, I've included a list of relevant URLs. I've accumulated and organized these in a Netscape Navigator bookmark file that you can retrieve from the WWW site associated with this book. This site is located at http://www.hayden.com/internet/intranetmac and contains files and other links relevant to the subject matter covered in this book.

The software described in this book is contained in a folder entitled Intranet Apps. This folder contains shareware, freeware, and demo versions of commercial applications. Your purchase of this book does not remove your obligation to pay your shareware fees. Think of this book's CD-ROM as a very mobile and very fast software archive. Just as you're obligated to pay for shareware you pull from an FTP archive, you are likewise obligated to pay for the shareware found on this disc.

The lightning pace of the Mac Internet environment has all but guaranteed that some of the software on this CD-ROM will be obsolete by the time you read this. You might want to check the Web and FTP sites associated with the various demoware and shareware applications on this CD-ROM for the latest versions.

A lot of the software found on the CD-ROM is discussed in the book. In those cases, a CD icon, such as that shown here, denotes the inclusion of the software on the CD-ROM. However, the software denoted by the CD icon represents subsets of the holdings on the disc. I put many more utilities and files on there in relevant places throughout the disc.

APPENDIX 

Establishing an Internet Presence

The cool thing about Intranets is that you use the same technology to develop them that you would use to develop a presence on the Internet. As a result, after you have developed an Intranet, you have most of the tools in place to adapt your Intranet services to the Internet community. In short, you're almost there!

You've probably fooled around with setting up public Web and FTP servers before picking up this book. This book has focused on harnessing Internet tools such as Web servers, CGI scripts, and email, to serve the day-to-day needs of your Intranet. However, these applications were originally designed to serve files and data via the Internet to hordes of Web surfers. You may have your own reasons for developing a presence on the Internet, and this appendix talks about how this can be achieved.

This appendix discusses the following topics that you'll need to consider when adding an Internet presence to your Intranet:

- ☐ Establishing your reasons for developing an Internet presence
- ☐ Changing your World Wide Web service
- ☐ Advertising your services to the Internet community

Exposing Your Intranet to the Internet

As stated in the Introduction, you have almost all the tools that you need to set up shop on the Internet. But before you go ahead and hang your cyber shingle, take a few minutes to reflect on why you want to develop Internet services.

It wasn't long after Mosaic and Netscape came into heavy use by the Internet community and public in general that people started creating Web sites. At first, these sites didn't tell you anything more than the name of the institution and a little about what it did. The first generation of Web sites quickly grew old. It wasn't much later that companies and organizations began asking themselves, "So, why do we need to have a Web site anyway?" Here's your chance to think about some of the confusing questions that confronted the early Web pioneers.

Why the Internet?

The Internet represents an entirely different medium from which to communicate with the rest of the world. For the first time, you can interact with someone on the other side of the world as cheaply and almost as quickly as you can flick an email message down the hall. With access speed and usage growing every year, the Internet is rapidly moving into mainstream society.

The type of service you provide has a great deal to do with who you are and what type of work you do. Your Internet audience can consist of potential customers, existing customers, potential students, or peers. Some of the advantages of Internet servers are described in this section.

Exposing Your Organization

The first and foremost effect of setting up a WWW or FTP server is that you provide exposure for your group, organization, or company to the Internet community. Regardless of the nature of your business, it's exciting to set up a home page and see the accesses stream in, knowing that you're attracting attention on the Internet. This titillating exposure that you provide to your group is really what fueled the initial growth of the Web.

Marketing Your Services

A medium such as the Web enables you to share a great deal of information about the work you do with the outside world. Furthermore, the Internet community consists of a wide variety of people. If the demographics of this group matches those of your target markets, the Internet gives you an inexpensive means of advertising your organization's services. This is true even if your business does not directly deal with the Internet. For example, Toyota (http://www.toyota.com) and Levi Strauss (http://www.levis.com) are two popular Web sites that market products, cars, and clothing, totally unrelated to Internet technology. Consulting and law firms also use WWW servers to display information about the capabilities of their organizations. Universities even do their marketing online; with so many homes wired to the Internet these days, many high-school students can substitute the standard college visit with a virtual visit to a university's Web site.

Interfacing with Customers

Let's say that you are using Web technology. You can provide even more sophisticated interaction with your customers. The following example demonstrates such a capability.

Think about the last time you pored through a catalog. Let's just say that it was a computer catalog from a large mail-order house, XYZ Communications, and you were looking to find out what prices they offered for a hypothetical 14.4 modem. You had to hunt around for a table of contents, looking to find the page where modems are listed. Then you had to thumb through the catalog and get to the modem pages. Finally, you found a paragraph of information about that modem—maybe two paragraphs if they used a six-point font. You called the toll-free number and the polite phone operator put you on hold for a few minutes. Twenty minutes later, you asked questions about the modem and were referred to technical support. After another minute on hold (ha!), you talked to someone who answered one of your questions but offered to research your other questions and fax answers back to you...as soon as possible. After the phone call, you felt vaguely unfulfilled.

Now imagine if you could access that store's Web page through your Netscape Web browser. You'd be able to do a search on the company's offerings. Just type **modem**, and on this hypothetical Web site a list of links to the various makes and models of modems would appear. At this point, you're thinking, "Whoa! I didn't know that XYZ Communications had a 28.8 modem! This is great!" Little did you know that a link was added soon after the store received a truckload of XYZ modems the previous day. You click on the modem link and you're presented with several paragraphs of technical description, as well as a picture of the modem. You notice that XYZ bundles the UFaxIt fax software with every one of its 28.8 modems. Hmmm, you've never heard of UFaxIt. Luckily, the mail-order house has that description hyperlinked to the Web pages of the company that makes UFaxIt. You notice that there are a slew of UFaxIt software updates available through the company's FTP server. You click on those links and download the software modules to your computer.

Moving back to mail-order company's XYZ modem pages, you realize that it's time to purchase the modem of your dreams. You click on a button that says, "Buy Me." You're presented with a new page of fill-in forms. You fill in your name, mailing address, and credit card number. You check the little key emblem at the bottom of your Navigator browser window, and you relax because you know that the server is using a secure connection protecting your transaction. You click the little button with the cash register icon and the transaction's a done deal. You get your modem in the mail a few days later. Along with the modem, the mail-order company has included a hard copy of its catalog. Ironically, you can't help but notice that at the bottom of the front page of the catalog, you see the company has printed their online catalog's Web address.

Types of Internet Servers

If you're interested in complementing your Intranet with Internet service, it's safe to say that you are doing this with some type of corporate sponsorship. Organizations like yours produce two types of servers; I like to call these *not-for-profit* servers and *corporate* servers. These servers maintain different content and are geared toward different audiences.

The Not-for-Profit Server

If your organization is a not-for-profit corporation, there are still valid reasons to develop a presence on the Internet. In fact, the Internet was developed so that non-profit organizations, such as government facilities and universities, could share and exchange research information. With the advent of the Web, the type of data that can be exchanged has become more sophisticated.

Universities can publish their research activities or even make admissions information available for prospective students. Also, academic departments can publish information regarding faculty research activities. For similar reasons, not-for-profit organizations can publish information relevant to their work objectives.

The Corporate Server

When you want to advertise your company or its products, you usually think about what type of potential penetration the advertising medium can establish. Now think about the millions of people in the country, not to mention the whole world, with access to the Internet. We're not just talking about expert users. The major online services, such as America Online, CompuServe, and Prodigy, have millions of customers, and most of them are average American families dripping with disposable income. Compared to traditional advertising media, the Internet offers the potential to connect with millions of potential customers.

The cost of maintaining a moderately sized server is a fraction of what it takes to advertise your company in the traditional print media. Furthermore, print media is limited to text and simple graphics. A useful feature of graphical Web browsers, such as Netscape and Mosaic, is that users can download a multitude of multimedia file types. Instead of a picture of your CEO on your company's home page, you can serve an audio recording of him welcoming the user to your company's Web site. Users also can download promotional movies provided by your site. Even if your business is not retail, advertising on the Web gives your potential and existing customers the impression that your group is quick to adopt emerging technologies.

Having a presence on the Web is the most visible presence you can give your company or organization. You can take advantage of the uniquely customizable features of HTML to configure your company's home page the way you feel most effectively communicates your company's image. Furthermore, Web administrators can rework their company's home pages more quickly and less expensively than they could redo their traditional advertising campaigns. With a few minutes of work, a page on your company's Web site can be altered to describe a new product or offering. The Internet community sees this change almost instantaneously.

Your Internet Services

The type of services you provide depends on the type of business you conduct and the nature of your target audience. This section looks at the types of WWW and FTP services you can provide that will draw attention to your organization.

Know Your Audience

Your Internet service will not only depend on your type of work but also, as mentioned earlier, your target audience. As with your Intranet design, you'll need to be aware of the needs and interests of your target audience. Your Internet server is just an extension of your organization's marketing efforts.

Web Services

After deciding to set up a WWW server, the next item on your agenda is to decide exactly what to put on the server. Whatever you do, you want it to be cool. You want to have the type of Web site that will draw users again and again. Some ideas regarding possible information served on a corporate Web site include the following:

- ☐ Company contact information
- ☐ Audio or video welcome
- ☐ Backgrounds of key personnel
- ☐ Company history

- ☐ Specific product information
- ☐ Current press releases
- ☐ Vendor location and information
- ☐ Online catalogs
- ☐ Links to relevant sites
- ☐ Description of consulting services

You may not possess the resources required to establish a high-volume Web site. Your Web site can act simply as an electronic business card. I've had my Web address on my business card for several years, for example. Once accessed, people can learn more about my professional interests and responsibilities. In addition, I have some educational background listed on my page so that my peers can become acquainted with my skills and abilities. My Web site is not a high-volume site, and I personally would not be served by developing it into a high-volume site.

Similarly, you may be part of a smaller organization, such as a law firm or a not-for-profit company. Users accessing your page may do so to learn more about your group. Your Web pages can contain information about the members of your firm or organization. You can post relevant information about the skills and background of your group's staff. The average Internet user may not be beating down the door to your site, but you may serve prospective clients in this manner.

FTP Archives

FTP remains a useful protocol for transferring large amounts of information. You can build links to your FTP site within your Web pages. The material you serve via FTP would supplement your Web site. For example, you might store an archive of company press releases in an FTP archive. You also can store reports or white papers produced in applications such as PDF, Microsoft Word, or Adobe PageMaker directly on your server. PDF's cross-platform readability makes it an ideal file type for archive documents. Your FTP server can serve any documents or files that you want to archive for reference purposes.

Your New Web Presence

To the uninitiated, the Internet and the Web are synonymous. As covered in Chapter 1, the Internet is comprised of many different services and protocols. Many of these services existed before the Web. However, the utility and innovation of the Web boosted use of the Internet.

As with your Intranet, your Web services will be the foundation of your Internet services. To set up your new Web pages, you'll need exactly the same tools and equipment you used for your Intranet. This section talks about how to adapt the style and direction of your Web pages to appeal to the users outside your organization.

Changes in Style

With your Intranet Web services, you had the luxury of a captive audience. In a sense, you were preaching to the converted. Your users will use your Intranet services as a matter of conducting business. Sure, people will like your pages more if they contain glitzy graphics and text, but they'll access your pages and services just the same.

Your Internet Web pages will require an entirely different focus. Your conventional HTML and drab company logos are not going to keep people from hitting the dreaded Back button once they hit your site. The fact that many people accessing your pages are accessing them through modems, rather than high-speed cable connections, also places a constraint on your content. You'll need to address some added security issues as well. Content is still the bottom line if you expect Internet visitors to return.

Content and Presentation

Your content and presentation will need to be slicker than what you have presented in your safe and secure Intranet Web service. For example, your Intranet users are interested in one thing—using your Intranet to simplify their administrative tasks. They don't care if you've got tons of graphics, audio, or video on your pages. Internet surfers, however, have different concerns. The average attention span of a Web user is small and growing smaller; to get your message out, you'll need to be concise and efficient in your presentation.

You'll need to use graphics efficiently. Many people may be accessing your page through a modem. Your Intranet is most likely wired with a higher-speed internal connection with high bandwidth in abundance. In every aspect of your Internet Web pages, design with the low-bandwidth user in mind. Pages with loads of graphics, for example, will discourage modem-users. Imagemaps are useful navigational tools, but make sure they are comprised of small graphics stored in GIF or JPEG files.

NOTE

If you do plan to use large amounts of graphics on your Web pages, remember that many browsers will cache frequently used graphics. A common occurrence of this is the ubiquitous ball graphic commonly used in lieu of bullets in bulleted lists. Once the ball is loaded from a Web server, it is stored and displayed from the browser's internal cache rather than called up each time it's referred to in the HTML code.

Whereas you may have presented long pages on your Intranet Web server, you'll need to break them up into smaller documents for Internet use. I consider a long Web page to be any page that is comprised of more than four browser window lengths from start to finish. Even if you just include text on these pages, they take time to download. Smaller interlinked documents are much easier to navigate. Remember that you are competing with thousands of other Web servers for users' attention. Anything you can do to make your pages easier to navigate will help.

Your Web page content also is going to be slanted to users outside your organization. Your Intranet offerings are likely to be more administrative and informative, whereas your Web pages will be more slick and efficient. You may want to use larger font sizes in your Web pages. Whereas your Intranet pages contain instructions and information geared to users required to use your pages, your Internet pages need to have plenty of white space so as to be more readable.

NOTE

For Navigator and Internet Explorer browsers, you can change the font sizes with the <FONT SIZE=n>...</FONT> commands. In this command, n is an integer that represents the increase or decrease in the size of the font with respect to the normal font size.

Security

You should protect your Intranet from attacks within your organization. Threats of disciplinary action or firing go a long way to secure your system from internal tampering. A firewall goes a long way to ensure protection from uninvited accesses.

NOTE

For more information on securing your network, see Chapter 13, "Intranet Server Security."

The situation changes once you advertise your presence on the Internet. People from all over the world will have access to your server. The MacOS provides few loopholes that can be compromised; however, with hundreds or thousands of external accesses each day, you run the risk of drawing the attention of someone who can exploit those loopholes.

Probably the most obvious and effective measure you can take to secure your new Web service is to run it outside your firewall. This means actually running your Web and FTP servers on separate machines; the disadvantage of this approach is that you require multiple Web and FTP servers. However, with this approach, you minimize exposure of your Intranet, running entirely within your firewall, to unwarranted access. Your Intranet users can access your external Web pages by going out through the firewall. While performance is impaired slightly, chances are that your users will find everything they need on your Intranet service.

NOTE

There may be some features on your external server that you will want to duplicate on your internal Intranet. It suffices to say that you do *not* want to rig up a special HTTP connection between the two systems. You must keep your Intranet and your external Internet servers separate at all costs.

Post as few real names as possible on your Internet Web pages. Hackers frequently try to determine passwords to systems by calling users by name and tricking them into revealing their accounts and passwords. One clever hacker was able to trace the keys that one user entered into his computer. Posing as a member of the technical support group, the hacker called the user and asked the user to type in his name and password. The user complied, and the hacker was able to gain access to the user's files, and from there was able to infiltrate the rest of the system.

NOTE

One trick that many system administrators use and that you might try is to set up a mail account for yourself as webmaster@your_company.com where you substitute your correct domain for your_company.com. In this way, you do not have to reveal your identity on your Web pages unless you feel comfortable doing so.

As with your Intranet machines, make sure that your FTP and Web servers reside on different machines. If a hacker compromises one machine, this method will prevent compromise of all of your data.

Handling the Bandwidth

Your connection to the Internet needs to be robust enough to handle the amount of volume you expect your server to generate. Nothing will turn off prospective Web surfers more than having to wait more than a few seconds to download a page or retrieve a file through FTP. The major bottleneck in your Web and FTP service will not be the speed of your server's CPU, but the capability of your server's network Internet connection to handle the excess traffic.

Your Server Deployment

Let's talk about how to deploy your servers so that you can get the most out of your resources. You need to look at the ways that you can provide safe and secure Web service.

Effective Server Topology

Drawing from my own example again, I started out running a small HTTP server and FTP server on the same Mac. This was fine because I was serving little more than a home page and maybe some pictures of my kids. Users can access my computer with either a Web browser or an FTP client, such as Fetch or Anarchie for the Mac. I used this computer for word processing and other office automation applications as well.

This arrangement worked for me because my server saw only a few hundred accesses each day. Unless you work for a small organization serving little more than your company's home page and a few GIF files, you will need a more expansive topology, or layout.

Figure B.1 shows the various configurations you can assume based on your resources. At the very least, you can house both FTP and HTTP servers on the same machine. As you progress in sophistication, you may consider moving your FTP server to a separate computer. This is so that your Web server and FTP server will not have to compete for the same processor resources. It's also a good idea if a lot of your traffic arises from FTP access, as is the case with a software archive.

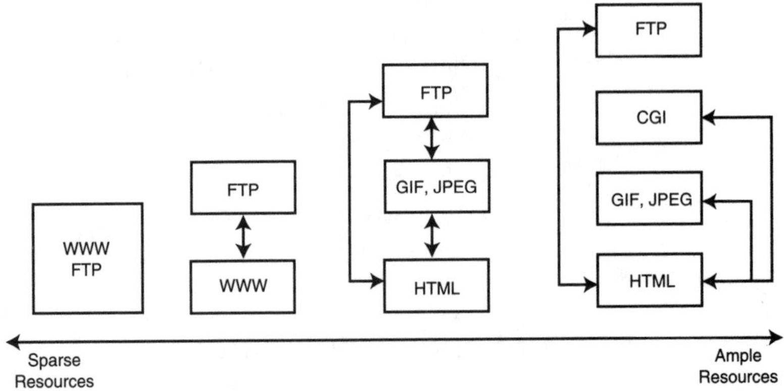

Figure B.1 *Depending on the number of computers and amount of resources at your disposal, you can deploy your Web and FTP servers in a variety of configurations.*

Well, that's great. Your HTTP and FTP servers are running on separate machines. Your FTP links are integrated into your Web pages using URLs addressed to the FTP server. Well, what do you do if your HTTP performance is still overloaded? One option is to move your graphics to a smaller machine that does nothing but serve graphics. Most HTML pages are 5 to 10 KB in size and require one download. However, each page might have 5 to 10 graphics files on it that can be 10 to 200 KB depending on the graphic. If you relegate the graphics to a faster machine, your primary HTML server can serve your home page, while your graphics server can handle the heavy-duty task of downloading graphics to the requesting browser.

NOTE 

> If you are planning to use a separate graphics HTTP server, make sure that you define the graphic sizes in your <IMG> tags (using the Netscape HTML extensions). Your HTML server will set aside the desired space in your pages as the graphics are being downloaded from the graphics server.

NOTE 

> RushHour, from Maxum Corp, is a tool that works with WebSTAR to serve graphics via a cache file. By loading graphics into RAM, the files are served more quickly. RushHour works best when running on a separate server. See the URL at the end of this appendix.

Finally, you may decide that all of your CGI scripts are slowing you down. You may decide to move these scripts to yet another server. Offloading these scripts to a remote computer means that they can be left running continuously so that execution is much quicker. This leaves more RAM on your HTML server to serve the actual HTML. Another option is for you to transfer much of your CGI functionality over to Java applets and JavaScripts. In this way, you'll be offloading the burden of running these applications on the client computers, again reducing the load on your server.

Isolating Your Server

You're going to want to put these servers outside your firewall. Any attempts to compromise the security of your HTTP servers will affect only the servers leaving your Intranet intact. Your users will have to go outside the firewall and back to access your home page, but that's the price you have to pay for added security.

Advertising Your Server

When you've finally completed your dream server, you want to get people to start using it. You can do this several ways. For example, you can advertise through the traditional advertising media. I cannot get through a full night of prime-time television without seeing at least one company list its server address in an advertisement. In computer and technical magazines, it's expected that not only will the advertising company have a Web site, but they'll include the address in the advertisement. As effective as traditional advertising media can be, with 40 million regular users, the Internet seems like a good place to start.

Using the Internet to Advertise Your Server

Nowadays, there are several means to advertise your server on the Internet. You can hang your Web pages without any fanfare, and sooner or later, a Web-crawling robot will stumble across your page. The content of your pages will get added to its database; someone searching for a string of text that's somewhere on your pages will be led to your site. If you don't mind waiting a few months for a robot to find your page, you're in great shape. However, there are more effective ways of alerting the Internet community to the presence of your Web page.

NOTE 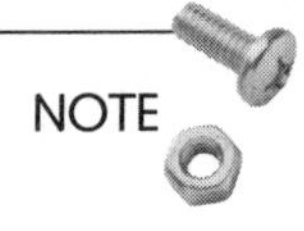

Several Web search applications spawn off processes that do nothing but scan the thousands of Web pages on the Internet and download their contents to a massive database. These applications are often referred to as Web-crawling robots. Some services that utilize this technique are WebCrawler (http://www.webcrawler.com), Info-Seek (http://www.infoseek.com),

Lycos (http://www.lycos.com), or Alta Vista (http://www.altavista.digital.com). All three of these services are available from the Netscape search page. This page is at http://home.netscape.com/home/internet-search.html, or accessible through the Search directory button at the top of your browser window.

What's in a Name?

A common convention for organizations these days is to set up their WWW and FTP sites with the following naming convention:

www.company_name.com

www.organization_name.org

or

ftp.company_name.com

ftp.organization_name.org

In this manner, you use the node name www.xyz.com for the XYZ Web pages. This aids the users who knows they are looking for the XYZ Communications home page but do not know the exact address. Try it out for a company such as Disney (http://www.disney.com) or a government organization such as NASA (http://www.nasa.gov). Sometimes organizations even set up an alias of their Web and FTP sites as company_name.com. The browser software then connects to the correct server depending on the service prefix in the server address.

Usenet

You should be visiting several newsgroups regularly. To keep up with the Mac Internet server community, scan the comp.infosystems.www.servers.mac newsgroup. To announce your server to the Internet community, submit the relevant information to the moderated newsgroup comp.infosystems.www.announce.

This newsgroup is accessed by thousands of users each day and is one of the quickest and most direct means of advertising your server.

NOTE 

> To find out the charters of the other newsgroups in the comp.infosystems.www hierarchy, check out http://boutell.com/~grant/web-groups.html. Instructions on submission to comp.infosystems.www.announce are included here as well.

Yahoo

If there's a Who's Who for the World Wide Web, it's got to be Yahoo (http://www.yahoo.com). Yahoo started out as a small index of useful Web pages at Stanford University, but grew too large for the academic environment and now is an independent service. You can request that your site be included in the Yahoo database. Yahoo operates under a strict hierarchy, so you'll have to characterize your server's function succinctly. Your server will get lumped into a page with other servers similar to yours. Yahoo also has a searchable query capability so that users do not have to burrow through the complicated hierarchy to find your server.

NCSA and Netscape What's New Pages

Both NCSA and Netscape Communications maintain What's New pages. Instructions are given on the pages shown here for submitting new sites.

Various What's New Pages

Netscape	http://home.netscape.com/home/whats-new.html
NCSA	http://www.ncsa.uiuc.edu/SDG/Software/Mosaic/Docs/whats-new.html
Yahoo	http://www.yahoo.com/new

These What's New pages are updated frequently and provide a means for you to advertise your server.

Keep in mind that in Navigator, the Netscape What's New page is accessible through the toolbar.

Cool Site of the Day

InfiNet, an East Coast Internet provider, operates the Cool Site of the Day page (http://cool.infi.net/). InfiNet staffers wade through email submissions and offerings on comp.infosystems.www.announce for sites that are the coolest. What makes a cool site? I don't know; if I did, my site would have made it on the list. You will have to check out this page for answers to frequently asked questions about this site.

NOTE 

> InfiNet claims that some sites experience about 175,000 to 200,000 hits on the day their site is selected to be a Cool Site. If you opt to submit your server as a Cool Site, be careful, you might get what you wish for.

Brad Schrick

Brad Schrick, a Palo Alto-based Mac Internet consultant, maintains an active list of Mac WWW server addresses at http://www.ape.com/webstar. The sites on this list have denoted that they are run using the MacHTTP or WebStar applications. Brad will accept postings if you are using another server application.

Internet Shopping Malls

If you want to offer your company's services to the Internet retail market, add your page to the Internet Shopping Mall at http://www.internet-mall.com/. The Mall is a way to buy products from companies who maintain a Web presence. There are other similar services on the Net that you access from this page.

Underwrite Someone Else's Web Page

Depending on how deep your pockets are, you may consider underwriting a popular service. For example, Yahoo and the Netscape Search page maintain small graphic images sponsored by advertisers. These images usually are hyperlinked to the sponsoring organization's home page. Many popular sites allow space for advertisers to post links, but it's not an inexpensive means of advertising your page.

Provide Ancillary Service

One of the big dilemmas facing the early television programmers of the 1950s was finding a way to fund initial television broadcasts. It wasn't long before companies determined which television programs were most heavily watched by their target markets. These companies then paid for advertisements during these broadcasts. This practice is still in effect today.

As much as we are used to free services on the Internet, someone has to pay administration, configuration, and maintenance costs for the cool things we see on the Web. Companies are learning to offer Web services valuable to the Internet community; these services are then heavily laced with the sponsoring company's logo and marketing propaganda. A good example of this practice is AT&T's toll-free directory service mentioned previously. During the 1995 Indianapolis 500 race, Valvoline maintained a home page (http://www.valvoline.com) that contained up-to-date reports and photographs from the time trials and race. They knew that people who were interested in the race could very well be potential Valvoline customers.

By offering a service unique to your target market, you can provide a lot of exposure to your Web site. For example, if your company makes athletic shoes, you may want to maintain links to track-and-field home pages. Or you may want to provide up-to-the-minute coverage of the track-and-field events of the latest NCAA basketball tournament. Build it and they will come.

Nurturing Your Web Site

Once your Web and FTP sites are up and running, you've only just started. In this dog-eat-dog Web environment, you will have to continuously work at keeping your site current, interesting, and exciting. Some of the tips in this section should give you ample food for thought with regards to nurturing your Web site and making it work for you.

Controlling Costs—Your Biggest Headache

Forget programming, learning CGI scripting, or understanding audio and video formats. Your biggest challenge as a WebMaster will be in controlling costs. Your Internet presence differs from your Intranet in that it will be harder for your Web site to pay for itself. We've already talked about how your Intranet services will trim some of your administrative costs, but the expense of hanging your shingle on the Internet may be somewhat harder to justify. An expensive Web server is going to show up like a sore thumb when your organization is looking to cut costs; if it's not producing a lot of interest in your organization, it'll be that much harder to keep your boss from shutting you down or relegating your WWW service to an SE/30 on the modem connection down the hall.

Your Two Biggest Expenses

Your two biggest expenses are simple—connection and staffing. Your connection to the Internet is a recurring cost and one that may not be easily justified. For example, your Ethernet costs go up according to the speed of the connection; furthermore, your connection is perhaps the single largest cost of your whole Internet venture. In a perfect world, you would string up a high-speed fiber connection and not worry about it ever again. However, in this imperfect world, such a move would be cost-prohibitive for all but the most active sites. Your connection must be robust enough to handle the traffic you expect, but it must be inexpensive enough to make your system viable.

Your next biggest cost is going to be staffing. As your Web service grows, it will become more difficult for one person to be in charge of hardware purchasing, network installation and troubleshooting, hardware installation, software installation, and programming. You may have to develop a staff to aid in these efforts. That's another recurring cost. Each member of your staff will have to be trained in their individual specialties, and those folks are not cheap. The upside is that with the rush to the Web, networking and programming experts are plentiful. Your best bet is to find individuals that can work at more than one task. I know of many network engineers who can program HTML and troubleshoot Ethernet cable problems. Unless your Web server evolves into a huge effort, you will have to work with a multi-talented staff that can juggle many tasks at once.

Using Consultants

If you're thinking of bringing in consultants, then I haven't done my job with this book! Seriously, if you're thinking of bringing in consultants, expect to spend several thousand dollars for startup costs associated with a large server and $100 per hour for programmers to update your server content. Graphic designers who specialize in Web graphics content also charge significant fees. Consultants take a lot of the grunt work out of the process, but at a high cost. The whole idea of this book is to put the knowledge of Intranets and Internet service in your hands, thereby making your investment easier to pay off.

Tips for Keeping Your Site Alive

Change is good in real life, but on the Web it's a necessity. Your site needs to be dynamic, interactive, and robust enough to handle the rapid pace of WWW culture and technology. We'll cover some of the means to do this in this section.

Start Modestly

The wonderful thing about using the Mac as a server platform is that you can start out small and cheap using MacHTTP or NetPresenz to establish a fledgling Web site. You can gradually increase your server processor size and speed and then switch to a commercial server. In this way, you can strike a chord with your audience and determine which features of your server are most popular and demand the most nurturing.

This also gives you the chance to grow with your server. The skills you need today will be dwarfed by the needs of your server tomorrow. For example, I set up my own Web server several years ago running MacHTTP and just serving up some text and maybe a GIF or two. Within a year's time, I had moved parts of the server to a Unix machine and had implemented imagemaps, Perl and Unix shell CGI scripting, and some fledgling database interaction. Fairly soon (hopefully by the time you read this), I'll be experimenting with Java and JavaScript. The key point is that I had time to grow with my server. Granted, you may not have a few years with which to grow with your server like I did, but avoid the temptation to embrace all the hot trends of the WWW at once. The last thing you want is to represent your company with a server that seems contrived and prefabricated.

Keeping Your Site Current

What's the first thing you think when you see a Web page that's five or six months old? You think that the site's pretty stale, don't you? Lots of WebMasters denote the modification date at the bottom of the page. It's a great feature but can be damning if you don't keep up with your pages.

NOTE 

> For discussion on using template files with the BBEdit HTML Tools, see Appendix C, "Perfecting HTML."

My advice to you is to use the templates in the BBEdit HTML Tools or some other HTML editor to allow you automatically to update your modification dates on your pages. Then, revisit them occasionally, adding new graphics and formatting. This gives users the impression that your pages are dynamic and current.

Getting Feedback

I often receive notes from users who have accessed my pages. I make it easy for them do to this by leaving mailto links addressed to myself sprinkled throughout my pages (see Appendix C, "Perfecting HTML," for more information on the MAILTO tag). These comments are often something substantial like, "Cool pages, man!" I have received feedback and even questions on some of the links I provide.

Your users have a chance to give you feedback, if you add mailto links on your pages. It's rare that this feedback is not constructive and is a way of gauging the relevance of your site on the Web.

Linking to Similar Sites

Back in the early days of the Web, the NCSA had an interactive posting board where you could leave your name, your server's URL, and a description of your server (the Free for All site is now no longer located at http://thphys.irb.hr/www.list.html). It wasn't long before people started streaming onto my little Macintosh IIci and then dropping my site into their list of bookmarks. From there, my site was actually incorporated into other HTML pages. One of the biggest thrills you can have in any vocation is to be recognized by your peers; so you can imagine my excitement at seeing links to my site in sites all over the world.

The Web community is so diversified at this point that different sites cater to different segments. Find out which sites members of your target market frequent and link to them from your page. It's only a matter of time before the other sites return the favor. This interlinking actually is what gave the World Wide Web its name.

Allow for Personal Home Pages

Personal home pages are some of the most accessed types of pages on the Web. In these pages, we learn a lot about people who we've never met, but whose picture (and sometimes voice) can be viewed at our discretion. People also put interesting links on their home pages. These links, or even the pages, eventually may draw attention to your site.

If the Web server exists outside your firewall, as it should, your users may have special access to that machine. You could give everyone in your organization access to your server, but this should not be undertaken lightly. If a mischievous file is somehow deposited on your server by an outside party, your intranet users could accidentally retrieve that file and compromise the security of your intranet. A better method is to set up a special connection between the Internet Web site and a mirror machine inside your firewall.

This mirror can have a special write-only privilege on your server and would be programmed to transfer user information once a day. Your intranet users would modify the files on the mirror computer; these modifications would be transferred to the server on a periodic basis.

Surfing for Ideas

One of the best ways to keep current on other trends is spelled out in three words—Browse the Web! Granted, your boss is not going to be thrilled to have you browse pages all day, but many of the new trends and buzzwords are hanging out there. Often when I see some interesting page, I'll download the source to see how the WebMaster accomplished a neat frame or cool JavaScript. By peeking out on the Web on a regular basis, you'll be able to keep abreast of changes in this dynamic environment.

Summary

I've skimmed many topics in this Appendix. My intent was to get you thinking about some issues involved in planning the Internet portion of your server. A haphazardly planned server can limit your options for growth in the future.

There are many reasons for establishing a presence on the Internet. These reasons, however, rarely overlap with the justifications behind your Intranet. Although the technologies are equivalent, your Intranet and Internet services provide two different functions.

In the next appendix, we'll talk about some of the advanced HTML programming features that you can implement in your pages. However, you can go back and look at some other related chapters.

- ☐ Chapter 4, "Macintosh HTTP Servers," to learn how to set up HTTP servers on your Macintosh.
- ☐ Chapter 5, "Managing Your Intranet Web Services," to obtain tips on efficient Web server management.

- ☐ Chapter 6, "Creating an Efficient Web Site," to learn about ways that you can develop a Web site that is easy to browse.
- ☐ Chapter 7, "Writing CGI Scripts," to learn about writing scripts for your Web site. These scripts allow you to process data from HTML forms and return customized Web pages.

Links Related to This Appendix

RushHour	http://www.maxum.com/RushHour
	Search Engines
Netscape Search Page	http://home.netscape.com/home/internet-search.html
Alta Vista	http://www.altavista.digital.com
Lycos	http://www.lycos.com
Info-Seek	http://www.infoseek.com
WebCrawler	http://www.webcrawler.com
	What's New Pages
Netscape	http://home.netscape.com/home/whats-new.html
NCSA	http://www.ncsa.uiuc.edu/SDG/Software/Mosaic/Docs/whats-new.html
Yahoo	http://www.yahoo.com/new

APPENDIX C

Perfecting HTML

Some of the more popular HTML editors are discussed in this chapter. There are several commercial, shareware, and freeware versions available for the Macintosh. In addition, we'll discuss some of the more popular Netscape HTML extensions that you can use to develop your Web pages.

Introduction to HTML Editors

I often think of a Web browser as an HTML interpreter, although somewhat limited in that capacity. The only way you can use a browser to validate your HTML is to load it. Standard interpreters, like Basic or Perl, will give error messages that aid you to correct programming errors. Browsers like Navigator and Internet Explorer will take their best shot at your code and will display what they think you meant on the screen. HTML debugging, especially for more esoteric constructs like forms and tables, can be arduous. For this reason, there are HTML validator applications and services available. These services are useful in that they analyze your code for syntax and logical errors. They are also useful in that they will check your code corresponding to the document type definition (DTD) associated with HTML 2.0, HTML 3.0, or the Netscape HTML extensions.

NOTE 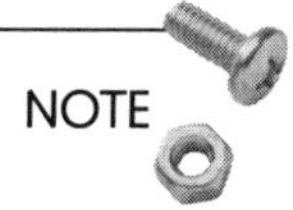

My recommendation is that you keep a copy of your Web browser running during your editing session if you have enough RAM to do so. You can tell the browser to load a local file, edit the file, and then tell the browser to reload the file. I prefer Netscape

continues

Navigator, as it's generally faster than Mosaic for local file access. Microsoft Internet Explorer is also a good browser to use for checking your HTML—you cannot beat the price (it's freeware).

When using Navigator to check your HTML code, make sure that you leave the Toolbar visible so you can easily hit the Reload button. Reloading a document is also performed by hitting Command-R.

HTML Web Weaver

HTML Web Weaver is a shareware HTML-specific editor. Like other HTML-specific editors, it's designed to aid in the development of HTML documents through the use of special buttons and icons. HTML Web Weaver version 2.5.3 makes use of icons and floating tag palettes as shown in Figure C.1. The main text window displays the HTML, while various icons and palettes aid in formation of the various HTML tags.

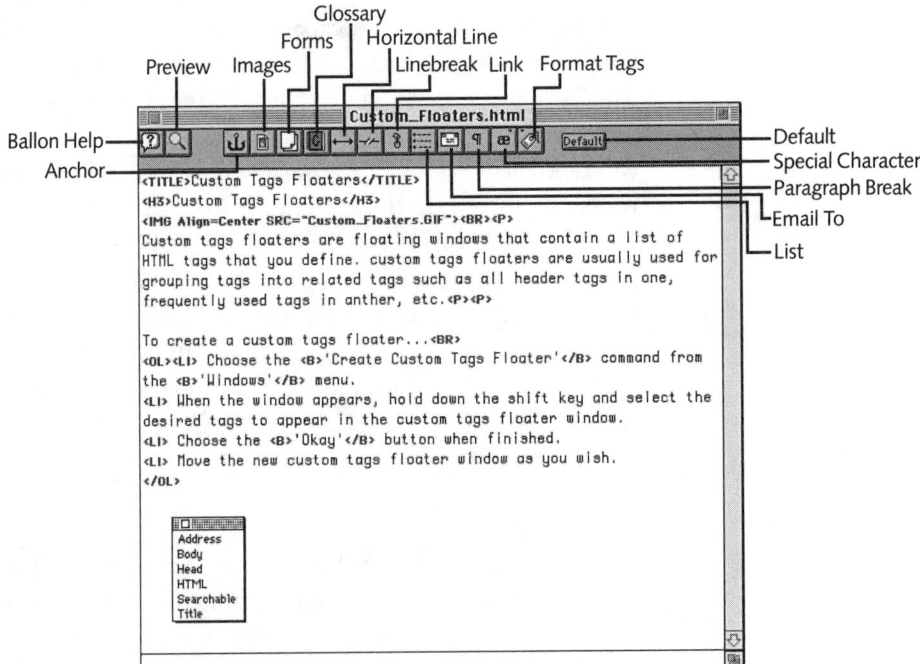

Figure C.1 *HTML Web Weaver v.2.5.3 sports an icon palette and floating tag table for use in HTML coding.*

As HTML Web Weaver uses the Macintosh TextEdit resource, it's limited to working with files that are less than 32KB. Many editors use this built-in text editing resource as a foundation. Commercial word processors use proprietary editing resources and are usually not constrained in editing file size.

The way Web Weaver works could be described as a "select-and-tag" method. You can select various portions of the text and apply the appropriate tags on the selection from either the icon or floating tag palettes. While your editor window will display both your text and your HTML commands, HTML Web Weaver makes it easy to differentiate between them. As seen in Figure C.1, HTML tags can be assigned a custom font, style, and color to differentiate them from normal text. This useful feature for beginners might annoy experienced HTML programmers.

The predetermined tags listed under the Tags menu are derived from HTML 2.0 along with some Netscape extensions; this version of the application did not have any HTML 3.0 tags included with the software distribution. HTML Web Weaver is geared toward beginning HTML programmers. There is ample Balloon Help with descriptions designed to appeal to the novice. Still, experienced programmers will find the application useful.

Furthermore, HTML Web Weaver allows you to quickly preview your code in a Web browser of your choice with a simple keystroke. HTML Web Weaver sends a temporary file over to the browser for display. Even though this process is performed very rapidly with this editor, it goes against my earlier recommendation of locally viewing the edited file in your Web browser. I find local viewing beneficial because:

- I can switch between my editor and my browser faster than my editor can switch over to my browser. It takes almost no time for me to pop over to Navigator and punch the Reload button.
- Switching between the applications forces me to save the file so that my browser can view the most recent version. Saving a

file repeatedly ensures that I won't lose my most recent document version in case of a system crash. Clicking the Preview option within my editor would cause me to grow fat and lazy and not save my document until it was too late.

Creating a New Document

There is no template capability in HTML Web Weaver. You must install the <HEAD> and <BODY> environments. By going up to the File menu and dragging down to Open, you'll be staring at a blank text field. You have access to the icon palette and the default floating tag tables, but you'll have to start from scratch. With the select-and-tag approach, you have to enter new text, select it, and apply the appropriate tag. The tags in the floating palettes are self-explanatory; a description of the various palette icons is given below.

Icon	Description
Balloon Help	Toggles Balloon Help on and off
Preview	Launches Web browser to view current document
Anchor	Creates anchor tag
Images	Establishes image tags using filenames and alignment
Forms	Creates the various forms tags and their attachments
Glossary	Sets up a definition list
Horizontal Line	Creates horizontal rule with Netscape options for width and size
Linebreak	Installs a line break tag
Link	Adds HTML link
List	Creates a variety of lists
Email to	Creates a clickable tag that sends mail to an address (mailto)
Paragraph Break	Inserts a paragraph tag <P>

Special Characters	Launches popup menu detailing all the HTML special characters. Click on a character and the HTML code is inserted in the document
Format Tags	Launches popup menu detailing all available HTML tags. Click on a tag and the resulting code is inserted in the document
Default	Assigns default style to selected text

Opening an Existing Document

Upon opening an existing document within HTML Web Weaver, you'll be queried as to whether you want the program to scan for HTML tags (shown in Figure C.2). If it finds any, it will change their appearance from the default font to the tag font that you've defined in the Preferences. I find this process to be slow and cumbersome, but if I don't click Yes to the query, a bug in the program causes the editor to disregard any text lying beyond the screen.

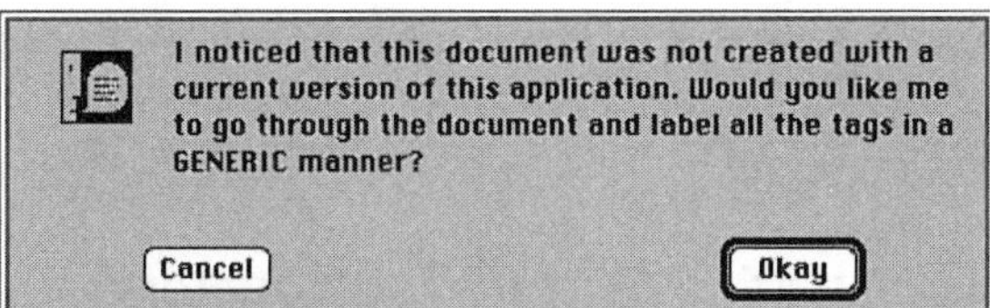

Figure C.2 *HTML Web Weaver will ask to scan for HTML tags when opening an unfamiliar document.*

Setting Your Preferences

By clicking on the Edit menu and selecting Preferences, you can bring up the Preferences dialog box, as shown in Figure C.3. The top two checkboxes in the dialog box deal with initialization of the program. If the bottom checkbox is checked, HTML Web Weaver will insert a carriage return after paragraph breaks, horizontal rules, and new lines. This does not affect the appearance of your code, but changes the way your document looks within the editor.

You can specify the default font and size with the top two popup menus. With the bottom four popup menus, you can specify the HTML tag font, size, style, and color. Again, these do not affect the document's appearance within a browser, but only within the editor. You have a choice of five colors to assign the tags; clicking on the Change Colors button allows you to edit those colors. Lastly, you select your Web browser with the Select Preview Helper button.

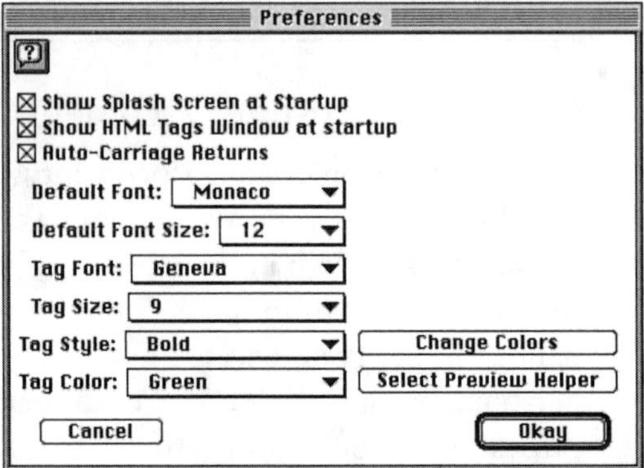

Figure C.3 *You can set default and tag fonts within the HTML Web Weaver Preferences dialog box.*

Creating Custom Tags Floaters

HTML Web Weaver allows you to create customized tables of your preferred tags; these tables, or floaters, will always lie on top of your desktop and editor window. By clicking on one of the tags within the table, you can insert the associated HTML code into the editor window.

To create a custom tag floater, click on the Window menu and select Create Custom Tags Floater. The Custom Floater Editor appears with all the available tags displayed in a scrollable list. You just click on the tags that you want to include in a table; in order to select multiple tags in a given window, you need to hold down the Shift key and click the various tags. When you're finished, click Okay, and a new custom tag floater will appear in the upper left of your screen.

Creating New Tags

Now that you've learned how to create custom tag floaters, you'll want to start populating your new floaters with new tags. New tags will come into use as the HTML standards or Netscape extensions develop. You can create these new tags without having to wait for new releases of HTML Web Weaver.

Under the Edit menu, select the Format Tags entry. You'll notice a sidebar pops up asking you if you want to create, delete, or edit a format tag. Select Create Format Tag and the HTML Format Tag Editor appears as shown in Figure C.4. You can give the new tag a name and provide its opening and closing tag, although a closing tag is not required. You also can modify the tag's appearance within the editor window using the popup menus inside the dialog box. Lastly, you can add descriptive text to the new tag. This text will be displayed when Balloon Help is activated. All of the active tags have some associated Balloon Help text.

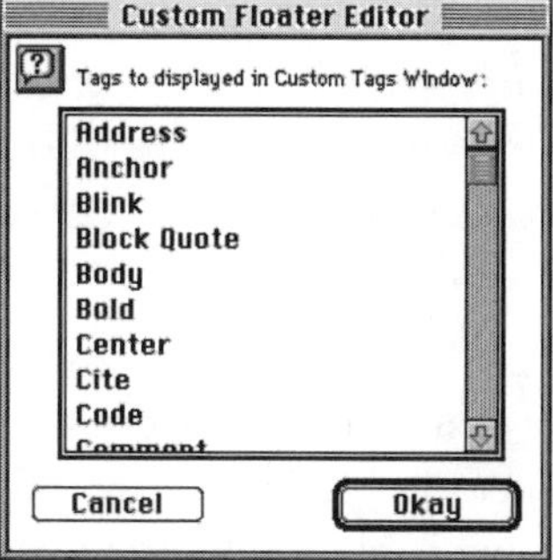

Figure C.4 *You can create your own HTML format tags with the HTML Web Weaver Format Tag Editor.*

NOTE

Each tag is contained in a separate file. This slows down the application startup, but it does make for a flexible means of exchanging tags with other HTML Web Weaver users. These tags are stored in the Format Tags folder of the HTML Extensions folder in the main HTML Web Weaver folder.

Adobe PageMill

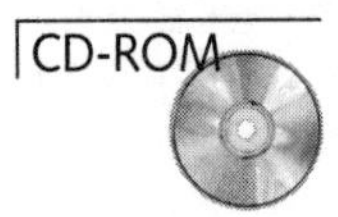

It's hard for me to exaggerate the advantages of the Adobe PageMill editor. I find it to be the most versatile and simple piece of software I've ever used. After months of working with shareware and freeware HTML editors, it was hard to conceal my glee after clicking through the PageMill tutorial.

Many people feel that PageMill is the hottest thing to hit the Web since...well, the Web. PageMill offers true WYSIWYG editing, totally insulating you from the rigors of programming with HTML. You move text around as if you were working in a conventional word processor. Forms and images can be moved around in a similar fashion. Images can be dragged from open applications and dropped into a PageMill window. It's no wonder that Adobe acquired Ceneca Communications, PageMill's original authors, back in late 1995.

The version of PageMill included on this book's CD-ROM is a demo version only. You will not be able to save any of your edited text. Contact Adobe at http://www.adobe.com for information on purchasing the complete version of PageMill.

An HTML document is shown in the PageMill editor window in Figure C.5. It looks, by design, very much like you are viewing the document in Netscape. PageMill was conceived as a one-stop Web authoring tool, in that no preview by an external browser would be required. Clicking on the icon in the upper right toggles an Editor and a Preview mode. While in the Editor mode, you can create and modify text and graphics. In the Browser mode, you can follow links to other pages that you created. The current version of PageMill does not yet support link access between remote sites.

PageMill users can upgrade to Adobe SiteMill, which is a Web site management utility. SiteMill has all the editing options of PageMill and also has several administrative functions as well, such as link checking and outline view.

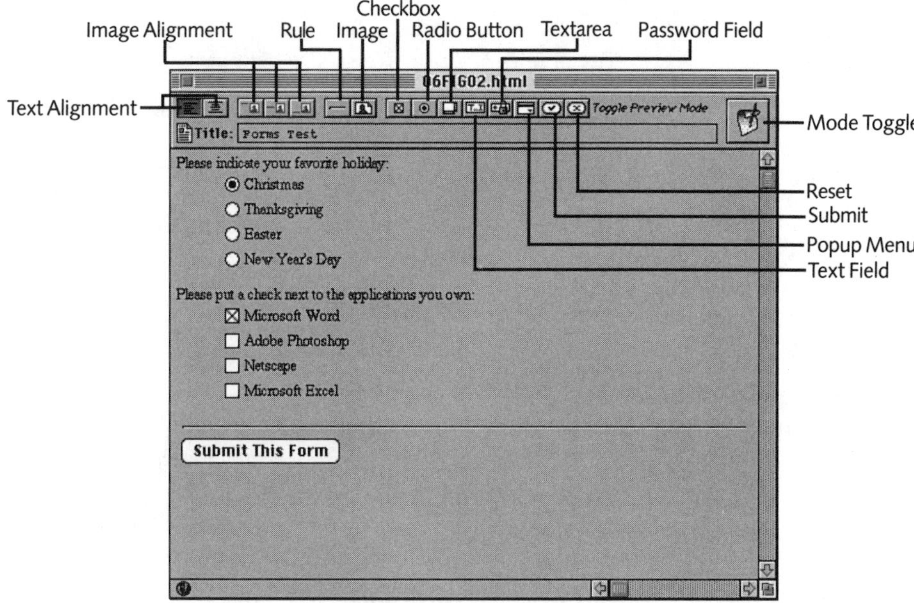

Figure C.5 *Editor or Browser? Adobe PageMill makes it hard to tell the difference.*

Creating a New Document

Creating a new document in PageMill is a matter of clicking the File menu and selecting New File. Initially, you'll be in the Editor mode, as signified by the Quill-and-Scroll icon in the upper right.

Icon	Description
Text Alignment	Left-justifies and centers text
Image Alignment	Text is aligned to top, center, and bottom of image respectively
Rule	Inserts horizontal rule
Image	Inserts image from disk file
Checkbox	Inserts forms checkbox
Radio button	Inserts radio button
Textarea	Inserts textarea

continues

Icon	Description
Text Field	Inserts text field
Password Field	Inserts password field
Popup Menu	Inserts popup menu
Submit	Inserts submit button
Reset	Inserts reset button
Mode toggle	Toggles between Editor and Preview mode

NOTE

The first couple of times that you try editing, don't become alarmed if you see that you cannot select or modify anything. You're probably still in Preview mode.

Opening an Existing Document

Opening an existing HTML document within PageMill will launch the Preview mode. You'll see the document much as it would look within a Web browser. Toggle into Editor mode and you'll be able to modify the document contents. If there are links within the page to files on your local computer, you'll be able to bring those files into PageMill just by clicking on the hypertext.

Using PageMill to Create HTML Documents

Let's try to develop a simple document in PageMill. First, let's enter the title Sample Title into the Title field in the header. Now type the following in the main text window:

```
This is my first PageMill page
```

This should appear with the default paragraph font. We can change that by clicking the Format menu and selecting Heading. A sidebar will pop up delineating six levels of headings from Smallest to Largest corresponding to the six levels of HTML headings. Just go for broke and choose "Largest." Click on the Center Align tool as well. We should have a centered headline at the top of the page.

Now go under Format again and select Paragraph to bring us back to the default font. Now add the following text:

```
So far, I like the following things about PageMill
No HTML!!!!
Drag and Drop text editing
No need to jump to Netscape for validation
```

After typing this, you decide that you want to make bullet items out of the bottom three items. All you need to do is highlight the last three items, select Lists from the Formats menu, and move over to the Bullet sidebar. You see that the bottom three items now have bullets preceding them.

At this point, you're just so thrilled not to be using HTML anymore that you want to move the second bullet item to the head of the list. You select the second item and drag it up to the top of the list.

Next, add a horizontal rule to the end of the list. Move the cursor to the end of the list and click the horizontal rule button—a rule appears that is the width of the window. Now, this looks nice, but a little humdrum. So click on the rule, and an envelope with contact points springs up around it. This allows you to adjust the width of the rule as well as its height à la Navigator. At this point, your page should look like the display in Figure C.6

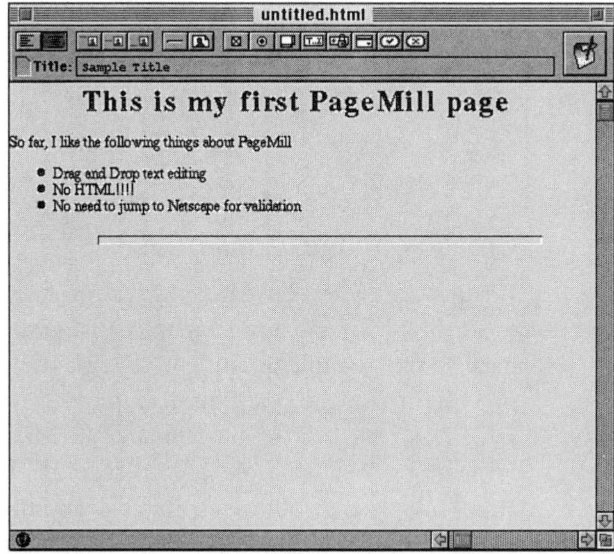

Figure C.6 *Elementary HTML construction is simple with PageMill.*

Creating Links between Documents

Well, what good is creating a Web site that has no links? Let's add links to our sample page. In the PageMill software folder, there are four separate folders. Open the folder entitled Self-guided PageMill Tutorial. In that folder, open a file called ReadMe.html.

Now go back to our example document. Underneath the horizontal rule, type the following:

```
Click to start PageMill demo
```

Then select the word `demo`. Now look back into the Readme.html file. Click on the file icon just to the left of the word Title in the window header. Drag that icon over to the selected word `demo` in your example document. Presto! You've just created a link! The word `demo` lights up and is underlined, linked, and ready to bring you to the PageMill demo. Just toggle back to the Preview mode and test the link for yourself.

NOTE 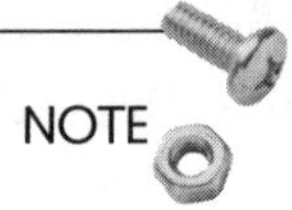

> Just dragging the link into a page that has no selected text will still create a link. The title of the link, however, will be the title of the linked page. This is a good way to compile a hotlist of pages on which you are working.
>
> Also, you can add remote links by selecting text that you want linked, and enter the remote URL in the text field at the lower left of the window next to the PageMill globe.

Creating Images and Forms

It's just as easy to construct images and forms in PageMill as it is to create links. To add an image into a PageMill document, lets go back to the example document. Toggle back into Editor mode and press Return at the point immediately following your newly installed link. Now go into the main PageMill folder and look for the How to get PageMill folder. In that folder, there's a file called PageMillSplash.gif. Once again, click and drag the file over to your example document and place the cursor after the last line. Upon releasing the cursor, you will see the graphic appear at the end of the file.

Click on the file and you'll see an envelope with contact points around the graphic. You can now grab one of the contact points and resize the graphic in either direction. The page should look similar to what is shown in Figure C.7.

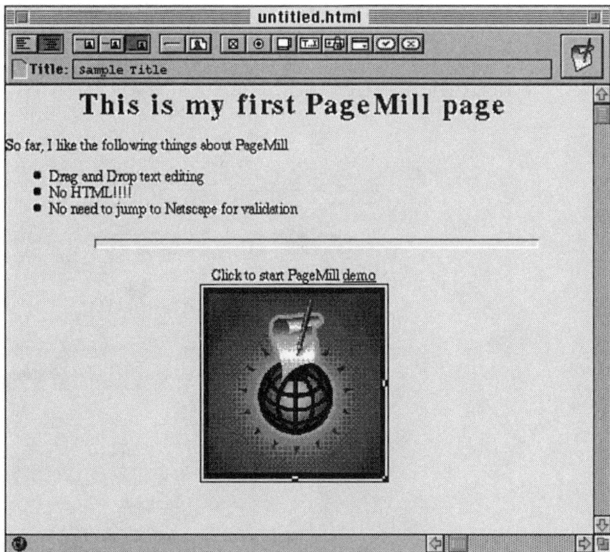

Figure C.7 *Graphics and links can be dragged and dropped into PageMill documents.*

As in all Mac graphics applications, you can scale graphics equally horizontally and vertically by grabbing the corner contact point and holding the Shift key down while you move it.

Forms elements are simple to add to your document by using the Attribute Inspector. However, the HTML behind form elements is not trivial. For a further examination of HTML forms, refer to one of the many excellent HTML books on the market or seek out some HTML tutorials on the Web. The W3C's HTML 3.0 home page is at http://www.w3.org/hypertext/WWW/MarkUp/html3/Contents.html.

Using the Attribute Inspector and Pasteboard

The Attribute Inspector is the one area in PageMill where the intricacy of HTML rears its ugly head. Still, it's an efficient means of designating attributes to some of the elements in your document. The Inspector is shown in Figure C.8; it's accessible through the Show Attributes Inspector item under the Window menu. The Inspector allows you to customize three different objects in your document: the page, the text, and any form element.

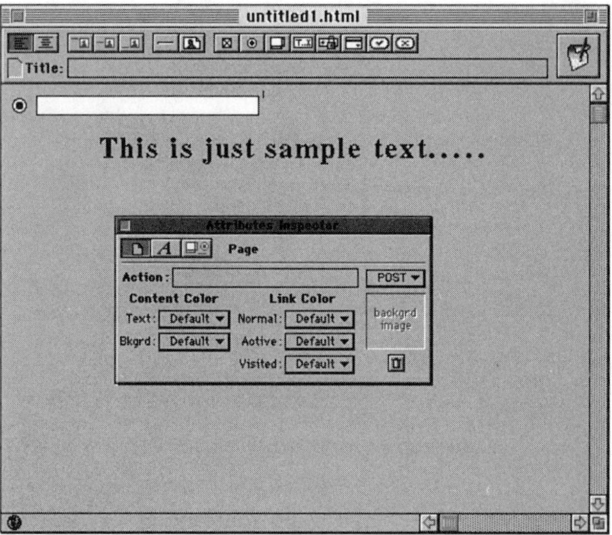

Figure C.8 *The PageMill Attribute Inspector allows you to assign HTML attributes to the various elements in your document.*

The three icons at the upper left of the box denote which objects the Inspector is modifying. To modify the document's background color or image, or text color, you would use the Inspector Page mode. You also can specify the page's CGI script URL, if there is one. The Text mode allows you to select text and modify its alignment, format, or markup. You can even edit or assign a URL if one is associated with the selected text. Finally, the Forms mode is active when a forms element is selected. The Inspector is context-sensitive; different attributes appear, depending on which element is selected. As a result, you'll see different attributes for checkboxes than you will for the password field.

Lastly, the Pasteboard is much like the MacOS Scrapbook, in that you can save PageMill items within the Pasteboard. In this way, you can reuse items like buttons and text for the purpose of standardizing your server's Web pages. Like everything else in PageMill, you just drag and drop text, graphics, or forms items into the Pasteboard and drag them back out for use. The Pasteboard is available under the Window menu.

Other Editors

Space limitations prevent a more comprehensive review of all the HTML editors. This is by no means the final word on Mac HTML editors. As awesome as PageMill is to work with, it suffers from several limitations in that there's no support for Java or JavaScript, HTML tables, or plug-ins. By the time you read this, Netscape may have released Navigator Gold, which is an integrated browser/editor that functions very much like PageMill. It seems that it will be hard to beat PageMill, but give the industry a few months. Links for alternative commercial HTML editors are given at the end of this chapter.

BBEdit HTML Tools

The specific HTML editors just described have no other function than editing HTML. There are existing text editors for the Mac that are used for a variety of purposes. These applications can be customized to aid in developing HTML code as well. The advantages are that these applications are inexpensive and flexible; the disadvantages are that many of the amenities in the specialized HTML editors are not present.

BBEdit stands for Bare-Bones Editor and may be, along with its freeware cousin BBEdit Lite, the second most popular text editor after SimpleText. Since it's not based on the TextEdit resource, you can edit files larger than 32KB. BBEdit Lite offers many editing amenities, such as a highly-configurable search and replace utility, word-wrapping, and tab control. The commercial version of BBEdit offers even more flexibility in searching and replacing,

AppleGuide help utilities, and more interfaces to established programming environments. The commercial version comes with a variety of tools and freeware on a CD-ROM, but for the purposes of HTML development, BBEdit Lite is more than adequate. For the rest of this appendix, we'll discuss HTML development in the context of the BBEdit Lite environment.

Figure C.9 shows a BBEdit Lite text window. In addition to the standard pulldown menus evident in other MacOS applications, BBEdit Lite provides some commonly used functions from the toolbar at the top of the window. Most significantly, the Saving tool allows you some flexibility in saving your document. Note that you have an option to save the file in Macintosh, Unix, or DOS format. The various operating systems differ in that the MacOS uses carriage returns to differentiate lines in a document, DOS uses line feeds, and Unix uses both. This difference in line termination is the largest obstacle to seamless ASCII file exchange between the three operating systems. BBEdit Lite's ability to write files in other OS formats is advantageous as it facilitates file exchange between Web authors who use different platforms to write HTML.

NOTE

You won't notice the different methods of line termination when you mix Web servers and browsers of different operating systems. As we've mentioned earlier, HTML ignores any formatting in the document that is not described using HTML. To a Web server, the difference between carriage returns and linefeeds is irrelevant.

BBEdit Lite functionality can be extended through the use of plug-in modules known as extensions. These utilities are accessible through the Extensions pulldown menu shown in Figure C.9. These extensions can be used as macros to perform various tasks on the file or its contents. Several sets of extensions have been developed to aid HTML programmers in developing Web documents. If you've used BBEdit Lite for any kind of text editing on the Mac, you're familiar with the interface; the use of either set of tools requires marginal training.

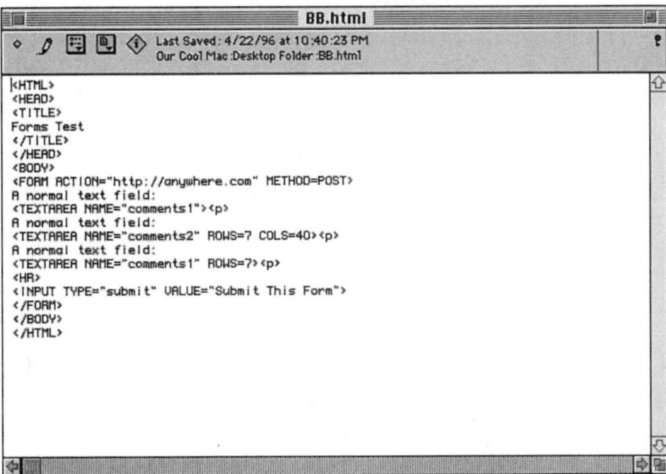
BB.html
Last Saved: 4/22/96 at 10:40:23 PM
Our Cool Mac:Desktop Folder:BB.html
<HTML>
<HEAD>
<TITLE>
Forms Test
</TITLE>
</HEAD>
<BODY>
<FORM ACTION="http://anywhere.com" METHOD=POST>
A normal text field:
<TEXTAREA NAME="comments1"><p>
A normal text field:
<TEXTAREA NAME="comments2" ROWS=7 COLS=40><p>
A normal text field:
<TEXTAREA NAME="comments1" ROWS=7><p>
<HR>
<INPUT TYPE="submit" VALUE="Submit This Form">
</FORM>
</BODY>
</HTML>

Figure C.9 *BBEdit Lite 3.5 offers a flexible HTML programming interface.*

Intro to the HTML Tools Extensions

The extensions that make up the HTML Tools are outlined in the following Table C.1. These extensions are extremely comprehensive. Most of them are self-explanatory, but there is ample Balloon Help available if you have trouble. Two of the more abstract capabilities available with these extensions are document creation through the use of templates and development of custom markup macros; we'll spend the remainder of this section focusing on these two areas.

Table C.1 *HTML Tools Extensions*

Tool	Description
Anchor	Creates an anchor tag <A>
Document	Macros to start a new document
Form Elements	Creates forms tags and environments
Heading	Creates heading levels from 1–6
Image	Formulates <IMG> tag and relevant keywords

continues

Table C.1 *Continued*

Tool	Description
Line Breaks	Inserts paragraph, line break, and horizontal rule tags
Lists	Creates the various types of lists
Preview	Creates either a graphically or text-based preview of file
Style	Creates logical or physical markup style tags
Translate	Translates between text and HTML
User's Markup	Employs user-defined HTML macros
Utilities	Assigns preferences; useful administrative utilities, such as HTML validation and URL-based browser launching

In the HTML Tools folder, open the "for BBEdit Extensions folder." Drag the contents of that folder into the BBEdit Extensions folder. When you launch BBEdit, you'll see these extensions listed in the Extensions menu. If you are running BBEdit 3.5 and the Internet Config application, you'll see these extensions in a menu entitled Internet.

Creating an HTML Document

Select New in the File menu. Next, you'll need to set up a document template. Document templates are the first place to start when building Web pages with the HTML Tools. These templates can be used as framework for creating multiple HTML documents. Before you can create these templates, it's a good idea to assign various preferences for the various extensions.

To set preferences, open the Utilities extension and click the Preferences button. From the pulldown menu, you see that you have four types of Preference options (see Figure C.10):

- **Addressing.** Specify your Web server URL.
- **Document.** Specify the folder that contains your template files.

- **Hotlist file.** Specify your hotlist file for possible URL insertion into HTML documents.
- **Web client.** Specify your favorite Web browser for use in document preview and other operations.

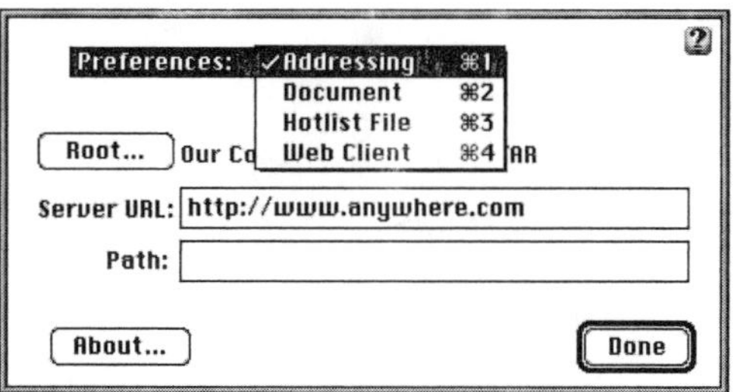

Figure C.10 *These are the Preferences options for the HTML Tools.*

NOTE

Clicking on the About button in the Preferences dialog box will present a splash screen with information about the HTML Tools. If your Web client is running, however, clicking on this button will launch the HTML Tools home page.

The most relevant preferences to establish for document preferences are the document and template folder options. By establishing the document preferences, you enable inclusion of your server and file locations in your document templates. This information will be inserted as HTML comments, but serves as a useful record. Setting up the templates preference provides BBEdit with the location of your template file.

At this point, you'll want to customize your templates file. An example template file, Template.html, is given in the Templates folder in the HTML Tools distribution. By opening up this file, you see that it comprises a framework for a sample HTML document. The code in Template.html is shown below.

```
<!DOCTYPE HTML PUBLIC "-//W30//DTD W3 HTML 2.0//EN">
<HTML>
<HEAD>
```

```
<!--
Author:        #THEUSERNAME#
Machine:       #THEMACHINE#
Created:       #THELONGDATE#
Time:          #THETIME#
Root:          #THEROOT#
Server:        #THESERVER#
-->

<BASE HREF=#BASE#">
<NEXTID N=#NEXTID#>
<LINK #LINK#>

<TITLE>#TITLE#</TITLE>
</HEAD>
<BODY>
<!-- #include "header.incl" -->
<!-- end include -->

#BODYTEXT#


<!-- #include "footer.incl" -->
<!-- end include -->
</BODY>
</HTML>
```

The variables in the template file are referred to as *placeholders;* these are denoted by an uppercase word bracketed by pound signs. These placeholders are either defined by the operation system, as in the case of #THEUSERNAME#, #THEMACHINE#, and #THELONGDATE#, or they are defined in the Preferences dialog box. Note that these placeholders are interspersed with HTML code. Using a little HTML know-how, you can customize the template code to present a distinctive and standardized look to your Web pages.

The template file also allows the use of headers and footers. Headers and footers offer you a means of adding standardized HTML code to certain parts of your document. The most common application of a footer is the datestamp; you could create a footer that imprints the date in which the page was last modified. To do this, you need to edit the footer.incl file also in the Templates folder.

Let's replace the contents of this file to include the following:

```
Page last modified by
<ADDRESS>
#THEUSERNAME#
</ADDRESS>
on
#THELONGDATE#
```

and then let's go back to the template file. The #include file_name.incl command is a means of inserting the contents of file file_name into your template. Therefore, the contents of the footer.incl file will be inserted into the new document when you exercise the template. Assuming that you have updated all your preferences, let's use the template file to construct a new HTML document.

Opening up the Document extension launches the dialog box shown in Figure C.11. You can enter the document title and the base URL. If you desire, you can enter a document ID and author information. At this point, you can press the Insert Template button, if you want to create a new document based on your template file. Based on the information within the computer's operating system, as well as in the preferences that you've defined, the template produces the following HTML code:

NOTE

If you just click OK when the Document dialog box is open, you'll get a bare-bones (pardon the pun) template. However, if you Option-click the Insert Template button, you'll not only get a document created from the full template, but you'll also cause the button to be the default option for the dialog box. Option-clicking the OK button will return the dialog box to its original state.

```
<!DOCTYPE HTML PUBLIC "-//W30//DTD W3 HTML 2.0//EN">
<HTML>
<HEAD>
<!--
Author:      Joe Smith
Machine:     Joe's Macintosh
Created:     Friday, December 29, 1995
```

```
Time:          12:11 PM
Root:          Our Cool Mac/Net Apps/WebSTAR
Server:        http://www.anywhere.com
-->

<BASE HREF="http://www.anywhere.com">
<NEXTID N=[undefined]>
<LINK [undefined]>

<TITLE>Sample HTML Document</TITLE>
</HEAD>
<BODY>
<!-- #include "header.incl" -->
This is an example of a header created on Friday,
➥December 29, 1995 at 12:11 PM



<!-- end include -->




<!-- #include "new_footer.incl" -->
Page last modified by
<ADDRESS>
Joe Smith
</ADDRESS>
on
Friday, December 29, 1995
<!-- end include -->
</BODY>
</HTML>
```

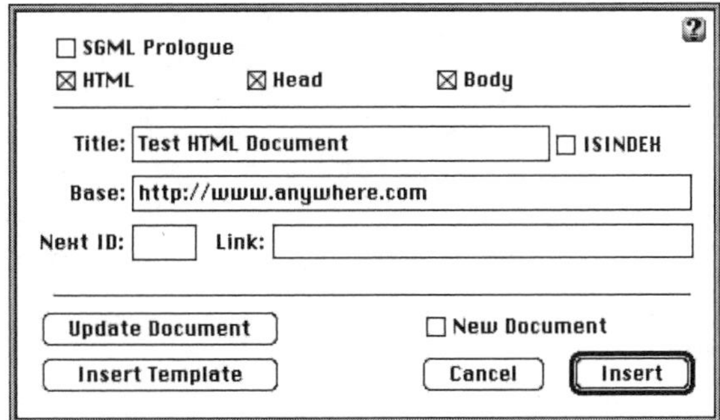

Figure C.11 *The Document dialog box provides several options for constructing and updating HTML documents.*

Presto, instant Web page! Now add some formatting to make the finished document look presentable. After the second header comment, add the following code:

```
<P>
This document was created with a BBEdit HTML Tools
➥template.<P>
```

The finished document appears in a Web browser, as shown in Figure C.12. As you can see, the footer information details the author's name and the date that the page was last modified, as specified in the footer.incl file. Another useful feature available in the Document extension is Update Document; this function allows you to install the values of any placeholders that have changed since the document's last modification. One placeholder that will invariably change is the current date that is stored in either the THELONGDATE or the THESHORTDATE variables. By using the Update Document feature, you can update the date and time listed in the document. This feature provides an easy means of publishing the last modification date of a Web page.

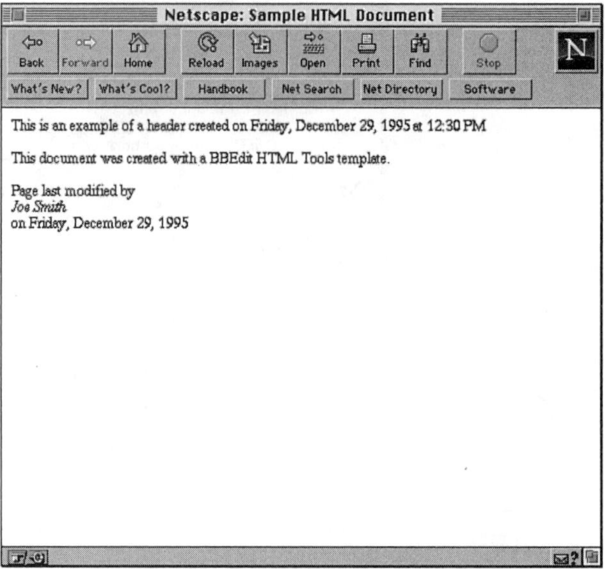

Figure C.12 *This page was created using the HTML Tools template feature.*

Creating Custom Markup Macros

The HTML Tools also offers a highly customizable macro language. Furthermore, in the latest version of the HTML Tools, the author has installed a much more friendly front-end to the macro language. These macros can be easily set up to perform a variety of complicated but redundant tasks. The interface allows the user the option of creating ten different macros numbered 0–9 (see Figure C.13).

To create a macro, click on one of the buttons. You then give the macro a name. Easy so far, right? You then assign the macro as a series of commands available from the down arrow next to the large text field. You have eight major macro topics, each with a variety of options. These topics and their associated options are described in detail in Table C.2:

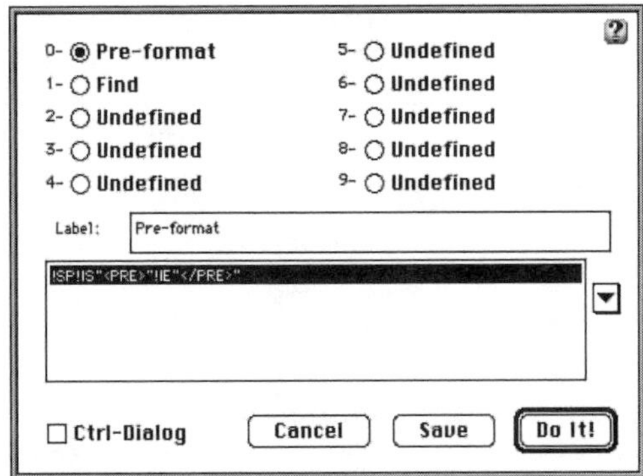

Figure C.13 *The HTML Tools' User's Markup extension allows you to develop up to 10 simple macros.*

Table C.2 *User's Markup Descriptions*

Selection	Option	Description
Select	Word	Selects word
	Line	Selects line
	Paragraph	Selects paragraph
	Document	Selects document
	Contents of container	Selects all text and tags of an HTML environment
	Container	Selects all text of an HTML environment
	Extend to xxx	Select everything from cursor to start of string xxx
Insert	Start of selection	Inserts string before selection
	End of selection	Inserts string after selection
	Replacing selection	Replaces selection with string
Find	Next xxx	Finds and selects next occurrence of string xxx
	All xxx	Finds all occurrences of string xxx

continues

Table C.2 *Continued*

Selection	Option	Description
Move insertion to	Start of selection	Moves cursor to start of selection
	End of selection	Moves cursor to end of selection
	Top of document	Moves cursor to top of document
	Bottom of document	Moves cursor to bottom of document
	Next line	Moves cursor down to start of next line
	Next paragraph	Moves cursor down to start of next paragraph
	Start of line	Moves cursor to start of current line
	End of line	Moves cursor to end of current line
Special characters	Date (Short) Date (Long)	month/day/yr Month Day, Year
	Clipboard	MacOS Clipboard Contents
	Buffer	BBEdit Buffer Contents
	Current selection	
	Return	Carriage return
	Tab	Tab
	Quote	“
	Slash	/
	Exclamation mark	!

Selection	Option	Description
Misc	Run macro X	Executes User Markup Macro X where X is 0–9
	Next default macro X	Set the next default definition to the number X (0–9)
	Beep	Execute beep
	3 Beeps	Execute three consecutive beeps
Copy	Copy to clipboard	Copy selection to clipboard
	Copy to buffer	Copy selection to BBEdit Buffer
	Append to clipboard	Appends selection to contents of clipboard
	Append xxx to clipboard	Appends string xxx to contents of clipboard
	Delete clipboard	Clears clipboard
Case	Upper	Raises case of selection
	Lower	Lowers case of selection
	Word caps	Capitalizes selection
	Make all tags uppercase	Raises case of all tags within selection
	Case sensitivity ON	Turns case sensitivity on
	Case sensitivity OFF	Turns case sensitivity off

NOTE 

Instead of searching for straight text, you can use Unix regular expressions in the Find macro.

Using HTML Tools macros, you can perform repetitive tasks. This sample macro converts paragraphs to HTML preformatted environments:

- ☐ Under Select, click and drag over to Paragraph. The macro !SP appears in the text field.

- ☐ Under Insert, click and drag over to Start of Selection. The command !IS“xyz” appears in the field just after the previous command. Change xyz to <PRE>.
- ☐ Under Insert, click and drag over to End of Selection. The command !IE“xyz” appears; replace xyz with </PRE>.

Okay, you’ve finished defining the macro; now give it a name like “Preformat.” The entire macro string should look something like this:

```
!SP!IS"<PRE>"!IE"</PRE>"
```

Close the dialog box using the Save button and give the macro a try. Just place your cursor within a paragraph. Run the User’s Markup extension and check the Preformat macro if it’s not already checked. You should see the entire paragraph installed within <PRE> and </PRE> tags.

By clicking the Ctrl-Dialog box in the User’s Markup dialog box, you can cause a specific macro (0–9) to run whenever you run the User’s Markup extension. To return to the dialog box, open the extension with the Control key held down.

Well, you get the idea. The HTML Tools documentation gives examples of more intricate macros, but you’re limited only by your imagination. The author has incorporated an extremely powerful tool through the use of this extension. The macros are virtually impossible to debug unless you have intimate knowledge of the individual macro commands. However, this capability is extremely useful, in that it’s not specific to HTML programming. You can define very useful macros for your normal text editing as well.

Miscellaneous Utilities

The HTML Extensions offer several utilities that aid in creation of your HTML documents. These are available in the Utilities extension. Selecting this extension brings up the dialog box shown in Figure C.14. The utilities are described in the following list:

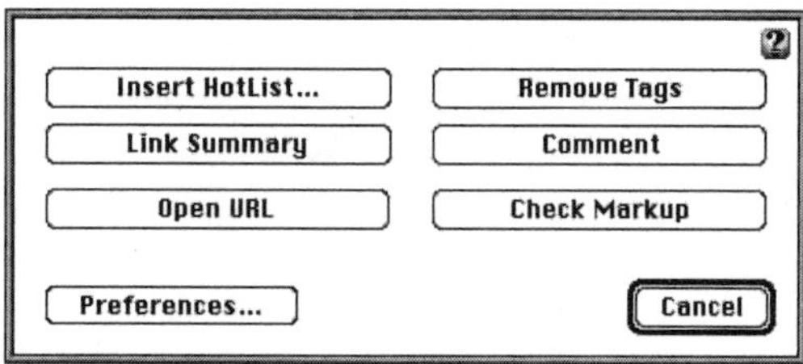

Figure C.14 *The Utilities extension offers many useful features in HTML editing.*

- **Insert Hotlist.** This utility will select the hotlist that you've designated as your default Web browser hotlist file in the Preferences dialog box. You can insert the list as a series of anchors, suitable for Web publishing, or in a textual definition list. This utility even handles Netscape bookmarks files, but ignores any hierarchy that you may have set up within the list. You need to have saved your bookmarks file to disk within Netscape.
- **Link Summary.** This utility creates a list of all the links, anchors, and images used in your document and places it in an HTML document.
- **Open URL.** If your cursor is inside a URL that can be interpreted by a Web browser, running this utility launches the URL in a browser that may be running.
- **Remove Tags.** This feature removes one tag on either side of the cursor. If a portion of text is selected, then all tags are removed from that selection.
- **Comment.** This utility converts selected text to an HTML comment. You can remove comment tags by Option-clicking commented text.
- **Check Markup.** The HTML Tools maintain the HTML Level 2 Document Type Definition as defined by the standards process. You can check your code again in HTML 2.0 syntax.

This means that this tool will object to nearly all Netscape HTML extensions. The output is not terribly informative and will just denote which lines have inconsistent notation. You'll need to turn on BBEdit line numbering to understand the error messages.

- **Preferences.** The HTML Tools preferences are described in the section "Creating an HTML document."

Using HTML Validators

There are several types of HTML validator capabilities available to you. Some of the more advanced HTML editors have validation services offered within the editor. Other services on the Web will check your code for you, provided it's available through a server. There is also a Mac port of a popular Unix-based HTML-checking application available as well.

Why Validate?

We talked before about the fact that Web browsers give very little feedback in the processing of HTML. Navigator will take its best shot at displaying what it thinks you want it to display. This often results in a lot of head-scratching on the part of the HTML developer. Validators can act as a source of the error messages that the Web browser cannot deliver.

Furthermore, it's important to keep in mind that the key to the versatility and popularity of the Web is its user accessibility, regardless of the browser and operating system. There are more browsers than just Internet Explorer and Navigator, and until there's a strict HTML 3.0 standard, there will be a lot of confusion as to what browsers can support what code.

Validators give you a chance to tailor your code to your Intranet users. You'll need to standardize on the type of browser to which you'll gear your Intranet pages. This is made difficult, as HTML standards and conventions change. Six months ago, Netscape Navigator owned the Web browser market; now it's head-to-head with

Internet Explorer, which contains its own flavor of HTML. Who knows what kind of HTML you'll be developing in six months or a year? Validators will enable you to check your code against the evolving HTML standards.

Doctor HTML

The Doctor HTML home page is shown in Figure C.15. This service asks that you enter the URL of the page that you want validated. This service is more robust than most services, and will check your spelling, your HTML syntax, and even the validity of your hyperlinks. The downside of this service is that only code that resides on established servers can be checked. If you are developing HTML documents on an isolated server, the Doctor cannot make a house call.

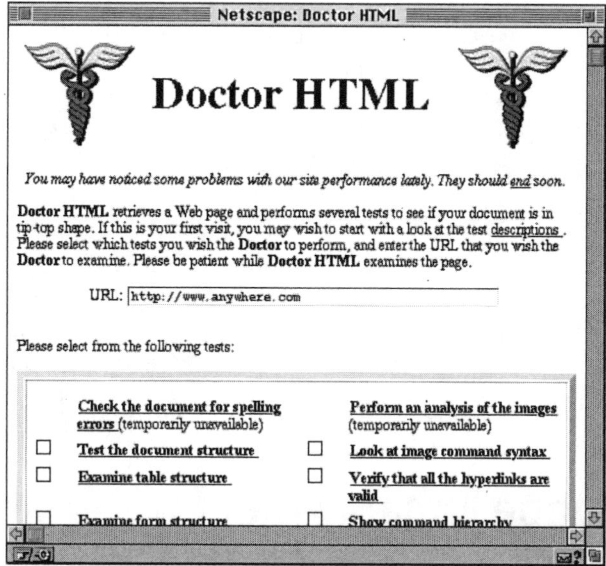

Figure C.15 *The Doctor HTML home page is at http://imagiware.com/RxHTML.cgi.*

MacWebLint

WebLint is a Unix program written in the Perl language. Similar to lint traps that trap fluff in your laundry machines, WebLint is designed to pick up fluff off of your Web pages. MacWebLint is a port of WebLint to the Mac. MacWebLint is based on MacPerl, which is itself a port of Perl to the Mac; the application requires MacPerl in order to run. Both of these applications are installed on the CD-ROM that comes with this book.

MacWebLint supports drag and drop testing of HTML files. Simply drag your HTML files onto the MacWebLint file; it will check only those files with .html or .htm suffices. The application will launch and evaluate your code. A file entitled MacWebLint Results will be created in the same folder as the MacWebLint application. This file is a text document that you can read with MacPerl or another text editor, which will detail line-by-line possible errors in your HTML file. Sample MacWebLint output is below.

```
test.html(9): unknown element <!FORM>.
test.html(11): the ROWS attribute is required for the
➥<TEXTAREA> element.
test.html(11): the COLS attribute is required for the
➥<TEXTAREA> element.
test.html(16): the COLS attribute is required for the
➥<TEXTAREA> element.
```

Valid HTML files return no error messages and the MacWebLint Results file will be empty. The MacWebLint source and configuration files (MacWebLint.pl-source and MacWebLint.rc) are available for your perusal. I wouldn't touch the source unless you knew what you were doing, but the MacWebLint.rc file has many options that you can turn on and off for error checking.

Netscape Enhancements

The developers of Mosaic left NCSA in 1994 and formed what has become the Wall Street and media darling, Netscape Communications. In reference to licensing disagreements with the NCSA, the Web browser was referred to inhouse as "Mozilla," which purportedly stood for "Mosaic-killer."

The Navigator browser became a wild success at the expense of Mosaic mostly because of its increased speed, its support for inline JPEG graphics, and what have been politely referred to as

"Netscape Extensions" to HTML. The Navigator browser sup-ported HTML 2.0 tags before HTML 2.0 was standardized. Similarly, the current version of Navigator supports many HTML 3.0-similar environments. In some cases, the browser has incorporated support for some of the proposed HTML 3.0 elements; in some cases the browser supports elements contradictory to the latest HTML 3.0 spec. Microsoft Internet Explorer also has some custom HTML extensions, with more sure to come as it continues to gain browser market share.

What does this mean for the future of HTML? Navigator being the 800-pound gorilla of Web browsers, it means that until HTML 3.0 is standardized, you may see a flourishing of "Netscape-enhanced" Web sites. Many sites on the Net now sport the Netscape logo with a disclaimer that the site contains HTML code with several Netscape extensions. Some browsers such as Mosaic do not support a good deal of the Netscape extensions; a Mosaic user viewing a Netscape-enhanced Web page may see a totally different layout from what the Web author had envisioned.

Modifications

This section deals with the Netscape modifications to HTML 2.0 tags. These modifications are similar to certain HTML 3.0 environments, but with more flashy attributes.

ISINDEX

Netscape's modification of the ISINDEX tag allows the author to specify the prompt to the input dialog box. The syntax is as follows:

```
<ISINDEX PROMPT="prompt_string">
```

Horizontal-Rule Attributes

Netscape goes several steps beyond the HTML 3.0 implementation of the horizontal rule. Netscape not only allows the width of the line to be specified in relative terms as a percentage of the browser window width, but also in absolute terms using the number of pixels. Horizontal rules also can be aligned flush left, center, or flush right. Vertical thickness of the horizontal rule can be specified as well. Several horizontal rule examples are shown in Figure C.16 as viewed in Netscape 2.0; the source code is given below.

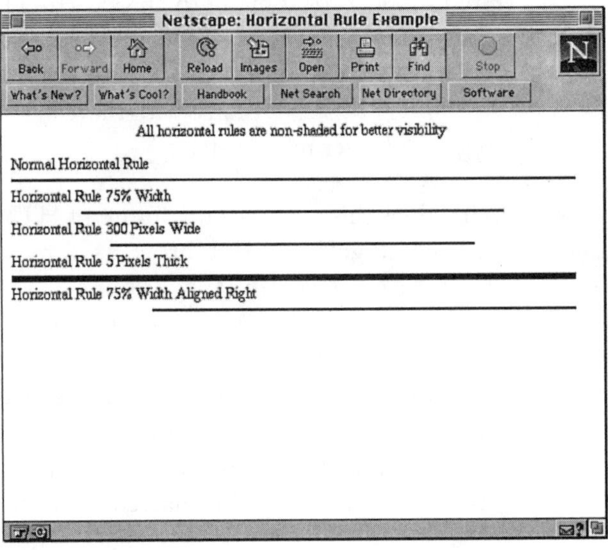

Figure C.16 *Netscape allows highly customizable horizontal rules.*

```
<P ALIGN=CENTER>All horizontal rules are non-shaded for
➥better visibility</P>
Normal Horizontal Rule
<HR NOSHADE>
Horizontal Rule 75% Width
<HR WIDTH=75% NOSHADE>
Horizontal Rule 300 Pixels Wide
<HR WIDTH=300 NOSHADE>
Horizontal Rule 5 Pixels Thick
<HR Size=5 NOSHADE>
Horizontal Rule 75% Width Aligned Right
<HR WIDTH=75% ALIGN=RIGHT NOSHADE>
```

List Modifications

With Netscape HTML, you can alter the sequencing scheme for ordered lists. Using the TYPE keyword in the OL environment, you can specify uppercase or lowercase lettering, uppercase or lowercase Roman numerals, or Arabic numerals. The syntax is shown below:

```
<OL TYPE=char>
<LI> First List Item
...
</OL>
```

where `char` consists of either A, a, I, i, or 1.

Unordered lists have the option of using a variety of bullet types. Examine the following syntax:

```
<UL TYPE=bullet_type>
<LI> First List Item
...
</UL>
```

where `bullet_type` consists of either `SQUARE`, `CIRCLE`, or `DISC`. The default bullet type is DISC.

New Elements

Navigator also incorporates several new HTML tags and environments. Note that I differentiate between tags and environments when discussing HTML. I refer to an HTML *tag* as a command that stands by itself such as <P>, <IMG>, or one of the HTML special characters. HTML commands that have opening and closing tags, such as headers and style markup, as HTML *environments.*

The Infamous Blinking Text

Perhaps no other Netscape extension has been more reviled on the Net than the notorious <BLINK> environment. Shortly after the tag was introduced, every other Web page was mind-numbingly blinking ad infinitum. You can make text blink by inserting it in the <BLINK> environment. However, no other tag will ignite the wrath of the HTML purist more than this little guy. As expected, the <BLINK> environment is nowhere to be found in the proposed HTML 3.0 specification.

Linking Mail with Hypertext

Netscape introduced the concept of linking email with hypertext by using the ersatz URL protocol MAILTO. The syntax of the tag is

```
Send <a href="mailto:joe.smith@anywhere.com">mail</A>
➥to Joe Smith
```

By clicking on the word "mail," a user can bring up a mail entry form. The user can enter the text of the message along with a subject and have Netscape send it off through a predefined SMTP host.

NOTE

> A common practice is for Web authors to include a MAILTO URL somewhere on the page to facilitate feedback from the user. Doing this will allow your Intranet users to get back to you with questions or feedback about your Web page content.

Line Breaking

Netscape also provides for line break control through the tags <NOBR> and <WBR>. You can prevent line breaks with <NOBR>; use of the <WBR> tag informs Netscape of locations where it can break lines, if needed.

Font Sizing

Netscape has the following environment used for font scaling:

```
<FONT SIZE=n>...</FONT>
```

where n is the relative size font. The default size is three, but it can be altered using the <BASEFONT SIZE=n> tag where n is the desired default font size. Relative font size can be manipulated using the

```
<FONT SIZE=±j>...</FONT>
```

sequence where j represents the number of level increase or decrease in size of the surrounding text font.

Centering

Centering is accomplished using the <CENTER> environment. This is in contrast to the <P ALIGN=CENTER>...</P> environment found in HTML 3.0.

New Characters

Netscape also introduced two new characters. In HTML 2.0, the trademark symbol, ™, and copyright symbol, ©, are expressed using the ISO 8859 character codes. These symbols have unique non-numeric tags in the Netscape HTML extensions, ® and © respectively.

Image Attributes

```
<IMG SRC="url"
[ALIGN=LEFT|RIGHT|TEXTOP|ABSMIDDLE|BASELINE|ABSBOTTOM]
➥[BORDER="#_of_pixels"]
[HSPACE="hspace"][VSPACE="vspace"] [LOWSRC="url"]
```

The Netscape HTML extensions offer a very flexible means of adjusting image positions. For an explanation of the various <IMAGE> keywords, observe the examples in Figure C.17.

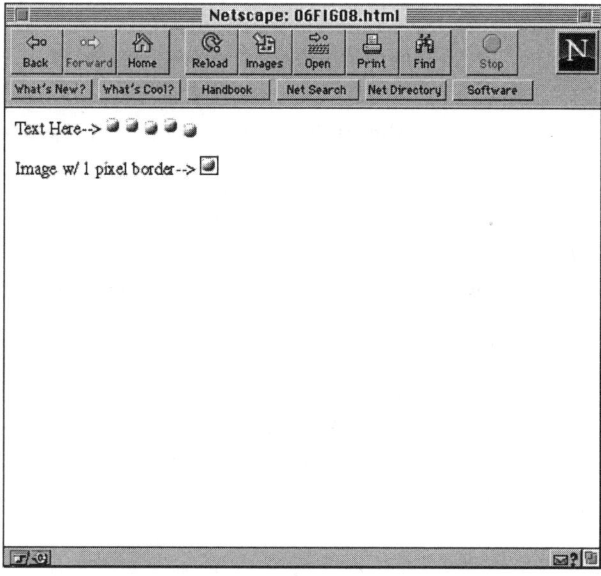

Figure C.17 *The Netscape <IMAGE> tag ALIGN attribute lets you align text and graphics in different ways.*

```
<BIG>Text Here--&gt</BIG>
<IMG SRC="bullet.gif">
<IMG SRC="bullet.gif" align=textop>
<IMG SRC="bullet.gif" align=absmiddle>
<IMG SRC="bullet.gif" align=baseline>
<IMG SRC="bullet.gif" align=absbottom><P></P>
<BIG>Image w/ 1 pixel border--&gt</BIG> <IMG
➥SRC="bullet.gif" BORDER=1>
```

The <IMAGE> keywords shown in the example include TEXTOP, ABSMIDDLE, BASELINE, and ABSBOTTOM. These keywords align the image with the adjacent paragraph text. Also, note the ability to put a border around an image with the BORDER keyword; the argument for the BORDER keyword is width of the desired border in pixels.

The keywords HSPACE and VSPACE are used to prescribe horizontal and vertical text-free margins. The LOWSRC keyword tells the browser to load a low-resolution proxy, located at the URL assigned to the keyword, instead of an original document. This document can be at a much lower resolution, and will therefore load faster because of its smaller size. After the page has finished loading, the high-resolution image is loaded.

Text and Background Color

```
<BODY BGCOLOR|TEXT|LINK|ALINK="color_code">...</BODY>
```

Since Navigator 1.1, the user has been able to specify background, text, link, and active link color. Mosaic also now supports these attributes. As mentioned previously, Netscape and Internet Explorer do support the HTML 3.0 background GIF and visited-text color proposals.

Client-Based Imagemaps

```
<IMG SRC="image_url" USEMAP="map_script#map_name"
➥ISMAP>
```

```
<MAP NAME="map_name">
<AREA [SHAPE="RECT"] COORDS="coordinate boundaries"
➥[HREF="reference"] [NOHREF]>
<AREA...>
<AREA...>
</MAP>
```

The HTML 3.0 proposals call for an alternative to the conventional imagemap designation using the new <FIG> environment. Netscape takes various exceptions to this new environment and has developed a fully client-based imagemap that also can work with a conventional server-based imagemap.

The new attribute USEMAP added to the IMG tag indicates that image specified in the SRC keyword is a client-based imagemap. The mapping between the image and associated hyperlinks is contained in a named <MAP> environment. The argument to USEMAP specifies both the file containing the <MAP> environment and the name of the particular <MAP> environment within that file.

The <MAP> environment is comprised of a variety of <AREA> tags. These tags map certain areas of an image to desired hyperlinks. The user gets to specify the approximate shape of the area. Currently, rectangles are the only polygons supported within the client-based imagemap. This is in contrast to conventional imagemaps that can support a variety of polygon shapes. The rectangle is specified through x-y coordinates of the lower left and upper right vertices. The desired hyperlink is entered in the HREF keyword.

Tables

```
<TABLE [BORDER="value"] [CELLSPACING="value"]
➥[CELLPADDING="value"]>...<TABLE>
```

Netscape supports the table environment defined in the HTML 3.0 proposals; however, new extensions have been introduced. Where the HTML 3.0 proposal calls for a border toggle, Netscape allows you to specify the width of the border in pixels using the BORDER keyword. Netscape allows you to control the amount of space between cells, and the amount of space between the cell border and using the CELLSPACING and CELLPADDING keywords; both options are expressed in terms of pixels. Some examples of use of these keywords are included in Figure C.18.

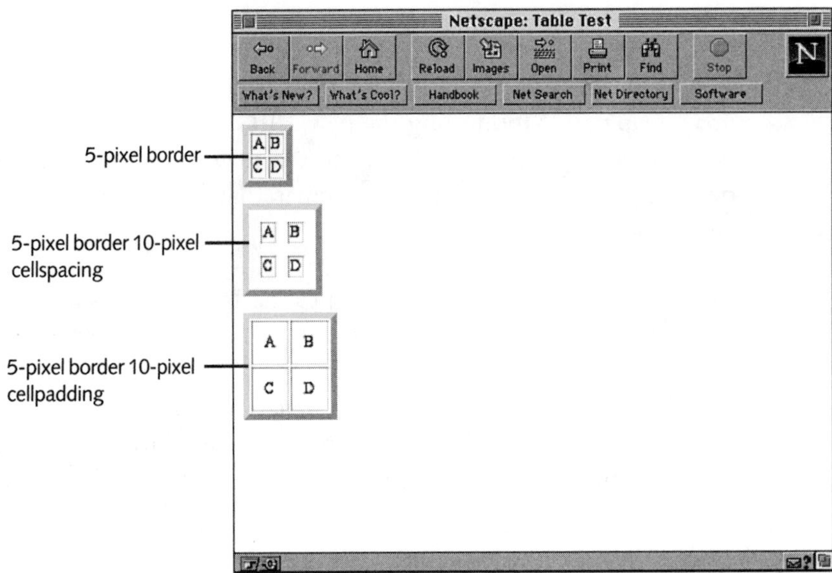

Figure C.18 *Tables can be configured with varying spacing and borders.*

```
<HTML>
<HEAD>
<TITLE>Table Test
</TITLE>
</HEAD>
<BODY>
<TABLE BORDER=5>
<TR><TD>A<TD>B</TR>
<TR><TD>C<TD>D</TR>
</TABLE><P>
<TABLE BORDER=5 CELLSPACING=10>
<TR><TD>A<TD>B</TR>
<TR><TD>C<TD>D</TR>
</TABLE><P>
<TABLE BORDER=5 CELLPADDING=10>
<TR><TD>A<TD>B</TR>
<TR><TD>C<TD>D</TR>
```

```
</TABLE>
</BODY>
</HTML>
```

Dynamic Updating

Dynamic updating is another browser feature that was initiated by Navigator but is also currently supported by Internet Explorer. With dynamic updating, the Navigator browser updates Web documents without intervention from the user. This functionality was added to version 1.1 of the browser. A possible use of this technique would be a hypothetical Web page that posted periodically updated news releases or stock quotes.

According to Netscape, dynamic updating can be accomplished using two methods: client pull and server push. In client pull, the browser, or client, takes the active role in updating the document; with server push, the HTTP server takes the active role in *pushing* the data into the browser. With client pull, the browser re-opens a connection to the server user-defined regularity. With server-push, the HTTP connection between the server and the browser is held open until it's automatically closed by the server or manually closed by the user.

Client Pull

As discussed in the previous section, the HTML 3.0 tag <META> can be used to specify browser- or server-specific information, which cannot be conveyed through conventional HTML. In this instance, Netscape makes use of the <META> tag with the HTTP-EQUIV option set to Refresh. The CONTENT keyword is set to the update frequency in seconds. A simple document that updates itself every five seconds is given below.

```
<HTML>
<HEAD>
<META HTTP-EQUIV="Refresh" CONTENT=5>
<TITLE>Dynamic Updating Test</TITLE>
</HEAD>
<BODY>
<H1>This is a dynamically updated document</H1>
```

```
This document is updated every five seconds based on
➥the value of the CONTENT keyword in the <META> tag.
</BODY>
</HTML>
```

This page will update itself every five seconds. It will continue to update itself until the server connection is broken or until the user closes the window or presses the Back button.

Server Push

Server push is the alternative means of dynamically updating documents. With server push, the connection is held open for a period of time; the server has total control over how often new data is sent down to the browser. The disadvantage of this method is that an IP connection is held open by the server, thereby constraining the server resources. In contrast to the client push, the server can be closed merely by clicking the Netscape Stop button.

Netscape implements the MIME message format to develop the server push. The MIME protocol is used by many Internet applications, most notably email, Gopher, and WWW clients, to package server data in response to a client request. Let's assume that a MIME header is included in a response from the server to a browser HTTP request. One MIME header type is known as multipart/mixed, which tells the browser to expect a variety of pieces of data within a single server message. Netscape implements an experimental MIME header known as multipart/x-mixed-replace where the x denotes the experimental nature of the header. Like HTML, MIME headers undergo a standardization process.

When a browser sends a request to an HTTP server, the response comes back in the form of response headers. Most of this response is formulated as HTML, which is then processed by the browser. However, the response headers included in the message direct the browser to do things other than process HTML. An example of a server-push HTTP response is given here:

```
Content-type: multipart/x-mixed replace;
➥boundary=BoundaryString
```

```
--BoundaryString
Content-type: text/plain

Text for the first update

--BoundaryString
Content-type: text/plain

Text for the second and final update

--BoundaryString--
```

Note that after the MIME header, we've included the boundary string BoundaryString; this string tells the browser when messages end and when new ones begin. After the first BoundaryString, you see the MIME header text/plain; this header tells the browser to expect pure text to follow the header and not to process it as HTML or any other format. The text is followed by a boundary string that concludes the first document. In this example message, the boundary string is immediately followed by a MIME header, notifying the browser that a new document is being constructed; new text follows the MIME header. However, the boundary string is now followed by a double dash that tells the browser that the HTTP message is over and no new data follows.

NOTE 

> The MIME header that tells the browser to expect HTML code is text/html.

In an ideal server push case, the server connection could be held open indefinitely. Using the multipart/x-mixed-replace header, the connection remains open until the HTTP message ends with the final boundary string. Furthermore, this header tells the browser to replace the document instead of adding to it; the browser will begin displaying the new document once the next MIME header is read. When the browser reads the intermediate boundary string, it dutifully sits and waits for the next data object to arrive.

Ideally, a server push connection could be maintained and initiated by a server script. The server would send down the appropriate

MIME headers, boundary strings, and HTML code in an HTTP message. You could do this easily with a CGI script on your Mac server. See Chapter 7, "Writing CGI Scripts," for more information about writing scripts.

One advantage of the server push mechanism is that you also can push an image to a browser, instead of the entire document. In this way, only the image is reloaded rather than forcing the entire document to reload each time. In an <IMG> tag, the SRC keyword can tie into a CGI script that commands that various GIF images be updated within a document window. In this manner, a crude form of animation capability can be added to a Web page.

Writing a CGI script to upload several images of a graphic for animation purposes and keeping that server connection open may be a labor-intensive way of doing animation on the Web. There will soon be an easier and more flexible way to perform animation and other such dynamic document updates. Navigator 2.0 browsers are able to process Java applets that can perform many online processes such as animation, calculation, and so forth.

Frames

Frames are yet another innovative Netscape HTML extension. It's interesting to note that as implemented by Netscape, frames are not included in the main HTML 3.0 proposals. Just as tables allowed partition data throughout your browser window, Netscape frames allow you to partition your window into a set of smaller windows. Each window can represent an independent interface, operating independently of the other frames within your browser window. Frames were first supported by Netscape 2.0.

An example of a site using frames is the Netscape Hall of Shame; its home page is shown in Figure C.19. Note that the window appears to be divided between two sections each with a left scroll bar. Each of these sections is called a frame. A user on this page clicks on one of the icons in the left-hand frame. The frame on the right-hand side changes content depending on which left-frame icon was clicked. Note that either the left or right frame can be scrolled independently of one another.

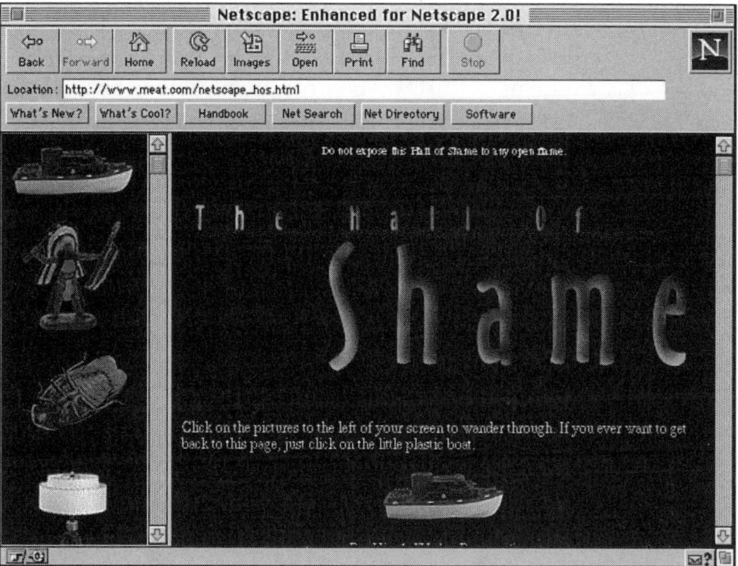

Figure C.19 *The Netscape Hall of Shame offers Navigator 2.0 users an interesting means of navigating through its Web site using HTML frames.*

NOTE

> Netscape maintains a list of companies and organizations who make use of frames at http://www.netscape.com/comprod/products/navigator/version_2.0/frames/frame_users.html.

Creating Framed Web Pages

Frames should consist of the following four components:

- <FRAMESET> environment
- a series of <FRAME> definitions
- the associated HTML code for each frame
- a <NOFRAMES> environment containing code seen by users without frames-capable Web browsers

Frame documents are constructed similarly to normal HTML documents except that the <FRAMESET> environment supplants the normal <BODY> environment. The individual frames are defined using the <FRAME> command. The source code for each frame is maintained in a separate file whose URL is specified in the <FRAME> tag. Lastly, provisions are made for frames-challenged browsers by inclusion of a <NOFRAMES> environment. This environment contains code that is processed by browsers that cannot process frame commands. Users with frames-enabled browsers cannot see the HTML documents created by code within a <NOFRAMES> environment.

The <FRAMESET> Environment

```
<FRAMESET COLS|ROWS="value_list">...</FRAMESET>
```

The <FRAMESET> environment is the main component of a frame document. Much like an HTML table, a framed document is composed of rows and columns. These rows and columns are defined using the <FRAMESET> ROWS and COLS keywords. The number of items in the lists that comprise the argument to these keywords defines the number of rows and columns in the frame document.

The ROWS and COLS keywords can be defined either by specifying absolute row and column widths in pixels, or by specifying row and column widths as a percentage of the related browser dimension. This is demonstrated in the document along with the source code (see Figure C.20).

```
<HTML>
<HEAD>
<TITLE>Frames Example</TITLE>
</HEAD>


<FRAMESET COLS="200,*">
  <FRAMESET ROWS="50%,50%">
    <FRAME SRC="cell.html">
   <FRAME SRC="cell1.html">
  </FRAMESET>
```

```
  <FRAMESET ROWS="33%,33%,33%">
    <FRAME SRC="cell.html">
    <FRAME SRC="cell.html">
    <FRAME SRC="cell.html">
  </FRAMESET>
</FRAMESET>


</HTML>
```

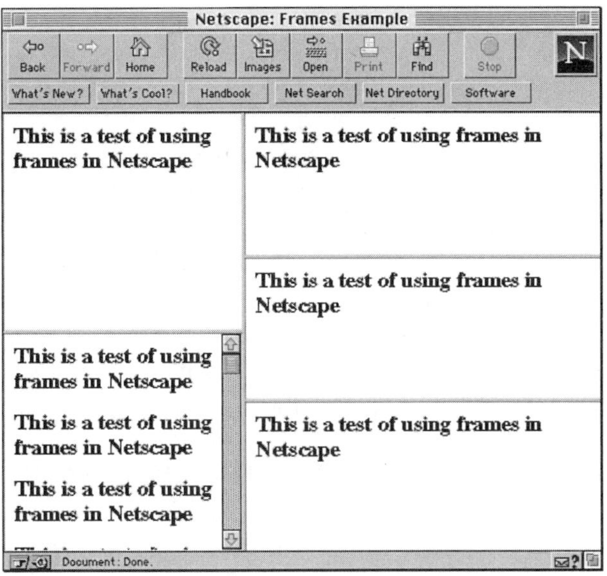

Figure C.20 *A framed document allows flexibility in Web page design.*

This example shows a frame with two columns—the left column contains two rows, and the right column contains three rows. Note the value for the COLS keyword in the first <FRAMESET> definition consists of a number, 200, and an asterisk. The 200 defines the left column to be 200-pixels wide; this column remains 200-pixels wide regardless of how the user resizes the browser window. In contrast, the right column has no specified width. The asterisk denotes the elasticity of the right-hand column width; as the browser is resized, the right-hand column expands to fill the window, whereas the left-hand column remains a fixed width. Note that the second <FRAMESET> environment defines there to be two rows to the first column. Each element of the list is 50 percent, meaning that the row heights each comprise 50 percent of the available window height. Similarly, the third <FRAMESET> environment assigns three rows to the second column; as a result of the 33 percent designation, the height of each column is designated to roughly one-third of the available window height.

Defining Frames

```
<FRAME [SRC="url"] [NAME="window_name"]
➥[MARGINWIDTH="value"] [MARGINHEIGHT="value"]
[SCROLLING="YES|NO|AUTO"] [NORESIZE]>
```

The <FRAME> tag defines the characteristics of the individual frames. The HTML that gets processed in each frame is located at the URL specified in the SRC keyword. The individual frame code used in Figure C.20 contains HTML listed in two separate files: cell.html and cell1.html. Cell1.html contains multiple copies of the single header contained in cell.html. The NAME keyword is used to assign a name to the frame, so that it can be targeted by links within the frame document or by links in other documents.

The MARGINWIDTH and MARGINHEIGHT keywords are means of manually determining the width and height of the individual frame margins in pixels. These keywords are optional; by default, the browser defines the margin width and height. Scrolling is enabled or disabled by the SCROLLING keyword; scrolling is enabled when the frame content exceeds the dimensions of the frame. The default value of this keyword is AUTO. Note that the lower left frame in Figure C.20 contains more code than can be displayed in the entire frame, so scrolling is therefore enabled. Some frames are resizable within the browser windows, simply by clicking and dragging on the boundaries with the mouse. Frames that are defined with the NORESIZE keyword are not resizable.

Linking to Frames

Before Navigator 2.0, new documents appeared either in the existing browser window or in a new window opened by the user. The new targeting feature in Navigator 2.0 allows windows to be opened as specified by the Web-site author. Now, Web pages can open within individual frames or automatically open inside new windows.

The TARGET attribute allows the HTML-site author to designate names to certain windows and can even specify that certain targeted documents only open in the frame or window bearing the matching name. This attribute manifests itself in four ways.

- **In the anchor tag.** The TARGET attribute can be used in the anchor tag as <A HREF="url" TARGET="frame_name"> Target Anchor</A>. Clicking on that link causes the link specified in the HREF keyword to be opened up in targeted frame.

- **In the BASE tag.** Specifying the target window in a base tag will cause all links in a document to be opened in the targeted window. This is of course overridden by specific uses of the TARGET attribute. The use is as such: <BASE TARGET="frame_name">.

- **In the AREA tag.** The Netscape tag AREA is an alternative to the current imagemap convention. Authors are able to target certain areas of an imagemap to open in a desired window. An example of this is <AREA SHAPE="shape" COORDS="coords" HREF="url" TARGET="frame_name">.

- **In the FORM tag.** The results of a form submission can be loaded into a desired window using the command <FORM ACTION="url" TARGET="frame_name">.

The TARGET names can be almost any string that begins with an alphanumeric character. There are reserved TARGET attribute names that load desired links into certain windows. A summary of these reserved TARGET names is given in Table C.3. All other TARGET names that begin with underscores are ignored by the browser.

Table C.3 *Functions of Reserved TARGET Attribute Names*

Name	Function
_BLANK	Causes link to be loaded into new browser window.
_SELF	Causes link to always be loaded into same window in which anchor was clicked. Used to override <BASE> TARGET definition.
_PARENT	Loads link in immediate <FRAMESET> parent frame.
_TOP	Loads link in full body of window, regardless of original frame definition.

Summary

HTML is an evolving standard, and the tools used to create HTML documents are evolving even faster. The line between browsers and editors is already blurred, and future developments promise to merge the two applications into a single entity. We already see that trend with Adobe PageMill; Navigator Gold and other editors will only refine the ways in which HTML editors allow you to construct your Web pages.

We also covered some of the Netscape enhancements to the HTML 2.0 standard and the HTML 3.0 proposals. Microsoft also has introduced some HTML enhancements for use in the Internet Explorer. As that browser becomes more mature, Microsoft may introduce HTML extensions that may further diverge from the Netscape extensions thereby shattering the standards process. Until things settle down in the HTML standards arena, you will need to standardize on a single browser within your Intranet and formulate your pages with those extensions in mind.

At this point, you've heard everything I've had to say. Feel free to peruse Appendix D, the glossary, for a refresher on the terms used in this book. Otherwise, you can hop back to any of the following chapters that are related to this one:

- Chapter 4, "Macintosh HTTP Servers," to learn about the different software you can use to set up World Wide Web services on your Mac.
- Chapter 7, "Writing CGI Scripts" to learn about writing scripts for your Web site. These scripts allow you to process data from HTML forms and return customized Web pages.
- Chapter 9, "Beyond HTML" to learn about ways some techniques to spruce up your Web site beyond just using conventional HTML and graphics. We'll discuss Java, RealAudio, and other cool topics.

Links Related to This Appendix

HTML Editors

Webtor	http://www.igd.fhg.de/~neuss/webtor/webtor.html
HTML Pro	http://www.ts.umu.se/~r2d2/computers/package/htmlpro_hel.html
Navipress	http://www.navisoft.com/products/press/press.htm
HoTMetaL Pro	http://www.sq.com/products/hotmetal/hm-ftp.htm
Netscape Navigator Gold	http://home.netscape.com/comprod/products/navigator/version_2.0/gold.html

Help with HTML Forms

Intro to CGI Scripts and HTML Forms	http://kuhttp.cc.ukans.edu/info/forms/forms-intro.html
NCSA Forms Tutorial	http://kuhttp.cc.ukans.edu/info/forms/forms-intro.html

Carlos' Form Tutorial	http://robot0.ge.uiuc.edu/~carlosp/cs317/cft.html

Netscape HTML Extensions

HTML 2.0 Extensions	http://www.netscape.com/assist/net_sites/html_extensions.html
HTML 3.0 Extensions	http://www.netscape.com/assist/net_sites/html_extensions_3.html
Dynamic Updating (server-push, client-pull)	http://www.netscape.com/assist/net_sites/dynamic_docs.html
Frames	http://www.netscape.com/assist/net_sites/frames.html

GLOSSARY G

10BaseT A 10 Mbps Ethernet transmission standard that provides data transfer over twisted-pair cabling.

100BaseT An Ethernet transmission standard that provides 100 Mbps data transfer over twisted-pair cabling.

100BaseVG-AnyLAN A 100 Mbps Ethernet transmission standard that is a competing standard to 100BaseT.

680x0 Describes the chip structure used by Apple to power older Macintosh computers. Has been supplanted by the PowerPC chip.

Apple Event Data structure used by the MacOS for communication between applications. Apple events are used to allow Web servers to communicate with CGI scripts.

AppleScript Apple's scripting environment bundled with System 7.5. It is a popular CGI scripting environment, but sees a good deal of use for building normal desktop-related scripts.

AppleTalk The MacOS native protocol. AppleTalk enables file sharing and printing between Macs.

applet Describes software application written in Java. HTTP servers send down Java applets in conjunction with browser requests. The applets can perform sophisticated processing on the browser display.

asynchronous CGI CGI scripts that can share processing with other tasks.

ATM A high-speed network transmission medium that offers greater reliability and performance than conventional networks.

backbone A high-speed segment of a local area network to which many ancillary network interfaces are made. The backbone usually transfers traffic into and out of large networks as well as throughout remote portions of larger networks.

bastion server A computer set outside an Intranet with the purpose to filter traffic from the Internet.

BinHex An algorithm often used to convert binary files to ASCII files for transmission over email and FTP.

bridge A piece of networking hardware that links two segments of a local area network.

browser Software used to communicate according to one of the TCP/IP layered protocols such as the Web and FTP.

client pull A Netscape-implemented feature which allows the Web browser to rapidly update Web pages without any intervention from the user.

client-server A term describing the type of application where a series of clients communicate and exchange information with a centralized server. A Web browser and an HTTP server have a client-server relationship.

client-side imagemap A type of imagemap in which the reference URLs are stored in the HTML text. These imagemaps do not require the use of a specialized CGI script.

cookies A feature introduced by Netscape which allows you to store information sent to the Web client by the server and/or CGI scripts. This information is then sent back to the browser when that user accesses the server once again.

Copland The next release of the MacOS (early 1997?). This OS will be a total rewrite of the Finder, making it PowerPC-native, multitasking, and more reliable.

domain An Internet cataloging system to manage distribution and placement of thousands of nodes.

domain name resolver An application that resolves names of the frequent DNS requests.

domain name server A computer that translates between IP addresses and Ethernet node names.

environment A pair of starting and closing HTML tags. <H1>... </H1> is an HTML environment.

Ethernet A cabling and network transmission standard.

FDDI A high-speed networking standard that runs over copper or fiber-optic cable. FDDI runs on many LAN backbones to funnel data through different portions of the network.

firewall A computer that lies outside your Intranet and regulates traffic running between the Internet and your Intranet.

frames A Netscape HTML extension that enables you to subdivide a browser window into scrollable subdivisions.

Frontier A PowerPC-native, multithreaded scripting environment for the MacOS that is fast becoming the CGI scripting tool of choice.

FTP (File Transfer Protocol) Used to transfer large files across the Internet and throughout Intranets.

gateway See *router*.

GIF (Graphic Interchange Format) File format used to display text and simple graphics. Commonly used to portray graphics on Web pages.

group scheduler A client-server application allowing users to compare schedules over a network for the purpose of scheduling meetings.

HTML (HyperText Markup Language) Programming language used to construct formatted text and graphics for display of documents via the World Wide Web.

HTTP (HyperText Transport Protocol) Underlying protocol behind the World Wide Web. Defines standard interaction between the Web browser and Web server.

hub A multiport network hardware device which coordinates traffic from many sources.

IETF (Internet Engineering Task Force) Industry consortium charged with development of Internet standards such as HTTP and HTML.

imagemap Clickable Web graphic that allows you to bring up different pages depending on location of click within the graphic.

Intranet The reason you bought this book. A TCP/IP network with many of the same services as those found on the Internet, but with a specific orientation towards a group or organization.

IP address A numerically unique address assigned to each node on the Internet or on an Intranet.

IP Port A means of differentiating TCP/IP communications through a server. Different services are channeled through different ports on an Intranet server.

ISDN (Integrated Services Digital Network) A protocol for transmitting information over a digital telephone connection much faster than conventional modems.

ISP (Internet Service Provider) A commercial provider of Internet services. An ISP usually has direct access to an Internet backbone. Users typically connect to ISPs using T1, ISDN, or conventional modems.

Java A programming language developed by Sun Microsystems that is being used in conjunction with Web browsers to write small, secure, cross-platform applications. Heavily based on C++. See *applet.*

JavaScript A scripted form of Java. Has fewer capabilities, but is considered easier for non-programmers to work with.

JPEG (Joint Photographic Experts Group) A rival format for GIF that is used primarily for storing complicated graphic images such as photographs.

KB 1 kilobyte or 1,000 bytes.

LAN Local area network.

MB 1 megabyte.

MacOS A synonym for the operating system running on the Macintosh computer.

MacPerl A Macintosh port of the Perl language. See *Perl.*

MacTCP An implementation of the TCP/IP protocol on the Macintosh. Recently supplanted by Open Transport as a means for running Intranet/Internet applications.

mailing list A means of sending and receiving email from multiple users.

Mbps 1 million bits per second.

MIME (Multipurpose Internet Mail Extension) A means of identifying information contained in a TCP/IP transaction.

NAP (Network Access Provider) A provider of the high-speed Internet backbones that carry large amounts of network traffic.

NCSA (National Center for Supercomputer Applications) Developers of Mosaic, the first cross-platform Web browser.

NIC (Network Interface Card) Used to connect desktop computers to a local area network.

node An active computer residing on an Intranet or the Internet.

Open Transport A new version of the MacOS networking software. Replaces MacTCP and AppleTalk for networking needs.

packet The smallest piece of data into which network traffic is disassembled and reassembled during a transmission.

Perl (Practical Extraction and Report Language) Heavily used in Windows and Unix environments. See *MacPerl.*

PGP (Pretty Good Privacy) An encryption program used to secure Net traffic.

Plug-in A software module that extends the functionality of the Navigator or Internet Explorer browsers.

POP (Post Office Protocol) Method used for email clients to retrieve mail from SMTP hosts. See *SMTP*.

PowerPC Microprocessor used to power late-model Macintosh computers.

PPP (Point-to-Point Protocol) Enables users to access TCP/IP services over a phone line.

router Networking hardware that directs traffic according to designations.

server Describes a computer which publishes information in a client-server relationship.

server push Netscape HTML extension that allows a Web server to update certain Web pages or portions of Web pages.

SLIP (Serial Line Internet Protocol) Similar to PPP. See *PPP*.

SMTP (Simple Mail Transport Protocol) Protocol used to transfer mail between sites.

SSI (Server Side Includes) Server-specific commands that add functionality to Web pages such as date, access counters, and email forwarding.

SSL (Secure Sockets Layer) Encryption protocol developed by Netscape that encrypts data being sent between Web server and Web client.

suffix mapping Process of examining a file suffix to associate data with a MIME type. See *MIME*.

synchronous CGI CGI processing where script blocks out all other processes until execution is completed.

T1 A high-speed Ethernet networking standard.

tag A single HTML command that needs no closing partner. <IMG> is an HTML tag.

TCP/IP Used to describe the combined effort of the Transmission Control Protocol (TCP) and the Internet Protocol (IP). Both protocols work to move network packets between destinations.

URL (Uniform Resource Locator) Used to identify specific locations on the World Wide Web.

video conference Remote audiovisual communication.

W3C (World Wide Web Consortium) Industry group charged with setting standards for the World Wide Web.

WAN Wide area network.

World Wide Web Conglomeration of servers, protocols, clients, and networks that exchange data using HTTP. See *HTTP*.

INDEX

Symbols

A

D

G

H

J

K

L

M

N

O

P

Q

R

S

T